THE HISTORIC WHITMAN

The Historic WHITMAN

JOSEPH JAY RUBIN

THE PENNSYLVANIA STATE UNIVERSITY PRESS
University Park and London

Library of Congress Cataloging in Publication Data

Rubin, Joseph Jay, 1912–
The historic Whitman.

Includes bibliographical references.
1. Whitman, Walt, 1819–1892—Biography. I. Title.
PS3231.R8   811'.3 [B]   72–1067
ISBN 0–271–01117–3

For Eleanore: One of the ways

CONTENTS

vii

The poet of A.D. 1855 will have his hands full with the men and women and things of 1855. . . . His hand and his heart find enough to feel and to do at his own door. There is poetry enough latent in the South Street merchant and the Wall Street financier; in Stewart's snobby clerk chaffering over ribbons and laces; in the omnibus driver that conveys them all from the day's work to the night's relaxation and repose; in the brutified denizen of the Points and the Hook; in the sumptuous star courtesan of Mercer Street thinking sadly of her village home; in the Fifth Avenue ballroom; in the Grace Church contrast of eternal vanity and new bonnets; in the dancers at Lewis Jones's and Mr. Schiff's and in the future of each and all!

George Templeton Strong
Diary, 27 January 1855

The relations that exist between the social and political condition of a people and the genius of its authors are always numerous; whoever knows the one is never completely ignorant of the other.

Alexis de Tocqueville
Democracy in America

PREFACE

At work that summer on *English Traits*, Emerson resisted the impulse to thank Whitman in person for the gift of a copy of *Leaves of Grass*. Rather than ride to an encounter with his benefactor, he remained at home to record memories of longer journeys to famous men. Wordsworth, upset by a broken tooth, had alternated schoolboy declamation of sonnets with disparagement of America—its people too much given to politics and the making of money, its communities toneless without leisured gentlemen. The mind once capable of sacred odes had softened into tame conformity and brooded over the fornications in *Wilhelm Meister*. Coleridge between pinches of snuff had inveighed against the quackery of Unitarianism, and speaking in printed paragraphs turned the occasion into a taxing spectacle rather than a conversation. Carlyle had provided a spirited interlude as he floated anecdotes upon streams of humor while satirizing contemporary literature. In the Scot's judgment rebellion was the basic American principle.

When Emerson, in preparing another chapter, turned to a reading of Victorian poetry after Whitman's thin quarto had fortified and encouraged him, he found that the aspirant Merlins lacked the stature to loom large as London: "How many volumes of well-bred metre we must jingle through before we can be filled, taught, revived!" Minus expansiveness and great design, they failed to exude the power of the Brooklyn poet who had honored his vow to incarnate the republic's vast geography in a psalm of praise, dilate the living, and drag the dead from their coffins. But the Concord referee—as though fearing to duplicate his Rydal Mount disillusion in Ryerson Street—kept to his task and thereby deputized later readers of the *Leaves of Grass* to search what he called the "long foreground."

On a Broadway saunter one afternoon in his early twenties, Whitman stopped at Colman's emporium to see the plates by Daguerre of Parisians, a Seine bridge, and the façade of the Louvre. In the young critic's judgment the new medium lacked the "filling up" that made the rounded portrait.

The Historic Whitman attempts a biographical filling up of the three decades from the Long Island beginnings to July 1855, the month in which he published the first edition of the *Leaves of Grass*—and buried his father.

To know those years is to possess the indispensable headnote to the *Leaves of Grass*. ("It were useless," Whitman insisted later, "to attempt reading the book without first carefully tallying that preparatory background.") But those years also offer autonomous excitement, for they served as his Antaean earth. Touching them he became powerful, gained purpose, vision, idiom. No other block of time—not even the Civil War—so stimulated and enlarged him through a succession of eclectic impulses.

The era's newspapers and journals yield the richest definitive material. Whitman's many editorships ranged from a tenure of mere weeks to over two years, with his principles and circumstances rather than ineptness or sloth the main causes of severance. At least half of the files have vanished, but his policies and solicitudes may be traced by joining the extant copies with hardy contemporaries. These fugitive archives show a compassionate, tender man who in a time of quickening social kindness was justified in claiming that he served the "most sublime reform, and the greatest truths connected with human freedom." (Bennett of the *Herald* and Bishop John Hughes of St. Patrick's would demur.) They illumine his motives in refusing to obey the orders of his compromised publishers to play the "bound booby." They reveal his heroes—among them William Leggett, leader of the Locofoco rump Democrats, Charles Dickens, and Jesse Talbot, a modest landscape painter; and his villains—Daniel Webster and Tammany Hunkers. And they prove his sustained though frustrated involvement in political affairs, whether of Long Island counties, Albany, Washington, or the Europe vainly bloodied by the revolutions of 1848. The dispatches from barricaded Paris that reached his desk at the office of the New Orleans *Crescent* brought him exultation at first and then grief.

The dictum that history is past politics becomes relevant in the span of *The Historic Whitman*. Pledged by inheritance and rationale to work to perpetuate the party that promised to shower the blessings of equal rights upon many rather than grant monopoly privilege to a few, he honored the memory of Jefferson and Jackson and campaigned for Van Buren and Polk. In the beginning he made the monster Bank and the humbug tariff, those twin bulwarks of Whig faith, prime targets. His speeches and editorials salted with approved epithets, his mature presence—that magnificent head, clear tanned skin that always seemed fresh-bathed, tall solid figure—

impressed his elders; they offered him the flattery of rally platforms and the security of jobs. But he eventually ended allegiance to what had become their coffle Democracy that lusted after Mexican acres.

Because of this fateful choice motivated partly—in the language of Mr. Hosea Biglow—by the fear that

> Chaps that make black slaves o' niggers
> Want to make wite slaves o' you

he scorned the congressional managers who voted into law the Compromise of 1850 and the Kansas-Nebraska Act of 1854. He saw war portended in these "doughface" depredations on free soil and cursed their agents as dis-severers of the Union. Ultimately *The Historic Whitman* becomes the record of a conversion to one of the many phases of abolitionism. What other tag for a man who shared a convention tent with Frederick Douglass, sent sympathetic letters to Senators Hale and Seward, contributed to the Washington weekly that first published *Uncle Tom's Cabin*, and joined Whittier in lamenting the rendition of the fugitive slave Anthony Burns.

Marked as a local Abdiel who refused to surrender to the specious terms of rigged caucuses, Whitman like other libertarians found himself "exfoliated," barred from tasting the pap of patronage, doomed to wait until the few voices that spoke for an end to punitive covenants became a dominant chorus. In this time of stress, as was his pattern since boyhood, he sought sanctuary in the ancestral countryside. Standing there on a Montauk headland in sight of bluefishermen trolling beyond the Atlantic surf, or musing over crumbled stones in a graveyard, or facing heaven at night from the deck of a sloop sailing out of Greenport harbor, he knew the peace that sanctioned meditation.

But Suffolk imagery and tranquillity could not efface the memory of metropolitan intellectual splendor. Returning to Manhattan, he exulted again in its lyceums where transcendentalists, geologists, feminists, and Egyptologists lectured; in its concert halls, galleries, daguerreotype parlors —and the new shelter where vagrants could bathe and launder their clothes. Lest oncoming generations be crowded into an airless Gehenna, he asked City Hall to open parks. The stiles of the glass and iron Crystal Palace never turned on a more appreciative patron. Relishing the tutorship in aesthetics they gave him, he played the role of Ruskin to his friends, the Turners of Brooklyn, despite the London *Critic* that would quip, "Walt Whitman is as unacquainted with art as a hog is with mathematics." He tried to ease his maimed, retarded brother Eddy by giving him a concept of Christ. Replacing his paralyzed father as provider for the stricken family, he began to print a weekly sheet that carried schedules of Long Island trains and stages; but the *Salesman* died at birth. Then he built and sold small wooden houses until depression ended this expedient.

Now in his mid-thirties, he refused to succumb to an inventory of apparent failure and bemoan the fate that rendered him, after fifteen years of service, an editor without a paper, a politician without a viable party, a poet without a publisher. Confident that he had absorbed the endless land with its pastoral beauty, its Five Points slums, its aspirations, crimes, charity, and cruelty, its history of heroes, martyrs, and apostates, its Arcade slave auctions, its grim chase after wealth and the resulting cycles of flush times, speculation manias, and bankruptcies, its music, humor—"Why is temperance a bar to friendship?" "It prevents shaking hands"—and its idiom vital for translating experience, he responded by ennobling its literature with the *Leaves of Grass*.

ACKNOWLEDGMENTS

The pattern of a major portion of the research for *The Historic Whitman* led me to ask often for the loan or microfilming of dispersed files of nineteenth-century newspapers. In all these transactions the Services staff of the Fred Lewis Pattee Library of The Pennsylvania State University, headed by Mildred L. Treworgy, served as gracious, efficient intermediaries.

Among the libraries that offered access to their resources or reading space were The American Antiquarian Society, Boston Public, Brooklyn Public, Catholic University, Columbia University, Duke University, Frick Museum, Harvard University, Haverford College, Kenyon College, Howard Memorial in New Orleans, Lehigh University, Library of Congress—where I found the *Letters from a Travelling Bachelor*, Long Island Historical Society, Massachusetts Historical Society, Newberry, New York Historical Society, Paterson Public in New Jersey, Philadelphia College of Physicians, Pierpont Morgan, Princeton University, Queens Borough, Smithsonian Institution, Swarthmore College, Tulane University, University of Maine, University of Montana, University of North Carolina, University of Pennsylvania, University of Virginia, and Yale University.

Charles E. Feinberg guided me through his matchless treasury of manuscripts and editions. The New York University Press, publisher of *The Collected Writings of Walt Whitman* under the general editorship of Gay Wilson Allen and Sculley Bradley, granted permission to reprint the letter to Senator John Hale. My gratitude goes also to John S. Carroll, Harold E. Dickson, Philip S. Klein, Charles W. Mann, Thomas Magner, Katherine Molinoff, Stanley Paulson, Jan S. Prybyla, Henry Sams, Harvey West, William White, and the staff of The Pennsylvania State University Press. My colleague, William L. Werner, anticipated the beginning of *The Historic Whitman* and his memory heartened the completion.

PART ONE

You know there are two great parties throughout Christendom. . . . One side is struggling to return to ancient usages, or abuses if you will, while the other wishes to go on with reform, or revolution, as the case may be. In Catholic countries the contest is between the priests and the unbelievers. To the former are joined the absolutists and ultras, to the latter the liberals. In Protestant countries the possessors of the monopolies contend with the outs.

James Fenimore Cooper to Charles Wilkes
Paris, 24 August 1830

1

DEMOCRATIC AND HERETICAL

CERTAIN of a Whig victory and a place in the Cabinet, Daniel Webster stumped across eastern states all summer and autumn of 1840, and with the fervor of a Methodist preacher exhorted citizens to elect William Henry Harrison. On Tuesday, 22 September he came to Long Island where farmers welcomed the chance to rest from harvesting the most abundant crops of grain and fruit in years.

Were he younger, the Massachusetts man assured the thousands assembled at Patchogue in Suffolk County, the prime lure for a visit would be trout fishing and woodcock shooting. Though disposed now to listen to his hosts, he knew they wanted his views of the gross conduct of the Administration. For the next two hours he told them that Van Buren had squandered thirty-nine million dollars. Customs officers and frontier land-agents indulged in arrant thievery, while the slow war in Florida that failed to uproot the Seminoles from hummocks in the Everglades enriched jobbers. The president's Locofoco henchmen in Congress had rammed through the Independent Treasury Bill, that portent of fiscal woes.

The way to domestic salvation, the "God-like" insisted, was to tax luxuries imported from Canton and France. "Do we want any more silks, or cloths, or cottons that flood in upon us, crushing our manufacturers?" He had a surfeit of foreign wares and preferred American comforts. Swelling this homely theme, the future secretary of state assured the country folk that Harrison still lived in a log cabin, though "he has made an addition to it, as many of us do." According to the New York *Herald*, whose relays of horses raced his words to the compositors, Webster roused laughter when he cautioned against the cant of the incumbent Pharisees. The word "Democracy, Democracy, Democracy" occurred as often among them as "ditto, ditto, ditto" in a tradesman's invoice or five shillings and eight pence in an attorney's bill.[1]

On Thursday he repeated his charges from a platform placed on a Ja-

3

maica green near Snedeker's famous inn and the Union race track. Then he rode to New York, where the merchants and brokers who thronged Wall Street welcomed his history of the debasement of the dollar by the folly of Van Burenite assaults upon a national bank: "WE MUST have one." The proper place to rebuild that citadel was here in the city and street of banks. Only then would the nation possess a uniform, stable currency.

Watching his triumphant progress, worried Democrats told each other that the election of a garrulous old woman like Harrison now seemed possible—even though it would prove the voters destitute of common sense. In concert they exposed the Whig's "rigamaroles," his cohorts' beer and brandy flattery:

> 'Twas Captain This, and Captain That
> And Cousin John and Uncle Nat. . . .
> And then they sung us pretty songs
> About our country's thousand wrongs.

At nearby Hempstead the attorney general, Benjamin F. Butler, dissected the character of Nicholas Biddle and then in a sublime peroration appealed to Jehovah for justice in November. Senator Silas Wright, who had guided the Independent Treasury Bill through Congress, was no less eloquent in Brooklyn.[2]

The Long Island *Democrat* of Jamaica spoke for the local party. Ever since James J. Brenton had started the weekly sheet in May 1835, he had made certain that it deserved patronage. From the first issue he warned that a monied aristocracy exerted a baleful influence on the country, and throughout the next four years renewed his vow to guard against unconstitutional acts prejudicial to wages and suffrage. He alternated eulogies of Jefferson, Jackson, and Van Buren with assaults on Hamilton, Clay, and sponsors of ruinous paper currency. When mobs rioted in New York to protest prices inflated fifty per cent, he charged that speculators rather than Administrative policy had caused the financial whirlwind. Before each election he summoned to the polls every friend of equal rights and traded epithets with the Whig *Farmer*, whose "*cur*-sory" policy branded all its rivals infidels, radicals, and agrarians. The *Farmer* proved an easy target and its publisher, the villager pharmacist, became Dr. Sangrado of the "pill and plaster popgun."

As the campaign swept toward a raucous climax and both parties, according to a current play, *The Politicians*, exposed voters to as much temptation as the lonely wife of a sailor long gone to China, Brenton brought into his

4

office a Suffolk native who had helped him before in local elections. The "smut machine," complained the *Farmer*, had opened its columns to "Tom, Dick, Jack—and Walter."

A sometime teacher in the schools of the area whose verse appeared in the *Democrat*, Walt Whitman had known Jamaica ever since childhood when he had ridden there from Cold Spring Harbor on his grandfather's stage and market wagon—though the lampblack and oil coating on the canvas frame sickened him. (Cornelius Van Velsor made the trip once a week for over forty years; in 1839 the *Democrat* would announce his death at eighty.) Though only twenty-one now, Whitman had gained technical skill as an apprentice and journeyman. Gifted with a sense of literary form, he was spared the chiding that Brenton gave other hands:

> Upon coming into the office the other day, we asked the "Devil" his rule for punctuation. Said he, "I set up as long as I can hold my breath, then put in a comma. When I gape, I insert a semi-colon; when I sneeze, a colon, and when I want to take another chew of tobacco, I insert a period."

Most appealing of all his credentials were his political ideals, based on what he himself called a "democratic and heretical" heritage.[3]

A curious—and unwelcome—spectator at the hustings, the young reporter expected Webster to display his legendary intellect in exploiting the strategy of palming off the Whigs as friends of the poor man. What he heard led him to raise his high-arched eyebrows. The orator's tone, he granted, was moderate and gentlemanly, free of the blackguardism that called Van Buren a lecherous sybarite who advocated the destruction of Christian morality. But the speeches were those of a dull intruder who had overindulged in one of Snedeker's choice dinners (cut-glass goblets filled with sparkling Heidsieck, brook trout and new potatoes, terrapin and golden sherry, chicken and asparagus, strawberries and cream, iced maraschino): "The man was sick. His cause was bad, and moreover his stomach was out of order . . . he neither suggested or mentioned, or made allusion to what he thought necessary *instead* of the policy of the administration. . . . From beginning to end he originated no system himself."[4]

By 1840 the Whitman family had lived on Long Island for almost two centuries. Joseph Whitman, the son of an Englishman from Buckingham-

5

shire, sojourned for a time in Connecticut and then joined one of the companies of eleven families that crossed the Sound and established the East Riding township of Huntington, whose records date from 1657. His name first appears there as a hired herder of cattle, but before long his rank rose to landowner, the profitable aftermath of grant and purchase.[5]

The settlers had chosen their site wisely, for the land dominated by central prairies and two axial moraines was fertile and would in time become the granary of the provinces. Clear springs that drought never dried flowed from glaciated reservoirs to water meadows and power mills. Oak, chestnut, locust, and pine provided houses, barns, ship timber, turpentine, and staves for Barbados rum casks. Fruit trees soon surrounded each farmhouse so that travellers marveled at their profusion; all her life Louisa Whitman remembered the size and beauty of a peach tree in her father's orchard. The soil, enriched by the annual burying of bony mossbunkers, produced wheat, maize, rye, barley, oats, and flax. Tall tales spread at harvest of carrots large enough to serve as liberty poles, and turnips used for targets by militia companies. Cattle and sheep found pasturage on the plains and salt marshes; seaweed served in place of straw as compost and litter for pens. Fowling and fishing seemed limitless; offshore whaling became possible with the use of swift cedar boats.

Anticipating war with the Indians, the settlers garrisoned stockades and drilled train bands. But the few thousand Algonkins, grouped in thirteen communities, fought each other rather than the invaders and surrendered title to their lands without bloodshed—in exchange for trinkets. From then to the end of the century the pace of their dissolution became so rapid that the settlers attributed the new burial mounds to the hand of God. (On a jaunt to Southold in September 1847, when Whitman met a lone Indian on this eastern end of the island, he meditated on the time when they were "as many as the spears of grass," but war, pestilence, and firewater had thinned the tribes until only a few families remained at Shinnecock and Montauk. He also scolded the Fulton ferry company for misspelling on its new boat the name of the legendary chief, Wyandanch, "the wise speaker" and lover of peace.)

Gaining a measure of importance as a landowner, Joseph Whitman was chosen constable, commissioner, leather-sealer, and grand juryman; he performed these duties with enough independence to be summoned before Governor Andros at the trial of the owner of a sloop charged with illegal trade. His children remained on the land and added to their heritage until the original "parsells" numbered five hundred acres located three miles south-west of Huntington village. They built shingled houses like those in Connecticut, with central chimneys and steep-pitched gabled roofs, and circled them with orchards and groves of black walnut. Sustenance came from the land they learned to till and from the Sound, visible to all who climbed the 428 feet of Jayne's Hill. (In flat New Orleans, Walt and his brother longed for the "little Steepe hills" of Suffolk.) New York, less than forty miles away, provided markets for their grain, which was then shipped to the West Indies and exchanged for sugar and rum. A ferry from Huntington to Norwalk also helped local farmers.

When the men married, they chose brides from the homes of the Whites, the Brushes, and other neighbors. That their courtship was not always exemplary may be gathered from a father's charge brought against an early Whitman for the "stealing of his daughter's affections contrary to her mother's mind and using unlawful means to obtain his daughter's love." The court found for the young couple. Sarah White, wife of Joseph's grandson, Nehemiah, and Hannah Brush, wife of great-grandson Jesse, were, by all accounts, superior helpmates; in their time the family fortune peaked.

Marriage and baptism were performed at the Independent Congregational Church of Huntington by the Reverend Eliphalet Jones and his successor, Ebenezer Prime, the two pastors whose combined service spanned more than a century. When Prime, a Yale graduate, preached his ordination sermon on 5 June 1725, four of the congregation of forty-two were of the Whitman family. Over the years the change to Presbyterianism by the church elders in 1748, in the hope of better preserving purity of doctrine and of establishing a more efficient discipline, the visit of Whitefield in 1765, the increase of Methodism, and the impact of Elias Hicks and other Friends widened sectarian differences. But when death came to members of this long-lived family, they were buried next to each other on a "gray and sterile" hill.[6]

The Revolution brought suffering early to Suffolk. Planning to hold Brooklyn Heights, the strategic key to the East River and New York City, General Washington ordered parapets and forts built along the western end of the island to reinforce in depth the natural defense line, and then with some 5000 troops awaited the attack of General Howe's 20,000. On 27 August 1776, British skirmishers surprised and captured outposts on the Jamaica road, moved through an unguarded pass, turned the American left flank, and overran the first lines. Smallwood's Maryland regiment in a rear-guard action held the enemy long enough to allow most of the American units to escape across the salt marshes and a deep tidewater creek; of 684 men, the Marylanders lost 256.

Whatever his reasons, General Howe withheld final assault on the Heights the next day, and ordered his engineers to build redoubts and prepare to initiate a siege. "There is not the least doubt," Whitman wrote after one of his many reflections on the battle, "that had the victors attacked in the dismay of that hour, they would have exterminated the Continental Army and taken Washington prisoner. But they hauled off." On 29 August amidst rainflooded trenches, Washington directed his men to abandon Brooklyn and cross the East River in the night. A heavy fog shielded the flotilla of whale boats, skiffs, and sloops until the last soldier left Fulton slip.

From then on, British, Hessian, and Loyalist troops quartered on Long Island and the fleet of Admiral Arbuthnot stationed in the bays could feast on the thousands of cattle and sheep, cut saplings and fence rails for endless fires, could seize grain, blankets, horses, and wagons while their officers raced and hunted foxes on Hempstead Plain. Because of the patriotism of its people and of Pastor Prime, Huntington seemed to invite looters. The King's Dragoon regiment of Colonel Benjamin Thompson, the Tory physicist whose experiments in heat and motion led him to be honored as a Fellow of the Royal Society, stripped the church of its timber and fortified the cemetery. Prime, who would not survive the war, hid the family silver in a well and fled, but the invaders ruined his library. Regulars, Loyalists in their green-and-white uniforms, Runners, and Cow-boys continued their depredations to the very end; outlaws from Delaware and Maryland beached their boats on the south shore, kidnapped Negroes, and sold them in their states. The hanging of Nathan Hale and the alleged sabering of the unarmed brigadier of militia, Nathaniel Woodhull, while he was driving cattle from the coast to the interior, provided memorable martyrdoms. During the six years of British occupancy the islanders lacked civil and church government, courts, and elections. The indignities they suffered—many perpetrated in the days of drunkenness after rations of spirits—became part of their lore; hearing them retold would always anger Whitman.[7]

The coming of peace ended the material and moral deterioration. Jesse Whitman, a militiaman, and his wife, Hannah Brush, daughter of a patriot, resumed normal married life, and by the time their son Walter was born in 1789 (also James Fenimore Cooper's birth year) the people of Suffolk, according to a happy legend, had recovered their industry and stability, with the result that the county no longer needed lawyers and the courthouse at Riverhead fell into ruins from disuse.

The insularity of Suffolk life seemed to preserve the best of its heritage. When Timothy Dwight travelled across the island in the spring of 1804, he observed the Indian remnants, the yellow sand, the fields distinguished by the stench of fertilizer, the string of dwellings along the stage road, the taverns with creaking sign boards, a church with a fish on its spire. All through Suffolk the Yale divine met with such kindness and good will that he concluded his hosts had remained New Englanders in every respect. "Descended from one source, they have to this day sustained one character." After completing his tour, Dwight was certain that they differed from the western counties in name, accent, manners, education, intelligence, morals, and religion.[8] Had he stopped to talk with Jesse Whitman and his fifteen-year-old son, Walter, he would have learned that they admired Elias Hicks, the Jericho Friend, whose teachings were honored at Meetings throughout the entire seaboard. Not from "Mexic hills" but from Suffolk would come the bard of the western world whom Dwight summoned in *Greenfield Hill*.

As Walter Whitman matured, he showed the massive physique of the men of his family; taciturn, he inherited little of his mother's geniality. Rather than remain on the farm, he hired out to his Uncle Jacob, a carpenter, and became a journeyman in New York. There he met Tom Paine through a cousin of Elias Hicks, and found the deist knowledgeable about carpentry; Paine had some time ago detailed a new method of building frame houses.

These last years of Paine's life were marred by a paralytic stroke and the abuse of Federalist politicians and orthodox clergy who stigmatized him as a revolutionist and anti-Christ, "a drunken, brutal infidel, who rejoices in the opportunity of basking and wallowing in the confusion, devastation, blood-shed, rapine, and murder." In 1809 he was consigned to an obscure grave by his few friends, but by then Walter Whitman, swayed by the concept of natural law rather than of supernatural revelation, had become "rather favorable to deism."[9] Afterwards as an independent mechanic he supported secular inquirers who attempted to perpetuate Paine's memory by opposing inherited privilege and defending equal rights. It was a time, complained Diedrich Knickerbocker, when "cobblers abandoned their stalls to give lessons on political economy; blacksmiths suffered their fires to go out while they stirred up the fires of faction; and even tailors . . . neglected their own measures to criticize the measures of government."

9

Returning to Long Island the carpenter followed his trade and soon gained a name as a skilled framer of barns and houses. He made them plumb by using seasoned timber for all braces and joints, and at times he would lie awake all night to form a complex design. Neither the Whitman family nor their neighbors suffered damage in these years during the dismal course of the second war with the British. Its one glorious land victory at New Orleans placed another hero by the side of Washington in their pantheon.

At Cold Spring Harbor, a few miles to the northwest on the edge of Dutch domain, in a region of millponds, medicinal sulphur springs, and thick woods, lived Cornelius Van Velsor, descended according to legend from a family with baronial rank in the reign of William of Orange. His wife, Naomi, whose garb evinced her Quaker persuasion, came from a stock of English sailors. The large house, the barn loaded with grain, and the sheds and pens with cattle and horses were evidence of a prosperity that the recent blockade of the Sound had not checked. Walter Whitman began to drive over the narrow road to court their Louisa, a girl with a splendid figure and abundant health. In June 1816, the year remembered for capricious weather that brought frost every month, they married and he took her to a new house he had built at West Hills near a great oak and a twenty-acre apple orchard. There within two years they celebrated the birth of their first son, Jesse. (Ill-fated, he would contract syphilis and die in an asylum.) In the spring of 1819 they awaited another child.[10]

Delighted with temporary sanctuary at North Hempstead, far from the threat of gagging bills against reformers that had led him to flee England, William Cobbett told his journal that it was impossible for any human being to lead a pleasanter life than on this Long Island. The soil responded to ample rain and sun and filled the rows with tall yellow corn. A watermelon runner stretched eighteen inches in two days; black and red cherries dropped in such abundance that thousands of pounds rotted unpicked. Wild strawberries and chestnuts were everywhere, the grass luxuriant, the straw bright as burnished gold, and the apples, fall pippins, the finest of all. The flowering locust, the tree Cobbett thought of surpassing beauty, spread to great height and girth. In March he found the roads as dry and smooth as the gravel paths in the garden of an English bishop, a newsworthy contrast to the bottomless mud of New Jersey.

10

Nostalgia brought other comparisons. Cobbett found few singing birds on Long Island, nothing like the hundreds of linnets that chorused from a single tree in Hampshire. Accustomed to rural order, he complained of a sort of out-of-doors slovenliness hardly ever observed at home: "You see bits of wood, timber, boards, ships, lying about, here and there, and pigs and cattle tramping about in confusion, which would make an English farmer fret himself to death; but which is here seen with great placidness." Local cheese lacked true flavor, but the beer and ale were superior and other liquors so cheap that one could drink oneself blind with six pence. The tippling of spirits was so common, he testified, that little boys under twelve stood in groceries and swallowed their drams.

The virtues of the natives outweighed their few faults. He found them civil but never servile, devout but tolerant. Within six miles of his study were Episcopal, Presbyterian, Lutheran, and Methodist churches, and a Friends' meeting house—"each larger and better built and far handsomer than Botley church." The versatility of local farmers and their capacity for sustained work surpassed any in his own experience. At Jericho Elias Hicks, now a man of seventy, cradled down four acres of rye in one day. Cobbett ended his recital with a hymn of praise, a benediction for the island and its people:

> Of the same active, hardy and brave stuff, too, was composed the army of Jackson, who drove the invaders into the Gulf of Mexico, and who would have driven into the same Gulf the army of Waterloo. . . . This is the stuff that stands between the rascals, called the Holy Alliance, and the slavery of the whole civilized world. This is the stuff that gives us Englishmen an asylum; that gives us time to breathe; that enables us to deal our tyrants blows, which, without the existence of this stuff, they could never receive. This America, this scene of happiness under a free government, is the beam in the eye, the thorn in the side, the worm in the vitals, of every despot upon the face of the earth.[11]

The boy born "on the last day of Fifth Month, in the year 43 of America" and named after his father shared the year with Victoria, George Eliot, Melville, and Ruskin; but bodings of disaster threatened to muffle the tone of rejoicing in these varied households. That May, Keats asked the nightingale to forget "The weariness, the fever, and the fret/ Here, where men sit and hear each other groan." In August, after Yeomanry and regular

Hussars killed eleven and injured hundreds of cotton spinners and weavers in the Peterloo Massacre, Shelley mourned them as "A people starved and stabbed in the untilled field" and urged the survivors to forge arms. Financial panic shocked both sides of the Atlantic as prices fell and bankruptcies increased. The long cycle of continental wars had reared an unstable credit structure; demand for wheat and corn in the post-Napoleonic years lessened; employers forced debased paper currency, the "Ghost of Gold," upon workers. Some Americans argued that their economy reflected an unbalanced foreign trade and inadequate protection for the new mills, while everyone agreed that speculators throughout the land had borrowed recklessly in seeking short cuts to fortune. The Second Bank of the United States, now housed in a Doric temple, became a prime target of antimonopolists when it initiated a policy of curtailment prompted by an illegal ratio of liabilities to specie; lesser banks with overextended credit suspended payment. In New York and other cities soup stations served hungry paupers.[12]

During the years of acute stress, Walter Whitman remained in the country. But in May 1823, sure of work as the number of new stores and houses built in Brooklyn rose from fifty the year before to over one hundred and fifty, he sold the homestead, moved his family there, and prepared to share in the new prosperity. There was a third child now, Mary Elizabeth.

2

OF OLD BROOKLYN

NOW A VILLAGE of eight thousand in a haphazard enclave a mile square, Brooklyn promised a livelihood to a sober mechanic, for civic leaders encouraged growth in a variety of ways. They advertised land protected against contagion by high elevation and natural drainage—though an epidemic of yellow fever that summer silenced those who boasted of total immunity for the area. They passed ordinances to rid slaughterhouses of noxious vapors and began tactical, though often futile, warfare to capture and pen hogs which in Manhattan roamed at large, under what sardonic observers called the flag of universal suffrage. They improved ferry service, built sidewalks and curbs, opened new streets, cleaned the old ones, and policed them at night to lessen the danger to pedestrians, who were forced to carry their own lanterns. The mayor tried to curtail the proliferation of liquor groceries by forcing owners to obtain licenses or face arrest. He fined drivers who, inspired by the Union track, raced their rigs at more than five miles an hour. Any militia company that fired at targets within bounds forfeited $25. The fire department began to add engines—though one September night twenty-five years later it still proved woefully inadequate.

A society to prevent and suppress vice, another to distribute charity during the winter, a book depot, a circulating library for whites and a separate collection for Negroes, the Hamilton Literary Society, two newspapers, and a permanent barber secured after diligent search—all reflected an enlightened response to the arrival of nearly a thousand new residents each year: tradesmen, carters, and laborers for the Navy Yard, the white lead and glass factories, distilleries known for mellow gin, tanneries, and ropewalks. Their owners and managers built homes on the Heights and reveled in the pure air, the incomparable view of bay, river, and islands. Adding to the natural beauty, they planted ailanthus trees, shrubs, and vines of Isabella grapes. Before long poets and artists circulated verse and aquatints inspired by this admirable community.[1]

13

Walt, as the boy was called, found a wealth of excitement at the foot of Fulton Street within range of home. Here began the enduring fascination with the ferry, for the gatekeeper at the landing allowed him to climb aboard the teamboats that were propelled by horses. A huge sign at the adjacent stage terminal listed Long Island places served; among them Quogue, Hopaug, Speonk. On winter days Grandfather Van Velsor and other drivers stopped at Smith and Wood's tavern, hung their greatcoats and whips in the wooden press of the public room, and warmed themselves at the cast-iron stove and the bar. Walt continued to wander down to the waterfront though the family moved to newer streets at least six times within ten years, for the carpenter followed a traditional pattern of buying a lot, building a house, living there until he sold it, then starting again.[2]

With a bent pin and a length of tow the boy fished ponds and creeks. He walked to the Wallabout road bordered by fields and the river; here the Walloons, ancestors of the Van Velsors, had settled. Immersion in vestiges of Dutch culture and love for Cornelius Van Velsor and Louisa Whitman, representatives of what he called that grand race, would lead him to lament the "shallow burlesque" of Irving's history "full of clown's wit." From early childhood he seemed to possess the perfect rapport with "Mammy" that endured until her death. When Louisa was seventy-six he told a friend that she "looks young and handsome yet."

On Sundays and holidays he raced along the beach at Coney Island with Jesse; on summer nights they played on the vacant lots. One of his friends, Levi North, always excelled in their games; in time he joined a circus and became a famous equestrian. Another playmate later became coroner of Brooklyn; a third, as a pen salesman, would send Walt samples of his wares to use on the editorial desk.

The boy learned the history of the embankments on the Heights and the stone house where Washington wept over the lost Marylanders. He talked with the guardian of the vault that held the bones of thousands of prisoners who died in the *Jersey*, the *Whitby*, and other hulks the British had anchored off an isolated stretch of the northeast shore. In their hot, crowded holds whose stench, according to a survivor, would have decomposed the olfactory nerves of a Hottentot, wretched men fought for air and waited for their brutal captors to dole out water while a few rods away bubbled pure springs. Vermin and disease, "carrion" food, and the nostrums of a Hessian quack took a daily toll. Vestiges also remained of crude defenses built in the summer of 1814 by "free people of color" and white volunteers.[3]

14

An encounter with Lafayette vivified the Revolution. On 4 July 1825, the hero came to Brooklyn as one of the fraternity of Free Masons to lay the cornerstone of a library for apprentices. Early that morning he rode in a yellow barouche drawn by four white horses through a twenty-foot lane formed by children and veterans of 1776. At Market Street he dismounted and led the procession to the building site. There, as he helped lift the smallest children to safety, Lafayette held Walt a moment and kissed his cheek. (When Lafayette reached Richmond he met the fifteen-year-old Lt. Edgar A. Poe of the Junior Volunteers, grandson of a comrade.) After the ceremony the elders joined the children in services at the Methodist church.

The library soon housed a thousand volumes lent with little charge to minors in the hope of "inducing among them habits of reading and reflection, which, if properly attended to, will enable them to support the honorable character of good citizens." The founders filled the shelves with Shakespeare, Milton, Addison, Scott, and Byron—who had inspired them to contribute a purse to help the Greeks defeat Turkish oppressors. Next to the *Edinburgh*, the *Quarterly Review*, and other British periodicals they placed a magazine with a New York imprint whose contributors thought it shameful that

> No native bard the patriot harp hath taken,
> But left to minstrel of a foreign strand
> To sing the beauteous scene of nature's loveliest land.[4]

In Lafayette's entourage was a young, tall, blue-eyed Scotswoman, Frances Wright, whom he called "ma bien aimée, adorée Fanny." Her extensive earlier visit had resulted in *Views of Society and Manners in America* (1821), a sympathetic analysis that anticipated de Tocqueville's. Wealthy, with an intellect that absorbed ideas from Epicurus to Jeremy Bentham and Saint-Simon, she had aroused admiration among her hosts with panegyrics on that "enlightened philosopher and generous friend of the human race," Jefferson, and the simplicity and purity of the Constitution. Unlike other travellers she found the unfinished Capitol sublime and prophesied that, "while this edifice stands, liberty has an anchorage from which the congress of European autocrats cannot unmoor her." In *Altorf* she announced that the thespian goddess would find a home here on the liberal plain and would mother a national drama.

Open and generous, Frances Wright refused to confirm charges by other foreigners of rampant licentiousness throughout the states, but ad-

15

mitted encountering one revolting fact—slavery.[5] After leaving Lafayette —her hosts now gossiped about her relationship with the 68-year-old-widower—she journeyed down the Mississippi and observed plantation life. Her fears confirmed, she vowed to attempt to emancipate the human chattels by building a model community at Nashoba in western Tennessee. According to a confidante, Frances Trollope, she planned to seclude herself in this deep forest of the western world and give her fortune, time, and talent to the suffering Africans. By offering equal education to a class of both black and white children, she sought to prove that the two races differed only in color and that the degraded rank always meted to the black was a gross injustice. Robert Dale Owen joined the experiment and Lafayette became one of the trustees.

Walter Whitman could not send his children to a private academy, but he did not allow them to join the many who roamed the streets and never entered a classroom. Either a payment of four dollars a year or the plea of poverty admitted Walt to Public School Number One, where under Selah Hammond and Benjamin Hallock he received his formal education. Their pedagogy reflected the acceptance in America of Joseph Lancaster's plan for instructing the children of the poor by appointing other students as "monitors"; this system combined expedition and economy. But in Brooklyn, as in London, those hostile to Lancaster maintained that a teacher whose overseers refused to hire assistants deputized pupils who knew little to teach those who knew less.

In 1826 the school at the corner of Adams and Concord had two hundred pupils: older boys and girls in the basement, small children on the first floor, and colored children on the second. In each room the desks formed a horseshoe with the monitor seated in the open front. Sessions started at nine in the morning with a Bible reading; then came dictation with rehearsal of words and their definitions. Arithmetic, geography, writing on a slate or in a copy book, and recitations in grammar and spelling completed the curriculum. At the end of the day the monitor reported each pupil's errors and the instructor recorded them.[6]

Followers of Lancaster had for their ideal the inculcation of habits of industry, order, and neatness through exacting discipline. The monitors kept the desks and benches unscratched and the floors spotless. Neither chance nor caprice interfered with their prime mission to let every child at every moment have something to do and a motive for doing it. Talking, swearing, fighting, and truancy brought "corporal chastisement," for Lancaster held that the rod was the master's sceptre. Whether or not Walt's experience matched the misfortunes of Smike in *Nicholas Nickleby*, he emerged with a hatred of floggings and an image of the male teacher as an oppressor cruel as Master Squeers, the tyrant of Do-the-boys Hall.

A lesson learned during a school recess also remained with him. At the Navy Yard a recruit had taken a candle into the magazine room of a new steam frigate and exploded the powder stores. As the burial procession for one of the officers marched through the streets to St. Ann's graveyard, the draped coffin, the slow tempo of drums, and the uniformed mourners taught Walt that death often had a compulsive ritual.

Gabriel Furman, the village historian, admitted in 1824 that his neighbors were not so rigid in religious matters as the saints of Oliver Cromwell's army; at least one boasted of infidelity. The oldest church was the Dutch Reformed in Joralemon Street near the Jamaica turnpike, a gray stone structure that seemed strong as its centuries of Calvinist tradition. Here prayed General Jeremiah Johnson, lineal descendant of the Jansens of New Utrecht, and other community leaders. Episcopal St. Ann's, second in seniority, had its share of wealth and power. The missionary appeal of Methodism to all who hungered for the language of brotherhood and salvation through visitations of the Holy Spirit added many converts during revivals that were held in the Sands Street chapel and that sometimes lasted an entire week. Descendants of the Presbyterians who had settled on the north shore of Long Island formed a congregation in Cranberry Street in 1822. They were followed by the Baptists and the Catholics. Seemingly an ecumenical model, the village did not escape intolerance, for before long nativist Protestants began to revile the followers of Rome. (Twenty years later a young editor echoed this ancient hostility.)

As part of the struggle to halt the legions of darkness, clergymen opened Sunday schools. In 1828 Walt began to attend the one at St. Ann's presided over by a vigorous young Episcopalian. The Reverend Charles McIlvaine, who would become bishop of the diocese of Ohio and president of Kenyon College, contended in his discourses against the "fearful assumption" of those men and women who denied that religion was the basis of the American social system. The stucco building set on a broad lawn that bordered a fine garden and the splendid church appointments awed the boy. The com-

munion table was of white marble and carved mahogany, the pews upholstered in leather; the organ and choir, typical of Episcopal excellence,
helped compensate for the lack of music in Mr. Hallock's school. Half a
century later, the memory of these Sundays returned when Whitman learned
that St. Ann's had been demolished to make way for the approaches to the
East River bridge.[7]

Though the family did not become communicants of any local church,
Louisa sometimes prayed with the Baptists in their small wooden house on
Pearl Street. She and her husband continued to admire Elias Hicks, and one
November when Walt was ten he spent an evening in the presence of the
aged patriarch. On the second floor of Morrison's Hotel in a room furnished
with velvet divans and crystal chandeliers—far more luxury than the Friend
usually knew—the Whitmans, officers from the Navy Yard, village dignitaries, and Negroes freed by the efforts of Hicks and other Friends assembled to hear him.

This was to be Hicks' last journey. Despite the weight of eighty-one years
and recent illness, he stood tall and straight, his eyes black and piercing, his
drab coat and broad-brim accentuating a shock of white hair and angular
features. His voice, tremulous now, was slowly emphatic and resonant; to
the boy it had a quality of "pleading, tender, nearly agonizing conviction"
remembered years later as worthy of ranking with those of Booth, Alboni,
and Father Taylor. Mature members of the congregation agreed that a
special eloquence rather than sheer reasoning raised Hicks high on the scale
of polemic divines.

Born at North Hempstead he had worked as a carpenter, surveyor, and
teacher. Fond of singing "vain songs," racing horses, fowling, fishing, and
dancing at country balls, late in his twenties while living at Jericho he experienced Divine Grace and joined the town's old colony of Friends. From
then on, like George Fox who had come to Long Island in 1672, he devoted
his life to apostolic visitation, despite the war which saw Tarleton's Legion
and Hessian Chasseurs stationed in Jericho and the later onslaught of schis-
matics who called Hicks a veritable Lucifer seducing followers because of
vanity rather than faith in Christ.

During more than half a century this tireless circuit rider had logged
thousands of miles, forded rivers at flood stage, slept in shelters so meager
that snow sifted onto his face. There were many months when he never saw
his home and four invalid sons whose life and death intensified his will to
act as a shepherd of Israel. From the beginning to the end, from the pulpit

18

or in his *Journal* or in letters, he proclaimed that "the mystery of our salvation is opened by the pure, unchangeable Light in the soul." Avowing the mystic nearness of a Creator, denying Calvin's "unsound doctrine of original sin and predestination," he lived to establish the dominion of humane truth, of private ecstasy and public charity. Because God resided within every man, Hicks like John Woolman fought the degradations of slavery, drunkenness, and ignorance. Like a young Unitarian minister in Boston, though long before him, he proclaimed in his own text the infinitude of the individual.

Hicks' exegesis of a Great First Cause coupled with scorn of what he anathematized as the departure from primitive purity and plainness among many professors of truth proved a source of increasing conflict in the Long Island and Philadelphia meetings. Visits by doctrinaire English Friends deepened the rift, and the charge became common that Hicks was a heresiarch who had abandoned belief in atonement and debased Jesus and the Scriptures. Nor could he silence the controversy by answering that he had placed both the Bible and Christ "upon the very foundation they each had placed themselves" and that he dared not place them any higher or lower. Some dissidents went so far as to accuse him of plagiarizing *The Age of Reason*; in fact he was the one clergyman to be honored by Paine's followers. In 1827 many Friends who had been united in gospel fellowship for more than forty years separated, and the orthodox shut their houses against Hicks and his disciples. "Yet they could not shut us out from the favoured divine presence."

In a final *Journal* entry Hicks wrote of the assembly at Morrison's as "large and very favored." He had spoken to the Whitmans and the others of "many things concerning the kingdom of God; and the only sure way by which an admittance into his kingdom of peace and joy may be obtained by the children of men." Two months later he was dead. He spent his last strength to indicate his hostility toward slave labor by pushing aside a cotton quilt.[8]

The secular speeches and writings of the "defamatory priestess" or female Tom Paine, as Frances Wright was now called, also stirred the Whitman conscience. In 1828 after leaving the floundering communal experiment at Nashoba she made her third tour of the states. Before, she had met official welcome everywhere including the Senate chamber; now those who interpreted "Wrightism" as "irreligion" and "free and fancy" sexuality kept aloof.

19

Rather than advocating irreligion, she explained in lectures at the Masonic Hall and the Park theatre that hers had been the first voice to protest against the very word. She admitted attacking sectarianism, rich churches, and hired clergy, but defined her aim as the separation of affairs temporal from ideas spiritual. Her intimacy with Lafayette and the publicized mating of a Nashoba overseer with a Negress prepared her antagonists to believe that she preferred an Eastern seraglio to a Western marriage. Answering them, she pointed to brothels and assignation houses as proof that marriage was legally and morally worthless. But she no more advocated the annulment of marriage laws than of those against thievery; she sought rather "to inspire women with dignity and self respect, and men—a thing yet more difficult— with honor."

Newspapers warned of her siren song. The *Evening Post* mocked the new Aspasia; others used cruder contemporary images in alleging subversion by a ranting female forgetful of modesty and respect for holy institutions. But crowds always came to hear her. Mrs. Trollope was revolted by the Scotswoman's use of that "phrase of mischievous sophistry, 'all men are born free and equal,'" but attested to her extraordinary eloquence and the wonderful power of her rich voice that enchanted every audience.[9]

Encouraged to find that throughout the East the mechanic and laborer sought to escape from grinding poverty, she decided to remain in New York and drop a spark from the torch of liberty until "it spread and burst into flame." With Owen she began to publish an eight-page weekly, the *Free Enquirer*, whose prospectus pledged that "religion, morality, human economy —those master principles which determine the color of our lives—shall obtain a prominent place in our columns. . . . We think meanly of man's present condition, and nobly of his capabilities." Among the thousand subscribers to whom the *Free Enquirer* came each Wednesday was Walter Whitman, who if taciturn and unable to voice his discontent and aspirations seemed eager to support those who wrote and spoke with power and passion.[10]

Like *The Poor Man's Guardian* and earlier working-class papers in Britain, despite the hostility of clergy, merchants, publishers, and politicians, the *Free Enquirer* for four years backed the struggles of mechanics to win and keep a ten-hour day. Through editorials by Wright, Owen, and Amos Gilbert (a Hicksite Friend), the weekly fought for equal rights without distinction of color and sex; for the abolition of capital punishment and of imprisonment for debts; for the easing of a burdensome militia system; and for nonsectarian, free and equal republican education that would give all children food and clothing as well as instruction. The children of the poor had no more eloquent champion until Horace Mann.

On Sundays and several weekdays the Free Enquirers met in their Hall of Science, a remodeled church near the Bowery where, according to worried opponents, they pushed their intellectual resources into the realms of atheism and sedition and doomed the future of the family by urging voluntary size limitation through "expedients"—their euphemism for birth control. One of the lecturers, Gilbert Vale, astronomer and biographer of Paine, later befriended Walt.

English travellers familiar with bookshops like Hetherington's in London and Heywood's in Manchester marveled at the rapid sale of every kind of heretical work in America. At the reading room of the Free Enquirers, those pursuing speculative wisdom found the two popular tracts that Walter Whitman brought home: Wright's *Epicurus, or a Few Days in Athens*, with its edict that "all existences are wonderful," and Volney's *Ruins*, an assessment of the impact of Osiris, Bacchus, "Boudh," and primitive phallic symbolism. According to clergy, the French scholar unchristianized thousands with his Jacobin doctrines that blamed organized religion for the decay of ancient civilizations.[11]

The Hall of Science inevitably became an assembly place for mechanics —among them many carpenters—and small merchants who feared the destruction of economic opportunity through the granting by venal legislators of monopoly licenses and charters to powerful entrepreneurs. Fusing with the followers of the pamphleteer, Thomas Skidmore, and the Brooklyn trade unionist, John Commerford, they scored enough success at the city polls in 1829 to insure their identity for several years as the Workingmen's Party.

"They convene their members," one opponent insisted, "to hear of 'equal rights,' 'rapacious capitalists,' 'grinding employers' "; others called them infidels. But their meetings contained pleas for the enactment of legislation vital to Walter Whitman. He wanted to work for ten hours rather than from sunup to sundown, to have his wages secured by a strong mechanic's lien and payment in specie. As a potential entrepreneur he sought easier credit; as a father he wanted a future for his sons and daughters. The first issue of the *Workingman's Advocate* in October 1829 summarized the utopian goal: "All children are entitled to equal education; all adults to equal property; and all mankind to equal privileges." Consummation would be slower than the editors envisioned.

21

In July 1830 with Nashoba closed and its blacks shipped to Haiti, Frances Wright sailed for France; an honor guard of Quaker women sat on the platform during her farewell address. (In Paris, American ladies snubbed her and their gentlemen marked the sexual infatuation that made Lafayette act like a youth.) Factionalism and quarrels soon destroyed the unity of the Workingmen's Party, but the aspirations of its onetime members for an egalitarian society endured.[12]

A committee of fifty journeymen, in their report that year on the causes of poverty, cited competition in the labor market from ever-available children. At eleven Walt ended his straitened days at the district school, whose classrooms and ferules had evoked his hostility rather than devotion. Fortunately, the community beyond its doors offered richer instruction. He first became an office boy to the Clarke family of lawyers in a building fronted by towering elms. On occasional errands he crossed the river with messages for a member of the New York Bar, Aaron Burr. The former vice president, not too far from the end of his shadowy anabasis, received him with the courtly manner that had charmed many men and women and rewarded the boy with a bit of fruit.

One of the Clarkes, a school inspector and vestryman at St. Ann's, helped Walt with his compositions and gave him a subscription to the circulating library. Now he read *Robinson Crusoe*, the *Mysteries of Udolpho*, and the *Arabian Nights* with "loving and greedy eagerness . . . surpassing the love for puddings and confectionary!" When he was a man of twenty-eight a new edition of the *Arabian Nights* gave him the chance to record his boyhood impression of its world of

> gemmed garments, the beautiful women, the slaves, the cutting
> off of heads, the magic changes, the dwarfs, the spiteful old sor-
> cerers, the dark caves, the cobblers transformed into princes—O,
> it was indeed gorgeous! Then that caliph always a-going through
> the by streets of the city at night—what on earth could become
> more novel and interesting? Certain moralists there are, of the
> vinegar complexion, who would forbid all works of fiction to the
> young. Yet such is always a foolish interdict. The minds of boys
> and girls warm and expand—become rich and generous—under

22

the aspect of such florid pages as those of Robinson Crusoe, the Arabian Nights, Marco Polo and the like.[13]

He walked with Jeanie Deans of *The Heart of Midlothian* on the perilous journey to London to save her sister's life, and continued to revere the courageous cottager all his life; in Scott's novel of the heroic Covenanters he found the fusion of history and imagination that resulted in the ideal national epic. When he began to versify, he followed the form he found in a volume he always kept at hand, Lockhart's octavo edition of the *Minstrelsy of the Scottish Border*.

After a pleasant year with the lawyers he worked briefly in the office and drug shop of the village health officer, Dr. Hunt, a retired naval surgeon who had served with Decatur in Algerian waters and on the *Chesapeake* during her bloody encounter with the *Leopard*. In the summer of 1831 the boy became apprenticed to a printer.

3

DEVIL AND PEDAGOGUE

A NATIVE of Suffolk County, where the legend persisted that every four years voters continued to cast their ballots for Jefferson, and a father who named his third son after that paragon and his fifth after Jackson, Walter Whitman inevitably subscribed to the Democratic Long Island *Patriot*. Walt came to know the publisher of the four-page weekly, Samuel E. Clements, and the shop in an old story-and-a-half building whose small bricks came from Holland. There in its basement, the boy began to learn the printer's craft under the guidance of typesetter William Hartshorne. Though not legally bound out, he lived with the other apprentices at Hartshorne's home next door to the shop.

A guild tradition defined the duties of a printer's devil—the apt term for the boy obliged to labor at dirty, exhausting tasks. Like young Franklin on the *Courant* he cleaned the floors, dampened paper, inked type by beating the forms with two ink-soaked sheepskins balls stuffed with wood and fastened to wood handles, and prepared the dried sheepskins by "treading out" the malodorous pelts. He learned to sort fonts of type and to identify the letter divisions, from the great "e" box to the quads in the right-hand corner; he handled the compositor's stick and rule, adjusted furniture, and planed the forms. He suffered exasperating moments with pi and long hours laying sheets on a wood-frame machine almost as primitive as the common press of the colonial shop. When Horace Greeley started his career in Vermont he found much of the work beyond his strength, but Walt had the power to pull impressions, the most strenuous of all chores. These years of unbalanced muscular stress overdeveloped his right side from shoulder to foot until he walked with the typical journeyman's gait, as rolling as a sailor's.

Since the welfare of an apprentice was solely the master's concern, one was fortunate to serve a respectable man. Hartshorne had come from Philadelphia at the turn of the century, and according to his devil the slight, fragile typesetter held to "the old school manner, rather sedate, not fast,

24

never too familiar, always restraining his temper, cheerful, benevolent, friendly, observing all the decorum of language and action, square and honest, invariably temperate, careful in diet and costume, a keeper of regular hours." His shop tolerated little of the drinking and gambling that made the trade notorious, though it was not too solemn for pranks to be played on a law student and writer, Henry C. Murphy, a future member of Congress and political leader of the Democrats of Brooklyn. In time Murphy would help Whitman into the editorship of the Brooklyn *Eagle* and then force him out of it.[1]

On Sundays Clements drove the boys to the Dutch Reformed Church, but Walt never found within that square fortress the drama staged by the Methodists in Sand Street when John Maffitt, after a decade of itinerant preaching, began a series of revivals to bring grace to the families of the laborers of Brooklyn. The wooden walls echoed daily with prayers, songs, exhortations—and the scoffings of sceptics in the gallery. The lure of spiritual holiness and the rhythm of hearty old hymn tunes, observed the apprentice, drew many witnesses to the altar—"and O, what pretty girls some of them were!"[2]

A sturdy physique helped Walt survive a national calamity. By February 1832 the cholera raging in Asia and Europe had begun to alarm America. De Tocqueville rushed to all the pharmacies in Philadelphia to find a reputed remedy, cajeput oil from a tree native to the Moluccas. In New York, debate over tariff and bank legislation ebbed as the disease engrossed conversation, though Mrs. Trollope's *Domestic Manners of the Americans* created a brief, angry diversion. By mid-spring the one hope of avoiding the fatal diarrhea and dehydration lay in the hypothesis that the disease was caused by atmospheric pestilence and poisoned air, whose virulence would lessen as it passed across the Atlantic. Coming home that May after seventeen years, Washington Irving found congregations joined in daily prayer and desperate municipal officials ordering streets cleaned and limed. But the pandemic horror arrived the next month. As cases multiplied a terrified exodus started from the cities; a fourth of Manhattan's 220,000 fled.

All the members of the Whitman family with the exception of Walt sought refuge in the countryside. "Revenge and Requital," his reminiscence of that traumatic season, explained that while many remained because of poverty, the "desire of gain, too, made a large number continue their business as usual, for competition was narrowed down and profits were large." He also found men and women "heedless of their own small comfort,

25

who went out amid the diseased, the destitute, and the dying, like merciful spirits—wiping the drops from the hot brows and soothing the agony of cramped limbs." During one hour in New York the revivalist Charles G. Finney halted his pleas for benevolent millenialism and counted five hearses at different doors within sight of his Chatham Street church.[3]

By October the contagion had ended, though health officials continued to warn of the danger in eating fruit. Among the local dead was Skidmore, the former leader of the Workingmen's Party. The phrenologist Spurzheim had bypassed New York on his lecture tour but collapsed in Boston.

Mrs. Trollope observed that every newspaper resembled a magazine "wherein the merchant may scan, while he holds out his hand for an invoice, 'Stanzas by Mrs. Hemans,' or a garbled extract from 'Moore's Life of Byron'; the lawyer may study his brief faithfully, and yet contrive to pick up the valuable dictum of some American critic that 'Bulwer's novels are decidedly superior to Sir Walter Scott's.' " In the *Patriot* each week the apprentice set imported literature as well as lines by Bryant and lesser local bards. One week he rimmed a column in black in memory of the creator of Jeanie Deans.[4]

Along with the opportunity to learn a trade and to steep himself in the most indigenous of literary genres, apprenticeship brought Walt further political awareness, for the prime concern of publishers since the days of James Franklin and Peter Zenger had been politics rather than literature or local events. "The two chief weapons that parties use in order to obtain success," observed de Tocqueville, "are the newspapers and public associations." A system of rewards often beyond a mere livelihood assured journalistic loyalty. Hezekiah Niles claimed in his *Register* that a corps of over one hundred and fifty Jacksonian editors had received offices or fat jobs of printing. Because of these prizes and the obligations they engendered, editors acted with a calculated bias that intensified over the years despite Jefferson's futile inaugural plea for the restoration of harmony and the cessation of pointblank fire by the artillery of the press. After Van Buren's Bucktails liberalized the state suffrage standards, almost every white male could respond to the campaign drama; in fact he became both actor and audience.

The publishers of the Brooklyn *City Directory*, in their election entry for 1828, had noted that the candidacy of Jackson and Adams deranged all old party lines until the destiny of the country hung in suspense. By the 1830's a condition existed that was both disgraceful and widespread. Writing to Irving who had entreated him not to contribute to a fractious sheet, James Kirke Paulding rationalized that if men of principle kept aloof, factions and demagogues would turn the press into instruments of mischief "and I don't know what will become of us." Visitors wondered why a civil, orderly populace appeared changed by print into a parcel of rowdy Hessians. The insults and calumnies with which party organs daily arraigned before the bar of public opinion the honor of families and the secrets of the domestic hearth shocked de Tocqueville; the first American paper he read called Jackson a heartless despot who governed through corruption. Some citizens tolerated the vilifications as the noise of a pre-election safety valve comparable to the hissing of a steam boiler, but those called pimps and thieves had less charity.

Cooper, who used the courts as a deterrent agency, blamed political adventurers for buying provincial hypocrites like Steadfast Dodge of *Homeward Bound* and *Home as Found* to pour "vapidity, malice, envy, and ignorance, on his fellow-creatures." One publisher, in rare accord with the litigious novelist, sold his shop and retired rather than endure the violent exchange between parties; in his farewell he expressed fear that unless the stridency ended it would "overthrow our splendid fabric, so that no state shall be left upon another."[5]

Other than a costly, slow libel suit, the only corrective to abuse was public assault upon the snide author. Bennett of the *Herald* became a frequent target for fist and horsewhip. Greeley's obituary on him was pertinent: "He developed the capabilities of journalism in a most wonderful manner, but he did so by degrading its character. He made the newspaper powerful, but he also made it odious." (In 1858, with the authority of twenty-five years of exposure, Whitman also editorialized on the danger to the nation in the habitual harshness of the political press, which called its opposition traitors, malcontents, renegades.)

On the *Patriot* Whitman helped set Jackson's challenge to the Charleston nullifiers and the notice of the veto that portended the end of the Bank. He responded to the solicitude that the President expressed for the farmer and mechanic in the credo that "there are no necessary evils in government. Its evils exist only in its abuses. If it would confine itself to equal protection, and, as Heaven does its rains, shower its favors alike on the high and the low, the rich and the poor, it would be an unqualified blessing." And he learned, as though in a catechism, the reasons why Walter Whitman helped elect Jackson to a second term: Time had revealed him to be a friend to universal education, who offered to appropriate public lands for this noble purpose. Respecting all religions, he negated legislation that sanctioned the unholy alliance of church and state. He sought to ease the plight of the debtor; all of his messages proved his hostility to licensed monopolies.

In June 1833 Walt joined "folks as thick as spruce trees in a swamp" in cheering Jackson as he rode through Brooklyn during a tour of northern cities. Partisans threw roses in the path of the barouche. Whigs satirized the frenzied receptions, the elegant "cooliations" and fried pork and bean suppers, the hours of handshaking more tiring than being dragged through forty knotholes. But the boy was not one to forget a day in the presence of a national hero.[6]

A bizarre episode cost Clements the *Patriot*. After scheming with a sculptor to exhume the body of Elias Hicks from the Jericho graveyard and make saleable casts, he quarreled with his accomplice; the resulting furor drove the editor out of Brooklyn. (Oddly enough, he settled in Camden, New Jersey.) The apprentice then found work on the only other paper in the village, the Long Island *Star*. In this shop his chores were eased, for publisher Alden Spooner owned a new Rust press whose motion operated a Spence inking roller.

Of the fourth generation of New England printers, Spooner attempted to identify the *Star* with worthy causes. Anticipating the incorporation of Brooklyn as a city in 1834, he pleaded that expansion plans include parks and promenades. Too many builders seemed content to cover every lot with meager houses; architects of public structures ignored grandeur and pursued a system of docking—good taste when applied to the tails of horses but hardly so for churches. A bookseller, Spooner helped to build the Apprentices' Library; an art patron, he was also an experimental horticulturist who wrote *The Cultivation of American Grape Vines, and Making of Wine*. As one who achieved mention in *The Croakers*, he insisted on standards of style and boasted that the *Star* always encouraged native authors. His friends agreed, for a poetess whose verse appeared in the paper became his wife and one of his sons sponsored the Hamilton Literary Society. Though not in full communion, Spooner supported the new Presbyterian church, but he also remained one of the few editors to tolerate Frances Wright. He printed antislavery tracts and sold *The Liberator*.[7]

Later Walt would be called an apostate for association with a publisher sympathetic to the coalition that adopted the name Whig, but Spooner was no extremist. With painful memories of a foray into Manhattan as a Clintonian in costly contention against Tammany, he now deplored rabid partisanship. In 1848 he and his quondam apprentice would embark on the same boat for Buffalo and the Free Soil convention.

The dollar the boy earned helped him enter early into what he called the mimic world of the theatre. A ferry ride brought him to Simpson's Park, a place of gold and crimson silks, and Hamblin's Bowery, rebuilt in 1828 after the first of several fires and equipped to equal any theatre in London. The popular literature of the era, according to one of its critics in 1834, was as flimsy as a house built for a short-term lease, but the stage escaped this censure since its managers produced a sequence of *Richard III*, *Hamlet*, and *The Lady of Lyons*, as well as *Maurice the Woodcutter*, equestrian plays, and other "high-seasoned novelties."

The eager apprentice arrived long before the doors opened at six to secure a seat among the other boys on the long wooden benches in the pit. Bryant, Cooper, Irving, Leggett, and Willis were often in the boxes; sometimes Clay or Van Buren. The notorious third tier always had its harlots; the smell of whiskey rose from the punch rooms. Then the curtain lifted and revealed a world beyond reality. (Unlike the graceful leap of the Bowery curtain, the slow, stiff canvas at the Park annoyed Whitman.)

Simpson recreated London until his theatre came to be known as Old Drury and nativists charged him with excessive deference to British taste and players. But he held firm, though New Yorkers rioted there after rumors of insults by one of his imports reached the streets. For the season of 1834 he imposed a series of tableaux upon each tier. Actors of earlier generations—Kean, Betterton, Garrick, Sarah Siddons—graced the dress circle; scenes from ten Shakespearian plays hung from the second tier, with relics of the Globe and Avon on the third. A portrait of the bard over the center of the stage completed the decor.

Here Walt saw players from both sides of the Atlantic. Charles Kemble did Hamlet and Romeo. His dark-eyed daughter Fanny as Juliet, then as Bianca in *Fazio*, Lady Townley of *The Provoked Husband* (with the peerless Placide), Belvidera in *Venice Preserved*, and Julia in *The Hunchback*,

29

established herself as a worthy niece of Siddons. The care-dispelling, mirth-inspiring Tyrone Power delighted thousands with his brogue. James H. Hackett, the Long Islander of Dutch ancestry, as Nimrod Wildfire in Paulding's *The Lion of the West* always delighted a full house with his brags: "Why, I'm the yaller flower of the forest. I'm all brimstone but the head, and that's aky fortis."

Cordial to young actors, Simpson engaged a twenty-one-year-old Bostonian, Charlotte Cushman, and for the next three years as Lady Macbeth, as Emilia denouncing Othello, or as Bianca she revealed the passion and swift change of mood, the perfect enunciation and dialect mimicry that became her hallmark. The roles of other actresses, in the metaphor of one of the audience, were watercolors; hers became oils brilliant with light and shade.

Hamblin, who had learned the profession at Sadlers Wells and Drury Lane, often lured crowds to his stucco "colosseum of the multitude" through dioramas of the North River and "that latest French frippery," the ballet. *The Lion Doomed*, advertised with bona fide lions, climaxed with the conflagration of an entire city. Equestrian melodramas made possible by the deep stage became a Bowery specialty, and Walt was one of many who offered "vehement tribute" to *Timour the Tartar* and *Mazeppa, or The Wild Horse*—no matter that the charger had the proportions of a donkey and dashed up an "awful precipice" that measured only ten feet "slantendiculously." (Fifteen years later in a time of harassment caused by his refusal to abandon his political ideals, Whitman paused to eulogize the several dead and the few survivors of the Bowery cast, "the delight of so many boyish days." Their parts in *The Last Days of Pompeii*, which earned ten thousand dollars in one week in 1838, remained fresh to him: Ingersoll as the gladiator Lydon; Hamblin as Arbaces; and Mrs. Flynn as the blind girl who carried a basket of flowers and guided her slow steps with a long staff. "There probably has never been a play and spectacle combined, possessing greater merit.") Another night he hurried between the Doric columns and through one of the three entrances to experience a Richard III by Junius Brutus Booth, who could be brilliant when sober or execrable when drunk.[8]

Though Hamblin now and then acted in a Shakespearian cycle or in *Rienzi*, he shrewdly fed the nationalistic hunger of his patrons. After an anti-British riot at the rival Park he added the epithet American to his marquee—not enough to stop a later mob also incensed by the same Anglophobia. It was here that the herculean Edwin Forrest with "powerful declamations" established his fame and ensured the Bowery's continued existence. Europeans remembering Talma and Kean could not endure his Othello and other roles because of his obvious coarseness; even some of his own countrymen found that his style propelled by a powerful torso became rant and claptrap. Seeking to show passion through extended expression, he often became ludicrous; the regular rise and fall of his voice led to monotony. He was prone to obvious gestures such as the constant elevation of his right arm which, complained William Leggett's weekly *Critic*, led to sympathetic pain in the shoulders of viewers. His left hand twitched too often at his belt. But that paper called Forrest the greatest actor in the country, and Dunlap ranked his *Lear* above all others. Whitman, too, testified that through Brutus, Spartacus, Jack Cade, Tell, and other libertarian roles the muscular stentor "filtered" into his "whole nature."[9]

When a copy of the play was at hand, the young patron read it before coming to the theatre. He bought a *Richard III* and carried it with him, for the many gas lamps made the ample vestibule of the Bowery as bright as a library. Nothing obliterated the memory of those nights.

In the summer of 1835 Louisa Whitman gave birth to her ninth child. An earlier nameless infant had died within months, but Edward was denied this fate though he soon revealed malformation of the left hand and left leg, and mental retardation. The unfortunate child and the ailing mother added to the insecurity of a household burdened by numbers and low income. In Brooklyn, as in other cities, prosperity had begun to prove elusive. Local bankers had responded to the extravagant speculation in real estate by issuing paper currency. After Jackson in October 1833 removed $10,000,000 of federal deposits from Biddle's Bank, in a "supererogatory act of tyranny" as Philip Hone called it, stocks fell and money became scarce; according to the diarist the president's killed and wounded, like those at New Orleans, lay everywhere.

Hoping to ease their common financial stress, the manufacturers, merchants, and mechanics of Brooklyn held public meetings in the winter of 1834, but without cash they accomplished little, and unemployment mounted. Walter Whitman then turned again with his family to the country near Hempstead, where good land and timber provided food and cord-wood and his sale of inherited acreage at West Hills brought $2250. Walt remained in Brooklyn to finish learning his trade.

When an apprentice rose to the intermediate rank of "three quarterer," he often found that he had outgrown a small shop. For a while the pub-lishers in Manhattan to whom the Napier steam press had begun to reveal its scope offered work to compositors. It seemed that a precocious literary aspirant might even find space in the elegant *Mirror*, whose editors pleaded that patriotism implied support for native authors. Here was the chance to meet the celebrated corps of literati and to absorb the advice dispensed in conversation and letters: "give us something new—something characteristic of yourself, your country, and your native feelings."[10]

But the unstable economy, cycling through inflation, crisis, and deflation, continued to restrict hirings. After money became plentiful again, specula-tion in stocks and land raced rampant, rising five-fold from 1834 to 1836; rents and food prices soared as banks flooded the country with paper. "Ameri-ca," concluded Cooper, "thinks, eats, talks, drinks, and dreams dollars." When Albany banned the issuance of bills under five dollars, out-of-state "shinplasters" crossed into New York; this currency was often worthless. The Specie Circular ordering payment for public lands in gold and silver was another measure that the many new enemies of the Administration found a harmful fiat rather than a panacea.

Other facts made a marginal existence in the metropolis difficult. On 12 August 1835 fire started in a bindery in the Fulton Street section, whose related crafts had formed a Paternoster Row, and destroyed about forty newspaper, book, and job printers. This crippling of the entire industry was followed in December by another fire that burned hundreds of stores and bankrupted insurance companies. Heavy snow and severe cold added to the general misery; capital crime became more flagrant than at any other time in the annals of the city. In April the hatchet murder of Helen Jewett in a brothel forced citizens to acknowledge the existence of "countless temples of infamy." When the jury returned within fifteen minutes to declare in-nocent—despite real evidence,—the wealthy 19-year-old patron, while another court that year convicted striking tailors, many lost faith in law enforcement. Editorials lamented the "seductive though meretricious allure-ment to ruin" met by thousands of youths without guardians; gangs of them, drunk and brutal, prowled nightly. (Six years later the vice and squalor frightened a mature visitor, Lowell.) The Five Points abounded in miserable dives beyond whose small bar and half barrel a door opened into a room where a woman—often a mere child—could be hired for a few cents.

During visits to Suffolk Walt found pleasure in the open landscape, in the white cedar swamps where thrushes sang, in fishing and swimming the bays and walking the beaches. He learned the Algonkin place names— Paumanok, Yaphank, and others; he met Samuel Mills, a veteran of the Revolution; Grandmother Brush, who lived until 1834, told him tales of Indian squaws; he talked with old Mose, once a slave to members of the family. The emotions Walt soon described in "Tomb Blossoms" became dominant:

> Man of cities! what is there in all your boasted pleasure—your fashions, parties, balls, and theatres, compared to the simplest of delights we country folk enjoy? Our pure air, making the blood swell and leap with buoyant health; our labor and our exercise; our freedom from the sickly vices that taint the town; our not being racked with notes due, or the fluctuations of prices, or the breaking of banks; our manners of sociality, expanding the heart, and reacting with wholesome effect upon the body;—can anything which citizens possess balance these?

Abandoning the boasted pleasure of seeing West's "Death on the Pale Horse" at the Academy, or hearing the *Messiah* at the Chatham, or talking to bookmen at Colman's about Irving's *Tour of the Prairies* or Kennedy's *Horse-Shoe Robinson*, he retreated into what seemed to be an island sanctuary.

But he found before long that tragedy also visited here. In November 1836 the new *Bristol* grounded at Far Rockaway and lost most of her passengers. Two months later the ice-encrusted *Mexico* beached in a gale at Hempstead. The surf and zero-degree cold prevented the rescue of over a hundred Irish immigrants huddled in a frozen mass on the forward deck.

Harriet Martineau noted in leafing through an almanac explicit directions for preparing a farm for winter. "Secure your cellars from frost. Fasten loose clapboards and shingles. Secure a good school-master." In turn Norwich, Babylon, Long Swamp, Smithtown, and others of the twenty-one towns of Long Island hired Whitman to teach their children. He may actually have answered advertisements like the one in the *Democrat* of 2 May 1838: "Wanted, a teacher in School District, Flushing."

To rural commissioners, education was less than the "shibboleth of our cause" proclaimed by the *Workingman's Advocate*. Their systems were built upon the haphazard combination of an itinerant tutor and a single classroom filled with boys and girls whose ages ranged from five or six to sixteen. After several years of experience, Whitman in 1840 deplored the quick acceptance of men "ignorant and stupid, of shattered characters, of questionable morality, of intemperate habits, of blasphemous tongues," and he estimated that two-thirds of the teachers had "raw and illiterate minds." Herman Melville in charge of a class in Pittsfield told his uncle, "Orators may declaim concerning the universally-diffused blessings of education in our Country, and Essayists may exhaust their magazine of adjectives in extolling our system of common school instruction,—but when reduced to practice, the high and sanguine hopes excited by its imposing appearance in *theory*—are a little dashed." [11]

Class, held in a church basement or an unpainted frame structure with a batten door and seats of rough slabs, lasted six days a week from eight in the morning until four in the afternoon; in winter until light failed. Sundays and alternate Saturday afternoons were free. When the boys responsible for the fireplace or box stove failed to do their chore, the teacher and pupils remained cold until one of them brought a burning brand from a neighbor. The girls swept the floor and cleaned the blackboards.

Throughout the day the master split and shaped goose quills, wrote specimens on the board or on slates, and—guided by the *Common School Assistant*—prepared as many as eighty-five charges for the unannounced visits of the inspectors by drilling them in Murray's *Grammar* and *English Reader*, Webster's *Speller*, Daboll's *Arithmetic*, and Mowbridge's *Geography*. There is little reason to doubt that the novice pedagogue deserved the wages that totaled $72.20 for a term of five months at Smithtown. A teacher also earned the dubious privilege of boarding at the homes of scholars, sometimes even sharing the same bed with a student.

Discipline could prove vexatious. Freneau escaped from Long Island after a frightening week with a "brutish, brainless crew." In Pittsfield one of the older boys challenged Melville to a fight. Because early maturation and hard work had made him six feet tall and husky, Whitman survived without resorting to the cat-o'-nine tails or imprisoning unruly scholars in a dark closet. Indeed, he announced his support for what he called a philo-

34

sophical system that repudiated lashes, tears, and sighs. In his words, a true teacher sought to open the sweet fountains in a child's breast with gentleness and kind words rather than with the rattan. Refusing to follow the common Lancastrian method, he enlivened the day with "twenty questions" and a game of baseball during recess. If he confiscated distracting contraband—marbles, fish hooks, knives, jumping jacks—he returned it as a reward for good behavior.

In addition to earning a living when all three banks of Brooklyn had suspended specie payment and an estimated fifty thousand walked the streets of Manhattan unable to buy food or pay rent, he found other rewards, especially in Smithtown. Despite a noticeable failure to attend either the Presbyterian or Methodist church, he abstained from tobacco and did not overindulge in liquor even when he lived at Hallock's Inn—whose sign offered "entertainment for man and beast." (Later, in 1840 during an exchange of insults, the Whig *Farmer* nevertheless called him a drunken pedagogue.) His simple dress, fine physique, and intellectual keenness brought the respect of inspectors and led to association with his peers, the grandsons of families that had survived the raids of the 17th Light Dragoons and De Lancey's Brigade of Loyalists.

One evening early in December 1837, he gathered with ten other young men in the schoolhouse on the Jericho turnpike to plan a debating society, the vehicle of self-improvement popular ever since the Philadelphia Junto. Passengers on transatlantic ships debated twice weekly, weather permitting, while seated on water kegs; Greeley listed his membership in a debating society, along with checkers and romantic verse, as his only dissipations; at Columbia College, George Templeton Strong and fellow Philolexians argued Fridays after supper; in Albany, Gansevoort and Herman Melville also "exhorted and beseeched"; at an academy near the Hudson, Stephen A. Douglas developed the skill he used to drive the Compromise through the Senate in 1850. A member of one society observed that this was the way the metaphysical nonsense of youth found vent—in trying to prove that a certain kind of timber composed the North Pole. But the societies also pondered topics of basic concern to the national welfare.

From December until March the Smithtowners debated questions chosen by a committee of three, including Secretary Whitman. He never missed an evening, kept the minutes for the ten meetings in a script as neat as that of his academy-trained successor, and spoke so forcefully, often against older men who were members of professions, that he won the majority of

35

his debates. In his reasoned judgment, the system of slavery as it existed in the South was wrong; the emigration of foreigners to America was not to be discouraged; capital punishment must be abolished; the arts and sciences flourished more under republican government than under any other.[12]

To work in these island towns by no means isolated him or barred an occasional jaunt to the city when simple country delights palled. After April 1836 the ten-mile track of the Brooklyn–Jamaica railroad opened, and an early-morning stage brought him to the eastern depot from which the new Baldwin locomotives, the *Ariel* and the *Hicksville*—barring encounters with wayward cows or flaming fields—pulled him to the ferry and New York. There, depending on bankruptcies and fires, he had the choice of two to five theatres. "Whoever denies himself the *Lady of Lyons*," exclaimed a reviewer in 1838, "diminishes the enjoyment of his life." A teacher could join the rest of the audience in weeping when Dickens' Smike died in Nickleby's arms. Niblo and other impresarios gambled and lost with the *Marriage of Figaro* and *Fidelio*, but "the fullest and most fashionable house" that included the schoolteacher cheered Fanny Elssler, filled her purse, and covered the stage with flowers in fifteen nights of Polish dances and the *La Tarantual* and *La Sylphide* ballets. Some of the press, shocked by a dress slit at the thigh, branded her "a gilded, glittering, shameless creature—the cast-off mistress of half the titled libertines of Europe." Wits riddled: "Why is a visit to see Elssler dance like going to an agricultural show? There is a display of fat calves." But only the arrival of the *Great Western* aroused as much excitement as the *danseuse* who confessed that her idea of ultimate joy was to please both God and men.

Sated after a time by these metropolitan spectacles and their endless replacements, Whitman returned to Suffolk.

4

A WELL-KNOWN LOCOFOCO

> In every hamlet, every trifling town,
> Some sly designing fellow sits him down,
> On spacious folio prints his weekly mess,
> And spreads around this poison of his Press.[1]

WRITTEN FOR an earlier generation, Freneau's lines now possessed added relevance as newspapers multiplied throughout the land. To become a publisher seemed so simple that the British visitor Hamilton concluded that every vulgar booby who could call names and procure type through a loan, had a fair chance of success.

Huntington with shipyards, fisheries, and a population of 5,000 in the environs seemed to promise success to a publishing venture, for no rival threatened competition. For fifty dollars the journeyman Whitman bought a used hand press and fonts at Bruce's foundry in Williamsburgh, rented shop space above a stable in Main Street, and assigned a younger brother the job of printer's devil. Some of the initial outlay may have come from his parents, who in January 1838 mortgaged the farm for $600.

On Tuesday, 5 June 1838, five days after his nineteenth birthday, "Walter Whitman, jun., editor and publisher," issued the first *Long Islander*. The next week the *Star* congratulated its former apprentice and wished that in time he might exhibit as many bound volumes as there were of the *Star*. With the wisdom of thirty years of experience, Spooner warned the neophyte that few country places provided adequate patronage.

Editing the *Long Islander* presented few technical challenges. As Whitman remembered the paper and others like it, they were "little dingy sheets, containing hardly anything but advertisements. Their conductors imagined they were doing all that was required of them if they scissored out a half column from the metropolitan papers and chronicled the details of a big pumpkin or a three-legged cow." In Massachusetts the "floundering car-

37

rier" delivered a similar weekly to the snowbound door of the Whittier farm. The first and fourth pages were printed on one side of the large sheet and the two inside pages completed the next day in time for delivery. The editorial or leader appeared in a column on the second page; advertisements, contributed or borrowed verse, tales, sermons, reports of fire, sinkings, and "horrible outrages" filled the remaining space.

The difference between temporary existence and permanent establishment depended upon the resourcefulness of the publisher. Ink, paper, an occasional dinner at Scudder's Huntington House, rent, and wages demanded income that could be secured by the job printing of sermons, almanacs, and directories. Joseph Smith's *Book of Mormon* came from a country shop; Spooner issued *The Hasty Pudding*, directories, and tracts for various societies; others solicited subsidies in return for the printing of taxbills and official lists. In the first months without such sources, Whitman needed and built a newspaper circulation large enough to keep busy for a day and a night delivering the *Long Islander* with the help of his white horse, Nina. The route through farm lanes was pleasant and provided lifelong memories of "stops by hay fields, the hospitality, the nice dinners, occasional evenings, the girls, the rides through the brush and the smell from the salt of the South roads." Huntington offered a delightful view from the summit of the village burying ground; its one flaw was a vile-smelling pond. The printshop became a gathering place for those drawn to the editor by his good cheer and his ability to hear them out and respond with informed conviction.[2]

Though the national economy sporadically showed more vitality than in the previous years, many families remained impoverished and *Long Islander* subscribers too often paid in cordwood and potatoes rather than in paper or specie. "Abundant experience has convinced us," advised Greeley, "that the cash system is, in the long run, the only one upon which newspapers and periodicals can be prosperously and independently conducted." Brenton dunned Jamaicans through doggerel:

> Pay the Printer, pay the Printer,
> All remember his just due,
> In cold winter, in cold winter,
> He wants cash as well as you.

But Whitman continued to be the captive of a lax policy. Eventually the discouraged publisher began to neglect his deadlines and several weeks often

elapsed before he and Nina carried copies to subscribers. Finally he closed the shop and sold his horse. In July 1839 when E. O. Crowell revived the *Long Islander* as an independent organ, he admitted laboring under a handicap "in consequence of the paper having been discontinued for so long a time."[3]

No file of Whitman's weekly survived and with few exceptions contemporaries failed to quote it. In August 1838 the *Democrat* copied from it an account of death by lightning, and in October it reprinted the editor's poem, "Our Future Lot." With thirty-two lines he consigned his "troubled heart and wondrous form" to decay in the "cold wet earth," but in the final stanzas rejoiced that his mind was destined to endure and its flickering taper would become "Radiant with pure and piercing light/ From the Eternal's eye!"

Excursions to the city enabled the islander to affirm his political identity. Frances Wright, aged not by making "desperate love" to Lafayette but ironically by an orthodox marriage, returned to stir new controversy over old issues. In Philadelphia, first the authorities and then a mob halted her lectures on religion and government. In New York, the mayor assigned police to control hecklers at the Masonic Hall where every Sunday night "Mad Fanny" condemned priests, banks, Whigs, and others creators of social convulsion.

In the long interval of her absence in Europe, Whitman had encountered the American political philosopher who became his exemplar. William Leggett found his most ardent admirers—"his peculiar party," a eulogist would soon say—among the young men of his native city, though Whittier and others far away joined in honoring him. An Easterner, as a boy he moved with his family to Illinois, then served as a midshipman until he resigned rather than tolerate the arbitrary discipline of a martinet. He clerked in a Fulton Street bank where he observed frenetic finance, then acted at the Bowery where he became intimate with Forrest. Indifferent at first to politics, he wrote two volumes of verse and one of fiction in which he used his knowledge of the frontier and the sea; Harper and Brothers would include his work in the *Tales of the Glauber Spa* by a group of Knickerbockers. In 1828 he started the weekly *Critic* and in a remarkable display of virtuosity filled the pages with his own essays and reviews. One day the anonymous *Fanshawe* reached his desk. There was no need to name the author, Leggett told his readers: "The mind that produced this little, interesting volume is capable of making great and rich additions to our native literature; and it will, or we shall be sadly mistaken." When Hackett offered a prize of $300 for the best comedy with an American as leading character, the actor asked Leggett to judge the entries with Bryant and Halleck. They chose *The Lion of the West*. When "The Last of the Boatmen" appeared in the *Western Souvenir* Leggett cheered, "Well done for the backwoods!" and reprinted that saga of the life and death of Mike Fink.[4]

Later as a journalist associated with Bryant on the *Evening Post*, Leggett began to sense the need to apply the "Jefferson touchstone" to local and national issues. A reading of John Taylor's *Injuiry into the Principles and Policy of the Government of the United States*, which he found one of the most democratic and eloquent books ever written in this country, gave him a strategic base: Taylor had exposed "in a masterly manner, the political evils of our unequal and oppressive banking system." Leggett's other mentors were Bentham, who had issued an imperative to good citizens to censure freely; David Ricardo, the free-trade doctrinaire and critic of the Bank of England; and Adam Smith, whose *Laissez nous faire* and *Pas trop gouverner* comprised for Leggett the vital lessons of political wisdom. *The Wealth of Nations*, whose 1776 publication date seemed more than a coincidence to one searching for an end to economic restriction, became the model for his indictment of the immorality of businessmen's combining to secure special-privilege monopolies.

In "unadorned, but free, hardy English, transparent as water," he attacked the Hamilton–Marshall doctrines of irrevocable contracts and vested rights, doctrines that he believed had created a banking oligarchy, steamboat monopoly, exclusive patent law, and incorporated colleges and churches. In the spirit of Jefferson he asked, "Can the dead bind the living?" When Jackson began to lay siege to the Bank of the United States, Leggett gave thanks to "the illustrious man who was called in a happy hour to preside over our country" and through whose courage the attention of the people had been "thoroughly awakened to the insidious nature and fatal influences of chartered privileges."

Those Democratic leaders who thought that in Leggett they had a hack willing to place party loyalty above principle had not read his essays on morality in politics. After Bryant sailed for Europe in June 1834, Leggett assumed chief editorship of the *Evening Post* at the time when the struggle against monopoly—which split the Democrats as well as separated them from the Whigs—reached its zenith. Repeatedly he warned that special charters invaded equal rights by creating a class of men distinguished from the mass by peculiar rights, powers, and prerogatives. Europe had forged a chain of ranks; America needed the lighter but stronger chain of brotherhood. In his judgment all special-interest legislation was immoral, and turned politics into a race for rewards and politicians into demagogues whose speeches had no more salvation in them than "Hail Columbia" or "Yankee Doodle." When a courageous investigation of "pet" state banks convinced him that they were signal failures, he accused the Democratic Albany Regency of growing fat on the drippings from this dish that was served to favorites. A port collector who absconded with a million dollars, a postmaster who confiscated abolitionist mail—these loyal Jacksonian henchmen proved to Leggett that there could be no morality, even in the Democratic party, until the nation returned to a pristine form of less rather than more government. Over and over again he stated categorically his conviction that the sole legitimate object of politics was the happiness of communities; a politician who ignored equal rights was an adventurer who "perverted the holy sentiment of patriotism."

His followers, including recruits from the remnants of the Workingmen's Party, became so formidable that in an election year they forced reform pledges from Democratic candidates. But victorious Democrats failed to ban rag money and restore gold currency—though Leggett made it clear that he was not for an exclusive currency but for one that would result from freedom of trade, "subject only to the natural influence of unbounded competition and enterprise." Nor did the "regular" Democrats slow the proliferation of charters. Vindictive, the radicals, visionaries, agrarians, Fanny Wright men, Jacobins—as they were called—vowed to elect only men from their own ranks. In addition to Leggett, they turned for guidance to the congressman who came from Whitman's Suffolk, Churchill C. Cambreleng.

The night of 29 October 1835 when Leggett lay ill saw the episode that gave another name to his adherents. A nominating assembly at Tammany Hall turned into an open conflict between the Equal Rights members and the Monopolists. After a riotous session, the Monopolists withdrew and turned off the illuminating gas. Then, according to the secretary of the group that remained, "Loco-foco matches are ignited, candles are lit, and they are held up by living and breathing chandeliers. . . . Reader, if this were not a victory over Monopoly, a blow at least, was struck upon the hydra-headed monster."[5]

The Locofocos, as a Whig paper named them in derision the next day, adopted their own Equal Rights ticket, and Military Hall rather than the hostile Old Wigwam became their headquarters. Though Leggett accepted the new tag, he believed that Locofoco, Whig, and Tory were arbitrary and inaccurate. "The true designation of the two great antagonistic political divisions of society is *democratick* and *aristocratick*." For the next two years, separate slates of Locofoco candidates appeared on the city and state ballots, though the strategy of hurting Tammany and Albany often dictated support for a senator or assemblyman who belonged to the Whigs or to other Democratic factions. In turn the regulars, abetted by their official paper, the Washington *Globe*, virtually excommunicated Leggett—a bull he had long anticipated.

On the slavery issue Leggett was as fiery as in his attacks on monopoly. In New York in 1834 when mobs sacked the homes of abolitionists and terrified Negroes, Leggett, unlike other editors, in the *Evening Post* condemned the hoodlums and demanded an end to the passivity of civil authorities. The next year, after slaveholders in Charleston burned mail they considered dangerous and initiated virtual censorship throughout all southern post offices, he denounced Postmaster General Kendall for allowing the publications of citizens to be treated as dispatches by foreign spies. That same year he published his concurrence with the program of the Anti-Slavery Society and held firm in the face of threats of business loss and party censure. "Every American," he answered, "who in any way countenances slavery, is derelict in his duty as a Christian, a patriot, a man; and every one *does* countenance and authorize it who suffers any opportunity of expressing his deep abhorrence of its manifold abominations to pass unreproved." Learning that friends who sought to send him to Congress were trying to gain votes by denying his abolitionism, he ordered them to end this folly:

> Let others twist themselves into what shapes they please, to gratify the present taste of the people; as for me, *I am not formed of such pliant materials, and choose to retain, undisturbed, the image of my God!* I do not wish to cheat the people of their votes. I would not get their support, any more than their money, under false pretences. *I am what I am*; and, if that does not suit them, I am content to stay at home.[6]

In December 1836, with the financial help of Forrest, Leggett started *The Plaindealer*. Every Saturday for the next ten months until it was destroyed by the panic he had worked to obviate, the journal expounded his faith that "little else is required to carry a state to the highest degree of opulence, but peace, easy taxes, and a tolerable administration of justice." He gave the most space to national issues but did not neglect the local butcher whose landlord charged exorbitant stall rent, and the laborer whose employer manipulated wages. "Combination" (he printed the "magic" formula in bold capitals) rather than single futile forays offered the poor a safe bulwark against predators. Leggett's vision was utopian—one of his essays used a text from Sir Thomas More—but his topics were current. To the dismay of Democrats he assailed Van Buren's inaugural address for its "cringing spirit of propitiation to the South," and he encouraged the "Massachusetts madman," John Quincy Adams, to resist the annexation of Texas. The way to lower the price of bread, he scolded rioters, was not by vandalism at the flour warehouse but through the ballot box.

When he found unused space in *The Plaindealer*, Leggett continued the literary program of his earlier *Critic*. He delighted in the poetry of Bryant, "far above the character of a mere contriver of the prettiness of rhyme," and he found in Catherine Sedgwick's novels, "that sort of American spirit which leads her to shape the incidents of her story, the sentiments of her actors, and all the various circumstances of the fable, according to the actual condition of things in this country, as they are modified by our political institutions." Avoiding chauvinism he became an early admirer of Dickens and saw in Martineau at least one traveller whose political morality was founded on "the greatest happiness principle"; the result was "a democratick book." As a critic of literature or of political institutions he remained primarily concerned with "the amelioration of the condition of manhood, and adding to the sum of human happiness."

Though beset by chronic illness and massive debt, he tried to rally his readers during the worst months of the economic crisis. Knowing that a party without office could not achieve its program, he urged union of the Democrats so that a single Whig ticket would not overwhelm split opponents. This was no abject surrender, for Locofocos claimed that they had gained their objective by showing politicians who had schemed to use the Democratic party for their own selfish purposes that they could not succeed. Lest there be conciliation based on corrupt bargaining, Leggett demanded the expunging of all traces of aristocracy that had crept into party creed or

43

practice, and the prompt return to the simple, sublime doctrines of Jefferson.

As he faced the end of publication and, in fact, of his life, he continued to extol the great maxim of equality "which considers the whole family of man as a brotherhood, the children of a common parent, and coheirs of a common destiny." In the last issue of *The Plaindealer*, he defined once again the Locofoco creed as the political morality which asserts the equal rights of all mankind.

Van Buren's conciliatory offer to him of a consulship to Guatemala, with the hope of a cure through a sea voyage and warm climate, came too late. When Leggett died in 1839 mourners everywhere paid tribute to this "warm and mighty heart," whose political faith, according to Whittier, coincided with the Gospel of Jesus. The Massachusetts abolitionist denounced Tammany for planting ploughshares of hatred "hot from hell" in Leggett's path and clamoring down "the bold reformer when he pleaded for his captive fellow men." Bryant's verses assured the community that his former associate's words of fire would continue to move the hearts of men "Amid a cold and cowardly age."

Theodore Sedgwick, Jr., author of *What Is Monopoly?*, collected his friend's essays into two volumes that became guides for all surviving believers in equal rights.[7] They searched them for epigraphs to place in new magazines and papers, and for wisdom with which to face the stress of later years. "Can we forget the career of the lamented Leggett?" Whitman, as editor of the Brooklyn *Eagle*, would ask in October 1846.

Sometimes guests offered the toast, "The village of Jamaica—very *near* a city." The six inns, ten groceries, the drygoods emporiums, and the two newspapers were signs of the prosperity brought by the hundreds of passersby who stopped daily at Jamaica station on the main railway route to Manhattan, and the thousands who came to cheer Lady Suffolk and other horses. Here Whitman worked on the *Democrat* published by Brenton, the Queens County party whip, who heeded his own warning and that of the Albany *Argus* that it was high time to counter the impact on the polls of the fabrications of "swig" cider politicians and of the ample money from the brokers of Wall Street.

The first foreshadowing of disaster for the vulnerable Democratic party had come in 1837 when the opposition gained large majorities in many parts of the state. "Can the Whigs maintain the high ground which they have won?" asked the startled losers. The disenchanted voters—who blamed the Panic on Administration policies rather than on the fall in the price of cotton, the hike in the Bank of England's discount rate, or the curtailment by Baring Brothers—then gave Seward the governorship and other Whigs the Assembly and offices long held by Jacksonians. Suffolk remained loyal thanks to the near unanimity of the Huntington vote, but Queens showed signs of disaffection. By August 1839 the *Democrat* had begun to cajole party members to awake and prepare for November. Soon the Whig *Farmer* complained of a young spaniel on the *Democrat* who "yelped till he turned red in the face. He is a dirty cur at best, and bids fair to make a worthless dogg." Whitman promptly countered these "vulgar allusions and low-bred attempts at wit" by the opposition editor-pharmacist: "A person had been to the New Drug Store for a dose of calomel and jalap. Instead of taking the medicine, he unfortunately swallowed the wrapper, which proved to be the *Farmer*. He did not discoved the mistake until he was afflicted with the most intolerable symptoms of nausea."[8]

Turning to the county partisans, Whitman attempted to rally their spirit with definitions of principle in the exalted tone he found in *The Plaindealer* and the *Democratic Review*:

> Democracy has its foundations in the very broadest notion of good to our fellow creatures and to our countrymen. It is based on the doctrine of equality in political rights and privileges; it overlooks the distinctions of rank and wealth; it comprehends in its protection all classes and conditions of society, nor allows that the refined and rich shall receive more consideration in its decrees than the poor and lowly born.[9]

By mid-October he had developed the theme he would repeat in New York two years later before a rally of thousands: rather than the advancement of an individual leader, the true Democrat sought victory for principles; the bond of party unity and the base of its strength lay in the will to benefit the people through the progress of popular and equal rights ensured by a prudent Administration.

In November, to the dismay of the *Democrat*, Queens sent a member of the King family, a "Federalist of the Old School," to the Albany legislature ruled now by Whigs. "The drams of gin and brandy—the bribes— the three dollar notes dropped here and there—the shaking of nasty hands

—have all told." What remained to be done now to counter fears of endless debt, liquidation, arson, and other spectres of continued economic depression was to avow faith in the outcome of the presidential contest by working with more spirit than ever before.[10]

That other teacher, Melville, after he had brought proper organization to his school, confided to his uncle that "a few intervals of time are afforded me, which I improve by occasional writing and reading." His contemporary, who returned to the classroom for the winter and spring of 1839–1840, also salvaged hours. Working near Jamaica, he had access to a variety of books, for Brenton's shop like so many others housed a small circulating collection besides Harper and Brothers' 100-volume school library. Exempt from the rental charge of six cents, he could read histories of Greece and America, biographies of Franklin and Napoleon, and the works of Irving, Miss Mitford, Burns, Scott, and Goethe.[11] Believing that Dickens, whose *Pickwick* brightened the depressed years, deserved greater praise than the average novelist, he reprinted chapters from *Nickleby* in the *Democrat*.

Access to books and press space was only partly responsible for the nine signed pieces he placed in the *Democrat*. According to metropolitan editors, several forces led them to publish "lines." As steam navigation lessened oceanic space, the British demand for American writers promised to increase, while at home the enthusiasm shown for Bryant and Halleck encouraged the collection of fugitive pieces by lesser reputations. "A scrap of good verse is not to be lost in these times so barren of the muses," wrote the New York *Review*, joining in the demolition of obstacles erected by those who thought it fashionable to sneer at modern poetry and utter "the most doleful apprehension for the prospects of young men who are allured into the pleasant fields of literature."

"The End of All," "The Love That Is Hereafter," and other vistas of the grave never quite satisfied Whitman, for he revised and retitled them. But the deletion of a phrase or a stanza did not lift their melancholy burden. Living in the midst of his vibrant island he chose at first to sing of stricken youth rather than of farm kitchens, headlands, morning glories, swimmers, and bluefish trollers. The news of the death of a schoolboy friend haunted him and led to recurrent visions of the body shrouded in white-lined coffin.

He also conformed to the numinous ethic of elder poets; again and again he visited the cemetery on the hill, mused on the common fate, strewed flowers, and then entered the family crypt. According to the *Democratic Review* the popularity of "Thanatopsis" had made this kind of pose, imagery, and tone proper.

The Suffolk poet did not spare his few exotic characters from death. In "The Spanish Lady," told in the manner of one of Poe's tales of revenge, an assassin's dagger sends the "beauteous" heroine to heaven. In "The Inca's Daughter," the captive princess, after a Metamora-like oration to her "paleface" captors, sheathes a poisoned arrow in her own breast.

Somehow robust "Young Grimes" survives. Brenton was fond of an old ballad honoring a member of the Long Parliament and had printed contemporary versions made popular by Albert Gorton Greene; these ranged from solemn eulogy to a parody on "Old Brindle's dead, that good old cow." In January 1840 he ran Whitman's verse biography of the paragon Grimes who "ne'er went to see the girls/ Before he was fourteen"; neither smoked, swore, nor indulged in extravagant clothes, and shunned "those dangerous rooms/ Where sin and vice abound." Marrying a prudent, chaste woman, instructing his children and honoring his aged mother, Young Grimes enjoyed the tranquil life and served as testimony to the worth of the farm over "the wide city's noisy din."

The *Democrat* also continued a prose series that Whitman had first placed in a Hempstead weekly. In nine "Sun-Down Papers—from the Desk of a Schoolmaster" he is in turn hortatory, melancholy, jovial, sedate. Repulsed by the sight of boys mouthing wads of tobacco or dangling segars from the corners of their lips, he indicts the latter combination as "a smoking fire at one end, and a conceited spark at the other." The gulping of gallons of tea and coffee by their elders seemed another fashionable way of suicide. Knowing the social aspirations of his milieu he warns mechanics of the peril to their families in emulating the "dissipation and miserable vanity" of patricians.

Coming face to face on the village street with a bitter adversary he meditates on the folly of hate and the glory of love: not the "sickly sentimentality" of a Bulwer but affectionate tenderness. He rejects the compulsive gathering of possessions—for "I have found out that it is very dangerous to be rich"—and offers instead a day spent in the surf and sun of a South Bay beach under an American flag hoisted by a companion on the handle of a clam rake.

Searching for Truth he wanders the world, through cathedrals, imperial courts, Brahmin temples, and other traditional repositories. At last aided "by the plain eye of simplicity" he finds Truth on the altar of Nature.

These early pieces are like many others that inundated editorial desks, but they contain personal revelations. Though Jamaica was the site of the Female Boarding School conducted by the Misses Zelia and Eugenia Edwards, late of Baltimore, the young man laments one May day that he has failed to find a single breast "where this tired soul its hope may rest." When a "sentimental fit" masters a Sunday night reverie and leads to the self-pitying cry "no one to care for, or to care for me," he remembers that "pretty little" Kitty Denton lives in the neighborhood. Rising from his elbow chair he takes his hat and goes out. But he does not call on Kitty. Avoiding her door, he walks the street till past midnight, when his melancholy lifts. Another evening he watches friends dance the sets of a fancy cotillion but does not seek a partner there or afterwards. Depressed, he admits missing thus far the "bloom and nectar of life," and then teases his married friends because they alone arrive breakfastless at the beach and they alone buy fish to ensure their suppers.

Another revelation is that Whitman, like Theon in Frances Wright's *A Few Days in Athens*, endured a recurring burden: the thrust of ambition. Proud of the capacity to achieve greatness he prophesies the writing of a "very pretty book" in which he will expose the "Peculiarities of men, the diversity of their character, the means of improving their state, and the proper mode of governing nations."[12]

"As everyone knows," Cornelius Mathews wrote in *The Motley Book*, "the advent of an election creates a general and clamorous demand for full-grown young men of twenty-one years of age." In the summer of 1840 Whitman found the clamor intensified as a result of recent Locofoco legislation. Silas Wright, Benton, Cambreleng, and other leading Administration men, after overcoming powerful opposition that included members of their own party, had convinced a majority in Congress that the depression proved the weakness of a fiscal system of paper notes and credit controlled by corporate monopoly. In their scheme, legalized after years of debate, economic salvation rested with the creation of an Independent Treasury that would separate the government and its gold and silver specie receipts from private commercial banks whose notes depreciated in time of stress. A victory for Harrison in November assured certain repeal of this key monetary reform.

The conduct of the local Whigs as they campaigned reminded Whitman of the Bowery stage during the last act of a melodrama, with its effects achieved by firecrackers, raised voices, and contortions of faces and limbs. He scorned as hypocritical the Whigs' offer of friendship to the poor while they deepened poverty by removing Democrats from jobs. Whig orators seduced mechanics with hard cider and promises of two dollars a day and roast beef, or frightened them with threats that Van Buren would give them ten cents and bean soup. Webster, King, and others who hungered for office had taken a respectable old gentleman and used him as a decoy duck. Who could believe that Harrison's home was so humble that he tended it with his own hand? Aware of slurs by the opposition journalists upon his limited experience, Whitman named Bryant and Leggett as the sources of his editorial argument for free trade, simplification of the duties of government, and opposition to paper currency. The *Democratic Review* also earned his tribute as a vital auxiliary in the reform movement.

Webster provided an ample target during his tour of Long Island in September, and the tyro did not hesitate to take aim. This "noted character," whose fame had been trumpeted throughout the land for years, lacked the anticipated glitter. In "exceedingly dull" speeches he had struck at the Independent Treasury and similar topics "which are doubtless quite new to us all, not having been treated in print and public more than twenty times an hour for the last six months." Within a fortnight after the departure of the visitor, the strenuous pen and voice of his Jamaica critic aroused "pursy" Whigs to written indignation. On 6 October the *Farmer* carried a letter by "Buckeye" charging that during a political discussion with Mr. John Gunn, "W. Whitman, a well-known locofoco of the town" and "champion of the Democracy was completely stumped . . . totally without any real proof, and to make it up he dealt in the most false and scurrilous assertions."

His blood tingling, the champion answered the "slimy backguard" that same day and accused the Whigs of spitting venom on individual reputations, "and of sending forth, week after week, the basest lies, upon the character of our country and countrymen. . . . I openly and without qualification assert that Charles King . . . in saying that Mr. Van Buren and the democratick party uphold the doctrine of a 'community of goods, wives, and children,' uttered a *lie*, and acted as *no gentleman* would act." [13]

49

Before the end of the month Whitman added a conciliatory postscript in the form of "The Columbian's Song." A proud nationalism rather than belligerence or self-pity flooded the patriot as he viewed the "fair and happy place" whose factions would unite to battle a threat to freedom.

Though the Whigs carried the nation in November, they lost Long Island. In Jamaica the Democratic vote doubled that of the previous fall; in Patchogue, the scene of Webster's first massive effort, it tripled. Whitman promised to provide lodging and a carriage for "the honorable senator's" use during the next campaign. By April the "well-known locofoco" and sombre poet pondered the symbolism in the cannon that was fired at the Navy Yard on the day of Harrison's funeral, then recharged and fired again to honor the ascension of Tyler.

The local victory continued to bring him pride. Two years later in New York, when he heard reports of apathy on Long Island, he wrote, "It's a pity the people of Queens have not some one to stir them up in the columns of the *Democrat* as in the fall of 1840, by a certain young fellow from the eastern part of the island, who . . . contributed materially to the unexpected triumph of the party at that period."[14]

5

ACTIVE YOUNG MAN

IN FIVE WEEKS fate replaced the fine day of President Harrison's inauguration with sudden snow squalls that marred his memorial services; hurrahs and waving handkerchiefs gave way to black festoons and a farewell salute of sixty-eight guns. The Whig program once seemingly secure lay splintered by their leader's death, for as a result of a blunder at Harrisburg they had chosen for vice president a politician now revealed as a Jeffersonian sectarian; rather than assistance from the White House in the struggle to recharter the Bank, they now faced hostility. According to the quip making its rounds, a prominent Whig, when asked how things were nowadays, answered, "I can hardly tell, for the Lord has got our President, the Locos our Vice President, and I believe the devil will get the rest of us."

Ignoring his own versified admonition to scorn the "bubble, fame," Whitman in May 1841 turned away from the pleasant towns, the meadows of salt grass and sedge, the deep bays and easy lanes, and joined the 300,000 in New York seeking the main chance. The time seemed opportune for one who had outgrown the random schoolhouse and the turnpike shop, and who had survived rural political skirmishes. A journeyman able to abide irregular hours and a wage scale somewhat lower than that of the daily papers could work for the weekly *New World*, whose publisher planned a spectacular series of supplements. A poet who had pleased rural taste could attempt to woo magazine readers and reviewers whose humbuggery Poe castigated in fire-and-fury critiques. Lured by the prospect of professional progress, he would suffer the discomfort of meager boarding houses, the heat and dust of what Melville called "the babylonish brick-kiln," the noise of streets, the odor of open gutters and ditches dug for Croton water pipes, the scavenger hogs, and the mock auctioneers. That August the body of Mary Rogers, the "beautiful segar girl," floated in the river near Hoboken; soon the Colt murder trial brought new sensationalism. When fire gutted an assignation

51

house, the *Herald* reported that five or six respectable citizens fled, "some with no boots, and some without breeches."

Manhattan seemed to offer what Lydia Maria Child termed vituperative alliteration: magnificence and mud, finery and filth, diamonds and dirt. It boasted the Battery rivaling Boston Common; a park like St. John's with ailanthus and catalpa trees, though only a few families in the neighborhood had the key to its iron gate; home gardens showing marigolds and poppies; and the portico of the granite Astor Hotel, haunt of beggars. Amidst the confusion of Broadway walked elegant ladies in gossamer Neapolitan hats, musicians with street organs and bagpipes. Shop windows showed everything from escritoires and chess sets to toothpicks. Corner stalls sold lemonade and ice cream; vendors sang "Lily white corn, buy my lily white corn"; fish hawkers blew horns; triangles rang from charcoal carts. The shrill sweep-ho of small boys, blanket and scraper in hand, marked them as chimney sweeps. Dog killers enlisted after a rabies scare every day clubbed hundreds of strays in the midst of strollers; loaded drays endangered a blind Negro. The new Gothic Church of the Ascension stood ready for worship, but Five Points in the sixth ward was worse than Hogarth's Gin Lane. In the harbor a clipper rode at anchor with more grace than any of the other ships, but it was the slaver *Catherine* captured by a British cruiser.[1]

For one who already described himself as a man who loved to examine "the uncouth, natural outpourings of the feelings of the heart," here was endless variety. Fascinated, Whitman wandered the different neighborhoods and observed them to be miniature worlds whose inhabitants ranged from the ignorant to the learned, the vicious to the moral, the impudent to the modest. On several mornings he spent hours examining classes at public schools and recorded in the Visitors' Book his gratification at the pupils' "understanding spirit." At night he basked in the artistic and intellectual effulgence of the metropolis.

With the exception of another engagement by the ballerina Elssler, the theatrical season was so dull at first that in desperation the Bowery held somerset vaulting matches; the winner flipped backwards sixty-one times. Hundreds rode the ferry to Staten Island and watched for one hour and three minutes until Yankee Sullivan stunned Tom Secor in the sixty-seventh round. Then in October, after its success at Covent Garden, came Bouci-cault's *London Assurance* with real rooms instead of sets, upholstered furniture, and yards of Brussels carpets rather than painted flats. Who could fail to respond to Charlotte Cushman as Lady Gay Spanker when she wished that creation had but one mouth that she might kiss it? Placide as Sir Harcourt and Browne as Dazzle aped the vices of the great in the delusion of gaining status.

A young man eager to absorb ideas could find them for pennies. The new *Tribune* printed parts of Henry Reeve's translation of de Tocqueville's noble *Democracy in America*, Emerson's "Man the Reformer," and gems from other essays, including a tribute to the artistic power of simplicity that Whitman would amplify fourteen years later. Lyceums came into vogue, partly because many people were hostile to the theatre; they vied with each other in offering lectures by Lardner the astronomer, Silliman on the structure of the earth, Fowler on phrenology, and Brownson, the "Locofoco philosopher," on the elevation of the laboring class and the laws of progress.

From Manhattan lecterns the self-taught Brownson, smitten according to his antagonists with the spirit of agrarian equality, deplored the widening chasm between wealth and labor that caused "bloated luxury and pining want" to exist side by side in every city. Seeking allies, he summoned writers to give their talent and sympathy to help end the calamity; only then would they create original, living work. Confessing ill temper and crudeness in his eagerness to enlist them in the cause of democracy, he pleaded for pardon in view of the desperate need for moral, intellectual, and physical amelioration. Becoming seer and guide, he charted the way for the twenty-two-year-old aspirant:

> It will be because a man has felt with the American people, espoused their cause, bound himself to it for life or for death, time or eternity, that he becomes able to adorn American literature; not because he has lived apart, refused to "serve society"; held lone reveries, and looked on sunsets, and sunrise. If he speak a word, "posterity shall not willingly let die," it will not be because he has prepared himself to speak, by a scholastic asceticism, but by loving his countrymen and sympathizing with them.[2]

Blessed for years by the absence of an international copyright law, at least one firm had amassed a fortune with the simple formula of reprinting foreign titles and selling them for twelve and sixteen shillings. By 1841 those who envied the Harper brothers had also begun, as they phrased it, "to enable the millions to share in the benefits of a splendid and inexhaustible fund of literature, which circumstances rendered so easy of access and at a cost so utterly insignificant." This euphemism signaled the start of a race for royalty-free profits by publishers of new magazines, like the *New World* for which Whitman began to work. Basing his analysis of the signs of the times on experience in three cities, Poe predicted accurately that "The brief, the terse, the condensed, and the easily circulated will take the place of the diffuse, the ponderous, and the inaccessible."[3]

Priced at a shilling, the *New World* and the *Brother Jonathan* were printed in a format acceptable for mailing to all parts of the nation at newspaper postage rates, even though envious rivals called them as large as sheep pastures and eventually forced them to be classified as pamphlets. To win market priority, their European agents bought sheets of novels by Bulwer, Dickens, and de Kock and shipped them swiftly to New York, where within forty-eight hours steam presses began runs of over ten thousand copies a day on special paper. The combination of a French novel and the small type in which it was printed led one reader to say that the *New World* and the *Brother Jonathan* had begun by corrupting morals and ended by ruining eyes.

These periodicals reached the streets embellished with woodcuts of celebrities and filled with "sixty or eighty square feet" of news, sermons, verse (the "Wreck of the Hesperus" first appeared in the *New World*) and the most profitable commodity, pirated fiction. Guided by editors as alert as Park Benjamin and John Neal, they succeeded in reaching an audience that found other publications too costly or too dull; they made the prices of the Harper list tumble and forced imitations by others. Greeley complained that the great beasts murdered his circulation by making so much noise and bluster that they bullied people into buying their trash if not into reading it.

Despite severe physical deformity, Park Benjamin had become influential through the combination Poe described as "ability, activity, causticity, fearlessness and independence." His literary taste and talent had been shaped at Harvard where he read compositions to Professor Edward T. Channing; he always kept out of his several magazines high-flown rhetoric and what he called perversions of language: "hideous hydra," "gent," "sass." He compiled a list of Americanisms and lectured on "going the whole hog," "raising the dander," and other locutions Dr. Johnson never dreamed of. Orthodox journals called Emerson's essays blasphemous rant, but the *New World* proclaimed support for their concept of the "independence and supremacy of the individual man in his spiritual nature." Benjamin also befriended

Hawthorne early in the Salem man's career and printed "Young Goodman Brown." An advocate of the proper mean in criticism, he anticipated receiving "more kicks than coppers" for his honest application of this concept; both came his way.[4]

For the *New World* Whitman set chapters of *Barnaby Rudge, Heroes and Hero Worship*, poetry by Wordsworth, Tennyson, and Mrs. Sigourney. Meanwhile he advanced his own political and literary careers.

All through July 1841 both parties in turn praised or protested legislation sponsored by Clay to create a bank like Biddle's. On Monday, 26 July the Whigs staged a climactic rally at National Hall to cheer its passage. Among them, according to hostile reporters, were the agents of foreign stockjobbers. That Thursday between eight and ten thousand Locofocos of "all conditions and occupations" filled the triangular park area in front of the white marble pillars of City Hall to hear speakers—ranging from "gray headed democrats" to those the *Tribune* scorned as youths with thin whiskers—denounce the Bank, national debt, protective tariff, and all other Whig schemes. The *Evening Post* reporter, with a privileged place on the platform, claimed that no political meeting in the city ever gave fuller indication of perfect unanimity.

Chairman Varian, the former mayor and onetime chief of the monopolist faction of Tammany, first introduced the popular Major D'Avezac, who had served under Jackson at New Orleans and at The Hague as *chargé d'affaires*. The outraged reporter of the *Tribune* departed when Judge Aaron Vanderpoel, the "Kinderhook Roarer," began "to beat the stand until the water tumblers hopped like mad," but loyal papers recorded the stentor's warnings to the Rothschilds and Barings abroad and the Astors at home that they meddled with stocks at their own peril. Any bank created by Congress under the pretext of serving the people would be strangled by the people.

The first speaker of the "active young men," as the *Post* called them, was Samuel J. Tilden, the author of a brilliant legal essay on finance. Then stood "W. Whitman Esq. of Suffolk," taller than all the others on the platform, skin darkened by the summer sun, bearded, dressed in a black broadcloth suit and white ruffled shirt. The care with which he had prepared his remarks was soon obvious.

First he reviewed the "mighty marshalling" of pre-election forces that had led the Democrats to hope for success last year. But "nations, like individuals, sometimes have their paroxysms of derangement . . . and a large portion of the people were untrue to themselves"—a fact that by no means caused his faith to falter. Here the Suffolk orator used funerary figures for the tragedy that came when the "ghastly finger" was laid upon the president and "he was put away to rest in the bosom of earth, the great mother of men. There let him repose, his name blessed and his memory honored; nor may any unhallowed hand presume to stir up for him the bitter waters of partisan strife."

Moving from past debacles to present struggles, "Mr. Whitman" gave thanks for the light showered liberally by education and a cheap, independent press. Citizens other than capitalists now knew the Whig threat to their thrift. A powerful bank had brought misery to masses in England and throughout the old world, crushed under the iron heel of poverty millions of men with hearts and souls, high and lofty desires. The same elements of tyranny, he cautioned, existed in this glorious palladium of freedom. Hundreds of domineering politicians loved to confer on corporate bodies "profitable and unjust immunities," and to turn the hand of government aside from its proper duties in order to benefit broken-down schemers and speculators.

To the delight of the sponsors who had invited Whitman to the rally platform, his summation was Locofoco doctrine worthy of a Leggett. This great land of unrivaled blessings, he told the throng, faced the threat of too much lawmaking and of legislative interference in matters best let alone. Any intelligent American knew that the panics of the past five years had come after officious meddling.

Because party leaders in many sections had begun to plan for 1844, he devoted his last words to their potentially divisive tactics. Expanding an editorial he had written for the *Democrat*, he urged them to lay aside the debate over the next presidential candidate and turn to the issues which demanded prompt action. "It is not to elevate this or that man to power that we are struggling. Our aim is nobler and higher; we are contending against dangerous errors and fatal measures; we are contending for the establishment of great and glorious truths." (Jackson had at times toasted "Principles not men.")

Gratified by the applause and by the press response that gave him more space than any other speaker, he later reprinted his conclusion:

My firm conviction is that the next democratic candidate, whoever he may be, will be carried into power on the wings of a
mighty reaction. The guardian spirit, the good genius who has
attended us since the days of Jefferson, has not now forsaken us.
I can almost fancy myself able to pierce the darkness of the future
and behold her looking down upon us, with those benignant smiles
she wore in 1828, '32, and '36. Again will she hover over us,
amid the smoke and din of battle, and lead us to our wonted victory, through the "sober thoughts of the people."[5]

Clay's bill reached the White House in mid-August. There, President
Tyler in the rapt image of a Locofoco, found one of Jackson's pens and used
it for his veto. New York learned of this astounding action within a day
when the last of the *Herald* relays arrived injured and lashed to his horse
"like Mazeppa." From now on Whitman counted Whiggery "a gone
coon"; the good genius had smiled again. The populace could turn to the
details of the death of Mary Rogers, reputedly violated by six or eight
ruffians.

The summer also brought his first large literary triumph, for in August the
Democratic Review placed the name Walter Whitman before a national
audience by printing "Death in the School-Room (A Fact)" a tale of a brutal teacher flogging a sickly pupil. The November and December issues carried "Wild Frank" and "Bervance and Son," narratives of domestic conflict
between unjust fathers and unruly sons. All of these, as he assured readers,
came from memory rather than imagination; he had heard them told in
low-roofed village taverns over brandy and sugar, or by a farmer's fireplace.
Whatever their origin, they traced a pattern of familial struggle between
the men and boys: a quiet, sickly mother "on whose lips Frank's kisses
seemed sweetest," and a widow who pressed "a long kiss on her son's lips."
Whatever their quality, they placed the author on the same title page with
Whittier, Longfellow, and Bryant. While Hawthorne worked as a weigher
in the Boston Customs House, too weary for other tasks, Whitman became
the leading contributor of fiction to the *Democratic Review.*

Obtaining Administration support in part because the Irish associations
of his father proved helpful to Van Buren, in four years *Review* editor J. L.

O'Sullivan, described by Longfellow as a young man with weak eyes and green spectacles, had redeemed his pledge to expound a theory of Jacksonian democracy that would ensure a return to the national starting point, the Constitution. A lawyer educated in Europe and at Columbia, since 1837 he had offered under the masthead motto, "The best government is that which governs least," an interpretation of American history that mourned the hour when "Hamilton's bold and powerful hand seized the helm of state, and—with honest, but radical, and most fatal, error or theory—gave it that false direction which it has taken fifty years of evil and struggle to correct." O'Sullivan augmented columns of historical or political theory with biographies and copperplate portraits of Benton, Wright, Cambreleng, and Congressman Ely Moore, once a journeyman printer and now devoted to equal rights for all men. O'Sullivan eulogized Leggett and with one exception traced most of his egalitarian ideas from their first statement, through official rejection and contumely, to their ultimate acceptance.

If the *Democratic Review* gave its strength to the "prostration of every institution which enables a few injuriously to offset the interest of others," it also spoke for a bipartisan and timeless philanthropy. Longfellow called him a humbug, but it was O'Sullivan as chairman of a legislative committee in Albany who wrote the *Report in Favor of the Abolition of Capital Punishment*, which remains a classic and moving marshalling of argument. With William Ellery Channing, a contributor to the *Review*, he held that the aim of civilization was the elevation of the laboring portion of the community. But he compromised his reforming zeal on one issue: from the beginning he announced that the *Democratic Review* would stand aloof from "the delicate and dangerous topic of slavery and abolition."[6]

Creator of the phrase "manifest destiny," firm in his belief that here was the "great nation of futurity," O'Sullivan honored the country's past and present. He brought to the magazine Catlin's Indian studies and an account of the massacre of Captain Fannin's rangers at Goliad. He gave Horatio Greenough space to expound ideas for buildings in which form followed function. Ambitious to promote native authors, O'Sullivan assured Hawthorne of a chance to gain distinction. "The Toll-Gatherer's Day" was the first fiction he printed, Bryant's "Battlefield" the first poem, and Emerson's *Nature* one of the first books reviewed. Along with his invitations to contributors came the imperative that the vital principle of American literature must be democracy, "the elevating principle of equality." Because most American authors had failed thus far "to comprehend the matchless sublimity of our position among the nations of the world—our high destiny," they continued to bend the knee to "foreign idolatry, false tastes, false doctrines, false principles." When, asked the *Review*, "will they be inspired by the magnificent scenery of our own world, imbibe the fresh enthusiasm of a new heaven and earth, to soar upon the expanded wings of truth and liberty?" After Gallagher's *Selections of the Poetical Literature of the West* with its Cincinnati imprint reached his desk, the editor exulted at the birth of a literature beyond the Alleghenies. Bryant's poems were fresh "like a young people unwarped by the superstitions and prejudices of the age"; the "holy instincts of democracy guide every expression and animate every strain."[7]

By the mid-forties O'Sullivan had relinquished control of the *Democratic Review*. From then on his faith in the fruition of American destiny expressed itself in his arguments for the acquisition of a sequence of territorial stepping stones: Texas, Mexico, California, Cuba, Nicaragua, Hawaii. He stood in the van of those who, according to the *Daily Times*, believed "the national horizon is supposed to stop no where short of the very verge of doom." In 1851 he was arrested in New York harbor aboard the *Cleopatra* and charged with planning to sail to Cuba to aid the invasion by General Lopez. Among his confiscated supplies were medicines, brass wind instruments, a printing press, and twenty-four kegs of powder. Long before then Whitman had turned to other political evangels for guidance.[8]

The Democrats regained control of the state in the autumn elections, but the active young man did not receive any plums. Spooner had cautioned him that it was easier to teach small children in the country than the big children of Tammany. On 20 November 1841, his status unchanged, he helped set in the *New World* his own temperance tale, "The Child's Champion." In a country tavern noisy with sailors and the music of Black Dan—a scene Mount painted—a drunkard attempts to force a thirteen-year-old apprentice, son of a widow, to drink a glass of brandy. A stranger exactly the narrator's age, dressed in broadcloth and clean linen, rescues the boy after a display of boxing skill. Then, aware that it is past midnight

> the young man told Charles that on the morrow he would take
> steps to have him liberated from his servitude; for the present
> night, he said, it would perhaps be best for the boy to stay and share

his bed at the inn; and little persuading did the child need to do so. As they retired to sleep, very pleasant thoughts filled the mind of the young man; thoughts of a worthy action performed; of unsullied affection; thoughts, too—newly awakened ones—of walking in a steadier and wiser path than formerly. All his imaginings seemed to be interwoven with the youth who lay by his side; he folded his arms around him, and, while he slept, the boy's cheek rested on his bosom.

Cleansed and inspired by this encounter with innocence, Charles' champion ends all association with blacklegs and swindlers.

In the first of two poems in the *New World*, Whitman singularized the bathos of the earlier "We Shall All Rest at Last" into "Each Has His Grief," inserted a few verbal variants, and a new stanza that revealed stress:

> And he who runs the race of fame,
>   Oft feels within a feverish dread,
> Lest others snatch the laurel crown
>   He bears upon his head.

The seventy-two lines of "The Punishment of Pride" served as a Christmas homily of an Angel-Lord, an aloof Abdiel, exiled from heaven to years of earthly penance until elevated by the "loveliest messenger," death. Though powerful again in full heavenly majesty, he now dispenses charity and pity rather than the scorn he meted to sinners before his fall.

His carpets ruined by retching guests, the Locofoco mayor of New York closed his office to all callers shortly after noon on New Year's Day. Throughout the day many well-dressed celebrants continued to stagger in the streets. While he enjoyed the carefree holiday in the sun, hearing and repeating the traditional greeting, "may your shadow never be less," Whitman could in all modesty believe that he cast a larger shadow on 1 January 1842 than ever before.

A host of anti-Benjaminites testified to the editor's irascibility; Whitman soon joined them. By 29 January 1842 his name appeared in the *Brother Jonathan*. Printed in what its rivals called a dirty little den on Nassau Street, this weekly gave its patrons under the motto "Cheapest reading in the World," the inevitable Bulwer, de Kock, George Sand, and a new French writer, Eugène Sue. According to Benjamin it also carried slang, slander, and dreadful murders. In turn the *Brother Jonathan* branded his verse sickening metrical balderdash, worthless as the advertisements of the abortionist, Madam Restell.

Though committed financially to an aggressive campaign to flood the nation with cheap reprints of foreign books—a main cause of the weakness of American literature, in Cooper's judgment—the *Brother Jonathan* also tried to reflect its homespun name. It published Mathews' *Puffer Hopkins*, the novel of a young politician who, like Whitman, made his city debut from a platform and pursued votes through caucus, oyster cellar, complimentary ball, and Chatham Street auctions. And the *Brother Jonathan* pleaded with writers to assert their independence:

> Let us have natural descriptions of American life and manners in your prose and poetry—passages from American history, the most romantic in the annals of nations, in your romance. Be no longer behind the age, and instead of serving us up old thoughts, antiquated even in Europe, in a new dress, let us have some of the freshness, freedom, and elasticity of the new world (the continent we mean) in your writing. Throw off servile dependence upon foreign schools and models, and you will not only command the American public as readers, but the whole world.[9]

John Neal, an editor of the *Brother Jonathan* and the third of the magazinists Whitman served, remained undismayed by the vicissitudes of a long career, and offered his staff the homely philosophy taken from an old farmer: "Ah boys, this is a hard world but there is a great deal of good cider in it." Lawyer, linguist, drawing master, phrenologist, boxer, fencer —Neal was the critic Poe thanked as the first to "jog" his career. In *Randolph* he made sensible judgments on Copley, Peale, and other artists a decade before Dunlap. Through essays in *Blackwood's Edinburgh Magazine* in 1824 he became the first historian of American literature. An ardent Benthamite who boasted of taking tea with the reformer, he told readers that the tremendous energy of the utilitarian's mind had revolutionized all social legislation. An advocate of women's rights, he insisted that those who denied equality used only one argument: "How is a woman to go aloft if she enters the marine service?" Defending self-praise, Jehu O'Cataract— as he was nicknamed—claimed that his own verse contained "more exalted,

61

original, pure, bold poetry, than all the works, of all the other authors, that have ever appeared in America." In his novel *The Down-Easters* he advocated the use of American language; in *Rachel Dyer*—one of the titles in the Jamaica library—he sought to show fellow writers the "abundant and hidden sources of fertility in their own beautiful brave earth, awaiting only to be broken up." And he spoke for an inspired concept of prosody:

> Will new poets never learn that *poetry* is always poetry—however it may be expressed; that rhythm, cadence, (regular cadence),—rhyme—alliteration, riddles, and acrostics, are all beneath poetry; that better poetry has been said in prose, than ever has been said—or ever will be said—either in blank verse or rhyme? Poetry and eloquence have a rhythm and cadence of their own; as incapable of being soberly graduated by rule, as the rambling, wild melody of an Aeolian harp.

As late as 1849 in the *Union* magazine which published his erstwhile journeyman's fiction, Neal again defined poetic form.[10]

Continuing to sense the inadequacies of his own verses, Whitman revised language and structure and placed two in the *Brother Jonathan*. But he did not attempt to lift "Ambition" and "Death of the Nature-Lover" from the fashionable tomb reserved by a popular aesthetic which held that the true sublime came from a spade, a youth, and a few crumbling bones. Bryant and Willis were exemplary celebrants; Poe staged dramas with the conqueror worm as hero and drew tears from adult audiences by reciting morbid fantasies.[11]

A prose defense of Dickens soon led Whitman to a declaration of faith in a doctrine vital to the living. On 22 January 1842 the British novelist landed at Cunard wharf in Boston. Angered by his estimated loss of $100,000, he had come to serve an author's bill of international copyright upon "unremunerating republishers." Whitman did not act as one of the 2200 hosts at the Boz Ball, the greatest affair in modern times according to veteran socialities of Manhattan, nor did he attend the exclusive dinner presided over by Washington Irving at City Hall. But no one would have received greater joy out of the *tableaux vivants* ranging from *Pickwick* to *The Old Curiosity Shop* than the unbidden admirer.

During those first days of welcome, tailors sold Boz breeches and confectioners made Samuel Veller candy, but initial gestures soon degenerated into what the *Brother Jonathan* called cap-pulling among the fashionables to play off the guest for theatrical, gastronomical, modish, or mesmeric purposes. As mutual disenchantment set in, the "Prince of Serials" began to be denounced as a knavish producer of trash. In February Whitman spoke up for the writer whom, he explained, he had "long considered a personal friend, and as a friend to his species."

The Washington *Globe* had charged Dickens with brutalizing democracy by delineating characters in the lowest stages of ignorance, vice, and degradation; exposure to *Oliver Twist*, the paper claimed, was as immoral as to the anatomy of Elssler. To show life characterized by grossest ignorance and brutality, Whitman retorted in the *Brother Jonathan*, did not militate against Dickens' claim for admiration from all true democrats. Characters like Twist and his mates in the poor house, and Squeers with his wretched scholars, forced every reader to reflect upon the inhuman society that spawned these evils, and to vow to uproot them. The literary fop spoke mincingly and delicately, "lest he should introduce a vigorous turn or idea, which should offend for its grossness," but Dickens had the courage to expose the tyranny of class-stratified society and to document "the philosophy which teaches to pull down the high and bring up the low." The defender concluded with a personal testimonial: "I cannot lose the opportunity of saying how much I love and esteem him for what he has taught me through his writings—and for the general influence that these writings have spread around them wherever they go." [12]

Two months later he championed Dickens' right to conceive a Quilp. After the *Democratic Review* in an otherwise favorable essay argued that the obvious exaggerations wounded moral sensibilities, Whitman answered that only a noble character like O'Sullivan could claim that the novelist resorted to hyperbole. "Why almost within reach," he explained, "there is the palpable counterpart to the worst embodiment that the brains of Dickens ever transcribed upon a paper." Risking a libel suit, he placed in evidence Bennett of the *Herald*.[13]

Before long this sincere advocate read *Martin Chuzzlewit* with its vindictive caricatures of Manhattan press corpsmen.[14]

6

THE WHITMAN

SIR CHARLES LYELL, in New York to lecture on fossil footprints, praised the early April weather. A few days before, snow had covered the ground but now the air was as warm as an English summer and leaves showed on the willows at the Battery. If Lyell walked along Broadway—and every visitor did, for the three-mile trottoir was famous—he came to an area as distinctive as any part of London. Passing Trinity Church where masons and carpenters were completing Richard Upjohn's Gothic plans; Colman's bookshop with its crowds examining the prints of the Madonna in the bow window; St. Paul's whose brown patina brought comparison with gingerbread; the resplendent Astor House; and that dirty-white "villainous specimen of architecture," the Park theatre, Lyell would have reached an open space within steps of Tammany Hall. Here in Ann Street the cries of newsboys identified the city's Printing House Square, formed by a cluster of offices. By close scrutiny the geologist might have observed the sign of the *Aurora*, though the name of the editor, Walter Whitman, was nowhere to be seen, for editorship was too fugitive an honor to be fixed in paint.[1]

For the past three years Anson Herrick and John F. Ropes had published the *Atlas* every Sunday. The prosperous weekly and an adequate shop gave them the resources to expand by adding a twopenny daily in November 1841. Their motivation, as they explained in the first *Aurora*, was patriotic, for with many others in these years of economic stress they feared the inroads of the immigrant, who, they charged, remained hostile to American institutions and people. They referred primarily to Bennett, from Scotland, and Benjamin, born in British Guiana; called one a disgrace to his profession and the other a literary charlatan. (They ignored the facts that Benjamin's ancestors had come to New England as early as 1632, and that Benjamin himself had been reared there.)

The first editor of the *Aurora*, Yankee Thomas Low Nichols of New

Hampshire, had forsaken the study of medicine at Dartmouth for journalism. His paper, he announced in a definition of policy, would be politically independent but "democratic in the strongest sense of the word." Free of the need to promote party fortunes, he gave little space to dispatches from Albany and Washington, and told instead of soirées at Charaud's and Carlton's, entertainment at Palmo's and the Tivoli, prize fights, lectures, and *La Sylphide.* This social coverage led the publishers to boast that the *Aurora* was the "acknowledged journal of the *beau monde,* the Court Journal of our democratic aristocracy." (Whitman's own prose soon contained fashionable French phrases, six years before his journey to New Orleans.) Rivals sneered that in reality bartenders of porter houses peddled the paper to the lowest echelons.

After three successful months in which estimated circulation reached a respectable five thousand, surpassed only by the *Sun,* the *Herald,* and the *Tribune* among the cheap papers and by two or three of the older, sixpenny, commercial Wall Street papers, Nichols resigned on 22 February because he had libeled electoral officials by charging them with pipelaying—the adding of illicit votes to ensure victory. The very next day the *Aurora* carried the first of six "Walks in Broadway," obviously Whitman's, and early in March printed his tribute to a friend, the "mad poet" of Broadway, MacDonald Clarke. Evidently this trial period satisfied the publishers that the young man of twenty-three could compete with Greeley, Beach, Bennett, Webb, and Noah. On 28 March they disclosed their decision:

> The publishers of the Aurora would respectfully announce to their friends and the public that they have secured the services of Mr. Walter Whitman, favorably known as a bold, energetic and original writer, as their leading editor. The addition of Mr. W. to the editorial department of the Aurora, the publishers feel assured, will enable them to carry out their original design of establishing a sound, fearless, and independent daily paper, which shall at all times and on all occasions advocate and sustain the dignity and interests of our country. The American public have severely felt the want of a journal which, in its sentiments and opinions, while it is biased by no undue prejudices against foreigners, will be far different from those newspapers which
>
> > "Bend the pliant hinges of the knee,
> > That thrift may follow fawning."[2]

65

The post his, Whitman soon knew that the conduct of a metropolitan daily could not be as casual as that of an island weekly:

> The consciousness that several thousand people will look for the *Aurora* as regularly as for breakfast, and that they expect in it an intellectual repast—something piquant, and something solid, and something sentimental and something humorous—and all dished up in "our own peculiar way" . . . implies no small responsibility upon a man. Yet it is delightful. Heavy as it weighs, we have no indisposition to "take the responsibility."

Happily professional peers observed a marked change for the better in "this spirited little daily since the accession of Mr. Whitman to the vacant chair. There is, nevertheless, a dash of egotism occasionally."[3]

By the standards of the day he merited praise, for the *Aurora* reached the streets as a well-printed sheet with a special *ton* attractive to "would-be *elegantes*." The front page often carried woodcuts of firemen, omnibus drivers, and other city types. (N. Currier advertised there.) Its leaders were individual and often moving, the exchange items exuberant: "The Yale Banner, a paper started by the students, and edited with great spirit, says, 'Yale has *turned out* some great men.' Pretty good for sophs."

From the very beginning of his editorship Whitman sought to make the city his major news beat. Having savored with maturing taste its vast resources these past months, he proclaimed New York "the great place of the western continent, the heart, the brain, the focus, the main spring, the extremity, the no more beyond, of the New World." After answering several misleading advertisements, he chose the boarding house of Mrs. Chipman, a "fleshy, red-cheeked woman" so genteel that the door carried no more than a brass plaque with her name rather than a vulgar solicitation to boarders. For $3.50 a week she gave him a room with "all the comforts of home" in a delightful location, good food, and conversation with a pleasant company of clerks, merchants, and several ladies. All the men came to the table with clean shirts and wristbands, though they probably ate with the spectacular speed that astounded Martin Chuzzlewit when he dined with the editor of the *Rowdy Journal*. Whitman became convinced of the comfort of Mrs. Chipman's when, after being locked out by accident, he spent a wakeful night in other lodgings listening to a quartet of snorers.

Though he missed the silence of the country where one could drowse with nothing louder than the bee hum, the piping of a locust, or bird song, the waking metropolis offered sights never met inland. The milkmen's carts, workmen with tin dinner kettles, newsboys with bundles of damp morning papers, and Irish women scrubbing marble stoops and sidewalks gave way by noon to strolling patricians. The "city lady" eclipsed all that poets and lovers wrote of her rural sister. Near Grace Church he met

> a pale, tall delicate girl, dressed fashionably, yet very neatly. She had her veil only half drawn over her face; and as we looked, we beheld one of the most lovely intellectually feminine countenances our sight was ever blessed with. We never professed to be very susceptible to the tender passion—but really those starlike eyes! and that queenly neck! and those luscious lips! O, we'd better stop—for if we go on, we shall. . . .

Flowers in a parlor window symbolized the presence of a nubile tenant and the passerby felt "greatly inclined to just step in, and see if there is any chance for a forlorn bachelor."

Because of their late shift employees on morning papers earned extra wages and Whitman could afford to follow fashion. Dressed in gray frock coat, boutonniere, high black hat, and a dark, hook-ended polished cane, he joined the promenade at the Battery and rejoiced, "Gods! what a glorious morning it was! Just enough of enervating voluptuous heat—and just enough breeze to feel the wings of the zephyrs—and just enough sunshine to reflect a sparkle in the eyes of beautiful women—and just enough people walking on the pave to make one continued, ceaseless, devilish, prevailing, delicious, glorious jam!" During the day he maneuvered among the bales and crates of an East River quay, and then watched steamboats race in midstream. Sometimes he meditated along the ocean shore: "We love to list to the deep and ceaseless tones of its music, when the repose of midnight has fallen upon it."

Varying the itinerary for the sake of his leaders, he visited a gymnasium and pistol gallery, took a few shots, and then watched rope climbers and boxers. His own melancholy banished, he recommended the routine to all "dyspeptic and misanthropic young gentlemen" and to those who desired to learn self-defense. Then he had a gypsy read his palm but did not reveal what she saw. At a food market he caught the "full, rich melody" of a butcher boy's whistle: "Perhaps, search the whole land through, you will not find a handsomer, more manly set of men than our butchers. They may be known by their clear complexions, healthy look, bright eyes—and by their saucy good nature, their bull dog courage, their impudent wit." When he gave two urchins half a dime to buy coffee and "kraulers," he knew more joy watching them eat "than if we had received sunny greetings from the proudest belle in Broadway, or heard that 'our party' had gained the gubernatorial contest."

He stopped in the park to watch a game of marbles played by a heterogeneous mixture of boys, varying from the "thick lipped negro sweep to the aristocratic truant from the college high school a few rods to the north." Their striving for a prize of ten or fifteen marbles seemed to mimic and foreshadow later struggles:

> In our greener age, we pursue shadows and toys; in maturity, the toil and the sweat and the fever are for benefits intangible, and phantom geegaws, intrinsically as valueless as the objects of our youth. . . . *We* daily chased gilded butterflies. In our common walks—in the path of ordinary business, we spend precious time, and god-like capacities, and advantages of fortune, to reach some goal, where, when we arrive, we turn sick with disappointment and disgust at its not conferring the blessings we most foolishly expect.

When the park custodians swung rattans to disperse the "poor ragged little devils," the *Aurora* pointed to other public places where the offspring of the fashionable rich played unmolested! Such favoritism "may hardly have the effect of teaching the proper moral to young *republicans*."

During other circuits he entered a daguerreotype parlor, attended a flower festival, and made a hurried survey of smoking ruins. He had enough curiosity remaining, as he left his office late at night, to scan the aurora borealis, "rolling up in waves, like an illuminated ocean."

Beginning to respond to the evangelical utilitarianism of articulate reformers, he asked why workers on their free Sundays could not enjoy trees and grass. The city had to provide more open places where brick walls, chimneys, and fences would not block a man's gaze. He stood on the steps of City Hall and watched firemen in close-fitting trousers and red shirts carrying banners inscribed, "Beware of the first glass." They seemed as courageous as Roman gladiators, and he may have joined in singing a chorus of the "Rum Drinker's Lament." At Temperance Hall he heard orators who at first sounded uncouth, but whose profound sincerity overcame his dismay at their unconventional language and made him admit that "we were never more interested in our life."

Hoping to attract a range of readers from "exquisites" in white kid who had attended the Boz Ball, down to the "heel and toe" gentry of Peter Williams' establishment, the *Aurora* tried to record every event which agitated the bosom of fashionable society. Rather than Bellini's *Norma* ruined by La Signora Fatoni Sutton, a prima donna he ridiculed as fat and forty, he found that the Swiss Rainers provided the musical joy of the season. The success of this group of four men and a woman in Alpine costume started the vogue of singing families. At the Chatham, *Macbeth* and *Coriolanus* alternated with *The Golden Farmer*. At the Bowery, Mrs. Shaw and Hamblin were so moving in *The Stranger* that Whitman could not keep from weeping during the last scene. But at the Park, *The Tempest* did not go well because the players seemed out of sorts; Mrs. Pritchard displayed "a pair of pretty legs" while walking and lying flat on the stage, but Mrs. Knight was not the Ariel of youthful dreams.

When the editor received a circular inviting him to join Charlotte Cushman in building a national drama, he answered that he had at all times been ready and willing to advance so worthy a cause, but could not afford to spend dollars any more than Benjamin could pay for contributions to the *New World* so long as Dickens and Bulwer cost him nothing. "Let us have an international copyright law, and we shall have a national drama, and literature also; until then, we must take what we can get, and be thankful."

Each week the outpourings from as many as ten lyceum platforms continued to justify his accolade to the city as the intellectual center of America.[4] Lardner, Lyell, and Brownson were joined by Bush on sacred symbols, Locke on magnetism, Schoolcraft on Indians. (Dickens ridiculed topics that stretched from the philosophy of the soul to the philosophy of vegetables.) At the end of February the *Aurora* noticed a series of six lectures on "The Times" to be read at the Society Library by Emerson. This event represented a victory for Greeley and other enthusiasts who had made the *Tribune* a virtual supplement to the *Dial*, and a rebuke to the hostile theologians of the New York *Review* who branded the *Essays* a godless book written by a blasphemous rhapsodist. As recently as January that magazine had compared the beauty of his *Nature* to a lovely flower whose scent is death.

On Saturday, 5 March, Emerson spoke on the "Poetry of the Times." Whitman's report in Monday's *Aurora* indicated that he had spent as much time in scouting the full house as in listening to the "quiet, easy speaker, with much grace, and a little of the Yankee twang in his voice." The few beautiful maidens were outnumbered by many homely bluestockings, physicians, parsons, young men with Byron collars, and "all other species of literati." Some of the audience wisely took notes, but when Whitman tried to recall the transcendentalist's comments for his column he found them elusive:

> He said that the first man who called another an ass was a poet. Because the business of the poet is expression—the giving utterance to the emotions and sentiments of the soul; and this expression or utterance is best effected by similes and metaphors. But it would do the lecturer great injustice to attempt anything like a sketch of his ideas. Suffice it to say, the lecture was one of the richest and most beautiful compositions, both for its matter and style, we have ever heard anywhere, at any time.

Later, after hearing "Prospects," he tried again to catch the essence of the Concord system. "In the language of Mr. Emerson himself—'This is the era of individuality. It is all Souls' Day.' "[5]

In a *Journal* entry the lecturer reflected that his ideas had about the same reception in Manhattan as elsewhere, "very fine and poetical, but a little puzzling." Greeley confessed that the hot, airless room in the Society Library turned his thoughts to nitrogen, carbonic acid, cigars, snuff, onions, and the quack architect. But Bryant congratulated both the subscribers and the visitor while Mathews' *Arcturus* relished the definition of the poet as the highest manifestation of the power of nature, given in a voice as mysterious as wind in a ruined abbey with imagery ranging from stars to moss. By the end of March the *Aurora* noted that the entire series, along with those by Lyell and Brownson, had given a "severe shock to the religious mind of the community."

Whitman had planned to write a weekly literary critique, but found time only for occasional comment. He continued to rate Dickens the greatest novelist of the day, but detested Charles Lever and Samuel Lover, the flippant perpetrators of *Charles O'Malley* and *Handy Andy*. He sided with Poe in the belief that compilers like Griswold were vampires who displayed depraved taste in their anthologies, but explained that national character and institutions thus far hostile to the cultivation of refined poetry bred spinners of rhyme rather than true poets. There was one exception: "Had his effusions the mellowness of age, and were not their author daily in the midst of us, people would look upon Bryant as the greatest poet of the time. In our mind he is undoubtedly so."

The *Aurora* carried only two of its editor's poems. In "Time to Come" he merely revised lines from the *Long Islander*, and in the second poem he parodied popular verses to describe a melancholy episode. For twenty years MacDonald Clarke, the tragic figure who called himself comfortably crazy, had both aroused pity because of his chronic destitution and served as a butt for pranksters because of his compulsive promenading of Broadway in search of pretty girls. Moved by the spectacle of a stricken soul Whitman read Clarke's verses written as the author admitted at

> a hundred lines an hour,
> With a rackety, whackety railroad power.

In them he found bold images and original ideas; the "jaggedness" of style did not prevent a response like that of a harp to the wind. In "The Death and Burial of MacDonald Clarke," formed after Wolfe's "The Burial of Sir John Moore at Corunna," Whitman escorted the cortege from the last lodgings at the Tombs to Greenwood cemetery:

> Ye hypocrites! stain not his grave with a tear,
>   Nor blast the fresh planted willow
> That weeps o'er his grave; for while he was here,
>   Ye refused him a crumb and a pillow.[6]

In his response to community issues Whitman sought to be "ardent without fanaticism." When a chartered company began to exhume and cart away skeletons and shrouded ashes from a Baptist graveyard prior to building there or when speculators sold land on the Brooklyn hill made sacred by martyrs for freedom, he cited this callousness as proof of the prevalence of an unholy spirit, a national character flawed by greed: "Let popular opinion show them what reward is meted out to soulless brutes who outrage every pure and gentle feeling of the soul—every sentiment of love, every remnant of the perfection that was Adam's in Eden!"

With few exceptions he refrained from abusing other editors. Bennett, the new recipient of Tyler's patronage, became a reptile whose path was marked with slime, a midnight ghoul preying on rottenness and filth. A woodcut of a jackass in the *Aurora* symbolized Benjamin, the "Great Bamboozle," now serving as a literary agent and allegedly fleecing those scribblers who faithfully placed their work in his hands.

At times he told of a petty slight. He had been stopped by the doorman at the entrance to a festival and forced to chaffer ten minutes before admittance. "When any one connected with the *Aurora* takes the trouble to visit places," he scolded, "he considers that if there is any favor in the matter, it certainly does not come from them to him." More typical of his daily encounters was the one with children in the midst of a sidewalk game who started to break their solid line because a gentleman was coming; he walked around them. "What wonderful powers children have of discriminating who is possessed of a courteous, kindly, manful and creditable disposition!"

All editorial restraint ended when Whitman enlisted in the momentous and unending religious war whose weapons were sectarian abuse, bigotry, and riot. The burning by a mob of an Ursuline convent in Massachusetts, and the brawls between Protestants and Catholics near the Catholic church in Chatham Street were recent skirmishes.

When de Tocqueville asked John Latrobe for information about the Catholics in America, this son of the famous architect told him of their extraordinary increase and their leaders' policy of turning all efforts toward education. But in New York City realization of this ideal met frustration or failure. Chartered in 1805 to administer to the destitute the Free School Society, a charity financed by public tax money to secure instruction for children unaffiliated with religious groups, was formed by private citizens. By 1825, with its expanded scope reflected by a changed name, the Public School Society served all children, though a city ordinance empowered the trustees to grant funds to applicants who maintained sectarian establishments. As enrollment began to outrace the scope of Lancastrian monitors, the Society started normal schools and a library; but because of organizational limitations it could not keep pace with a population growth five times the national average.

In his first message Governor Seward, who corresponded with Horace Mann, acknowledged the imbalance created by immigrants and asked for generous treatment of their children—many of whom spoke only German —in new schools where they could enjoy education "equal to our own, with free toleration of their peculiar creeds and instructions." He also proposed changes in curricula and administration, and additional space for Negroes. Little resulted except the suspicion and anger of bigots. Again in January

1840 he recommended that along with the generosity that had opened the nation to the oppressed of Europe, the electorate of the state display the wisdom to provide the education needed to qualify all children for the tasks of citizenship.[7]

The trustees of the seven Catholic schools in the city petitioned for funds, only to be refused. A Presbyterian and a Hebrew congregation also failed to move Common Council. When the Catholic vicars continued to demand money and itemized their objections to the reading of the King James Bible in the schools and to the use of texts with slurs on the Papacy and undue praise of Luther, a storm of obloquy broke.

Xenophobia had been overt for years. The hostility against the Irish startled Mrs. Trollope, who learned that many employers hired them only if assured they did as much work as the Negro. "The foreigners," as Cooper saw them, "have got to be so strong, among us, that they no longer creep but walk erect. They throng the presses, control one or two of the larger cities, and materially influence public opinion all over the Union. By foreigners, I do not mean the lower class of Irish voters, who do so much at the polls, but the merchants and others a degree below them." The *Protestant Vindicator* and Maria Monk found a large audience prone to believe in deadly plots by Austrian Catholics and in pornographic revelations of the escapades of sinful nuns and priests in Canada. Now, many friends of the Society suspected a vote-capturing alliance between Governor Seward and Bishop John Hughes, who had assumed leadership in the effort to save Catholic parishioners' children from idleness in the streets or from exposure to an education he denigrated as "practical infidelity." In fact, Seward admired the prelate and hung his portrait on the same wall with one of Washington. Others saw a resurgence of a notorious anti-Masonic clique. Whigs and Democrats motivated by religious and ethnic hatred joined those with faith in the ideal separation of state and church to resist the proposed legislation, and remained unmoved by Seward's avowal that the rescue of twenty thousand untutored Irish and German children was his sole concern.

The powerful *Journal of Commerce* found no reason to reward Roman exclusiveness; Protestant clergy joined the press in vowing enmity to a foreign hierarchy, with at least one minister announcing that he preferred infidelity to Catholicism. Samuel F. B. Morse diverted some energy from his artistic and scientific projects to lead the American Protestant Union in its opposition "to the perversion" of the Common School fund for sectarian

73

purposes. But Seward persisted in his plan to provide the children with amenable education for the sake of good citizenship, and maintained a cordial relationship with Bishop Hughes.

This vigorous, courageous prelate, born in County Tyrone to a father who taught his son that in politics a Catholic farmer ranked lower than a Protestant laborer, had come to Chambersburg, Pennsylvania, as a young man and had worked in quarries, on roads, and as a gardener at Mount St. Mary's College. Ordained in Philadelphia, he quickly countered Protestant polemics with his own newspaper, tract society, and sermons and became the leading church controversialist in the state. Though neither orator nor prose stylist, he reminded literary parishioners of Dr. Johnson's estimate of Burke: "no one could meet him by accident under a shed to avoid a shower without being convinced that he was an extraordinary man." He was summoned to Manhattan in January 1838 to be consecrated Bishop and Coadjutor in the old St. Patrick's Cathedral in Mott Street—he would lay the foundation for the new St. Patrick's—and began at once to administer a diocese that included all New York state and part of New Jersey, some two hundred thousand people.

His survey of Catholic education in the diocese revealed that overcrowded classes were held in church basements or storerooms. Debt-ridden congregations lacked money for teachers and equipment; nor did they all agree on a solution. Meanwhile the numbers of illiterates and godless multiplied.

In September 1840, Bishop Hughes petitioned the Public School Society for relief from a syystem that doubly taxed Catholics "for the purpose of destroying our religion in the minds of our children." The Society and a group of Methodist and Episcopal pastors answered with a publicized "Remonstrance." Visiting City Hall, the prelate and prominent laymen debated with the Society's lawyer, Theodore Sedgwick, and a Protestant minister, but this session and a second ended in refusal by the Society to honor the prayers of the petitioners.

A favorite text for the bishop's sermons was the combination of civil and ecclesiastical power in the governments of the Middle Ages. Now, seeking its current application, he memorialized Albany. Governor Seward encouraged the submission of a proposal in April 1841 by his secretary of state and ex-officio superintendent of schools for changes that would transfer the power of the Society to elective commissioners. But the Senate voted to postpone a decision until after the election in November of a new legislature.[8]

All that summer and autumn Bishop Hughes carried the issue throughout the diocese and demanded that his people ignore party ties and "look well to your candidates; and if they are disposed to make infidels, or Protestants of your children, let them receive no vote of yours." On 29 October, four days before the election, he assembled communicants at Carroll Hall and gave them the names of Assembly and Senate candidates whom their votes could help send to Albany. This "bold, daring, reckless" move, according to the *Herald*, "fell upon the great body of the community like a clap of thunder in a clear sky." In the judgment of Mayor Hone, to distribute public money according to the dictates of a religious sect was tantamount to preparing the way "for that formidable old lady, the whore of Babylon."

The fact of a committed bloc of Catholic votes no longer angered Tammany. In its first decades the Sachemship and other offices had remained the exclusive domain of native Americans, but the massive influx of new potential voters whose allegiance would ensure victory changed the biased attitude to an expedient tolerance. Many Democrats, however—including Whitman and his publishers—remained hostile to the Catholics. Orangemen and Protestant natives left the Wigwam and made the North American hotel their headquarters; there they waited, ready to sally into the streets. Bennett, long afflicted with bias, thought that Bishop Hughes had become blinded to all facts and truths "save the dogmas and drivellings of the Catholic Church in the last state of decrepitude." Other editors charged that the priest had been seduced from his holy office and deserved to be unfrocked. Moderates welcomed a change that would be helpful to many children who now lived beyond the pale, but cautioned against damaging an admirable institution; they feared to widen the door lest the interior of the edifice be destroyed. Heeding the uproar, some of the candidates named by Bishop Hughes repudiated his support. After the Democratic victory in November the press intensified its assault upon him for political tampering, but Governor Seward promised to submit another education bill to the new legislature and asked Senator Maclay of New York City to prepare it.

Unchecked by threats or by pleas not to bind the sceptre to the crosier, Bishop Hughes with the power implicit in his control of six wards intensified his efforts in the next months. By March 1842 those who first believed that the Maclay Bill would fail began to note mass meetings on its behalf and the establishment of an Irish Catholic newspaper, the *Morning Pilot*. Then, as the elections for mayor and aldermen neared, Bishop Hughes published a Carroll Hall slate headed by one of his supporters.

Whitman entered the fray with an editorial, "The System Must Stand." He told *Aurora* readers that in establishing his role as an expert witness, he had visited every public school in the city, read official reports, and talked with many parents during the past six months. This scrutiny added to long experience teaching in country districts gave him a base for "wholesome judgment." In every classroom he found "bright-eyed, healthy, fine look-ing fellows" who answered all questions "with a degree of promptness, good breeding, and intelligence that cannot but astonish the interrogator." It was obvious that the Society system was unsurpassed.

He went on to refute charges of monopoly. Every inhabitant found a welcome here whatever his rank, trade, or creed. Common Council, the people's agent, voted every cent of appropriations and elected all supervisors. The fact that pupils filled the buildings to overflowing was the ultimate proof of success. As for the cries of intolerance raised by "a certain reverend bishop"—in four of the schools up to two-fifths of the children and "no inconsiderable number of the teachers" were Catholic.

His wholesome judgment gave way in the next days to near-hysteria, whose origins lay in the conviction Whitman shared with other Protestants that the school skirmish was part of the strategy of European "magnates" to further Romanism in America. Citing evidence that men and women were brought "like cattle under their drover" to St. Patrick's and forced to sign petitions that the cunning Hughes sent to Albany, the *Aurora* called for a watchman on the walls of the threatened city to sound the alarm bell. An officious priesthood must be stopped from swaying civil policy by cor-rupting the ballot box. The nation had long been a blessed Eden where no church attempted to influence matters of state. Now a reptile infused "foul feelings, envy, malice, and all other uncharitableness in the minds of his disciples."

The watchman Whitman kept a nervous hand on the bell rope. On the afternoon of 16 March he left his office and walked to City Hall Park, where he joined thousands gathered to defend the Society; twenty minutes after the meeting had started violence erupted near the platform and en-gulfed the crowd. According to the *Aurora*, squads of "the lowest class of foreigners" drilled by "the hypocritical scoundrel Hughes" and other "jesuitical knaves" were guilty. The one way to deter these "Romish priests" and their "degraded creatures" was to follow the examples of western communities and revenge all outrages.

When a friend of Bishop Hughes protested the malevolence of the *Aurora* and asked if the editor did not fear its consequence, Whitman retorted by claiming enough bravery to support to the last all holy and patriotic causes. "But there is one thing in which we *are* a coward. . . . We allude to any attempt to infuse religious sectarianism in the making of our laws—and poisoning of the constitution with taint from a meddling priesthood." Encouraged to persevere by new allies, he continued to confront "the reverend and hoary hypocrite."

In the last week in March news arrived from Albany that the Assembly had passed the Maclay Bill on to the Senate, but in recognition of varied and relentless pressures had amended it—no one could tell whether for good or evil. The *Aurora* now tried to counter the faction of Catholic foreigners in Tammany that was allegedly dictating policy. Possessing "an ineradicable yearning toward the time honored institution," Whitman advised its leaders to be bold and adhere to the teachings of Jefferson rather than to treat the malcontents in the manner of parents playing bo-peep with their children. The *New Era* attempted to speak for Tammany; but in Whitman's judgment, acceptance of this sheet was comparable to allowing the dullest "supe" at the Park to represent the stage. Democrats who refused to barter their honor needed the guidance of a newspaper "bold, manly, able and *American* in its tenor"—like the *Aurora*. But Tammany ignored his advice to risk losing mayor and aldermen rather than establish a precedent for the introduction of sectarianism into politics. According to the embittered editor, it bowed to the very dust:

> The bulwark of truth—the "unterrified democracy," ruled by a tattered, coarse, unshaven, filthy, Irish rabble! Americans, high in reputation, degrading themselves worse than the slavish nobles who of old kissed the toe of the triple crowned? *They* knelt to the Pope himself; *Americans*, to the abjectest menials of the Pope.

Taken to task once more by some of the moderate press for "gross, beastly, shocking . . . unjustifiable barbarous attacks," and by a correspondent who told him he might as well deprive the tree of its sap as America of its influx of foreigners, Whitman answered that his love was capacious

77

enough and his arms wide enough to encircle all men whatever their native land. Yet he warned again of danger spread by every packet and steamer, threatening to deter "a continent peopled by *freemen*" from the high destiny of perfecting human nature and self-government. All the "poisonous atmosphere" of European philosophy, all the "fallacious glitter" of literature patronized by prince and church were not fit for this beloved nation.[9]

As he heard of frantic scurrying by envoys to Albany and the promise to withdraw the Carroll Hall candidates in exchange for senatorial support of the bill, he became increasingly apprehensive. Early in April word arrived that with deliberate, last-minute absenteeism by a Democrat the Senate had passed by one vote what the *Aurora* called a statute for the fostering and teaching of Catholic superstition. Others read the many pages of the Maclay Bill with more care and found less than a complete victory for the governor or the bishop. The new law did end the monopoly of the School Society by transferring administrative power to a board whose members were to be elected by voters in each ward; but a major amendment withheld public money from all schools in which "any religious sectarian doctrine or tenet, shall be taught, inculcated, or practiced." The *Brother Jonathan* asked all true friends of religious liberty to rejoice that their schools were to be preserved from becoming engines of proselytism.

Though Bishop Hughes scratched the Carroll Hall slate, Whitman branded the city election anticlimactic and spent his anger in hurling invective at those he judged guilty of treasonable maneuvering. He vowed to stay away from the polls and asked other New Yorkers to withhold their votes in protest:

> We love (why should we conceal it?) we love the name democrat. It has been our pride and glory to keep the title untarnished, as we inherited it from those who carried the then opprobrious term amid the stormy political tempests of Jefferson's day. But we cannot flatter the base, and fawn to hypocrisy, and wriggle out and *lie*, for the interests of any petty clique. True democracy requires such things of no man for any purpose.

On Monday night, election eve, he wandered from a Tyler meeting in the park to Tammany Hall. Lights flooded a great transparency in front of the building, and crowds milled in the room where stood the memorial to

Leggett—who also had filled columns in an attempt to keep state and church separate. The speeches of "fifth rate pettifoggers" who "soft soaped the foreigners" drove the disconsolate editor away. He tried one ward meeting after another but found them slim affairs. He remained in the streets until after midnight, watching torchlight parades and listening to band music.

The next day a large majority gave the mayor's office to a Democrat, while the Whigs gained some power in the Common Council. When all the returns came in, the *Aurora* repeated the wish that Tamany had met total defeat, so that Catholic priests could not say in the future, "Behold what might we have to sway your elections!"

The ugly time continued. In the metaphor of George Templeton Strong, the first fruit of that "very abominable tree," the Maclay Bill, was a series of "no popery" riots that started late Tuesday afternoon with a fight between natives and Irish near the Tombs. Then the Spartans, a gang led by the tipsy pugilist, Yankee Sullivan, and Mike Walsh, roistered through the "Bloody" sixth ward seeking Catholic victims and shouting, "Americans stand firm!" Reinforced, the Irish fought back with stones and wood billets; by midnight both sides had made a battlefield out of the streets and turned the police station into a hospital. From his window Whitman watched two mounted companies of Washington Greys arrive to calm the area.

Violence flared throughout the week. Patrols surrounded and garrisoned St. Patrick's to keep it from being sacked, but bricks smashed Bishop Hughes' windows in his Mulberry Street house. "Had it been the reverend hypocrite's head," the *Aurora* told its readers, "we could hardly find it in our soul to be sorrowful." The paper went so far as to suggest a plot: "We shouldn't wonder if the Catholics themselves started the whole rumpus, merely to generate sympathy for their cause."

Because the policy of the *Aurora* paralleled that of the Native American party, burgeoning as one of the results of Carroll Hall, Whitman found himself first accused of "roaring" on their behalf, and then invited to join the Nativists in helping disenfranchise the foreign-born and exclude Catholics from office. In the calm after the riots he repudiated the accusation and rejected the invitation. He had lifted his voice, he explained, to counter servility to an alien gang and to imbue Americans with confidence in their republic. The same motives, he added, led him to refuse to accept the dicta

79

of Old World critics. As for the Nativists, he thought their doctrines were also flawed:

> We could see no man disenfranchised, because he happened to be born three thousand miles off. We go for the largest liberty—the widest extension of the immunities of the people, as well as the blessings of government. Let us receive the foreigners to our shores, and to our good offices. While it is unbecoming for us to fawn upon them and flatter their whims, it is equally unnecessary that we should draw the line of exclusiveness, and say, stand off, I am better than they.

To a young man with an eye for the future, the Native Americans offered power and respectability; in two years they would elect as mayor the publisher Whitman admired, James Harper. But Whitman's motivating political philosophy, unlike theirs, was the anticlericalism common in Volney—whose *Ruins* he reread that spring—Paine, Wright, Owen, the other Free Enquirers, and the original Locofocos. The *Aurora* carried Jefferson's plea for "the absolute and lasting severance of the church from the state," and rephrased it in editorials that vowed to uphold the letter of the Constitution and always to oppose sectarian political measures, be they introduced by Episcopal, Presbyterian, Methodist, or Catholic.[10] In the midst of this tumult, President Tyler also recorded his conviction that any merger of church and state would be an unholy alliance.

At no time did Whitman war against piety. On the contrary, he often revealed religiosity in ecstatic thanks to "the All Bounteous" for "balmy air, and the fantastic drapery of clouds, and the sight of mighty waters, and a thousand influences, solemn and sweet, that forbid their entertainment to no man, but are spread by God, as a banquet where they may all come, and none shall be thrust aside." Swedenborgian lectures at the Lyceum threw "the camp of old theological church militants into utter confusion," but he did not censure a faith that removed the fear of death, saw correspondences—as he would—between the material and the spiritual, and taught that the greatest things visible instruct humanity of the least, of the smallest invisible.

On Saturday with a Jewish friend from Mrs. Chipman's, he attended services at Shearith Israel, the oldest of the five synagogues in the city. There he recognized the most famous member of the congregation. Wrapped in prayer cloth before the ark stood Mordecai M. Noah, playwright, diplomat, editor, sheriff, judge, ingatherer. Early in the week the *Aurora* carried the visitor's account of the morning:

> And there we were amid the Jews worshipping in their temple. The people of Solomon and Saul, of Ruth and Mary Magdalene, of the traitor Judas, and John, the beloved son of God—the people of the very Christ himself—these were they who stood around. And they were speaking in the same tones as those which at night bade the shepherds to follow the guidance of the star in the east— the same tones which Jonathan and Saul used in the beautiful friendship—which sounded out from the plaintive Hagar in the wilderness—through which Absalom, "that too beauteous boy," made rebellion against his father—with which the widow's son, who was dead and brought to life again, gladdened his desolate mother's heart;—the tones and the native language of the holy Psalmist, the lovely Rebecca of Scott, and the malignant Shylock of Shakespeare.

During the chanting of the Hebrew liturgy his fancy lifted again from Crosby Street to Jerusalem, where along the thoroughfare came the burdened Christ.

Sundays often found him at church, though he never identified the denomination to his readers. After hearing "the best worst sermon ever delivered," he told them to attend an Indian powwow rather than the services of a "prosy, whining, seesaw" preacher who began with Adam and ended "we hardly knew where."

If he spent the weekend on the island with his family, he devoted hours to Eddy, his deaf-mute brother. When the seven-year-old boy seemed to respond to a portfolio of religious engravings he had bought at Colman's, Walt tried to explain the idea of a God. Through gestures and an illustration of the crucifixion, he preached a silent sermon on the "Man of Grief" and the resurrection. Encouraged by what seemed to be the intuitive affirmation of the little congregation, he went on to show "the affectionate disposition of the Great Master of the Apostles—how he gave assistance to the poor—how he comforted the sorrowful, and soothed the pains of sickness and guilt—how he called little children unto him—and how he met with no resting place where to lay his fainting limbs—and was at last cruelly put to death, by agony the most excruciating—and scoffs and re-

81

vilings and ridicule." All this, the fraternal minister wrote, "seemed to touch the child, even to his inmost heart."

During the remaining weeks of his tenure, no other local or national issue roused the editor to the vituperation that marked his defense of secular education. In a reasoned way he supported the suffrage revolt led by Governor Dorr in Rhode Island against an obsolete charter. Were he a resident he would be "a revolutioniser, in the front rank," for one-sided laws could not take "natural prerogatives" from man. The *Aurora* also exposed the protective tariff "humbug," and suggested that voters reform Congress by electing mechanics, merchants, artists, and manufacturers rather than talkative lawyers. Fewer, shorter sessions at Washington, Albany, and all other capitals would be wise, since national and state affairs were obviously worse by adjournment time; moreover, the "law-making powers" were too officious, meddling with everything from foreign empires to the oyster trade. His summary of the ideal state was in the tradition of Leggett: "Government is at best a necessary evil; and the less we have of it, the better."

Though the Bowery theatre, overrun by prostitutes, had become "an immense house of ill-fame" which no respectable person could visit "without shame for the frailty of poor humanity," he opposed punitive legislation; statutes would neither remake man nor supersede nature. He was beginning to feel, he explained in defending what seemed a permissive stance, "not in theory merely, (that has long been the case), but in reality, that every being with a rational soul is an independent man, and that one is such a man as another, and that all sovereign rights reside within himself, and that it is a dangerous thing to delegate them to legislatures."

For the two months of his editorship, despite Bishop Hughes, inexorable deadlines, and many inches of space that had to be filled, he was "*The* Whitman," proud of his station, handsome in finery, and happy with the glow of youth: "Wasn't it brave! And didn't we laugh (not outwardly—that would have been vulgar; but in the inward soul's bedchamber with the very excess of delight and gladness?) O, it is a beautiful world we live in, after all!" But on 3 May a squib in the *Aurora* revealed that the publishers were disenchanted: "There is a man about our office so lazy that it takes two men to open his jaws when he speaks. If you kick him he's too idle to cry, for then he'd have to wipe his eyes. *What* can be done with him?"

His daily policy conferences with Herrick, usually held after he returned from a walk on Broadway or down by the Battery, had survived the Maclay Bill because the two men concurred in their opposition. Then came the fatal hour, as Whitman recalled it three years later, when the *Aurora* "became lost in the storm and darkness of Tylerism." Promised a place in the Customs House by the President's managers in return for support, Herrick abandoned his pledge to avoid partisan involvement. But his editor had little enthusiasm for the "milk and water" incumbent whose chances of remaining in the White House, he believed, were as safe from demolishment as a roast duck served at a corporation dinner; in all his conjectures for 1844 he ranked Van Buren, Benton, and Calhoun higher than Tyler. When he refused to conform to the new policy, his position became untenable.[11]

On 16 May the publishers announced that "Mr. Walter Whitman desires us to state that he has been for three or four weeks past, and now is, entirely disconnected with the editorial department of the *Aurora*." Later that summer they described their former hand as "a pretty pup" whose "indolence, incompetence, loaferism and blackguard habits forced us to kick him out of office." In turn he flung his own epithets:

> There is in this city a trashy, scurrilous, and obscene daily paper, under charge of two as dirty fellows as ever were able by the force of brass, ignorance of their own ignorance, and a coarse manner of familiarity, to push themselves among gentlemen. Not capable in their own sconces of constructing two lines of grammar or meaning, they are in the habit, every month or so, (for no man can remain longer than that time in their concern,) of engaging some literary person to "do" their paper. *We*—ill-starred by Fate—were, some six months since, unfortunate to allow ourself to be induced by the scamps in question to take the editorial charge of their sheet. During the few weeks we continued there, we saw, in the instance of these two ill bred vagabonds, more mean selfishness—more disregard of all manliness and good manners —more low deceits—more attempts at levying "black mail"— heard more gross blasphemy and prurient conversation, than ever before in our life.[12]

The "scamps" refused to allow the quarrel to end with this version. "We were fine fellows," they answered, "as long as we consented to pay him for loafing about our office; but we didn't happen to want him, and, 'of course' we are 'dirty fellows.'"

In 1860, aware of the growing reputation of his former editor, Herrick noted in the *Atlas* that "Whitman's poetry is very bad, and so are his garments—but his heart is sound enough."[13]

7

POPULAR AMERICAN AUTHOR

DILLON AND HOOPER, publishers at 27 Ann Street, accepted the pretty pup's version of the rift and by June he wrote for their *Evening Tatler*, a "bulletin of horrid murders" (according to Herrick), and soon edited their *Sunday Times*.[1] That autumn in a prospectus for a weekly *Tatler* to be circulated in the country the name Walter Whitman stood with Hawthorne and Bryant in the list of the ablest American authors promised to subscribers.

To support this ranking he contributed the "Gad Correspondence" to the *Times*. Here he commended Niblo, who had brought French opera from New Orleans, scolded the vulgar for eating ice cream during the band concert, and reminisced of lonely nights as a schoolmaster when he played solitaire checkers, manufactured hot toddy, and responded to a "literary fit" by writing "Death in the School-Room." Under an epigraph from *The Old Curiosity Shop* he printed his blank-verse poem "No Turning Back," in which a Leggett-like figure, once famous but now scorned by the masses, rallies devotees:

> O, youth, a weary road
> Spreads out before you! Hidden grief lurks there,
> And burning fires of vice lie smouldering there,
> And disappointment's clutching fangs wait there:
> But far ahead, up in the height of heaven,
> Glitters a star. O, let thy constant gaze
> Be fixed upon that star; step not away,
> But gazing on the brightness of the guide,
> Press forward to the end and falter not!

With a mere fragment of the *Times* extant, there is no certain way of following the editor through his tour of duty. Governor Dorr, now a fugitive from Rhode Island after an abortive revolt, aroused his sympathy;

85

the Democrats at Tammany—the dateline for the Gad letters—campaigned to elect William Bouck governor and to return beloved Silas Wright to the United States Senate. Heavy rains brought good crops; disenchanted Whigs named the fever and ague that swept the country the Tyler grippe. Lectures on mesmerism convinced Whitman that there was such a thing as mesmeric sleep. Forrest gave *Venice Preserved*, the city drank the sweet water of the new Croton reservoir, and the ten-gun brig *Somers* cruised toward the coast of Africa.

If their man's literary reputation did not merit the superlatives of the publishers' blurb, he had placed at least ten tales by autumn 1842 and could say with candor that they were "pretty popular and extracted liberally." "Death in the School-Room" ran in several papers; the *Sun* and the *Tribune*, with a combined circulation of some thirty thousand, printed "A Legend of Life and Love" on their front pages within the same week. The *Post* considered all of his "very neat and fanciful performances" newsworthy and read them "with pleasure."[2]

Though Lowell described the fictions as done "a la Hawthorne," no single model dominated their composition. The force that shaped manuscripts in the 1840s, as the author of *Tales of the Grotesque and Arabesque* had discovered some years before, was the market that awaited them. If "The Angel of Tears" approximated the popular type that Poe described as the singular heightened into the strange and mystical, the white hair and stone tablets of death in "The Tomb Blossoms" followed another respectable formula. Their author also sold pieces germane to the furtherance of temperance and the abolition of capital punishment.

Often he resorted to observation and traditional reminiscence rather than invention, and in prefatory notes acknowledged sources and disclaimed fancy: "If the reader supposes that I am going to tell a story full of plot, interest, and excitement, let him peruse no further." Then followed a case history of grief caused by drunkenness. Anecdotes gathered on Long Island from old men whose fathers served in the "Sacred Army" became tributes to General Washington: "The model of one pure, upright character, living as a beacon in history, does more benefit than the lumbering tomes of a thousand theorists." Revering the veterans of the Revolution for breaking chains forged by "kingcraft and priestcraft," he envisioned an era when nations would discard war and its train of sanguinary heroes.

The tales lack the structural skill of Poe or the sustained symbolism of

Hawthorne, but they offer personal revelation. Their compassionate author is concerned with the widow and—inevitably for one who believed that Dickens became the great novelist of the day with Oliver and Nell—is made solemn by the "ashiness and moisture on the brow, and the film over the eye balls of the sick child." He abhors brutality, greed, and domestic bickering; a frequent theme is the son driven from home by a cantankerous father. He delights in landscape, the locust and the oak, garden and pasture, a farmhouse with a huge fireplace, the quiet village and old church, the air that clears vision and ends the city-induced headache. Old women, grandsons, farmers, and a Negro musician serve as characters, with twenty-year-old Nathan receiving the most sensuous description—glossy hair, eyes soft and liquid "like a girl's," lips that "curled with a voluptuous swell." Promising to avoid scraps of sentimental fiction, the author nevertheless fondles the love of the aged for lifelong companions, of the living for the dead, of a young man for a boy.

As Hawthorne discovered, the promise of lavish returns for publishing in the *Democratic Review*—or any other periodical—often proved illusory. O'Sullivan sent him twenty dollars for an entire story, not three to five dollars a page, and paid this small sum, according to Sophia, in a sadly dilatory manner. After Poe had received two dollars a page for one work of fiction and ten dollars for all of "The Tell-Tale Heart" he summarized the random policy: "They graduate their pay by mere whim—apparent polarity—or *their own* opinion of merit." With little assurance of a living income from the sale of short fiction, authors found regular employment imperative.[3]

On 9 November 1842 the *Herald* listed the fifty-two newspaper writers of Manhattan, "a very important and numerous class of *literati*, whose labors, genius, and talent are gradually giving a tone and coloring to the age." Years ago Irving, Halleck, Verplanck, and Cooper had formed an aristocracy of letters that exercised dominance through books, but now these fifty-two reigned with their daily leaders, paragraphs, squibs, reports, and reviews. In the attempt to prove their talent superior to that of the London press, the *Herald* promised a biographical sketch of each man, embellished with wood engravings of the "face divine." But the biographies never appeared.[4]

Among the fifty-two were Bryant, Godwin, Noah, Brisbane, Greeley, Bennett, and Whitman.

The Pewter Mug, one of the remarkable taverns in the city, served as a border post where all parties met, compared notes, and settled affairs. Here Whitman sometimes sat with a shaggy, red-haired survivor of a decade of political forays, Levi Slamm, editor of the new *Daily Plebeian* whose motto was "Press Onward." A leader of the original Locofocos and friend to Leggett, whose memory he invoked, now as then secretary to sessions of mechanics at Tammany Hall, the onetime locksmith whose fervent rhetoric had made him a byword continued in the *Plebeian* to assail aristocratic inroads on the Democratic party. "Slamm, Bang" editorials scorned monopoly in every form and all so-called protective tariffs that added to the wealth of the wealthy and the poverty of the poor. In Slamm's judgment, the gulf separating the two groups had widened fearfully since the Revolution. Striving to recapture man's primordial rights, he printed columns of Fourieristic plans that would elevate the worker to real liberty and provide scientific, practical education for his children.

Slamm's trade unionism, antimonopoly bias, and egalitarianism made him a ready target for numerous antagonists; even former cohorts impugned his motives and character. But none of these swayed Whitman who found the editor an earnest, tireless advocate of the Democratic cause and a legitimate Jeffersonian.[5] After the suspension of the *Tatler* and the *Times*—"the murders did not make the pot boil"—he became a penny-a-liner for the *Plebeian*. A party paper in the midst of a campaign had space for an experienced whip. This time November brought the elation of a triumph that seemed to justify his brag that "coonery" was totally used up.

One day that autumn Parke Godwin found the penny-a-liner at the Pewter Mug. A Princeton graduate, author of a fine essay on Shelley, a Germanic scholar who translated Goethe, Godwin was taunted for acting as a local Luther determined to reach an American Diet of Worms; in time he would indeed get to Brook Farm. When he began to publish *The Pathfinder* its espousal of progress made the periodical a legitimate heir to Leggett's *Plaindealer*, for Godwin also sought political reformation to consummate change in communities and individuals. Now he asked Whitman to write a temperance novel.[6]

Whitman's acceptance was not dictated merely by Godwin's eloquence or offer of seventy-five dollars—enough to cover expenses for three months.

Like so many others Whitman was already a participant in this phase of the international struggle for the amelioration of humanity in general and father, brothers, friends in particular. That August in Wiscasset, Maine, the *Washingtonian Temperance Journal and Family Reader* reprinted the "Legend of Life and Love." His "Wild Frank's Return" placed the wayward boy in a tavern, tossing down brandy and sugar with a hanger-on whose face "told plainly enough the story of his intemperate habits—those deeply seated habits, now too late to be uprooted that would ere long lay him in a drunkard's grave." In "The Child's Champion" the profligate was armed by the magic of the phrase, "I have promised my mother not to drink." In "Reuben's Last Wish" the boy dying because of a sotted father's abuse found enough strength to point to the blank space at the bottom of the temperance pledge and to urge his father to sign.

Extreme addiction to the Bottle Demon, as Melville called it, was common throughout the land; in some towns more than half the men were drunkards, while many others spent their days and nights in the condition known as "half and half." They took drams in grogshops or from the keg placed on free tap by riverboat captains or in western doggeries. The Brooklyn directory for the year when the Whitman family arrived listed over a hundred tavern keepers, while thousands of saloons across the river made pertinent the supposed translation of the Indian name Manhattan: "The place where all get drunk together." The pathetic wretches in Five Points rarely drew sober breaths; de Tocqueville's companion Beaumont, who mingled in Boston's elegant society, noted three characteristics of this set: intellectuality, snobbery, and heavy drinking. Harriet Martineau testified that in otherwise enlightened communities she encountered ladies of station and education intemperate as their gentlemen. College students boasted of becoming "philanthropically cocked."

Some blamed heredity; others cited the extremes of climate or the over-indulged European tastes of immigrants. National customs were also suspect, since whiskey, brandy, and wine were served free during hotel meals or placed habitually on the family table; during harvest lunch Suffolk farmers brought to their hands jugs of spirits distilled from ample orchards. (Mason Weems wanted to award a civic crown to the man who popularized coffee at dinner.) Fourth of July and New Year turned into debauches. In the judgment of responsible observers the campaign of 1840 was a vast spree; ward clubs served cobblers and brandy smashes on key days, beer and crackers followed routine meetings. The number of toasts at any banquet mounted in ratio to the number of guests; at a dinner attended by Jackson there were twenty-four toasts before Old Hickory rose. Visitors wondered at the fatally cheap price of Monongahela whiskey, Yankee rum, and corn liquor served in half-gill bar glasses; a man could get drunk twice for six pence. The *Aurora* reported that the nightly receipts of the three-cent shop next door to Tammany Hotel averaged twenty-five dollars. When de Tocqueville asked why legislators failed to tax liquor and lessen its availability, his hosts answered that those who voted for that law would surely lose their seats.[7]

The temperance movement had received a powerful thrust in 1825 when Lyman Beecher, then in the first years of his pastorate at Litchfield, began to preach on the nature and evils of intemperance. After these sermons were circulated throughout the nation, the American Temperance Society was organized and by 1830 claimed hundreds of branches and salaried field agents. De Tocqueville placed one of their tracts in his trunk as a souvenir of a remarkable force. George H. Cheever, Mrs. Sigourney, and other popular writers lent aid; at age seventy Dunlap wrote *The Memoirs of a Water Drinker*. Phrenologists, imbued with faith that self-improvement was the leading characteristic of the century, lectured on the need to abandon a habit that added fuel to the fires of passion and weakened moral and intellectual power.

All the years of Whitman's boyhood in Brooklyn temperance was a political issue as well as a social problem, owners of the distilleries and the rum shops contending against men whose modest hope was to suppress drunkenness on the Sabbath. During his apprenticeship on the *Star* he witnessed an election with liquor control through licensing as the main issue. Though Spooner was a connoisseur of wine, he helped the reformers elect a mayor and printed their tracts. While Walter Whitman framed houses in the village the *Star* reported that local carpenters had vowed to abstain from drinking on the job. In rural Long Island repentant bartenders visited Cold Spring; at Jamaica, home of one of the first temperance societies in the nation, two rival editors shared the same platform to urge sobriety and both printed Lamb's *Confessions of a Drunkard*—from which Whitman would borrow a paragraph. The publisher of the revived *Long Islander* attempted in every issue to reach the conscience of Huntington's tipplers.

From the time of Dr. Rush and his *Inquiry into the Effects of Spiritous Liquors* (1784), reformers had tried to ban whiskey and rum but had sanctioned fermented liquors because they believed these would not cause addiction; indeed for the sake of digestion they urged moderate use of beer, ale, and cider rather than water. Churches and genteel society also sanctioned this middle way. In the depths of depression when Wall Street knew many bankruptcies the auctions of celebrated cellars brought bidders eager to pay exorbitant prices for old madeira and sherry. Unfortunately, time revealed that these drinks also led to alcoholism. By the 1830s temperance workers decided to insist upon total abstinence.[8]

The scope of the new pledge led at first to theological controversy, since those who insisted that a drinking Christian was as paradoxical as hot ice or cold fire faced charges of blaspheming Christ, who had blessed wine along with bread and oil. But Manhattan's leading wine merchant, Henry Delavan, in a startling repudiation of his business interests, announced that chemical analysis proved that modern wines contained damaging adulterants, unlike the pure vintage of Judea. He then emptied every one of his casks into the sewer and distributed thousands of drawings of a ravaged human stomach. When Irish immigrants brought word that Father Theobald Mathew had saved many of their countrymen by keeping them from whiskey and Guinness, American clergymen attempted similar mass conversions. The most spectacular success came, however, from the mission of men who were neither repentant merchants nor ministers, though they offered a secular sacrament that had the impact of baptism.

A carpenter, wheelwright, tailor, blacksmith, and silver-plater who were drinking the night away at Chase's tavern in Baltimore, 2 April 1840, brawled with the bartender. Sobered and shamed by the episode, they formed a fellowship open to all who pledged not to drink spiritous or malt liquors, wine, or cider. A wise clause in their constitution required each member to bring a drunkard to the frequent meetings; in this way they converted John Hawkins, a hatter, who became their most valuable proselyte. To add dignity, they called themselves the Washingtonian Temperance Society. In less than a year they "saved" a thousand men.

News of their good work sped northward and brought invitations. Starting in March 1841—the year the Secretary of the Navy admitted the increase of drunkenness among officers—Hawkins and four others spoke in theatres, halls, and churches, but wherever their platform stood they made it neutral ground so far as sect or politics. Within days after reaching Manhattan, they inspired the formation of a local chapter that claimed ten thousand members by the end of the year. "I used to say," Lydia Maria Child told a correspondent, "that I knew not where there were ten righteous men to save the city; but I have found them now. Since then the Washingtonian Temperance Society has been organized and alive in good works." Ladies of the Martha Washington Auxiliary entertained converts; Governor Seward removed all bottles from the executive mansion; a committee of fifteen printers walked with Greeley from shop to shop and secured pledges; sailors, firemen, members of Congress, faculty and students at Yale and Dartmouth joined. When John Gough, one of the Washingtonians' most persuasive agents, visited Princeton, the students elected him to a literary society. The popular Hutchinsons added "Plow Up Your Hops" to their musical repertoire.

Moving through the nation the Washingtonians reached multitudes with a formula that seemed infallible. The *Brother Jonathan* described it as "free, unpredictable, hearty, and of the genuine Crockett character—'Go ahead!' "[9] The missionaries entreated and encouraged, never frightened or denounced. Believing that reclamation came through cheer rather than compulsion their language was not "Avaunt! Ye miserable," but "Approach, men!" They sought former companions and wooed them by appealing in a friendly way to motives of duty and self-respect, rather than by force.

Whitman like many others succumbed to the hypnotic fervor of their patterned sessions which opened with songs. With bars they fight bars, punned the *Aurora*. From the time of Anacreon poets had apostrophized wine, but here drinking ditties gave way to glees that warned of the effects of the first glass. Then came pathetic confessions and anecdotes out of the speaker's dissolute past. The promise of a new life followed, the Washingtonian standing before the audience as a living sign of resurrection. As the inebriate moved with tottering limbs and trembling hands to sign the pledge the audience cheered and waved banners like the one picturing an ear of corn whose motto impressed the young editor: "If you eat me I am life; if you drink me I am death."

The reformers also used the holiday parade as an adjunct. On 4 July they formed a three-mile column in Manhattan, and Whitman applauded a line of children holding high their placards, "We would be pure." From his hotel window in Cincinnati Dickens watched Washingtonians drag a wagon that held an allegory of the steamboat *Alcohol* bursting her boilers.

In Springfield Abraham Lincoln met the crusaders on the birthday of their namesake and told them that in the time "when there shall be neither a slave nor a drunkard on earth, how proud the title of that land which may truly claim to be the birthplace and the cradle of both of those revolutions that shall have ended in victory!" (In 1863 he signed the bill that banished the grog ration from the Navy.)

As momentum gathered, men and women from all levels of society sought the cure. Congressman Thomas P. Marshall of Kentucky became known as the Mirabeau of the teetotalers; when he came to New York in 1842, he searched for addicts all the way from the Tabernacle to City Hose Company 33.

That September a tragic ending to a sports event added evidence to justify legal intervention. The pugilist McCoy collapsed and died after being pounded for 120 rounds—two hours and forty-one minutes—by the fists of Christopher Lilly. Because the match had been arranged in a porter house, the press blamed liquor sellers for the death and clamored for their suppression. The next month brought a practical ally, potable water.

At dawn on 14 October one hundred cannon sounded and church bells rang as all the fountains in Manhattan gushed with the first flow from the Croton aqueduct. From now on, purists predicted, men would drink water rather than spirits; grog shops as well as contaminated pumps at street corners and rainwater caches were obsolete. The seven-mile parade that afternoon included journalists, firemen, butchers, and a float adorned with a thousand dahlias.

Tireless, the Washingtonians went far beyond halls, parades, hymnals, and periodicals for adults and children. "The teetotalers," Whitman noted, "have caused to be produced a tragic play, illustrative of the ten thousand ills that flesh is heir to by its too frequent moisture." When *The Blighted Hope* was staged at the Bowery, a Brooklyn bartender spoke the prologue. One of the few reviews in the *Aurora* was of T. S. Arthur's *Six Nights with the Washingtonians*, "a well told and interesting tale." As signs mounted of the success of the crusade, the danger now lay in excessive zeal. In Boston one Sunday the consecration cup presented to communicants contained water and barberry syrup; cynics anticipated the use of Graham bread for the sacrament. In New York someone spread the rumor that Hamblin intended to close the Bowery and become a saint. Punsters seized their opportunity to ask, "Why are temperance societies a bar to friendship?

93

Because they prevent shaking hands." Or, "Why should an Israelite signing the pledge be prohibited from kissing his wife? Because he is forbidden to touch Jew-lips."

On 22 November 1842 Jonas Winchester announced the addition of a temperance novel to his weekly shilling series that included *The Western Captive* by Seba Smith, Liebig's *Agricultural Chemistry*, and Dickens' *American Notes*:

> Tomorrow morning will be issued in an Extra New World, an original and beautifully written novel, by a popular American author, entitled Franklin Evans, or the Inebriate, A Tale of the Times, dedicated to the friends of Temperance. The incidents of the plot are wrought out with great effort, and the excellence of its moral, and the beneficial influence it will have, should interest the friends of the Temperance Reformation in giving this Tale the widest possible circulation.

The novel appeared as a buff, paper-covered, royal octavo pamphlet with thirty-one, double-columned pages printed in new minion type. The title on the wrapper was "*The Merchant's Clerk,/ in New York;/ or the/ career of a Young Man from the Country;/ by Walter Whitman/ Author of "Death in the School-Room"; Etc. Etc.*" The first page had "*Franklin Evans/ or/ the Inebriate/ A Tale of the Times.*" The rapid printing of which Winchester boasted was manifest, for his pressmen had reversed the twentieth and twenty-first chapters.[10]

Each Washingtonian came before his audience as a living parable of the lost sinner found, redeemed, and now worthy of emulation. Whitman defined his novelistic task as a comparable one to be performed by a similar technique known "to the earlier teachers of piety." Rather than attempt to win the approval of critics "with profound reflections," he sought to stir "The People" with the tested formula. After reading of the alcohol-induced fall of a young man, extended degradation, and ultimate ascension through total abstinence, the inebriate would sign the proper pledge and rejoice over a cup of pure Croton water.

As recently as that spring, the novelist had spent an hour with the prototype of Franklin Evans. Strolling the Battery during a pleasant afternoon, he learned that a boyhood friend lay dying in a slum room. While he hurried through the iron gate and across the city in search of the shabby address, he thought of the years when Lively Frank delighted everyone on Long Island with his vivacity and extraordinary intelligence. Coming now to a dirty, narrow street, Whitman entered a blackened, miserable house and climbed to the attic where "Upon a thing, which, for want of some other name, we suppose must be called a bed, there lay a human form." He did the little he could to ease the terminal agony and after his farewell pondered this "tale of chances thrown away, industry contemned, extravagance indulged in, and utter desperation at last."[11]

With little time for invention, Whitman reached into memory and into his files for the exemplary details. Evans had been apprenticed at eleven by a carpenter father who receives an authorial rebuke: habits of drunkeness in the head of a family "are like an evil influence—a great dark cloud, overhanging all, and spreading its gloom around every department of the business of that family, and poisoning their peace at the same time that it debars them from any chance of rising in the world." Coming of age, the islander with an old black leather valise in hand climbs aboard a country market wagon like the one Cornelius Van Velsor drove and begins the ride on the same Jamaica turnpike toward the "mighty labyrinth." He is "Youth" in Thomas Cole's four allegories of *The Voyage of Life*; the placid river that takes him from Eden will change in "Manhood" to a dark turbulence with shores patrolled by demons of intemperance and lust.

To the jog of the horses the passengers talk about the local Indians and their ruination through rum. An antiquary tells of Wind-foot, a boy of fourteen with graceful figure and soft, beautiful lips who is killed by a vindictive brave. Then the antiquary warns the young traveller of the wicked city where there are a thousand things no man is the better for knowing. But Evans will not be deterred for he has lifted the sheet-anchor, Hope.

Like the apprentice in Lillo's *George Barnwell*, often performed to teach boys to avoid the sequence of sin, he takes his first false step soon after reaching Manhattan. Enticed into a cabaret he enjoys the music and the pretty women but succumbs to liquor. His shame does not last long and he returns often, and then moves on to the theatre to see a play like *London Assurance*, with its flippant society and dialogue tainted by "the most nauseous kind of mock aristocracy." Fascinated by an actress, Evans pursues her backstage but at close range finds her coarse and masculine. Soon, with evil companions, he is following the "red circle" of ruin. Too drunk to execute an

95

important mission for his employer, he is fired, then tends bar in a cheap hotel until he is revolted by the realization that he is selling jugs of brandy to children.

As a sober factory hand, he marries the landlady's daughter, buys a lot, and begins to build a house. But he is forced to sell because he cannot afford to complete it, and he turns again to drink. When his wife dies broken-hearted, he tries to kill the demon who first tempted him. Non-Washingtonians fail to save Evans because they ignore the fact that low as the drunkard falls he "is a *man*" and will not respond to injudicious severity. He leaves New York but continues to drink while living in a village, for vice is not restricted to an urban locale; there he finds fellows like the schoolteacher with "bright black eyes and very long fine glossy hair" who lies in a stupor beside a haycock.

Swindled by a villager he returns to the city and, like one of the young boarders at Mrs. Chipman's, becomes a thief. Here Whitman calls in the hero of an earlier tale, a reformed drunkard now a prominent citizen, who acts as Evans' benefactor after the young man is arrested and secures a suspended sentence for the culprit. Taking the old pledge that outlawed only the most ardent kind of liquors, the chastened man travels on business to Virginia and begins to share a bottle of wine with new companions. Before long he is, "to use an expressive word, *obfuscated*." Sexually aroused by a Creole—"I don't know whether I have intimated, in the . . . course of my narrative, that my nature was not wanting in susceptibility to female charms"—he marries her. The epigraph from *Othello* becomes apt, for the jealous wife murders a fair rival and then commits suicide.

At last after five years of torment Evans is convinced by a Washingtonian that *total* abstinence is the only safe course. He signs the "holy charter" and sure of grace and sustained sobriety ends by literally waving the temperance flag.

All the way from the chapter epigraphs taken from Lamb, Dickens, Shakespeare, lecture-hall ballads, and Cheever's *Commonplace Book of American Poetry* (Poe thought the title reflected the contents), to the concluding tribute to the Washingtonians, the novelist admitted shaping his 60,000 words to "do good." In addition to the young clerk, other characters make the fatal journey. A "sickly-looking, red-nosed" barkeeper is his own best customer; the Indians justify the narrator's comment that "Rum has done great evil in the world, but hardly ever more by wholesale than in the case of the American savage." For readers who failed to find their own biographies, he enclosed little lectures: "Intemperance destroys even the resemblance of love."

Winchester advertised *Franklin Evans* as the creator of a sensation "both for the ability with which it is written, as well as the interest of the subject." Reviewers accepted the novelist's admonition that he wrote not for them but for the People; the *Tribune*, always in the van of reform, heartily commended the novel's circulation "to the friends of Temperance, for the good it must effect, to the novel-reader for its exciting scenes, and to all for its intrinsic worth. . . . There are thousands who will read a novel who would not touch a Temperance tract or periodical, and many villages in which a few copies would do silently the work of an efficient lecturer. Give it a trial." The *Brother Jonathan* called it a clever story; the *Aurora* thought the former editor's fiction was worth more than the price. A future employer, the Brooklyn *Eagle*, added a personal note: "We have not found time to read it yet; but the known ability of Walter Whitman is sufficient guarantee of its high character. If successful now the author promises to 'try again.' The price is only *one shilling*—cheap enough in all conscience." [12]

The *Herald* headed its review "American Literature," and linked Whitman with Cooper and Cornelius Mathews as authors of new, light books. *Le Feu Folle, Puffer Hopkins,* and *Franklin Evans*

> will all be read by a large number of persons, but we doubt whether they have but a brief existence. When we read them closer we shall speak of their merits and defects. We have classed Cooper with the others, because they are contemporaries; yet it must be remembered that whilst he usually writes like a finished workman, the others are mere apprentices, having just shed their feathers as penny-a-liners. [13]

Had the *Herald* made the promised reading, there would have been a paragraph of praise for Whitman's use of the city he called a brick-and-pine Babel, with its boarding houses and streets that he knew intimately, and for his compassion toward the many unfortunate inmates. Once again he wrote tenderly of children and accurately of the theatre. In a manner to please O'Sullivan and other expansionists, he carried Evans beyond Long Island and New York to a world of distant towns and vast stretches of territories and states "away up in the regions of the frozen north, and reaching down to the hottest sands of the torrid south—and with the two distant oceans for its side limits." And for the first time he confronted slavery and some of its attendant evils.

Metropolitan papers advertised *Franklin Evans* all through the next year and into 1844. In time, stores offered it with Scott, Dickens, Bulwer, and Frederica Bremer in a packet of twelve books for one dollar, and then dropped the price to 6½ cents for each title. Two facts may have combined to slow, then end sales: the Post Office raised rates on "extras" to equal those for books and, with profits cut, Winchester sold the *New World* which soon suspended publication.

In a military metaphor Whitman concluded that the dominion of the Liquor Fiend had been assaulted and battered, but asked "Will the old fortress yield?" The disheartening answer came early. New Year's Day was cold. Snow fell in the morning and made fine sleighing all through the city, but along with fun and frolicking the day seemed to be filled with rowdyism. If there were fewer visits from house to house, there were more to rum-shops, private drinking clubs in back rooms, and Bowery cellars whose habitués showed dull eye, bloated cheek, and quivering lip.

Within three months Whitman readied a second temperance novel, *The Madman*, for the New York *Washingtonian* and *Organ*, two papers published weekly by Colonel E. Snow and sold "for the lowest price of a glass of ruin." Only two short sections of *The Madman* survive—the title may have come from a popular ballad—but they contain the profile of young Barcoure, who is more intellectual than Evans. Familiar with Volney, Paine, and Frances Wright, he has inherited his father's "fierce radicalism and contempt for religion," and like a true Free Enquirer has built his own system of morality that rejects all the superstitions of mankind. In Barcoure's code each religion "contained more or less excellence—and more or less fanaticism." [14]

Mathews' *Puffer Hopkins* had been admired for its local color. In *The Madman* a character named Irish John serves pork and beans in a Fulton Street eating house.

The populace continued to need salvation, but deliverance was elusive. An epidemic of influenza cast suspicion upon the purity of Croton water; there were whispers that Hibernian laborers had used it as a latrine; rumor spread that ex-drinkers of alcohol became chewers of opium. Lobbyists blocked prohibitive legislation, their task aided by ample budgets and disillusioning episodes like the backsliding of Gough. Missing for days, he emerged from a brothel claiming that he had been abducted and carried there after accepting a drugged soda, but sceptics held that chemical analysis of the drink would reveal a base of brandy. Whitman was more credulous and cited a comparable episode as proof of the evil beneath the surface of Manhattan. Temperance inns closed, while taverns continued to sell mint juleps and champagne for the genteel beginner, punch and port for the moderate drinker, "sword fish gin" and other lethal materials for the "confirmed and seedy soaker." All political parties increased their use of alcohol; Clay Clubs, Empire Clubs, Ash and Hickory poles combined to make saturnalia out of campaigns; their three months of electioneering undid three years of Washingtonianism. Guests at the official reception on the Fourth of July 1843 found full hogsheads, tureens, ladles, tumblers, and crockery: "Never since punching was invented, were a Governor and suite, and Mayor, Common Council, and friends so punched."[15]

When Whitman again controlled a paper he reprinted *Franklin Evans* and wrote sobering editorials.[16] The pleasure he took later in life in baked shad and champagne suppers shared with Philadelphia hosts cannot erase his sincere work for temperance. This crusade which enlisted the great men and women of the day along with the humble, he served without hypocrisy or recourse to the bar of the Pewter Mug.

99

8

AN HUMBLE BUT EARNEST INSTRUMENT

"DIRECTLY the acrimony of the last election is over," Dickens wrote in his *American Notes*, "the acrimony of the next one begins; which is an unspeakable comfort to all strong politicians and true lovers of this country: that is to say, ninety-nine men and boys out of ninety-nine and a quarter." The campaign of 1844 had started in 1841 after the first of Tyler's vetoes, when a caucus of fifty congressional Whigs proclaimed the end of allegiance to "His Accidency." The severance statement came from the pen of the novelist John Pendleton Kennedy, whose *Quodlibet* satirized Democratic fiscal policy from the time of Jackson's withdrawal of the deposits and the coddling of pet banks that proliferated like "new Egyptian plagues."[1]

Now both camps resorted to the semantic tactics identified by the Quodlibertarian philosopher, the Hon. Middleton Flam:

> In our country, especially amongst the unflinching, uncompromising democrats . . . a name is always half the battle. For instance, sir. We wish to destroy the Bank; we have only to call it a Monster: We desire to put down an opposition ticket, and keep the offices amongst ourselves; all that we have to do is set up a cry of Aristocracy. If we want to stop a canal, we clamor against Consolidation: —if we wish it to go on, it is only to change the word—Develop the Resources. When it was thought worth our while to frighten Calhoun with the notion that we were going to hang him, we hurraed for the Proclamation; and after that, when we wanted to gain over his best friends to our side—States Rights was the word. Depend upon it, gentlemen, with the true Quodlibertarian Democracy, Names are Things.

Tyler's exchequer system continued to stir revolt within his party because it included opposition to a higher protective tariff. As a result, according to

100

the *Herald*, for the first time since the founding of the nation its president lacked a party in Congress to support his measures or befriend his administration. When Whitman, on one of his habitual rambles, passed Whig headquarters, he mused that no politicians had ever come into power under more favorable auspices, but now they were broken and scattered—the tidal wave of 1840 had subsided. Veteran correspondents in Washington confessed that they had never before known the despondency manifested by men willing to discharge their duties but thwarted by their titular head.

Those who attributed Tyler's vetoes to a plot calculated to insure a second term in the White House cited other maneuvers on his part to gain Democratic support. When Mike Walsh, the leader of the sixth-ward Spartans, visited Washington, the president invited that hero of the unterrified to dinner. Walsh boasted in letters sent home of sitting with the honest patriot and enjoying a sublime segar served on a silver platter by a black boy. Not too long ago this guest in tarpaulin hat and frock coat had driven a cart daily through the streets of Manhattan.

Surveying the "regular" Whig candidates, Whitman credited Webster with no more than third-rate talents: "We heard what were considered his best speeches previously to the election in 1840; and, though biased in favor of his oratorical powers, we could see little more than the mere commonplace politician." When the *Tribune* unfurled Clay's banner, he understood the enthusiasm kindled by the man's lofty carriage, suaveness, and sincerity; but the Kentuckian's forte was a bold, dashing kind of warfare with little caution: "He resembles some fire brained political Murat, riding gallantly into the midst of the enemy, pressing on their very bayonet points, with cuts and thrusts to the right and left, but fearing nothing, and heeding no warning, whether it comes from friend or foe."[2]

The Democrats had not united on a nominee. Van Buren, leader of the largest faction, faced Benton, Calhoun, General Cass, Buchanan, and Richard M. Johnson, always popular with eastern workingmen. Benton, whose "mint drops"—new gold coins symbolic of the Missourian's advocacy of hard money—brought support from the South and West, seemed to Whitman to be the man to come to the post with ribbons flying. But the talk at the Pewter Mug turned often to Calhoun. The *Democratic Review*, in January 1843, lauded the South Carolinian's advocacy of free trade and the separation of bank and government; Harper issued a biography the next month; Calhoun's managers bought a Washington weekly and attacked Van Buren and Clay. In Manhattan the *Herald* began to echo the adulation of the Charleston press for its idol; Walsh and his Spartans, shirt-sleeved with "long niners" in their mouths, also became henchmen and brawled on the steps of City Hall. Whitman acknowledged that the pride of southern chivalry was a great man but found the record flawed:

> We admire his spirit, his vigor, his fiery breath, and his brilliant eloquence. We admire his very faults—his devotion to his native south, and his ardent advocacy of her interests above all else. But his *nullification* conduct—there we stop; we can never admire anything which puts in jeopardy the well being of our beloved Union.[3]

His candid estimate of Van Buren, composed with memories of nights watching Shakespeare, dwelled on the loyalty of the old adherents he met at Tammany and at ward meetings. These disciplined regulars remained faithful through "triumph and doubt, despair and glory, sunshine and tempest, rank and retirement." If no other man had ever gained high office with so little personal enthusiasm, few had retired leaving so many warm friends. And like Richard III he possessed the king's name. Frequent encounters with this coterie added to the young analyst's conviction and he soon joined them.

On Monday morning, 14 March 1843, appeared the first issue of the New York *Statesman*, a daily published by Kraft and Lamb and edited by "Walter Whitman." A contemporary succinctly summarized the editorial policy: "It supports Martin Van Buren for the next Presidency, with much spirit—denounces John Tyler."[4] Unfortunately, not a single copy of the *Statesman* survives.

In addition to politics Whitman had the opportunity to chronicle the other events Manhattan considered newsworthy. March was the most miserable month in years, with wind that reached a velocity of fifty miles an hour and piled heavy snows everywhere, but the weather did not stop the rhythmic progress of a new social exercise—the waltz. A grimmer diversion, the trial of Captain MacKenzie of the *Somers* for the hanging of three of the crew, became public domain; those who considered his action a courageous command decision applauded the acquital verdict while others deplored as another miscarriage of justice the exoneration of a cold-blooded lyncher. An officer of the *Somers*, Lieutenant Guert Gansevoort, could relay first-hand testimony to his cousin, Herman Melville.

At Niblo's the popular Russell sang the temperance ballad, "The Dream of the Reveller"; Rossini's last pupil, Calvé, performed her master's arias with a voice lovely as a flute. Among the serene landscapes at the Academy of Design Whitman discovered a Columbus in chains. Gliddon, former consul at Cairo, lectured on Egypt, a country whose antiquities contained new excitement for Americans. Mathews argued for international copyright; Emerson explained politics, a field more actively tilled by the editor of the *Statesman*; Lowell started the *Pioneer* as "a rational substitute for the enormous quantity of thrice-diluted trash in the shape of namby-pamby love tales and sketches poured monthly" by magazines. The *Tribune* read fiction by a newcomer to the city and liked its imaginative power: "Mr. Poe writes effectively, though not always discreetly." (For a post as government inspector the desperate Poe promised in March to forgo mint juleps and join the Washingtonians.) To wake on the morning of 23 April was in itself news, for Whitman and all other journalists had listened to Parson Miller interpret recent meteors as portents of the second coming of Christ and the end of the world on that date. Instead, everyone passed what the press called an ordinary sort of a day, and the ascension robes sewn from white muslin by the gullible remained unused.

At Tammany Hotel where good dinners were inexpensive, Whitman's table companion was often an elderly, white-haired constable of the city court rather than a party official of high rank. Several times a week he sat with Colonel John Fellows and listened to the octogenarian deist's reminiscences of Paine, Volney, and Elihu Palmer. At age seventeen Fellows had served in a regiment of minutemen and witnessed the battle of Bunker Hill. Graduating from Yale after the Revolution, he corresponded with Jefferson and Madison, met Volney when the *philosophe* toured America, joined Palmer's circle of free thinkers in New York, lived with Paine and attended his deathbed. As a bookseller and publisher he reprinted *The Age of Reason*, wrote texts on astronomy and Egypt, and edited the monthly *Theophilanthropist* whose motto from Pope identified him as

> Slave to no sect, who takes no private road,
> But looks thro' Nature up to Nature's God.

Still lucid and alert he had helped Gilbert Vale recently with a biography of Paine meant to erase Cheetham's portrait of a drunken sloven. Now he

103

told the young editor that the libertarian Paine had been slandered and denigrated by leeches on society who feared that the advent of equal rights would force them to yield their hold on selfish privilege and ancient prejudice.[5]

The *Statesman* did not last longer than two months. It was mentioned in one list of Manhattan papers on 22 April 1843 but excluded from another on 30 May. The backers counted their investment profitable, however, for in the spring elections the Democrats won easily. Jubilant leaders in New York called the result annihilation for the Whigs and the foreshadowing of disaster for Clay.

In the flush of this triumph, Walsh started the weekly *Subterranean*. Spokesman for what he called the Young Democracy—Mayor Hone described them as rag, tag, and bobtail rabble "vile and savage as the canaille of the Faubourg St. Antoine at the start of the French Revolution"—he continued the strong-arm tactics he had displayed during the School Bill riots. With his Spartans he raided ward meetings and terrorized Tammany with physical and verbal assault; in turn he called Slamm a noxious stinkweed and a vain imbecile incapable of writing a soap-boiler's advertisement. But in his strenuous way this self-styled champion of the shirtless honored the "immortal" Leggett. On a tour of Philadelphia he stood before the Bank and ignoring the rain exulted that its doors remained closed. He echoed the right-to-land program of George Evans and soon merged the *Subterranean* with the *Workingman's Advocate*. Convinced that monopoly of public lands would lead to war and starvation of the many for the gain of the few, he demanded equal rights to the soil. In his own verses published by the proud Spartans he exhorted:

> Through the ages thou has slept in chains and night,
> Arise now Man and vindicate thy right.[6]

The first issue of the *Subterranean* on 15 July carried the "Lesson of the Two Symbols" by Walter Whitman. Written in the season of the dedication of the Bunker Hill Monument, the sixty-six lines of blank verse were suffused by the "glow of holy patriotism" emanating from Boston. After a Volneyesque view of the ruins of mighty empires the poet saluted a new nation

> moving like a beauteous youth,
> Vigorous with strength, fresh bloom upon his cheeks,
> And ardent heat swelling in every vein.

Lest its citizens defect through selfishness or sophistry, he commanded the acquisition of knowledge and strength. The passing ages would then show that "the light of lands,/ The refuge of mankind" need not fear the rest of the world.[7]

That summer Whitman became one of the eight reporters on Moses Beach's penny *Sun*. Covering the police stations and the coroner's office, he learned the accuracy of the contemporary estimate of a reporter's work: "The horrible is his true forte. The pathetic is his element." Reduced income forced his acceptance of a less fashionable address than last year's; but at Browne's, 68 Duane Street, a coincidence helped him to score a beat over every other newsman in Manhattan. One of his fellow boarders was a boy of seventeen employed as a junior clerk at an auction house. A theatre lover, Henry Saunders had joined an amateur group and often disturbed the other boarders by "loud-mouthed and dying performances." One day in August he collected his baggage and absconded with thirty thousand dollars taken from his employers. But he never had the chance to play his favorite role of Claude Melnotte, for the police captured him in Boston harbor aboard a ship ready to sail for England, and returned him to New York and a cell in the Tombs.[8]

Liberation from editorship gave Whitman the time and incentive to further his literary career. He finished four tales and sold them to Israel Post, a former mechanic now hailed at oyster and champagne suppers for publishing the new *Columbian Lady's and Gentleman's Magazine*. Post boasted of surpassing *Godey's* or *Graham's* by obtaining material from the best authors at a "liberal cost" of two to twelve dollars a page. Poe published in all three and found them so nearly alike that he wagered no one could distinguish one from the others if the covers were changed. They featured the mezzotints and line engravings of Sadd and Smillie, vermilion or azure title pages, and fashion plates on fine paper.

The four tales demonstrated the range of Whitman's fiction. In "Eris: A Spirit Record" he returned to the fantasy of the "Angel of Tears." Here the disobedient sprite is blinded as a portent to those "whose selfishness would seek to mar the peace of gentle hearts, by their own unreturned and unhallowed passion." In "Dumb Kate," a reminiscence of Long Island (the

Columbian that July ran an engraving of the landscape near the Van Velsor home), he wrote of a familiar tavern, huge buttonwood trees, and a long porch with a grape vine "wreathed around it like a tremendous serpent." Like so many of his young characters, the mute girl meets early death, but her seducer escapes to the city and becomes rich. Though he chose a pleasant playground in Manhattan for the locale of "The Little Sleighers: a Sketch of a Winter Morning on the Battery," the self-styled sombre moralist refused to be cheered by the sight of healthy youth clad in pert costumes of satin cloaks, kid shoes, and gloves. He concluded in funereal cadence that "all, all will repose at last." Like T. S. Arthur he also sold the *Columbian* a retitled temperance tale, "The Child and the Profligate," with a byline that identified him as the author of *The Merchant's Clerk*.

Lamb's "Dream Children" inspired a reverie which he placed in the weekly *Rover*, edited by Seba Smith (the humorist Jack Downing). Homesick for the family now living at Dix Hills, the twenty-five-year-old bachelor boasted of brothers with patriotic names. He had carried Washington on his shoulders, taught Jefferson to spell, and wrestled with Jackson. He worried over the future of a very beautiful young sister, and he mourned the dead in the graveyard on the Suffolk hill. Saddened by the knowledge that one brother would never gain normal use of mind and body, he ended by wishing, "Had I any magic or superhuman power, one of the first means of its use would be to insure the brightness and beauty of their lives."

Victory for the Democrats in 1843 had failed to bring the harmony they needed to pick a presidential standard bearer. From his own biased vantage point Whitman observed "the tricks, the clap trap, and the wire pulling" as managers—and Walsh—sought ascendancy for Calhoun or for General Cass, idol of the "Jack Casses." When the skill of Van Buren's disciplined regulars won him the city and state delegations, his return to the White House seemed certain, but opponents elsewhere in the nation succeeded in delaying the convention at Baltimore until May 1844. The intervening months saw the emergence of the issue that would keep Van Buren at Lindenwald.

Early in February, the publication in the Washington *Globe* of a three-page letter by Senator Robert J. Walker of Mississippi brought the case for the annexation of Texas before the electorate. As thousands of copies of the letter circulated in a special edition, each candidate faced a virtual plebiscite on gaining a powerful new slave state through certain war with Mexico and possible dissolution of the nation. When that same month the explosion of the twelve-inch "Peacemaker" on the *Princeton* killed the secretary of state, Calhoun accepted the post and completed negotiations with the Texas envoy. In mid-April Tyler sent to the Senate a signed treaty.

Men who shared no other opinion joined the attack on what seemed to be the consummation of an outrage. Whittier warned the Southerners,

> Work the ruin, if you will!
> Pluck upon your heads an ill
> Which shall grow and deepen still.

In New York Whitman watched protest meetings attended by Greeley, Bryant, and other former antagonists now united; and he read the letter from the Kentucky abolitionist, Cassius M. Clay, who called annexation treason. In Brooklyn, William Henry Channing, editor of the transcendental *The Present*, refused to be gagged with cotton and urged disunion rather than the offering of an immense bribe to the South.[9]

Late in April, Van Buren sent the inevitable letter to the *Globe*. Instead of "the lust of power, with fraud and violence in the train" that annexation implied, the ex-president asked for reason, justice, and a postponement of action. When his opposition to the present confirmation of the treaty became public, his career was aptly described as in the sere and yellow leaf. At Baltimore the next month, pro-Texans insured his defeat by imposing the two-thirds rule on the nominating process, over the objection of the New York delegation. Once again, as in 1840, saddened friends listened to derisive ballads. The noblest act of his political life had destroyed it. The convention chose on the ninth ballot one of the earliest annexationists, Polk.

The first editions of the papers printed the day of Polk's nomination named Silas Wright for vice president. Greeley thought the New Yorker worth two of Polk; Bennett called him the only pure high-ranking politician of any party he had ever known in the state. To many the ticket had assumed the shape of a kangaroo and walked upon its hind legs. But Wright refused to accept office from those who had abandoned Van Buren; in fact, before the final ballot, he turned away firm offers for nomination to the presidency. Not long after the new telegraph in Washington had transmitted his emphatic no to Baltimore, he repeated his rejection in a letter sent by wagon. Polk's managers then turned to Dallas of Pennsylvania for the vice presidency. Wright soon began to be mentioned as a possible nominee for governor, for among his unique assets was the ability to rouse the support of all sections of the community, bankers and merchants as well as mechanics and farmers. But since the divisive problems faced by the party in the state seemed insuperable—even to one known as the Cato of America—he also declined this candidacy. His one flaw, quipped a newsman, was the habit of refusing high office.

By July 1844 wider rifts separated the Democrats of New York. That most promising partisan, Gansevoort Melville, had addressed harmony meetings and with the family gift for rhetoric had eulogized Young Hickory (Polk) as a tall sapling from the same staunch stock of Old Hickory, destined to reach as lofty a growth. But these conciliatory efforts seemed failures. Rejection by the Senate of the Texas treaty had intensified the fervor of its advocates and the fears of its opponents. The new epithets of Hunker and Barnburner, like those of Conservative and Radical, or Monopolist and Locofoco, described old issues kept current by the very diversity of mercantile, manufacturing, agrarian, and working-class interests. As far back as Whitman's birthyear the Bucktails of Tammany had rebelled at supporting the building of distant canals; the intervening years added the irritants that led to the outcry against monopoly, charters, and rag money. Governor Seward in his two terms borrowed, spent freely, and allegedly damaged the fiscal position of the state; but his Democratic replacement in 1842, Bouck, a popular commissioner of canals known as Old White Horse (and described as a tolerable mixture of common sense and common place) from his inaugural message onward also pained those hostile to incurment of debt for internal improvements. When he continued to support the expansion of canals and railroads and to appoint men from the Hunker clique and his own family to office, the Barnburners began to seek ways to turn Old White Horse out to pasture in 1844. This would not be easy, since the strongest Hunker, William L. Marcy, defended Bouck; to attempt to send an unwanted Democrat to Albany risked the loss of thirty-six electoral votes.

On 17 July the *Post* ignored Marcy's protests and editorialized that the whole party could be united upon Wright. With the nominating convention scheduled to meet in Syracuse within two months, there remained the considerable chore of overcoming his published reluctance. Party leaders resorted to a standard campaign practice. "Political papers are coming out as thick as blackberries," reported the *Atlas*, "and office holders and those who hope to hold office are bleeding freely, if not willingly, to support them."

The next day came the announcement of the establishment of the *Democrat*, a morning paper supporting party principles and candidates, and edited by Whitman. "The matter in this number is principally political, and its editor engages in the warfare with heartiness and spirit. Besides putting up the names of Polk and Dallas as its candidates for President and Vice President, it sets before its readers the name of Silas Wright as its candidate for the office of governor of this state."[10]

The *Tribune* characterized the 20- by 15-inch, two-cent *Democrat* as "a not at all scrupulous Loco-Foco daily," because it predicted that Polk would carry Tennessee by a majority of ten thousand, although he had been beaten there twice. If readers could humor the joke, the *Tribune* declared, they would find the *Democrat* quite a pleasant paper.[11]

The first editor in the state to name Wright at his masthead as candidate for governor, Whitman supported his choice with "a series of able and judicious articles." He abjured intemperate personal attacks on the kindly Bouck and accusations of violations of republican principles, and wrote rather of the folly of renominating him when reelection seemed impossible and the electoral vote in doubt.[12]

Within a fortnight, eleven papers in the state had followed the *Democrat*. Gratified to learn that no difference existed among those who desired a Democratic victory, Whitman entreated prudent politicians to nominate the one man who was both certain to secure it and trustworthy enough to execute party principles. He estimated that a Wright victory by 15,000 votes would sweep Polk and Dallas into the White House. In August and September ward caucuses added their acclamation to the editorial pleas. When the convention named Wright as David to walk among the Philistines, he accepted the nomination as a mandate. Half an hour after the Albany boat with the news reached the Manhattan wharf Democrats, according to the opposition press, "in all their picturesque haunts of elegance and vulgarity, were perfectly crazy with delight."

Papers in Richmond and Washington quoted Whitman on the strategy certain to win in November:

> Almost every democratic paper we open, responds to our recommendation of union and harmony in the democratic ranks, *oblivion* to the past, energy and zeal to the future. Throw open the doors of Tammany Hall, broadly, for all the tried friends of John Tyler to enter—pass the word throughout the State and

109

Union, that we are *one and indivisible*, that the old Democracy is again united and powerful, and we shall then sweep everything before it.

Channing asked politicians to avoid staking their country in a game for the presidency with Texas as a trump card, but the editor of the *Democrat* and his sponsors, hungry for victory, accepted annexation and the occupancy of Oregon.[13]

A veteran Whig thought it always possible to tell the nearness of an election by the conduct of the lower strata of Locofoco journals, for at that time "they always eschew the lie circumstantial as too tame and prosy and adopt the lie direct." Greeley, who had worked himself into an infection of boils to elect the Mill Boy of the Slashes, now accused the *Democrat* of the lie direct in what *Niles' Register* called the case of the confidential letter "purloined and published."[14]

In September Henry Clay had written from Ashland to his kinsman, the abolitionist Cassius M. Clay, and chided him for harming the Whig cause in the South by undertaking to speak the candidate's private feelings. Perturbed by earlier blunders, Clay went on to clarify his position: "At the North, I am represented as an ultra supporter of the institution of slavery, while at the South I am described as an abolitionist; when I am neither one nor the other." Mailed to an intermediary in New York and then entrusted to Greeley for delivery, the sealed letter vanished from the *Tribune* office. Within days it appeared in the *Democrat*, with Whitman defending its publication because the author was a public figure dealing with vital public matters. The Whig press refused to believe the explanation that a laborer had found the letter soaked in the mud of Canal Street, offered it first to the *Post* and *Morning News*, which suspected a forgery and refused to print it, and then to the *Democrat*. Greeley alleged a plot tantamount to naked felony and threatened all culprits with state prison, but he never started suit or consulted a local Dupin.[15]

On the morning of 16 October the editor of the *Democrat* told his subscribers—he claimed six thousand—that "the end of our enterprise has been achieved." With Wright nominated and the state "beyond the danger of capitulation to our Federal opponents," the paper would merge with the *Plebeian*, for Slamm also ardently believed in "the sublime principle of equality" and had sustained it "in the teeth of every aristocratic influence, whether in or out of the party." The valedictory closed by bidding Slamm

110

"God speed in the glorious cause of Oregon and Texas, Polk and Dallas, Wright and Gardener." In turn the *Plebeian* blessed the patriots who had sustained the *Democrat* and labored in the same cause. The suspension of the *Democrat* may have also resulted in part from the inability to compete with the well-staffed *Morning News*, started that year by Tilden and O'Sullivan.

In the hours after Tuesday's balloting both parties claimed victory. As late as Thursday morning, some Whig papers announced that Clay had won New York and with it the White House. Whitman and many thousands spent the warm, sunny day waiting for the final count to arrive by steamer from Albany. At six-thirty they knew that Polk had carried New York by some 5000 votes, while Wright had doubled that margin in defeating Millard Fillmore. Analysts in both parties credited the new governor with saving Albany and Washington for the Democrats; Whitman, therefore, felt justified in naming himself "an humble but earnest instrument" in this triumph.

Tammany celebrated the return to power with a splendid ball. There were men among the guests who saw portents of increased strife between Hunker and Barnburner; but none knew that the beloved mediator, Silas Wright, and the young leader, Gansevoort Melville, would not live to see the next presidential campaign.

After the loss of the *Democrat*, Whitman worked that autumn for Nat Willis, who added a daily evening edition to his weekly *Mirror*. Touched by a visit in September by the long-suffering Mrs. Clemm, Willis had hired her son-in-law, Poe. Whitman saw his colleague often, since Poe attended to his duties faithfully at a corner desk, and both frequented the oyster cellar conducted in the heart of the Ann Street printing district by a Washingtonian famous for terrapin stew.

Even a young man who tagged himself a sombre moralist given to "mottled reveries" could indulge in the pleasures that made Manhattan tolerable. According to one paragrapher the usual outcry of strangers amidst its crowded 350,000 was "God bless us, what a filthy city!" But for a shilling on weekdays and eighteen pence on weekends, Whitman bathed in soft Croton water at the Knickerbocker. At the Battery he exulted in the beauty of the sun on the waves, the many ships, the haze over the shore of Staten

Island. Nights, he avoided the drinking clubs, the many blackleg hells, the thirty faro banks like the one at Park Place where some players lost $3000 a session. It was healthier and cheaper to walk the fine graveled paths around the fountain at Castle Garden.

Macready played Shakespeare, but the theatre in general had fallen on evil days: burlesque, fire eaters, a troupe of fifty-five horses, and a "romantic ballet" in which a Hungarian noble was turned into an African eunuch. Frequent scandals erupted at the houses; a manager's wife stabbed a dancer; the greenroom was rumored the locus of scarlet behavior. Admission cost more than books.

Party regulars admonished every member to hang in his home Danforth's engraving of the Dodge portrait of Jackson, but lovers of art leaped over parochial boundaries. Whitman could tour the Gallery of Fine Arts, hung with canvases collected by the late Luman Reed, and muse before Cole's "Course of Empire." Audubon's watercolors were at hand; a retrospective show of Inman contained 120 paintings. Masons placed the first flying buttress against Trinity Church.

Blessed with a sensitive ear and a good voice, Whitman hoped to save enough money to buy a piano and indulge his passion for music at home. Meanwhile he rejoiced in the procession of European virtuosi and native choristers, in opera by Bellini, Rossini, and Donizetti, a Beethoven symphony, and a Mozart requiem. After the debut of Ole Bull in November 1843, the press hailed this new star as higher in the heavens than Paganini. The flaxen-haired Norseman's recitals, featuring the "Carnival of Venice" and the "Psalms of David," soon included his own "Niagara" and "Solitude of the Prairies." Another celebrated violinist, Henri Vieuxtemps, also deferred to his hosts by variations on "Yankee Doodle"—after sonatas.

The limited repertoire of the Hutchinson family brought complaints at times that they might as well sing the Ten Commandments as "Excelsior," and that their nightly use of the "Old Granite State" threatened to wear it out; others wanted melody rather than the piety of "My Mother's Bible." But the ensemble of three brothers and sister Abby enthralled Whitman, who agreed that

> they are nationalizing our sentiments and making us feel that America need not look abroad for noble deeds to celebrate, or inspired bards to commend them to the popular heart. . . . We want something that is all our own, fearless, republican, out-

112

spoken and free—the musical embodiment of the American character—and the commencement of this we see in the enthusiastic
reception invariably accorded. . . .[16]

With cries of "Vive la musique" the press toasted the "great musical
caterer" Niblo for serving *La Fille du Regiment* and the momumental *Anna
Bolena,* but he sold more seats for the gymnastic Ravels and a "regular rib-
shaker," *She's Not a Miss,* with the comedian Sefton. Undaunted by the
popular taste, Palmo opened an opera house in 1844 and gave *I Puritani* and
The Barber of Seville. "The scenery is very handsum," wrote Major Jones,
"the action is good and the fiddlin is first rate; but so much singin spiles
everything."

A sound unknown in Europe began to be heard in the concert halls Whitman frequented. After the successful tour of the Virginia Minstrels, a blackface quartet, the Ethiopian Serenaders filled the Apollo. Burnt cork and
wooly wigs could not disguise the pronunciations of these Down Easters;
and like all other troupes, too often they sang "unmeaning and ungram-
matical words, purporting to be niggerish," set to music "that Negroes of
the South never heard or uttered." But the author of "A Critique on Nigger
Melodies" in the *Plebeian* acknowledged the beauty of the few "pure Negro
airs" and their value in helping lay the foundation of national music. Becoming fashionable with those who found opera "a everlastin caterwaulin,"
the Ethiopians opened their own hall. Bankrupt, Palmo went to work as an
assistant chef at a hotel.

As the author of a novel selling for six and a half cents, Whitman sym-
pathized with publishers who confessed that competition had driven prices
below costs, but as an avid reader he could choose widely and buy cheaply.
Sartor Resartus, Schiller's *Poems and Ballads,* and other imports accom-
panied the splenetic *Martin Chuzzlewit.* It seemed that Dickens had caused
irreparable damage to his popularity by calling the United States a loathsome
country, but soon *A Christmas Carol* earned forgiveness. Appleton's edition of Leigh Hunt made available "What Is Poetry?" with its affirmation
that all truths belong to the poet and that "the simplest truth is often so
simple and impressive of itself, that one of the greatest proofs of his genius
consists in leaving it to stand alone, illustrated by nothing but the light of
its own tears or smiles, its wonder, might, or playfulness."

Some churchmen, who claimed that men and women with the intellects
of dancing masters and the morals of whores made the "cheap and nasty"

113

school of Bulwer and de Kock profitable, added Eugène Sue to the proscribed index. *Arthur* was filled with rakes, courtesans, seductions, and adulteries, and in his *Mysteries of Paris* the heroine lived as a prostitute among murderers and thieves. (The Chatham hurried a version onto the stage.) But when Winchester issued a translation of *The Wandering Jew*, hostility toward the author often expressed by the wish that he commit Sue-icide turned to praise in which Whitman joined.

Those who longed for the victory of elegant letters took comfort in Verplanck's illustrated Shakespeare and the plans announced by publishers for other editions of the classics. Prescott's *Conquest of Mexico* brought justified pride to American literati, but Margaret Fuller writing for the *Tribune* refused to believe that a revolution in taste had started. She gave as evidence the history of the *Dial* "published four years in the midst of our hundred thousand liberally educated men, ten thousand professed scholars, and over one hundred colleges and universities without winning more than *three hundred subscribers*." In her opinion the public would continue to gloat over scabrous fiction and "dispose of every new thought by calling it Socialism, Transcendentalism, Germanism or Mysticism."[17]

In the summer of 1844 Whitman found himself a spectator in the midst of a debate begun when a British periodical charged American poets with servile imitation rather than original creation. Their defenders gave the customary rebuttal: men without a legendary past and presently absorbed in a powerful struggle to free humanity could not both act and write the epic at the same time. In August the *Herald*, in a series of editorials, agreed with the *Foreign Quarterly*—Poe also thought the article told "much truth"—that while Bryant, Halleck, Longfellow, and half a dozen others composed passable lines, none showed indigenous mastery. The spiritless effusions that filled the pages of Griswold's compilation by no means represented the mighty continent.

As a corrective, the *Herald* printed on its front pages the "pure, original, and really inspired" poesy of national politics. "The Coon's Lost His Tail" and other ballads of the hustings were rude but vigorous and original. Using the past, they promised a future. Through wit and bold metaphor the balladeers turned their countrymen into Homeric types:

> Adams is a turkey hen, boys,
> From his wings he shakes a quill,
> And scratches 'gainst bold Tyler. . . .

> Dan Webster is a proud cock,
> That has some Yankee game,
> But he's too much fed, boys. . . .

To hear these ballads was to know the heroic soul of the republic at last gushed forth in song.[18]

Margaret Fuller also spoke for the fruition of native talent. She ended a review in December with the sibylline utterance that Emerson's *Essays* "will lead to great and complete poems—somewhere."

9

HURRAH FOR HANGING

AS FAR BACK as Wednesday evening, 17 January 1838, the Smithtown club with Secretary Whitman for the affirmative had debated, "Ought capital punishment to be abolished?" According to his minutes, the decision went to the negative—the fate jurists with mature skill met elsewhere. Edward Livingston, who corresponded with Bentham, could not convince Louisiana legislators to beware how they sharpened the axe; New York twice rejected bills for abolishment of the penalty; and Massachusetts remained unmoved by Robert Rantoul, Jr., who in the spirit of Montesquieu argued that punishment not dictated by absolute necessity is tyranny, and that no social compact authorized the ending of life.[1] The one triumph for opponents of capital punishment came when Maine postponed each death sentence for a year, with execution then subject to review by the governor.

Since the Manhattan courts and the Tombs were his beat, the "law of revenge" seemed as immutable to Whitman as in the era of the stoning of Faithful in *Pilgrim's Progress*. But the cumulative force of those hostile to it had brought a degree of change. In Europe after the Padua graduate, Cesare Beccaria, published *On Crimes and Punishment* in 1764, Russia and Tuscany had abolished hanging. Men in England also began to feel the same enlightened impulse to ease harsh statutes, and in the first decades of the next century Sir Samuel Romily and his followers petitioned Parliament to replace Draconian severity with the code of Solon. Bentham through pamphlets and the *Westminster Review* inspired his countrymen—and Americans—to believe that it was better for a hundred guilty men to escape than for one innocent to suffer. Parliament at last struck the death penalty from scores of minor offences and prepared for further amelioration.[2]

In Pennsylvania Dr. Benjamin Rush circulated his cogent *Considerations on the Injustices and Impolity of Punishing Murder by Death*. Kentucky, Ohio, and several other states reduced the number of capital crimes, but the insight of the physician failed to achieve national acceptance for the ultimate

116

compassion. According to the *Mirror*, "While the community has grown too tender to cut off the hand, it is yet willing to break the neck; its humanity will not allow it to put out an eye, or to slit a nose, but it will, from expediency, reduce the whole man to a clod of earth."

The irrevocable severity of the death sentence hampered juries. Harriet Martineau attended a trial in which evidence was suppressed, false alibis given, and the accused murderer freed to travel west. Assured that the case was typical, she predicted that such impunity would end only with the abolishment of capital punishment.[3] Some placed the cost of freedom in New York at fifteen hundred dollars—the retainer fee for the celebrated firm of Maxwell, Price and Hoffman. Moreover, execution did not always follow a verdict of guilty. "Mitchell was convicted yesterday," announced the *Aurora*, "but will not be sentenced now—probably never." From his experience in reporting cases at City Hall, Whitman knew that judges often fixed the sentencing date far in the future, while sheriffs gave romantic penny-a-liners and sympathetic old ladies every opportunity to visit the cell of the condemned man.

Because the logic of a code based on deterrent terror implied a direct ratio between the number of spectators at the gibbet and the effect on public morality, mobs turned the scene of each hanging into a Tyburn. In 1741 thousands watched the thirty-two executions that followed the alleged Negro plot to burn Manhattan and kill its whites. Livingston testified that he witnessed hangings that had the holiday aspect of a county fair with a sinister exhibit added. Prayers were often offered that the land be cleansed of this voyeurism and its cause, but every new case seemed to surpass all others in sensationalism.[4]

A series of gruesome episodes in different parts of New York led Governor Seward to refer petitions for penal reform to a legislative committee. In April 1841 he made public the 164-page *Report in Favor of the Abolition of Capital Punishment* by the committee's chairman, O'Sullivan of the *Democratic Review*, who was serving a term in the Assembly. Whitman read the *Report* and thought it would create a sensation.

Because vigorous opposition to reform often came from clergymen who cited texts from Genesis and Leviticus, O'Sullivan turned to the precept "thundered over the world from Mount Sinai" and then to the tenderness he found through the New Testament. In the image one of his readers used years later he concluded that "the fair twin sisters," Christianity and Democracy, had been sent to walk hand in hand over the earth in the harmony

117

of a common origin and a common aim. To replace the gallows, he proposed a sentence that combined the three classic aims of punishment—retribution, deterrence, and reformation: "imprisonment for life, at labor, in solitude, and beyond the reach of executive clemency."[5]

Made timid by sneers at laws shaped to please "the mawkish sentimentalism of an affected and spurious philanthropy," Albany refused to accept the *Report*. Whitman urged the reformers to try again: "Let not those who have been active in the movement to abolish that relic of barbarism and blood, hanging, be discouraged by their late failing in the Assembly of this state. A good cause can bear being beaten twenty times, and still remain as good as ever." O'Sullivan began a series of debates with the aid of the *Tribune*, which confronted the relentless *Herald*.[6]

Two new trials that Whitman—and everyone else—followed avidly added evidence for needed change. Convicted of murder and of the cutting up, salting, and crating for shipment the remnants of his victim, John Colt spent his last earthly day in the Tombs while the entire city swarmed in the surrounding streets. All legal appeals having been refused, the sheriff had issued formal invitations to the sunset hanging. But Colt, never swerving from his plea of innocence, plunged a dirk into his own heart. After disclosure of the tragedies on the *Somers*, sympathy for reform widened as testimony from the court of inquiry at the Brooklyn Navy Yard filled columns in every paper. The *New World* issued an extra charting the ship's itinerary and describing the captain's act as "offensive to the laws of God and man."

Writers on both sides of the Atlantic committed themselves to this crusade with the same enthusiasm they had given to temperance. Manhattan bookshops carried translations of Victor Hugo's *The Last Days of the Condemned*; Longfellow in "The Ropewalk" asked the breath of Christian charity to blow the gallows-tree from the earth; the Reverend Charles Spear's essays on the "humane side" went through eleven editions within four years. Bryant became the first president of a society dedicated to ending the death penalty; the tireless O'Sullivan edited its *Anti-Draco* bulletin and brought Whittier to meetings at the Apollo, where Whitman took pride in counting the assemblage of remarkable heads.

Serving as a national rostrum, the *Democratic Review* ran Lowell's rebuff to Wordsworth for sonnets that warned lawgivers not to debase the public by sparing murderers:

> And always, 'tis the saddest sight to see
> An old man faithless in humanity.

Simms sent word from South Carolina of his willingness to help with the indictment. Whitman also vented anger on the poet who had given an entire generation a sense of nature as refuge and healer, and called him an abominable tory; the merciful Thomas Hood replaced the fallen laureate in Whitman's affection.

In 1845 Whitman sold the *Democratic Review* a "Dialogue" and "Revenge and Requital."[7] Both illuminated O'Sullivan's *Report* and the substance of many lectures and editorials: crime often results from one wicked impulse; a gross, lawless act sometimes reforms the perpetrator; evil cannot be abolished by legislated horror; certainty of prompt punishment through life imprisonment would be more effective than haphazard severity. But knowing the dark horrors of the cells at the Tombs—they made Dickens shudder—Whitman exclaimed in the "Dialogue":

> Good God! we are almost shocked at our cruelty when we argue
> for such a punishment to any man! Looking only at the criminal
> in connection with great outrages through which we know him,
> we forget that he is still a duplicate of the humanity that stays
> in us all. He may be seared in vice, but if we stand invisible by
> him in prison and look into his soul, how often during those ter-
> rible nights might we not see agony compared to which the moans
> of the slain are but a passing sigh!

Those who attempted to silence sanguinary clergy often proposed that they act as hangmen. Through the protagonist of the "Dialogue," Whitman branded the use of the Bible to justify capital punishment a prostitution so foul that he trembled in anger. When he passed a church he found himself wondering whether the walls did not at times echo, "Strangle and kill in the name of God!" In spiraling indignation, he claimed that the clasp of a minister's hand gave him a choking sensation, and that a ghastly gallows blocked the pulpit from his view.

To illustrate the reformation thesis Whitman in "Revenge and Requital" evoked the cholera plague of 1832. The escaped killer canceled his crime through martyrdom as an angel of mercy searching the noxious alleys, cellars, and garrets surrounding Chatham Street, and carrying medicine and food to the abandoned victims.

119

In their scrutiny of the prospects for American letters, some reviewers contended that the advent of a new magazine provided an index to the era, whose proliferation of learning and readers created a need for intellectual light artillery as well as heavy Peacemakers. If the *Rover* and the *Columbian* represented the first category, the *Aristidean* and the *American Review* belonged to the second.

The first issue of the *Aristidean* scored high for material that included Whitman's *Arrow-Tip*, a 17,000-word novella. The editor, Thomas Dunn English, a Philadelphia Quaker known for "Ben Bolt," had survived a brief turn on the *Aurora*. Those who never lacked an explanation for the unseating of an editor found him pompous and didactic; Poe told him to go home and try his father's job of ferryman on the Schuylkill. But English remained in New York where he supported capital punishment reform by writing "The Gallows-Goer" and printing *Arrow-Tip*.

In *Arrow-Tip* Whitman dramatized the utter finality of the "awful method." An Indian, the title character, is accused of killing a white man after a quarrel in the forest, and the lack of any trace of the body is cited as proof of the crime. But the supposed victim, whose own violent temper provoked the quarrel, has staggered to the cave of a monk who nurses him and sends a half-breed—the monk's deformed, malevolent son—to tell the truth to the settlers. Filled with jealousy for the strong, well-born Arrow-Tip the half-breed delays his errand of mercy. The executioners realize their irrevocable error when the supposed dead man arrives—"all too late."

Since *Franklin Evans* the fictionist had become more conscious of technique. "The plot of the narrative," he told his readers, "makes it preferable not to detail minutely here all the events that took place during the day." By confining the setting and limiting characters and episodes, he gained sharper definition. Resisting digressions and lectures, he created a sense of climax. In at least one passage, the hunt, he wrote an ode to the majestic frontier.

He knew many writers who had used the Indian: among them Leggett (whose tale "The Rifle" is *Arrow-Tip* with the innocent men saved in time) and Snelling, with whom he had worked on the *Tatler*. As early as 1837 George Catlin had brought to Clinton Hall his Indian Gallery of hundreds of drawings, costumes, and artifacts collected through years of research among western tribes. When the pioner anthropologist published his *North American Portfolio* in 1844, Whitman sensed the artistic, historic value of this material "so emphatically American," and joined other

120

admirers in urging the purchase of the entire Gallery as the base of a national museum that would preserve the memory of the red man, who was "melting away like the snows of spring." But only a baker's dozen responded to the graphic narrative of these vanishing aborigines. Whitman envisioned the advent of some itinerant bard or novelist as gifted as Catlin who would gather their legends and create the legitimate romance of the continent. What nobler subject than the Indian, "whose existence was freedom— whose language sonorous beauty?"[8]

The compassion he gave to Arrow-Tip and to the bereaved tribesmen may have been intensified by a recent tragedy. Under the roses, honeysuckle, and creeping ivy of Greenwood Cemetery, near the grave of MacDonald Clarke, lay the Sac princess Do Hum Me whom Whitman had seen often with fourteen of her tribe at the American Museum. The dignity of the Sac braves and the beauty of the girl had impressed him and her sudden death saddened him.

The *Mirror* found *Arrow-Tip* too long, but the editor of the *Aristidean* answered that he could not bear to cut the piece in half or omit it. The *Plebeian* agreed that here was an exceedingly well-told tale of frontier life with an appalling catastrophe.

The case of the *Somers* not yet closed, Whitman turned to a historic precedent, the Nore mutiny in Pelham's *Chronicles of Crime*, and wrote "Richard Parker's Widow" for the *Aristidean*. In this sketch Parker, the mutineer, remained as poised at the approach of death as Billy Budd. Poe called the piece admirable.[9]

From now on Whitman would continue his arguments in O'Sullivan's *Morning News* with "Revenge and Requital," and in his own papers where he reprinted *Arrow-Tip* and items by other reformers. Reading of a sentencing, he exclaimed in irony, "Hurrah for Hanging"; the rearing of the scaffold in the yard of the Tombs brought from him renewed exhortations to erase the "blood-written statute." The elation that came when Michigan in 1847 became the first state to abolish capital punishment gave way to resignation, for legislators elsewhere chose to side with editors like the inflexible Bennett who tagged the work of the compassionate men "nothing but leather and prunella—the puny efforts of empty heads and shallow brains, trying to get up a war of words." Soon the warden of the Kings County jail invited three hundred Brooklynites to witness an execution in its yard.

In later years Whitman often told the story of a shipwrecked sailor who, wandering over a strange coast, came upon a gibbet holding a corpse. "Thank God," exclaimed the castaway, "at last I am in a Christian land."

In other prose, directed by what he described as the sublimest of impulses, good will to man, he also tried to foster thoughts that would make a moralist smile. Increasingly responsive to the charismatic power of Christ, he used "the pen's prerogative to roll back the curtains of centuries," and in "Shirval: A Tale of Jerusalem" retold Luke's account of the miracle Christ performed in raising a widow's son from the dead. Willis had turned the same episode into verse and earned Lowell's scorn:

> And he ought to let scripture alone—'tis self-slaughter,
> For nobody likes inspiration—and—water.

But Noah, whom Whitman had seen reading the Pentateuch in the Crosby Street synagogue, thought "Shirval" a "touching and ingenious sketch" and reprinted it.[10]

In "Some Fact Romances" Whitman rummaged through memory and came up with a drowning near Huntington, a deaf girl helped by a Negro widow, and a macabre trip by an insane man and his dying wife. During a visit home he sat with Louisa Whitman, and over a cup of coffee learned of a frightening night she had once endured. He used this anecdote and one told at the Tombs by the forger Saunders whose escape had been foiled through time lost in redeeming his mother's keepsake.

The *Aristidean* suspended publication after the December 1845 issue, because the "bold, racy, and fearless expositor of critical judgment" failed to meet expenses. Its advocates blamed the five-dollar subscription rate or the title that was difficult to pronounce and easy to ridicule. English had chosen the motto "Men call me cruel;/ I am neither: I am just." Poe suggested, "Here the two monosyllables 'an ass' should have been appended." In its six months Whitman placed more fiction in the magazine than any other of the sixteen collaborators the editor thanked in the valedictory.

Whitman's contributions to the *American Review*, a new "Whig journal of Politics, Literature, Art and Science," led the Brooklyn *Advertiser* to call him a political apostate.[11] But Whitman in his denial could show that his name had appeared at the same time in the pages of the arch-rival *Democratic Review*. Of the three pieces he sold at two dollars a page to the

American, two represented familiar phases of his art. Knowing that the editor, George Colton, author of "Tecumseh" and a rhapsody to the blue Ontario, encouraged the use of native materials, Whitman turned to *Franklin Evans*, lifted the Indian episode, and sold it as "The Death of Wind-Foot." His reminiscence of an ethereal girl entombed early, "The Boy Lover," belonged to the domain of another contributor, Poe.

"Tear Down and Build Over," the third piece, was an essay on the preservation of St. Paul's and other antiquities. Every spring the city saw extensive razing that Whitman thought brought joy to every jolly Irishman who owned or hired a dirt cart and a horse. With unabashed emotion he said farewell to venerable structures "rough-coated on the outside, but stout and sound at heart, like the men of the former age!" The threat to St. Paul's involved personal associations, since he often visited the chapel where Washington had received communion, and the graveyard whose old elm with "blistered weather-beaten trunk" shaded the graves of two soldiers and the cenotaph Kean had placed to honor George Frederick Cooke. In April 1844, during the funeral of General Morgan Lewis of the Society of Cincinnati, he had sat in one of the side pews and counted the few survivors of Bunker Hill and the battle of Long Island. After the services he had listened to their reminiscences of that paragon of men, Washington.

Within the year Whitman concluded that the *American* lacked the noble scope of the *Democratic Review*, "for democracy is closely identified with a developed literature—and it has always been the highest pride of the best writers to advance the claims of liberal doctrines in government." However, he continued to read the Whig periodical with enough care to make marginal notes. In it he found clarification of transcendentalism ("that form of philosophy which sinks God and Nature in man"), a review of the Hindu *Institutes of Menu*, and in September 1845 an essay on "The Bhagvat Geeta and the Doctrine of Immortality," with excerpts and an explanation of the creation and transmigration of the soul.

As a magazinist Whitman had ranged from Jerusalem to London, from wigwam and hut to an alehouse on the banks of the North River, from the Manhattan of the stock jobbers of Wall Street and the wealthy residents of the Astor House and Washington Place to that of the stevedores and ships at Whitehall wharves and to the squalor of Five Points. He had memorialized Christ and Washington, mutineers and forgers. He had placed his name next to those of Poe, Hawthorne, and Longfellow. All in all he was

123

justified in calling himself "a pretty fair writer," but when he counted his earnings he was dismayed to find they totaled less than five dollars a week. "True men of letters," wrote John Bigelow in January 1845, "not unripe literary adventurers, or vain, pretentious scribblers," were too often starved into silence.[12]

As evidence Bigelow cited the Harper list, with its disproportionate number of imported titles among 1500. The four brothers, including the Nativist mayor, proud of their new steam presses, guided visitors through the great Cliff Street plant and showed them every stage of bookmaking from the casting of a single letter, through the composition, stereotyping, and folding, to the stamping of the gold imprimatur on the spine. But it seemed a rarity when a Prescott came from their bindery. No one questioned the value of an encyclopedia which diffused knowledge cheaply throughout the land, but a lover of literature could suggest support of native authors as the most honorable way of showing attachment to America. Had Dickens lived here the penny-a-liner and essayist would not have emerged into the novelist, the historian and friend of universal humanity; Grub Street would not have put on "the winged life of Parnassus." Treated coldly and deprived of confidence, Boz would have turned cotton merchant or rusted in neglect.

Nor had his four years in New York assured Whitman of an editorial career. Campaign sheets like the *Democrat* were doomed at birth to be short-lived; out of eighteen different papers issued from one building in Nassau Street in the last twelve years, only five survived. For some reason he missed the chance to work and rise in stable establishments like the *Sun* and the *Mirror*; he had never worked for the paper whose editor, associates, and policies were ideally compatible—Bryant's *Post*. "If we attempt to classify the journalists," wrote one of his contemporaries, "we should simply divide them as they do almonds and Baptists at the South, into hard-shelled and soft-shelled. The former know how to make the most of their position; the latter allow their good nature too often to run away with their interest as well as their judgment—and might as well have no pockets." Apparently Whitman was soft-shelled.[13]

Not even the memory of his first major press role remained unsullied. When he heard in January 1845 of the demise of the *Aurora*, he turned back in nostalgia to the days when "it flourished bravely among the would-be *elegantes* of the metropolis" and was read by all ball-goers. "Fatal hour, when it withdrew from this brightest circle, of which it was the cynosure,

124

and became lost in the storm and darkness of Tylerism." But the *Herald*
on 6 January used its obituary notice to warn politicians not to attempt to
manufacture public sentiment by purchasing rickety newspapers. As illus-
tration here was a little sheet which had fallen into the hands of a Mr.
Whitman "who commenced an outrageous system of blackguarding the
Catholics and the Irish, and soon ran the paper down to low-water mark,
when the emissaries of Captain Tyler, casting about for a tool within their
means of purchase, stumbled upon the *Aurora*, and the bargain was struck
at once."

The prospect of remaining in New York as a journeyman lacked en-
chantment. Its 250 printing offices in 1845 ranged from mammoth plants
with half a million invested to dens whose type and press would not bring
an auction bid of fifty dollars. A fortunate compositor could earn from nine
to fifteen dollars a week if he set his several thousand ems daily for a book
publisher or a morning paper. But three-fourths of all journeymen earned no
more than $300 to $450 a year, and their Typographical Society, because
of a restrictive clause in its 1818 charter, lacked the power to fix a uniform
scale or control the ruinous competition of the new graduate apprentices.

Whitman decided to return to Brooklyn, even though its papers, in the
view of worldly Manhattan professionals, were conducted in a sleepy fashion; he would work for Spooner's *Star*, on which he had had "his brought-
en's up." Unlike a Herrick or a Bennett, this publisher lived by the noble
creed that men are not enemies because their opinions differ. Whitman's
wages, according to an angry rival, were only five dollars a week, but he
could board with his family now back from the country—Walter Whitman,
with his son's help, had bought a lot on Prince Street and built a house. And
the chance still remained of following the advice Poe's Thomas Bob gave
Thingum Bob, whose career as a politician had thus far failed:

> The trade of editor is best:—and if you can be a poet at the same
> time,—as most of the editors are, by the by,—why, you will kill
> two birds with the one stone. To encourage you in the beginning
> of things, I will allow you a garret; pen, ink, and paper; a
> rhyming dictionary; and a copy of the "Gad-Fly." I suppose you
> would scarcely demand any more.[14]

125

10

HUMANE CORRESPONDENT

IN THE YEARS since Whitman's apprenticeship Alder Spooner and his son Edwin had built the *Star* into the ranking Brooklyn paper—"though this is not saying much," noted the New York *Atlas*. The publisher whose favorite maxim was "Be thoughtful of the coming generations and they will bless you," had space for works like Prime's *History of Long Island* and the verse inspired by Guy's period painting of the village

> With houses, horses and snow,
> As seen some thirty years ago.

He sent potential patrons to the National Academy to see Mount's "Eel Spearing at Setauket" and asked them to start a regional collection with similar canvases. He respected the new churches rising in rapid sequence but questioned why Common Council built neither hospital, public walk, or park. The *Star* fought for riparian rights and potable water, urged the widening and cleansing of the narrow, filthy route to the river, and complained that other streets were in an "offal" condition and that pigs, like editors, should stick to their pens. Hostile to capital punishment, the *Star* reprinted Whitman's "Dialogue." Reports of immorality in Washington brought the editorial opinion that more than any other place in the world, that city needed the pure influence of womanhood. No humorless prig, Spooner accepted absent-mindedness as the source of Bishop Onderdonk's suspect behavior with female members of the diocese: "The Bishop frequently does not know where to put his hands." He chided the vulgar aristocracy at an Astor House ball for stopping Whitman's friend, the musician Dodworth, from dancing with guests because he had been hired only to lead the orchestra.[1]

Married to a poetess whose *Gathered Leaves* would appear in 1848, Spooner lifted the literary taste of his subscribers. The *Star* endorsed Hudson's lectures on *Hamlet* and mourned that the Park was now a tanbark and sawdust circus where Shakespeare from his pedestal above the arch endured the antics of Billy Button, the tailor, and listened to the stale jokes of the clown. "So much for the legitimate drama. Who will write its epitaph?" This lover of Addisonian simplicity blessed the vernacular for its capacity "to express fully, and earnestly, and heartily what one thinks," and scolded literary fops who mangled the best language known since the confusion of tongues at Babel.

"Spooner's weakness," complained the Brooklyn *Eagle*, "is the presumption—nursed by long habit, into a sort of belief—that politics may be separated entirely from our city affairs." When a Whig mayoralty candidate like Francis Stryker—a journeyman carpenter earning twelve shillings a day—lacked the experience to head a city of 60,000, the *Star* withheld support. Though convinced that a conservative press guaranteed the safety of the country, when other editors berated Robert Owen and the National Reformers for a "hellish scheme" to establish joint-stock communes, Spooner defended the Grand Regulator as a humanitarian he had known for twenty years and reported the meetings in Manhattan as deliberations over grievous inequalities and the oppression of wealth. (Both Whitman and O'Sullivan were dismayed when they attended these meetings to find that many of the participants were old men, each with peculiar ideas—except the daily appeal for funds.) Admitting sympathy for the Nativists, the *Star*, unlike the *Aurora*, did not hurl insults at Catholic leaders but praised the neighbors who helped Irish laborers, and cited Scripture when a samaritan sheltered immigrants stranded at Fulton ferry: "I was a stranger and ye took me in."[2]

Though he was on leave because of a tour of duty in the surrogate's office, Spooner resumed editorship in May 1845. Rejoicing in his lucky escape from partisan strife, he vowed to serve merely as a mediator rather than to succumb again to the lures and falsehoods of "that ugly monster, Politics, about which every fool becomes wise, and every ignoramus can talk." But international and domestic issues would bar isolation or neutrality.

An indication of the beat the *Star* assigned the former apprentice came in September with the first of the columns initialed W.—a plea to spare old trees, Brooklyn's "pride and beauty," and to plant willow and chestnut in the new sections. If this were done "we shall quite rival New Haven—and in due time we are not without hopes of going ahead of that far-famed city in this kind of verdure." Then followed reflections on the Gough scandal, with W. arguing for rigid abstinence but refusing to join in calling the disappearance of the temperance orator into a brothel a drunken and unchaste frolic. He had less tolerance for militia training, a senseless farce and burlesque of soldiery. By October, with Horace Mann on his way from Massachusetts in fulfillment of his pledge to speed radical school reforms, the columnist also joined in the effort to change what he described as the seminaries where the future masses of the republic were formed.

Common Council, always his target, showed miserable petty economy by holding to the ridiculous rule of requiring each scholar to furnish books and materials. The new three-story building Whitman inspected in Middagh Street was well ventilated, but the chairs were narrow and armless; a playground ten times larger would have been fifty times better. Most of the classrooms in the other thirteen schools needed high ceilings, valves, or other devices for purifying air. Travelling through Queens and Suffolk in search of evidence, he found dilapidated structures defended by stubborn trustees who argued, "They were good enough for us." All districts suffered from the haphazard hiring of young men on vacation from college, "poor students, tolerably intelligent farmers, who have some leisure in the winter, and want to make a little money,—and so on." (He did not extend the list to itinerant journeymen.) As a possible solution he suggested the increased hiring of women: "If boys were more generally brought under the gentle potency of female polish, how few would be those awkward gawkys, those blustering ill-favored juvenile rowdies, that swarm now in every street." But when he learned that one of the women on the staff of a school in the sixth ward had whipped a child, he accused her of attempting to form a monstrosity worse than any in anatomical museums.

On 20 October Whitman went to the Tabernacle and heard the exemplar of the "sacred cause" of education denounce "the old fallacies that unfortunately are by no means yet completely routed from among us." Secretary to the Massachusetts State Board of Education since 1837, Mann had gained a national reputation through annual reports and lectures delivered, according to admirers, in epigrammatic phrases whose antitheses rose like stones and came down sparkling like meteors. ("To prepare children for resembling the philosopher, rather than the savage, it is well to begin early, but it is far more important to begin right.") Refusing to surrender to dismay after examining eight hundred systems and finding that many states spent more money for railroads than for education, he sought to elevate the character of the common school by demanding the hiring of trained teachers to staff comfortable rooms and to inspire pupils rather than intimidate them. Consulting physicians, surgeons, chemists, and phrenologists—Dr. Samuel Gridley Howe was his intimate friend and he toured with Combe—he relayed their observations on ventilation, seats, lights, and heat in the hope of replacing individual caprice with guidance by valid law. To support the thesis that no teacher could funnel knowledge into the mind of a child like fluid being poured from one vessel to another, he observed the treatment of young inmates at lunatic asylums and at the Swiss school founded by students of Pestalozzi. His *Seventh Report* praised Prussian teachers for avoiding useless "ding-dong" repetition and degrading canings.[3]

On 22 October the author of "Death in the School-Room" quoted the educator: " 'Those who expel wrong by means of physical chastisement,' said Mr. Mann, 'cast out devils, through Beelzebub, the prince of devils!' Are not some of our Brooklyn teachers a little too profuse of this satanic power?" The next week Whitman alluded to *Nickleby* when he assaulted the nearby Squeers and parents who turned Brooklyn schools and homes into penitential purgatories dismal as those of Yorkshire; he claimed that these furies of orthodoxy administered the same cure-all whether the boy "says 'damn' or breaks a glass—whether, tempted by God's beautiful sunshine and air, he plays 'hookey,' or prompted by hunger, eats the forbidden pound-cake, kept for 'company' only—whether he invents a falsehood or loses his pocket handkerchief."

Letters to the *Star* promptly charged him with sanctioning anarchy and quoted Biblical justification for the rod. Always angered when opponents turned to this tactic he deplored the consequence if every petty tyrant, every lazy pedagogue were to barricade himself behind the gospel. From what he called his own considerable teaching experience, he knew that a master's platform was no "bed of flowers," but asked once again for the "*entire* abnegation" of the whipping of "those of whom the Divine Founder of our religion said, 'Of *such* is the kingdom of Heaven.' " A Christly ministry of love rather than the hourly lash would melt hearts.

He also sought to follow Mann's admonitions to end the rote drilling of boys and girls as though they were soldiers on parade; the "monotonous *old*" must give way to the "fresh philosophical *new*." The way to impart the missing grace and elegance was to add music and kindred arts to the curriculum—and he cited as his authority a Manhattan professional who assured him that elementary pupils could be taught to sing by note. After a concert given by a chorus of eight hundred children, he exclaimed, "Indeed it was a holy sight!"

Because he believed that one of the cheerful duties of the press was to encourage all that could ameliorate the morals and conditions of the new generation this "humane correspondent"—as one of the letters to the *Star* called him—wrote a series of six *Hints to Apprentices*. He had long been irritated in the streets and on the ferry by "collections of smartly-dressed, good-looking, bright-faced young fellows—indulging in low conversation, licentious jokes, and puffing the smoke of cheap cigars in the face of every passerby." Now in the role of a William Ellery Channing whose *Self-Culture* he called an unsurpassed piece of wisdom, or of a Beecher whose *Lectures to Young Men* he quoted by the page, Whitman tried through miniature tracts to turn each loafer into an ideal mechanic of impeccable habits who would find no fault with his employer, refuse to succumb to gross desire, never dominate a group by rowdiness, never dress beyond his means, and seize every chance to develop mind, spirit, and an affectionate heart.[4] Evidently the *Hints* went unheeded and within a year he told Brooklynites in rounder language to stay away from bars and gambling hells.

The extravagance of four families out of five and the preying upon others by those who lived in unwonted style also served as a text for this lay preacher: "What a rivalry there is among us in furniture and dress!" Potential dangers loomed in his own home. Walter Whitman now in his mid-fifties was no longer hale; one brother had become a wayfarer; another remained crippled and retarded. To help Eddy, his special charge, Walt spent evenings at the exhibition of the American Institute and examined prosthetic devices. The artificial teeth seemed so beautiful, he confessed the temptation to knock out his own and replace them with Dr. Dodge's.

To his discomfort, he discovered that the thousands of items made by native workers to satisfy every taste, "from the philosopher to the humblest laborer," drew unruly crowds:

> What a silly propensity it is in people who go there, to push and squeeze as if life depended on their getting along so very quickly!
> —And, by the by, how some women *can* push! There was a pretty creature, in whose track we had the fortune to get, with

an utter impossibility of advancing or receding; and the way her elbows and bustle "gave it" to us, was quite a caution!

But his good humor returned when Niblo displayed fireworks. By closing time, pride in the skill of native craftsmen made the reporter feel taller.

In 1845 a lover of music did not depend upon amateurs or children. At the Tabernacle he heard Ole Bull play compositions inspired by Niagara, General Washington, and the Fulton ferry. "What music came from those thin fingers," he exclaimed after a performance by the pianist De Meyer. He sat among four thousand while three hundred musicians gave Haydn's *Creation*. All summer at Castle Garden with its cool promenades he attended fifty-cent "undress" operas and heard Borghese, "so perfect a union of the cantatrice and actress," and Pico, who "like a bird from a sunny clime left her voice in our souls."

But no *bel canto* troupe from Italy and France cast in *Semiramide* and *Les Huguenots* stirred him more than the Cheney family of Vermont. At Niblo's one Monday in November he listened to the four ruddy, stout-shouldered brothers and their sister sing "The Irish Mother's Lament" and "Nature's Nobleman." They seemed strangely simple and awkward, but on Wednesday he told *Star* readers that the Vermonters were the first musicians he had heard worth the aid of those who always asked for someone "to put freshness, newness, and freedom in this department of American art." Hearing their second concert confirmed his initial impressions and he went on in "Heart-Music and Art-Music" to cite the five as a "starting point from which to mould something new and true." The rustic girl so genuine in these days of humbug touched him more than the dancing-school curtsies and gloved kisses of European prima donnas; her lyrics had meaning, while the librettos of operas were "a mass of unintelligible stuff." He asked the Vermonters to continue to build a repertoire of simple songs infused with genuine American feeling, and to sing them without tinsel embellishment. By no means were they to engraft foreign airs upon domestic stock.

Because the Brooklynites had stomped and thumped throughout the evening, he scolded them: "No thorough-bred person now-a-days ever expressed appreciation with his feet. Your hands—give your hands, ladies and gentlemen, where your hearts prompt you to give anything."

On 22 November in his *Broadway Journal* Poe offered "many thanks to

131

W.W." and in the next issue printed the tribute to the Cheneys with a prefatory note:

> The author desires us to say for him, that he pretends to no scientific knowledge of music. He merely claims to appreciate so much of it (a disdained department, just now) as effects, in the language of the deacons, "the natural heart of man." It is scarcely necessary to add that we agree with our correspondent throughout.

Endorsing homely, natural entertainment rather than the "stale, second-hand, foreign method, with its flourishes, its ridiculous sentimentality, its anti-republican spirit, and its sycophantic influence, tainting the young taste of the republic," Whitman also struck at venal metropolitan critics who puffed jaded imports whose cracked voices deserved derision.

That same season another form of "true American" singing again earned his accolade. On twenty-eight successive evenings the Ethiopian Serenaders delighted Broadway audiences who found the rhythm of banjo, accordion, tambourine, and bones irresistible. Walking from the Battery to Washington Square the *Star* reporter could hum the tune Dodworth's Cornet Band had borrowed from these "sable" artists:

> New York gals have pretty faces,
> Bran new frocks trimmed with laces.

Another quartet, the Harmoneons, with a treble "higher, clearer, and sweeter than ever we heard before," pleased his self-avowedly somewhat fastidious taste by eschewing the crudities shouted by many blackface minstrels. They proved that talent could lift a "low" subject: "Nigger singing with them is a subject from obscure life in the hands of a divine painter: rags, patches and coarseness are imbued with the great genius of the artist, and there exists something really great about them."

Fortunately his program of refined enjoyments permitted variety. In November of 1845, when he heard the Sacred Music Society give Mendelssohn's *St. Paul*, he confessed the oratorio awoke within him a yearning after beauty and perfection. Leaning back in his chair he closed his eyes to avoid seeing the spasmodic beat of the conductor:

> We went with Saul on his wicked journey, but the still soft voice
> of God spoke by the way side, and a bright light shone around.

132

The heavens opened, and we saw the serene love-beaming eyes of the Atoner, and his features of immortal beauty. Then in due time the regeneration of goodness took place in the angry heart—and all was mild and calm again.

Afterwards he found it impossible to transfer to the *Star* all the emotions Mendelssohn stirred: "Who shall define the Cabalistic signets of the undying soul? Who shall sound the depths of that hidden sea, and tell its extent from a few dim and dull reverberations?" Apologetic for indulging a transcendental ecstasy that most readers would not understand, he rationalized that there were others who had similar experiences.

The lover of drama omitted the theatre from his round of refined pleasures, since he was in rare accord with the *Herald* that dramatic managers and authors were investing a trifling amount of brains. At the Chatham and the Bowery (risen from ashes the fifth time) newsboys ate peanuts in the pit and cheered stale melodrama staged with "an extra quantity of terrific combats and American flags, and traded off with a few commonplace appeals to 'patriotism' and 'freedom.'" A person of taste, Whitman concluded, became "completely nauseated with the stuff." The Park fared no better, despite pretensions to quality, for Simpson remained guilty of importing antirepublican plays and staging them with London and Liverpool castoffs.

The *Star* critic joined other nationalists and moralists who opposed the building of a theatre in Brooklyn until assured that its stage would remain clean of both the threadbare robes of foreign fashion, and of the licentiousness as rampant as in the Restoration but possessing none of the wit of that era. A letter to the paper complained of a young female dressed in gauze for what was billed as a dance, but which to country folk seemed ground and lofty tumbling: her dress "owing to its thinness and the rapidity of her movements frequently rises to a very indecent height, although much to the gratification of the spectators, if the waving of handkerchiefs, clapping of hands, and stamping of feet that follows the performance is any evidence."[5] Epes Sargent's Prologue to *Fashion*—the saving grace of the season—satirized this animus:

> Well, sir, and what say you? And why that frown?
> His eyes uprooted, he lays the paper down:—
> "Here! take," he says, "the unclean thing away!
> 'Tis tainted with a notice of a play!"

As befitted a bibliophile's employee, Whitman spent hours at Taylor's literary depot in the Astor House. Because the *Star* never afforded him the space the *Tribune* gave Margaret Fuller, he could not attempt essays like hers on Dante, Shelley, Michelet, Hegel, and Bailey's *Festus*. In random paragraphs he mentioned Parke Godwin's translation of Zschokke's *Tales*, touched by the gentlest spirit of love and liberty, and asked for publication of more titles in Wiley and Putnam's new American series that included Simms' *Views and Reviews in American Literature*.

The lyceum brought Vandenhoff who read Byron, Longfellow, and lectured on oratory. The *Star* noted his belief that an orator is made, a poet born. To hear Poe, whose "Raven" published that winter had in the metaphor of Willis embroidered him at once upon the quilt of poets, was worth a ferry ride on a February night. Some two hundred sat in the Society Library while Poe berated "dunderhead" critics and publishers, and pricked the bladders of anthologists and poetasters. Then he dropped into the melting pot the copperplate five—Bryant, Halleck, Longfellow, Sprague, and Dana. A dozen of these critiques, in the opinion of the *Mirror*, would make a readable, saleable book:

> He becomes a desk,—his beautiful head showing like a statuary embodiment of Discrimination; his accent drops like a knife through water, and his style is so much purer and clearer than the pulpit commonly gets or requires, that the effect of what he says, besides other things, pampers the ear.[6]

Thirty years later this image of Poe reappeared in Whitman's dream.

To round out an aesthetic program for *Star* readers, he sent them to their Institute to see canvases by Huntington and Durand; nor were they to miss a local engraver's version of "The Last Supper." He greeted as a "great desideratum" the first number of *The Artists of America*, for this overdue supplement to Dunlap's fragmented survey seemed to presage better days for painters and sculptors.

Two aspects of science also touched the Brooklyn newsman that season. From Fulton slip he could watch workers try to stretch a telegraph cable across the floor of the East River. And at the local lyceum he covered a series by Professor Asa Gray on the antiquity of the earth as revealed through fossils in rock strata. To soothe restive fundamentalists he cited the botanist's assurance that no conflict existed between the data of natural history and of Scriptural revelation.

The defeat in April 1845 of the Nativists and Whigs by the Democrats had firmed Spooner's plan to isolate the *Star* from local politics, but the boundary crises with Mexico and Great Britain soon prompted pleas from him for peaceful diplomacy. When the Empire Boys exploded gunpowder to honor annexation, he deplored such bravos who "tired of peace and prosperity— tired of a dull democratic life" chanted

> I wish Mr. Polk would but get up a war—
> I care not who with, nor what it is for!

Turning to their irate antagonists, the separatists, the *Star* advised the latter to leave the Texas business to cool-headed men: "Slavery is bad, and annexation is bad, but the people are not foolish or wicked enough to sacrifice all the blessings which we enjoy in Union, because of those evils!"

On behalf of the mechanics who hungered for western freeholds George Evans had started a newspaper and named it after the catch phrase of the expansionists, *Young America*. When politicians with exalted continental aspirations appropriated the same name for their own cohorts, the *Star* challenged them: "Precisely what the title assumed by a party of men who are anxious to get hold of their neighbor's lands, by a process not exactly in accordance with the teachings of old-fashioned honesty or morality, is intended to signify, we are at a loss to discover." But by July the *Morning News* boasted that Texas was sure, "and now, as the razor-strap man says, 'Who's the next customer?' Shall it be California or Canada?" O'Sullivan wrote of his supreme faith that a fearful power—"the Democratic Energy" —would perform territorial miracles. Bennett concurred: "It is our firm conviction—that, sooner or later, not only Texas, but Mexico, Canada, Oregon, and all, will be absorbed in the mighty bosom of the North American Republic. It is destiny." In Beckman Street a cook nailed a sign over a door, "The 54° 40′ Eating House"; here, according to a cynic, lovers of patriotism and pudding took their fill.[7]

Rejection by the British of the White House offer to divide the Oregon Territory at the line of 49° and Polk's subsequent insistence on the land on both sides of the Columbia filled the nation with a degree of Anglophobia unknown since the McCleod affair a decade ago. Reading the December *Democratic Review*, Whitman became angered by a "loud-mouthed bully" and retorted with "Some calm hints on an important contingency." He too believed in a glorious future for the republic, but no outrage cried now, as in '76 and '12, for vengeance on despoilers of the land or its liberty. Rather

135

than gain national fame through "cannon fire and dead men," we could turn our face aside and almost say, " 'let us never be a great nation! Our policy is peace.' " Everyone chilled at the thought of a scalpel probing a child's club foot or a woman's tumor, yet "we can deliberately and even eagerly advise the prosecution of steps which will result in horrors compared to which those of the surgeon's table are as a key-hole draft of air, to the hurricane in its hottest fury."[8]

Admiration for Queen Victoria strengthened his pacifism. This inheritor of faith in equal rights continued to hope for the end of all monarchy, but he sensed the improbability of major change in the British government. Meanwhile he asked men who hated tyranny to pray for amelioration by degree, in order that this young and amiable queen escape doom.

A calamity to a colleague rather than the course of the cisatlantic political contest changed Whitman's fortunes. One day that winter he ferried to Broadway to see the "things of beauty" at Plumbe's daguerreotype gallery, and then the engravings and embellished volumes at Colman's Emporium. Coming home late, he learned that William Marsh, the thirty-three-year-old editor of the Brooklyn *Eagle*, lay ill of liver congestion. Marsh's friends talked of a rally but by Wednesday, 25 February 1846, his name had disappeared from the masthead and on Sunday mourners filled the Universalist church where the Reverend Mr. Thayer wept as he eulogized this model young man. The choir ended the services with

> I would not live always; I ask not to stay,
> Where storm after storm rises dark o'er my way.

Braving the harsh wind a large cortege that included Walt Whitman, the new editor of the *Eagle*, followed the hearse to Greenwood. On 3 March he published in that paper a personal plea for aid to the bereaved family.[9]

PART TWO

The true poem—epic, didactic or lyric—is the daily paper. The true poet—*poietes*, is the daily Editor.

New York *Daily Times*
22 April 1852

They've such a passion for Liberty, that they can't help taking liberties with her.

Charles Dickens
Martin Chuzzlewit

11

DAILY COMMUNION: THE *EAGLE*

AT THE WHITE HOUSE one Friday evening in February 1846, President Polk was escorted from his office by Secretary of the Navy Bancroft to the parlor below to watch a sleight-of-hand artist. The forty or fifty ladies and gentlemen present enjoyed Herr Alexander, but the president found little edification and, as he explained in his *Diary*, rued the time lost: "I, however, was thinking more about the Oregon and other public questions which bear on my mind than the tricks of the juggler, and perhaps on that account the majority of the company might think my opinions entitled to little weight." These public questions also perturbed the new editor in Brooklyn who had helped elect Young Hickory.[1]

The *Eagle and Kings County Democrat* started in October 1841 by Isaac Van Anden had prospered through patronage; larger quarters in the slate-colored building at 30 Fulton Street would be ready by May and a Napier press was on order. Marsh, who had learned his trade from Greeley and Bryant, reflected these dignified mentors while holding over the years to the pledge in his first editorial to devote the *Eagle* to the sacred preservation of all the fine old landmarks of the Jeffersonian school and to be "vigilantly zealous for equal rights both great and small, particular and general." Though opposed to legislated monopolies and special privilege, he withheld —to the dismay of some ultras—doctrinaire support for what he called political fanaticism and crude, impracticable theories.

In the last months of his life, Marsh stood accused by the *Subterranean* of serving Hunker "*Dim-Ocracy*," and by the *Morning News* of editing a conservative organ that was the mouthpiece of Senator Lott who was said to be scheming in Albany to effect an alliance of Whigs, Nativists, and anti-renters to defeat the "Radical Democracy."[2] Marsh retorted that Lott never contributed a cent to the *Eagle*, and dismissed the name-callers as demagogues ambitious for pap. This type of internecine warfare among the Democrats had intensified with charges that the state's financial resources were

139

being exhausted upon utopian schemes for internal improvements. Too many politicians at the state capital, in the view of the *News*, remained "the immemorial friends of all the old abuses, errors, corruptions—the banks, charters, monopolies and special privileges—the wasteful public works, expenditures and debts." As the rift widened over Governor Bouck's purported abuse of patronage and his program of canals and roads, each side identified the other by pejorative epithets.[2]

Those angered by the passage of "stop and tax" legislation that curbed construction stigmatized their intraparty rivals as "Barnburners" who were willing to burn the entire party structure to rid it of a few rats. In turn the Barnburners called their antagonists "Hunkers"—who, as Senator John A. Dix defined them, kept to their homes or "hunks" and as a result never knew what was going on in the world.

While Whitman, through his *Democrat* in 1844, helped replace Bouck with Wright and boost the national ticket into office, the Hunkers kept control of Albany for another year; then after losing power in the state, they joined the dissidents in New York City and successfully pursued federal patronage. Polk named Marcy secretary of war and appointed a Hunker banker to the rich collectorship of the port; the Hunker bloc also retrieved a vacant seat in the Senate for Daniel S. Dickinson who was anathema to all Barnburners and to many outside the party who knew him as "a cleverish sort of buffoon in a bar-room law suit."[3]

When Polk who was sensitive to the charges of favoritism made conciliatory overtures, the Barnburners spurned them; the one assignment Whitman applauded was Hawthorne's to the Salem port. The president also endured a span when the Hunkers showed him their resentment. By 1846 the entire nation knew of the discord in the state's Democratic party; but as elections neared conciliators tried to minimize the strife, resorting to a purification metaphor of a floating scum forced naturally to the surface by the constant motion of the great body of Democracy. The image proved inadequate to dispel the truth that the Hunkers continued to refuse to abide by decisions made in caucuses; furthermore the burgeoning slavery issue threatened to destroy the few remnants of harmony, the Hunkers preferring silence to debate.

Rather than continue the verbal exchange from a dead man's desk, Whitman refused to speak for faction or clique. He suppressed—for a while—his loathing of "Scripture Dick" Dickinson, he never mentioned the influence of Senator Lott, he denounced O'Sullivan for lacking Leggett's sincerity, and he identified himself neither as Hunker or Barnburner but as a Democratic Republican—an heir to the Jefferson who knew the rights of the people. He belonged to a class "who wished to deal liberally with humanity, to treat it in confidence, and give it a chance of expanding, through the measured freedom of its own nature and impulses." By his standards Whigs continued to regard men as things to be governed, for they followed the formulas compounded by Hamilton and the elder Adams and applied to the Alien and Sedition laws and a vexatious fiscal policy. As editor he would echo choruses of the campaign song:

> The Mechanic and the Farmer
> Both have buckled on their armor. . .
> Against Bank machination
> And high-tariff taxation.

Biddle lay buried in St. Peter's graveyard and his Bank served as a subject of musing for passersby like Dickens who in *American Notes* wrote of it as the tomb of many fortunes and the catacomb of investment. But the evil of financial oligarchy continued to serve as a text for political sermons. The first weeks of his editorship gave Whitman the chance to iterate the gospel he had heard from Locofoco economists in the depressed years of his youth. Not even the paragon Leggett had called more stridently for a ban on shin-plasters, the small notes bought by some employers at a discount from unsound banks and then foisted upon the workingman, who often found them as worthless as the paper of an embezzler. The way to end this gross breach of contract, tantamount to robbery, was to insist upon payment in cash and to support Polk's revival of the Whig-repealed Independent Treasury, "the noblest and most Democratic reform of the age," designed to divorce state from bank and to end political interference by financiers. The resulting legislation, in the judgment of the *Eagle*, did not follow fully the Jeffersonian ideal that all government agencies receive and pay only in gold and silver, since Secretary Walker, aware of accusations that he was trying to create a monster with an iron chest, had provided for the continuance of payment in treasury notes as well as in specie.

Guided by the inevitable motto from Leggett, "we are for free trade," Whitman approved Walker's plan to replace the "exorbitant and most abominable tariff of '42" with one based on uniform ad valorem percentages designed for revenue rather than for protection. Because the secretary's search for data on the excesses of the Whig "black" tariff had disclosed that

141

some of its duties totaled over two hundred per cent, the *Eagle* called the protests of Massachusetts cotton lords and their satellites ludicrous and their protective doctrine as great a humbug as Millerism. He was not privy, of course, to the entry Polk made in his *Diary* describing the tremendous lobbying efforts by coal and iron masters, who "swarmed" over Washington badgering senators and Vice President Dallas; but while the bill hung in the balance the editor remained constant in his advocacy and marshalled allies on both sides of the Atlantic: Cobden, Hume, Boz (another show of the novelist's "generous sympathy for humanity"), Leggett, Bryant, and "that staunch free trader," David Wilmot, soon to be identified with a more momentous cause.

In 1844 no other man in the party had contributed more to the defeat of Van Buren at Baltimore than Walker, but now Whitman hailed the Mississippian (transplanted from Pennsylvania) as a true liberal to whom Democrats owed a debt of honor for untiring devotion to progress. His opposite, Webster, took shape in Fulton Street as "the real representative of the conservatism of the Past—a man of High Tariffs, Banks, and a stiff-handed government," whose speeches were "egotistical silliness," whose private character was "miserably bad." Before long the *Star* scolded the *Eagle* for "Mr. Tyro's vulgarism and low imputations" in gossiping about Webster's alleged assault upon the pretty wife of a clerk.[5]

When Congress aided by the votes of a senator intercepted at the depot where he waited to take the train back to Illinois, and by Dallas who defied his own Pennsylvania industrialists, passed the Walker tariff the *Eagle* exulted. Then a careful reading of Schedule C with its thirty per cent duties on metals, wool, leather, and paper led Whitman to admit that he had hoped for more liberal reductions and he pledged to work for them. For the remainder of his editorship, while attributing the country's increased prosperity to the new law, he continued to call for free trade that would allow the energies and workmanship of the American people to expand boundlessly.

Through the winter and into the spring of 1846 the clamor for "All of Oregon," the platform slogan of the Democrats at Baltimore which had been repeated by Polk in his inaugural address, resounded from Congress as the Administration proposed to terminate the treaty of joint occupancy that had been a frontier fact for years. Senator Cass, spokesman for the Northwest, proclaimed in his voice known for its apoplectic tone that the American claim was as patent as that to Bunker Hill and New Orleans. In Brooklyn Whitman stopped work to watch the Eagle Guards of Engine Company 4—"stout handsome young fellows"—march past his window on their way to target practice with the precision of well-drilled soldiers; exchange papers from London told of the sailing of men-of-war and the building of a fort at the mouth of the Columbia. But the editor certain of the future greatness of America saw no need to shed blood for a few million acres that involved neither national power nor honor in any degree worth serious attention.

Reading Washington dispatches, he thought Polk gained stature through cool nerve and the willingness to be the man of the entire country, not just a portion of it. Calhoun's conciliatory speech to a crowded Senate on 16 March, motivated in part by the need to save a key market for southern cotton, led Whitman once again to rank this advocate of "wise and masterly inactivity" as a great statesman; later that week after a second reading he expanded the salute to a warrior "whose ponderous hand lifts up the clearest, most useful principles of political truth, and rallies in their belief a support of intellect and heart-eloquence surpassed by hardly any man living."

On 30 March Cass spoke against concession: "And if war come, be it so." In rebuttal Benton, according to the increasingly apprehensive editor, joined Calhoun and spoke for peace, compromise, and the 49th parallel. The *Mirror* on behalf of literati, agreed that "All of Oregon" had the large sound of mountains, rivers, and deep harbors; but territory mattered less to the integrity and greatness of America than an international copyright that would bless all and ruin none.

The ebb and flow of oratory led Polk to a rare display of wit at the expense of senators more concerned about the next election than about settling the Oregon situation either at 49° or at 54° 40′: He quipped that 'Forty-eight' has been with them the great question, and hence the divisions in the Democratic party." On 23 April Congress voted to give Britain notice of termination of the United States adherence to the treaty of joint occupancy, but two days later an episode on the southern border dramatized the need to avoid hostility on two fronts. After Mexican troops crossed the disputed Rio Grande and fought American dragoons near the town of Matamoros, the fate of Captain Thornton's men became prime news. By mid-June the Senate had voted approval for the Oregon compromise negotiated between

Secretary Buchanan and Lord Aberdeen. Abandoning title to what he called a few miles of pine swamp, the foreign minister accepted the 49° line and recognized American rights to the Columbia, in return for free navigation on the river for the Hudson's Bay Company until 1859. Whitman promptly unfurled a new flag at Fulton Street to honor ratification of the treaty. In the meantime another candidate for "Forty-eight," General Zachary Taylor, had begun to outdistance all those in Washington.

On Sunday, 10 May 1846, the editor attended services in the new Episcopal church in south Brooklyn and found the brownstone façade and the plain oak pews beautiful. He complimented the congregation for resisting the "showy" fashion of Renwick's Grace Church, whose Gothic vaults, polished white marble, carved tracery, and sybaritic upholstery made him question how one could "*worship* God there." Back in his office he pondered the skirmish on the Rio Grande and composed Monday's editorial, "Shall we fight it out?" and answered with a resounding yes. "Let our arms now be carried with a spirit which shall teach the world that, while we are not forward for a quarrel, America knows how to crush, as well as how to expand."

President Polk also had an interlude at church and then completed drafting the war declaration for presentation on Monday, with the plea "to vindicate with decision the honor, the rights, and the interests of our country." When Congress in two days approved it, Whitman was swept up in the excitement that made the slack time between dispatches from New Orleans intolerable. "It is like the appearance of a great actor, half the week; all the off nights are heavy, and the players mouth it to empty benches." In the thrill of General Taylor's first victories at Palo Alto and Resaca de la Palma, he chided Brooklynites for failing to mount a celebration equal to the one across the river where some fifty thousand exulted in City Hall park. Young townsmen were told to emulate some of the most respectable people and volunteer for service. The Navy Yard, always one of his favorite rambles, added to its attraction the lure of the *Preble* and other sloops of war being fitted for action.

At first he spoke as a patriot who turned from peace because of the need to avoid national disgrace by quelling Mexican insolence—Paredes was "full of spite," Santa Anna "a bloody monster, and cowardly as he is bloody." He sought revenge for the massacre a decade ago of Captain Fannin's rangers at Goliad and retold their history in the *Eagle*. As the roster of American victories swelled he began to wonder if "annexation of Mexico might be

144

good." But when General Taylor's column marched deeper south Whitman showed a measure of restraint and became apprehensive over the price of conquering enemy soil; the *Eagle* now asked Washington "to reserve the very first proposition for peace." Then Monterey and other Mexican place names in the dispatches revived his editorial exultation and brought a prophecy that a Republic of the Rio Grande would be the stepping stone to a new cluster of stars for the Spangled Banner. General Taylor began to assume the stature of that earlier fashioner of a nation, Washington.

Through the early stages of the campaign the *Eagle* called the antiwar Whigs demagogues who disguised selfishness under the mantle of preachers of peace. Greeley, admirable in so many ways that Whitman prayed for his conversion to the Democratic party, earned censure for pro-Mexican sympathies. But by the start of the new year Whitman's paper indicated that the time had come for all citizens to speak candidly and end the war. Offended honor had been avenged, the enemy punished enough. From now on the *Eagle* supported vigorous prosecution of the war for only one reason, the "obstinate refusal" of the Mexican government to negotiate a proper peace. Whitman honored each new conquest with superlatives and invited other patriots to gather in Fulton Street under his window to cheer the "brilliant and manly" General Scott who was retracing the route of Cortez through Vera Cruz, Contreras, Churubusco, Molina del Rey, and Chapultepec. But in the aftermath of each victorious dispatch he searched for auguries of peace and waited hopefully as Polk's plenipotentiary, Nicholas P. Trist, beset by command squabbles and other obstacles, took the slow and tortuous path toward armistice. Long before it came Whitman joined with those men pledged to oppose the exploitation of the new-won empire. Rather than join the train of conquering generals, he followed the civilian member of Congress from Pennsylvania, David Wilmot.

The editor faced his test at the polls in the local elections of mid-April 1846, confident that the string of victories throughout the nation would extend to Kings County. Thus far he had supported Young Hickory and avoided seconding any duels between Hunker and Barnburner. None— with the exception of "Gowanus," the correspondent of *Young America*[6]— could find fault with his civic program for parks, better and cheaper ferry service, and cleaner streets ("the only things stirring in Brooklyn today is dust—dust—dust"). He had guided local mechanics, laborers, and trades-men to honor Secretary Walker's pending fiscal legislation, and assured them of his faith in a Jeffersonian concept of government that protected weak minorities from the impositions of a strong majority. Before the bal-loting for the mayoralty and other offices he filled the *Eagle* with traditional imperatives: "Go immediately! Now's the day and now's the hour!" Then he waited for the official count to confirm his predictions of victory.

To his chagrin the Whigs elected their man to the mayor's office by a majority of over 1200 votes. Conceding that the opposition " 'chawed' us up pretty handsomely," Whitman ferried to New York where he found that the Democrats had routed the Whigs and the Nativists. Pained by the con-clusion that he had failed in a major editorial function, he thought of escap-ing to Connecticut. He returned instead to a sober analysis of the defeat, concluded it was caused by petty family feuds, and asked ruefully, "Is our great and holy cause—including the most sublime reforms, and the greatest truths connected with human freedom—to be trailed in the dust?"

His spirits revived when a special election at the end of the month sent three delegates he favored to a constitutional convention at Albany. "Will any body deny now," he crowed, "that Kings county is democratic." He attended the fifty-eighth anniversary festival of Tammany and had a fine time for a while. However he later pierced the surface of the social ameni-ties and saw that the factions were beyond reconciliation, with the Hunkers now seeking reprisals for the decision of the Albany convention to forbid an increase in debt without a referendum.

Throughout the summer the editor told his readers that he would hold fast to his "prodigious fancy" for keeping the *Eagle* aloof from this ruinous struggle, but a national issue debated just before the summer adjournment of the Twenty-ninth Congress demanded commitment. On 7 August he sided with the legislators who had risen in the House to oppose the ex-tension of slavery to Oregon:

> Though our cool and sensible men at the North look with infinite
> contempt at the fanaticism of sundry Northern "abolitionists,"
> there is no denying the pernicious evil of strengthening an institu-
> tion which Washington and Jefferson condemned, and expressed
> the most ardent desire to meliorate. —If the "abolitionists," and
> their foolish encouragers, would only hold their tongues, and let
> the slow but sure and steady spread of political and moral truth,

do its work among the people, all that ought to be done in reference to slavery, *would* be done; which, by the way, does *not* in-
volve a sudden abrogation of it. *That* would be a great curse to
the country, instead of a blessing.

Late that evening David Wilmot, the new representative from Bradford
County in Pennsylvania, took the floor and began to speak in the full, rich
voice that was his hallmark. In less than ten minutes he offered an amendment concerning the southwest similar to the one for Oregon: except as
punishment for a criminal act, "neither slavery nor involuntary servitude"
should ever exist in any part of the territory to be taken from Mexico. Polk
promptly branded the proposed legislation mischievous and foolish, but Whitman boasted later that he was the first editor to endorse the Wilmot Proviso.
Mandatory adjournment on 10 August prevented a vote.

When the advocates of the Proviso resumed what was to be a long, fruitless struggle to secure passage, Whitman again clarified the position of the
Eagle which favored the exclusion of slavery from new states rather than its
destruction in the old. His predecessor Marsh had condemned both the "dangerous fanatical insanity" of abolitionism and the other extreme, but had
printed Longfellow's moving summons to the skeletons in sunken slave ships
to serve as witnesses to sanctioned murder. Whitman also called the slave
traffic the most abominable of all schemes for making money; but when a
Syracuse paper denounced the Southerners who voted against restriction of
slavery in Oregon he counseled Northerners to remember "that our fellow
citizens at the South by nature and education view things differently from
what we view them. Let them endure their notions as far as they wish, and
can constitutionally do so—and let us do the same. Have we any fear but
that right will eventually triumph?"

This tone of patient, confident tolerance would soon turn harsh as he
joined other spokesmen who feared the fate of the impoverished mechanic
and farmer doomed to compete in lands monopolized by slave owners with
their chattels. Parke Godwin, congressional candidate of the National Reform Association, had placed free soil high on a platform years before the
Proviso. George Evans, editor of the revived *Workingman's Advocate and
Young America*, cited Leggett as a "free land man" and directed broad-
sides toward saving western territory for squatters rather than slaves. If King
Cotton, that selfish monarch, pre-empted the fertile acres of the new public
domain the dream of relocating families from Five Points and other eastern

147

THE HISTORIC WHITMAN

slums and rock farms would fade. Whitman agreed that white emancipa-tion had priority over black.

To his dismay as secretary to the Democratic party of Kings County, Whitman began to hear rumors that enemies schemed to unseat Governor Wright who had not enjoyed the same success in Albany as in Washington. The Rensselaer anti-renters whose violence Wright suppressed with troops after they had fired on sheriffs called him King Silas who jailed martyrs to patroonery and feudal land tenure; moreover, the recommendations of his committee to ease the long controversy did not earn him many upstate votes. He held aloof from patronage squabbles, yet intensified the hostility of the Hunkers by vetoing their canal and bank legislation. To Whitman how-ever he remained a hero deserving a second term. When Tammany finally instructed its delegates to vote for Wright, the *Eagle* applauded, though even a tyro could sense the bitterness of the opposition. As a conciliatory gesture Whitman printed a Leggett essay that defined the sole legitimate object of politics as the happiness of communities.

Auguries of catastrophe began to appear when the party lost Pennsylvania and Ohio. Worried about the outcome of the clash between the "liberal democratic principles on one side" and the "conservative hold-back, or rather go-back, whig principles on the other," Whitman surveyed the nation and found assurance that "the Great West—that lap of the future powers of the republic" remained Democratic. But as November 1846 neared, a sense of crisis entered *Eagle* editorials which entreated dissidents to close ranks and march united to the polls. "Don't flunk!" he exclaimed. "With energy, vigilance and activity, victory is certain." (A shrewder politician, Marcy, believed that "Things will not get right till we are whipped—but when and under what circumstances the whipping shall take place is a question of grave importance.")[7]

Weather rather than riots or pipelaying frauds marred election day, "one of the wettest, sloppiest, drizzliest." The count stunned faithful party men. The *Herald* aptly wrote of a rain of hostile votes that quenched locofoco matches and turned the governor out of Albany. Whitman sought comfort in the oyster house of his friend, Dominick Colgan, at 196 Fulton Street where he found a warm fire and savored "something nice." In this time of loss he clung to a slender statistical straw: unlike the rest of the state, Kings had given Wright a larger majority than in 1844.

Lifting his vision beyond the darkened political horizon Whitman prophesied the perpetuity of democracy and its dominance, certain as in the time of Jefferson, over all foes of equal rights:

> We think so from two simple facts. One is that the great body of workingmen are more enlightened and more powerful than they were. . . . The other is, that there is a mighty and resistless energy through the length and breadth of the nation, for going onward to the very verge with our experiment of popular freedom.[8]

Polk hastened to express regret at the defeat of the statesman whose career personified integrity and principled loyalty. Condemning the Hunker officeholders for their bad faith, he vowed that this faction "shall hereafter receive no favors at my hands if I know it." The Democrat who had shared a platform with Whitman in 1841, Tilden, began to work on a biography of the unseated leader.

Longer than de Tocqueville or von Raumer (the German historian whose *America* he read twice),[9] Whitman pondered the character of the press. Why in a country "newspaper-ruled" were there few—almost no—perfect specimens? Why the lack of "high-toned gentlemanliness" or elegance or politeness? Why the lack of depth, force, power, and solidity? Why, he asked out of experience that now encompassed fifteen years, were editors flippant, superficial, vague, and verbose? When one of "lofty faith and stern virtue"—Leggett—had arisen, why had the community rewarded him with hostility and contempt, rather than with the honor due a fearless patriot, a Christian who was "filled with a strong sense of the responsibilities of human existence"?

For answers he cited opinions gathered in talk with exceptional professionals—Greeley, Bryant, Godwin, Bigelow: Because American society required no more, more had not been done. Considered a mere agent for transient pleasure, the press aspired to no higher function. "It has failed to perceive its real nature; it has failed in asserting its claims; it has failed in discharging its duties as an instructor; it has failed in becoming the moral power of tremendous force of which it is capable." A true editor required a union of rare qualities: general knowledge, a fluent style whose attributes like those of impromptu political oratory were sincerity and truth rather than polish or elaborate finish, a temper beyond that of Job (who never suffered pied type or press stoppage), the endurance to handle six tasks at once, and a sharp eye to discriminate "the good from the immense mass of unreal stuff floating on all sides of him—and always bearing the counterfeit present-ment of the real."

Undismayed by these formidable specifications, the editor vowed the *Eagle* would not be printed for the mere sake of nine pence. Whatever its drawbacks, he would place the paper in many homes and exert a potent influence for "much good." An admirer of the Reverend Mr. Thayer's sermon on a text from Second Corinthians, "Behold, now is the accepted time! Now is the day of salvation," Whitman revealed himself day after day in a manner that assured his acceptance by the community and praise from his colleagues across the river. Indeed, Concord would have welcomed the man who, unswerving in his faith in human goodness and progress, hung a transcendental aeolian harp in the Fulton Street window.

On a spring-like day after weeks of ice and gale he rushed to the South Street docks to help greet overdue packets long believed sunk by a north-easter. His "beautiful favorite," the *Roscius*, was now a battered hulk, but others had fared better thanks to Him who rules the storm. The waterfront always alluring teemed with stevedores, cartmen, and immigrants; "spite of Nativism," he welcomed "a robust set of Hibernians." At Fort Hamilton he said farewell to friends in the regiment outward bound for war service in California; they planned to settle there. He stood by during the launch-ing of the *Washington* and noted proudly that she had five kelsons of solid oak.

Brooklyn, he reminded subscribers, is shaped like a gigantic heart, and he hoped the resemblance would always be borne out. Touched by the orphans at the county home he took them in a coach called Excelsior for an afternoon at Greenwood. For one who wept easily over the sorrows of youth, there was cause for tears at the Blind Asylum, though one of the girls sang "In God Is My Help" for the visitor. He grieved over the suicide of a young man, a briefless lawyer, and wondered what motivated another deed of darkness—the throwing of a stone through the window of the chapel of Holy Trinity. In the heat of summer he scolded carters who drove their horses until they panted and reeked with sweat. The coming of winter meant misery for the impoverished and the jobless; he extended pleas for charity to them and to stricken Ireland.

In the judgment of the erstwhile humane correspondent no more than half the children in the county attended school. Hours spent visiting class-rooms—"we have never before seen so many beautiful little children"—led to renewed demands for banning the rod, improving curriculum, staff, buildings, and beginning free evening instruction. The trustees ought to stock the libraries with Harper's *New Miscellany*; among its many titles was one on a "new rich theme," Mrs. Farnham's *Life in Prairie Land*.

Violent crimes by drunkards led him to reprint *Franklin Evans* but he chided the "intemperance of temperance" when the Fall River railroad banned shipments of liquor or when legislators restricted local vendors: "In awakening great moral reforms, we have very little faith in statutes." He offered zealots a bit of levity:

> Why is it that on Emma's cheek
> The lily blooms and not the rose?
> Because the rose has gone to seek
> A place upon her husband's nose.

The carpenter's son and long-time journeyman followed the struggle of mechanics and artisans to raise wages and reduce hours. After the striking tailors of Cincinnati were jailed he asked, "How happens it that when em-ployers *unite* together as they frequently do, to settle the prices they will pay, nobody ever thinks of arresting them for conspiracy?" He encouraged dock workers who sought to lift their pittance of 64½ cents a day to 87 cents to stand against their "grinding bosses," and with heavy irony congratulated the owners of the white lead factory, notorious as the place where almost certain death came to old hands, for their frugality in lowering wages by 12½ cents a day: "We hope that the country may now be considered safe." He joined Manhattan papers in exposing the desperation of girls who could not earn a decent living with a long week of sewing umbrellas, parasols, and vests. "No wonder that pest houses and brothels are increasing."[10]

With Secretary Bancroft and the author of the forthcoming *White-Jacket* he sought to stop the flogging of seamen. An admirer of Dorothea Dix and Elizabeth Fry he joined these philanthropists in the heroic attempt to im-prove prisons and mental institutions like the one where his brother Jesse had been committed after supposedly suffering a head injury in a fall from a mast. He appealed to wardens and keepers to abandon their regimen of terror and filth and to lean on the great strength of Christ's mild precepts: "We call upon those who have any faith in human goodness—any abhorrence of brutal cruelty—any honor for Him who, amid the agonies of the Crucifixion, turned His dying sight upon a felon, with words of promise."

Whitman's religiosity pervaded the *Eagle*, for the image of a benign Christ, codifier of "a law of love and forbearance and charity," led him through all crusades. No single sect or ritual dominated his faith. This erstwhile arch-enemy of the priests who agitated for parochial schools rejoiced at news from Boston that Unitarians had tolled their bells to honor the funeral of a Catholic bishop. The ecumenical gesture seemed like an oasis in the midst of sectarian wilderness. Amidst the pomp of the consecration of a turreted chapel, his memory turned to Greenport, where surrounded by great trees stood a simple church "which a property speculator would not own, as an investment, if he had to pay taxes on it." Sundays he sat among different congregations and waited during this "holy siesta" for the mystic ecstasy that came one June day at the Presbyterian church when the Reverend Mr. Spear, a pale, thin man, turned to Matthew's account of Christ's words at Gethsemane: "My soul is exceedingly sorrowful, even unto death: tarry ye here, and watch with me." That Monday the editor published his tribute to one of the most eloquent discourses he had ever heard—a judgment he repeated three years later. Dr. Mason came from New York to the Episcopal church and made a morning memorable with a sermon on immortality. Starting with Job's "But there is a spirit in man," he went on to excoriate the "absurd" materialism of the era and "to make *palpable* the nature of the soul." Another visitor, Dr. Bush, taught Swedenborg's doctrine of the correspondences between the natural and spiritual worlds.

Each Monday amidst the street sounds that swirled around his office— the horn of the brewer's yeast man yelling "wide-awake, wide-awake," the piping of the chimney sweep, the cries of the oyster vendors and auctioneers, the rush of thousands on their way to the ferry and their jobs in Manhattan —the editor dispensed secular exhortations with Bagley's gold pen, the gift of a schoolmate and far better than crispy, good-for-nothing steel. He confided one morning,

> There is a curious kind of sympathy (haven't you ever thought of it before?) that arises in the mind of a newspaper conductor

with the public he serves. He gets to *love* them. Daily communion creates a sort of brotherhood and sisterhood between the two parties.

On behalf of these loved ones he petitioned Common Council to end the Egyptian darkness by using pressed sperm oil in street lamps. He called on the inspectors and the mayor to sweep the garbage-littered streets whose stench marred May mornings fresh with moist grass, the blossoms of peach, cherry, and lilac, and the green of leafing horse chestnuts. He pointed out that new residential areas wanted pavements and plantings of ailanthus. Surrounded by family illness that did not respond to therapy, he showed his lack of faith in the efficacy of doctors, drugs, and bleeding, published the Hutchinson parody on calomel, and suggested blackberry syrup as a cure for dysentery. But he allied the *Eagle* with the *Star* to obtain a hospital, a sanitary market, and a reservoir to replace the wells tainted by drainage from some six thousand cesspools.

Like Augustus Graham he sought to change the national diet and told pale clerks to rise no later than six and breakfast on brown bread baked from unrefined flour. The Indian pudding served in the farm kitchens of Suffolk was a healthier dish than the refined delicacies of the French chef at the Astor House. "Above all, don't bolt your food like the anaconda." A reader of the *Water-Cure Journal*, he insisted that everyone should put his "carcass" under water every day. If visits to Gray's Swimming Baths at the foot of Fulton Street were impractical—he enjoyed them regularly with his printer's devil, Henry Sutton, who worked the handles of the shower—one could bathe in his own room with "a couple of towels and sponge, soap and a basin of water." After Mrs. Gove lectured on physiology (she was the wife of his predecessor on the *Aurora*), Whitman told mothers how to dress babies, "if a bachelor may be allowed such a presumptuous liberty." To counter sedentary habits he suggested wrestling, leaping, and pitching quoits. A new game intrigued him; in sundown walks in open fields he watched youngsters play " 'base,' a certain kind of ball. We wish such sights were more common."

He attended some of the soirées at Tammany and the Tivoli but objected to the late hours and heavy food. Why not start at eight and end no later than midnight? He may have felt too heavy to dance gracefully, for his six-foot frame carried nearly two hundred pounds. But he violated his own precept one July night—possibly after lessons from Mr. Whale at Gothic

153

Hall—and sailed up the Hudson on the *Excelsior*. He waltzed, did polkas, quadrilles, and Virginia reels until four in the morning without ill effects. (On a later excursion the *Excelsior* sailed without him, exploded, and went to the bottom.)

There was no obvious reason for Whitman to avoid the company of women. Now in his twenty-seventh year he was worthy of a portrait by Inman or a daguerreotype by Plumbe. The medical examiner for the company that insured him for $500 reported the applicant to be healthy and a good risk. Lees of the *Advertiser* spoke in honest admiration of his rival as a "handsome, well-built fellow (no flattery)." Occasional remarks in the *Eagle* suggested that its editor agreed: "There is one young rascal in Cranberry street who insists on calling us always 'Uncle Tom,'—though heaven only knows why. Perhaps his ma once had some good looking brother, yclept Thomas, and the child saw him but a short time—and thought—resembled him—ahem!"

Not that he dwelled Narcissus-like on his own charms. Protesting the evil men inflicted, he concluded that "with all its failings, its affectation, and its fickleness—the female character is surpassingly beautiful." On the ferry he ogled the belles with those "lithe graceful shapes such as the American women only have—the delicately cut features, and the intellectual cast of head." At a clambake he toasted his townswomen unsurpassed in virtue and unequalled in beauty. He published letters sent from New Orleans by his friend, the painter Theodore A. Gould, with their injunction to "Give my best respects and choicest compliments to the Brooklyn girls, and kiss them all for me." A walk on Broadway was pleasant in part because one could see "*the ladies*."[11]

His experience may have been more intimate than chance observation. First love, he mused, is invariably a milksop affair. "Who can recollect anything about his earliest development that way, without a blush? Ah, it is only when the full strength of the passions is matured—when the inner nature of the man is all grown—that we really *love*." At a wedding he shared cake and champagne and wished that half a dozen matches would come off every night, for he was no Malthusian. But "O, hevings, the idea of an editor taking unto himself such a precious and costly treasure as a wife!" Meanwhile he continued to ponder the source of feminine attraction for men of sense and decided it was neither shiny dress, expensive shawl from Stewart's new store, or cameos, or gold wristlets or necklaces sold at

Banks' for ten years' salary. "They look beyond these. It is your character they study."

Much of his joy came from outings in the "luscious air, mellow as a full-ripe peach." For a dollar the railroad took him on a "flying pic-nic" to Greenport, where he dug clams, trolled for bluefish, and ate sumptuous chowder. To escape from "city brick and pine" at four in the afternoon, when the single-cylinder Napier had ended its run, he climbed into the East Brooklyn stage, gave six pence to the polite driver, settled back on the thick velvet cushions, and rode for two hours. Then he dismounted, walked, and returned home by eight, relaxed and sleepy.

With its swift expansion Brooklyn would soon hold a hundred thousand. Where, asked the *Eagle*, will there be "a resting spot for nature" or "lungs" for its inhabitants? Houses and stores filled the play spaces of the 1830s; gone were the elms near the Clarkes' and the magnificent horse chestnut in front of Dr. Hunt's office. In a "glance ahead" he projected an apocalyptic vision of

> hundreds of narrow streets, thickly packed with houses, and densely populated. The air is dead, and dry—in the summer, hot and offensive. The gutters are—city gutters, (we can't find any simile for *them*). You travel block after block, corner after corner —and the same dreary stretch of the *artificial phases* of humanity stares you in the face. —Plenty of children there are perhaps; but they play under the glare of the sun and in the mud or dust, or on the walk—or, which is quite as bad, they are cooped up in the houses. Your spirit, your very breath, feels suffocated with the pressing weight of the deadened aspect around you. O, then for a dash of nature's greenness—a patch of sward, a tree, a grassy knoll!

To forestall this Gehenna he joined with the *Star* in petitioning Common Council to build a park upon the Fort Greene encampment where every visit was an encounter with the Revolution and one stood literally upon the bones of history. Atlantic wind cooled the summit and on a clear day one saw six counties. Landscaping would achieve the only thing lacking: add rows of shade trees, terraced paths, and "Glorious! is the word which irresistibly falls from your lips!"

He tried to convince voters that the entire cost would be no more than

155

two or three cents for each hundred dollars of taxes, and that in return they and their children would inherit the double blessing of health and hallowed ground. But he could not overcome the opposition of dilatory politicians and "Gowanus" of *Young America* who asked landless toilers to choose between enlarging their heavy debt for a gravelled path over pale grass "that looks as though it had strayed into town and was in pound," and owning their own home and eating their bread in peace: "What is a path or two to a people pent up in city walls, amidst din, tumult, and smoke, and wasting life by dreary and excessive toil, compared to men being on their own freehold, being their own masters, as they might be, if the public lands were made free." [12]

Seeking ways to fan regional pride, Whitman printed the obituary of Samuel Mills and told of his talks with this revolutionary, who had enlisted in the summer of 1776 and who often boasted of having given a glass of cider to Washington. On the seventieth anniversary of "the saddest fight" the editor eulogized the troops whose courage put to scorn "the vaunted things of Greek and Latin story"; surely Brooklyn could do no less than reserve one spot of land as a visible token. He scolded other papers for neglecting to honor

> Evacuation day,
> When the British ran away

and described that epiphany of the entire war, the victorious commander's farewell to his soldiers.

Analyzing his own penchant for attempting to awaken patriotism, Whitman concluded that it was the inevitable counter to the gross selfishness of contemporary politics. An unabashed hagiographer, he memorialized a trinity of national saints. Washington had moved amidst elemental circumstances with serene strength and "God-like calmness." Jefferson, that searchingly philosophical mind, cut like a scimitar through "the flimsy covering of mere precedent and law." Jackson, a "massive, yet most sweet and plain character," had "entrenched himself on his deliberate understanding of right and the country's truest interests, and *there he stood*." Serving American democracy Jackson had endeared himself to freemen of the entire world. On the anniversary of the Battle of New Orleans Whitman sang the appropriate march at the breakfast table, cried "Hurrah for Hickory!" and then climbed the roof of the *Eagle* building to watch the thirty-gun salute from the Battery. The wind "whistled right sharply athwart" his nose but he steeled himself by reflecting that bullets thirty-two years ago had whistled much sharper "nigh One whose spirit now rests in Heaven!" To ensure his remembrance of the birth and death of this heroic apostle of the great cause of political reform he marked the dates on his calendar.

On Saturday, 4 July 1846, he woke early and by seven had reached the National Hotel, where he joined the Union Blues, Columbian Riflemen, Fusileer Guards, and other civilians. Marching to the "place of places," Fort Greene, citizens heard a reading of the Declaration of Independence. Then, to the tune of "The Star-Spangled Banner," Mr. Freeborn sang odes written by Walter Whitman and the Reverend Mr. Thayer. As *Eagle* readers knew, the first ode was another editorial urging preservation of this "sanctified earth." Rain shortened the program, but the patriot's celebration of the "advent of Freedom" did not end. On Tuesday he attended services at Trinity Church and then walked among St. Paul's ancient graves. At night, with 30,000 other Brooklynites, he watched fireworks.

The seasons moved on but Common Council delayed voting for the park. On the Fort Greene hill, after trudging through February snow, the editor vowed to "stick to it" and to end this insult to "that Immortal Patriot whose sacred sword flashed in battle here." The next 4 July he served as secretary to the holiday committee and wore a blue ribbon over his heart.

12

FUNNY JUDGMENTS

IN THE QUICKENED first weeks of his editorship of the *Eagle*, Whitman responded with a customary explanation (given ten years before in Smithtown debates) to the commonplace remark that America failed to encourage the fine arts: "Perhaps this is unavoidable; for in the course of our national existence—the subduing of wild territories—the prosecution of two heavy wars, and the general turmoil incident to the first fifty years in the life of an empire, we have had little time to attend to the finer and more polished enjoyments of existence." But to identify the cause was not to accept the result. Refusing to wait silently for fruits slow in ripening he acted as a cultural courier who led the "common people" of Brooklyn to seek refinement through prints, daguerreotypes, cheap casts of statuary, and music.

Inspired revelation rather than media or technique mattered to this aesthetic guide. Artistry would emerge

> in all spirited transcripts of God's works—whether in the style of etching, engraving, or what not—so long as they evince a true idea in the mind of the sketcher and are done with merit. For, if we go to the bottom of the matter, the excellence of a work of art consists principally in its capability of producing thought and pleasure in the mind.

If families hung Dick's engraving of the "Last Supper" and spent days "with the divine face and expression of the Guileless Man beaming down upon them, who could let meanness, selfishness, and passion, get such frequent mastery of reason?" (Shortly after completing the engraving, Dick, who lived in Brooklyn, became blind.) Flipping the folio leaves of Harper's *Pictorial Bible* with its 1600 engravings by J. A. Adams they would come upon Christ healing the beggar Bartimaeus.[1] Whitman ignored clerical protests that the landscapes of Paradise with naked cherubs and scantily clad

158

Adam and Eve were obscene. Secular portraits by Inman and landscapes by Doughty brought him to wish for permanent free exhibits.

Looking through daguerreotype parlors, he remembered the first plates sent from France by Gourand and Daguerre of Seine bridges, the façade of the Louvre, and the rose window of Notre Dame. It had seemed to him that the bare outlines lacked the "filling up" needed for portraiture, but in the next years technicians with new chemical compounds had refined and quickened the process; the sitter no longer donned a head vise or remained motionless in the direct rays of the sun for five to fifteen minutes. When Plumbe of Boston, the first organizer of an intercity chain of shops, opened in Brooklyn, he showed work that Whitman judged almost perfect—"*almost* we say, for that there will be some important development . . . we have no doubt. The perseverance of some Yankee artist will yet attain the power of rendering daguerreotypes indelible, and of transferring, through the camera, natural and combined colors." Meanwhile Plumbe, Brady, and Stanberry held "the mirror up (the nearest) to nature."[2]

In their parlors at last he could satisfy an abiding passion for "that masterpiece of physical perfection, the human face." At home he spent hours gazing at the miniatures in his own collection, for an "electric chain seems to vibrate, as it were, between our brain, and him or her preserved there." Time and space were annihilated as the semblance merged with reality. An oil of Frederica Bremer at the Institute had the same magnetism, but what display equaled Plumbe's where in every direction from ceiling to floor he saw President Polk, John Quincy Adams, Calhoun, Benton, the "storm king of the piano" De Meyer, Ole Bull, Robert Owen, brides, matrons— and an Indian girl? The composite effect of this "great legion of human faces—human eyes gazing silently but fixedly upon you" created an "immense Phantom concourse—speechless and motionless, but yet realities."

He had long considered music to be the cheerer of the festive scene, the lightener of life's cares. Admitting his technical ignorance—the *Star* suggested that he consult a music dictionary—he defended occasional gaffes by claiming that most audiences blindfolded could not tell the difference between a tolerable amateur and a Sivori or De Meyer; the important thing was to attend concerts faithfully. The *Eagle* carried his joy in Granger's brass band and in madrigal choristers. The Cheneys and Ethiopians singing "Alabama's Sunny Shores" prolonged his conversion from "Italian artificiality" to music "intended for the natural ear." Handel's *Elijah* seemed

159

too heavy, unrelieved by lightness and melody. But when the daughter of a neighborhood dentist sang "Parting" she "wrapped" him in "voluptuous harmony." He cautioned the manager of a popular troupe of Yankee children to avoid straining their valuable voices. By the start of the new year, though, he asked Simpson at the Park to resume English opera with Ann Bishop whose soprano reminded him of the gyrations of a bird.

No concert piece pleased him more than Félicien David's *The Desert*, first played by De Meyer and then transcribed by George Loder. When Whitman heard the symphonic ode with its Oriental melodies which programmed the progress of a caravan he sat enchanted at the Tabernacle. Within a fortnight he attended three other performances and thought the work more beautiful with every repetition. Part of *The Desert*, he explained, consisted of recitative in the manner of a chant "which demanded elocutionary as well as musical power." He vowed not to forget this "triumph of the divine art."

While treasuring his memories of Booth as Lear, Forrest as Jack Cade, Cushman as Nancy Sykes, the mentor of the Brooklyn masses balked at sending them to the theatre. As an ideal agent in the creation of a "democratical" atmosphere the drama could teach Americans to preserve their independence. Where else could one see domestic problems enacted and solved, the failings of parents revealed, the young spared grief by revelation of the toll of sin? But a pernicious combination of factors blocked realization of this potential. At the Park, Simpson used the star system to the detriment of stock players. After thirty years in New York, according to the second generation of his assailants, his taste remained as foreign as though he had just landed from an immigrant packet. Decor and costumes were those of a place on the verge of bankruptcy (though John Jacob Astor owned the building) and had turned Old Drury into Old Dreary. Its liveliest regions were the third tier, harlot territory, and the punch rooms, the scenes of drunken brawls.

Simpson could defend himself by pointing to the playbill of the premiere of Mrs. Mowatt's *Fashion* on 26 March 1845, and the reviews of that brilliant night when ladies and gentlemen filled the house—the third tier had been barred to its customary tenants and allotted to students. Poe returned to the next seven performances to watch Adam Trueman best

160

Dimple, and in two critiques named *Fashion* as clear proof of a revival of American drama. Whitman also found the play delightful.[3]

After more than half a century the theatre had a companion piece to Royall Tyler's *The Contrast*, but the next months failed to add a third. The dramatists, according to Poe, piled underplot upon underplot. Willis thought his fellows prone to step too precisely in yesterday's footprints, and as a result there was "less originality—less independence—less thought—less reference to principles—less effort to keep up with the general movement of the time—more suppineness—more bullet-headedness—more rank and arrant conventionality in the drama, than in any single thing in existence which aspires to the dignity of art." Not until dramatists burned their old plays and wrote new ones derived from principles of dramatic composition based on nature and common sense, would the theatre merit support.

Meanwhile the Richmond and the Chatham offered voluptuous tableaux and spectacles with props that seemed as lurid to Whitman as the summer sun over the deck of a ferry in midstream. The obituary of an actor from the company of the old Bowery filled him with nostalgia for a matchless Audrey, now dead; an inimitable Nurse Evans, retired; Hamblin, older and poorer; Mrs. Flynn, grown fat; Thorne and his wife, careworn. Then two imported players gave him cause to confront managers, stars, and their allies, the puff writers of Manhattan.

When the *Herald* previewed the season of 1846–1847, it reported that "illiberal and blackguard critics" of London had humiliated the touring Forrest, but New Yorkers were to shame British audiences by giving Charles Kean and his wife, Ellen Tree, a cordial reception in *Richard III*. In January after the sixteenth performance, the *Herald* described the run as a brilliant spark to a revival that could possibly give birth to a poet with more liberal feelings and more soaring exploits than Shakespeare. Ignoring its own earlier ranking of Kean as second- or third-rate, the paper cried down oyster-cellar litterateurs who ridiculed the way he tore passion to tatters.

"Ah, Kean's *Richard* again," sighed the *Morning News*, and charged a claque with forcing Edmund's son down the throats of the public. The *News* asked theatre-goers to save their patronage until the advent of American plays planned "to build a national drama by interlocking American authors and actors."[4]

When Simpson advertised a second cycle of his stars, Whitman insisted that the "true old stock" of native actors was superior to these imports, who were "fifth-rate artistic ? trash." In the entire history of the stage he found

161

few instances of greater business done on such "infinitely little capital" as Kean's. His manner, gait, and constant wrenching of eyebrows were unnatural; his nasal huskiness made a handkerchief rather than a sceptre more appropriate to his hands. Ten years ago when Ellen Tree toured America she was an elegant young woman of genius, but now the figure that Hazlitt and Park Benjamin admired had thickened until she was "*merely* the frame and thews of that time, with none of its pliant grace, its smoothness, its voluptuous swell—(merely ex-Tree, and *not* extra)." Lest he be branded an anglophobe Whitman praised a lyrical performance of Ion by young Anderson. Then he listed Americans who surpassed the Keans: Mrs. Shaw, Mrs. Vernon, Susan Cushman, Scott, Placide, and Chippendale, creator of Adam Trueman.

Manhattan papers pounced upon these "funny" judgments. "Is it possible," one asked, "that a sensible man, such as we know the editor to be on all other points, is really weak enough to write and avow such ridiculous stuff as that?" A second suggested that the best way Whitman could ensure the survival of American drama and players was by silence. Greeley, rarely cordial to the theatre since he believed it to produce evil rather than virtue, now called the *Eagle* items on Ellen Tree "by far the most unmanly as well as unjust piece of newspaper writing it has been our fortune to encounter." The *Mirror* mocked Whitman's taste and style:

> "The decline of the legitimate" has long been a favorite phrase with theatrical critics, but hereafter the elevation of the stage, the dawn of the legitimate, the progress of the theatre, and similar phrases will be in vogue. One of the most encouraging signs of the times, as the reformers say, is the appearance of a new critic in one of our evening contemporaries, whose criticisms are modelled after the classical examples in the Little Pedlington Gazette.

Lees of the *Advertiser* congratulated his rival on at last gaining proper appreciation.[5]

After hearing all charges Whitman remained unimpressed by the "tawdry glitter" of foreign fame and held firm to his "honest opinions." However "ridiculous and funny" to metropolitan critics they were his own, and "that's more than a man would get from the New York papers in a month of Sundays." He committed no libel in charging other papers with venality. Managers traded gifts, suppers, and money for praise; one veteran testified that five dollars bought a notice and ten dollars a review. Documenting his claim that five-sixths of the reviews were written before the performance, Whitman cited a column in the *Herald* that described a play "which accidentally didn't come off." The gentleman who would soon carve *New York in Slices* agreed that impartial, independent theatrical criticism was out of the question. Because he respected Greeley the beleaguered editor denied any intent to be unmannerly; the Keans were but prominent examples of "the almost unmitigated falseness to nature which the drama presents." He had used "the sharp knife and the heavy axe" to keep the theatre from failing its greatest office—"enlightening, purifying, ennobling, and making poetical, the souls of men."[6]

The *Mirror* turned from prose attacks upon the valiant to parody. With the aid of puns an anonymous versifier grafted the names of Whitman and Ellen Tree to the popular song by George P. Morris:

WHITMAN, SPARE THAT TREE!
BY A PUFF CRITIC.

> Whitman, spare that tree,
>   Touch not a single leaf!
> In youth it oystered me,
>   In age shall give me beef.
> 'Twas my forerunner's hand
>   That placed it in a puff,
> There Whitman, let it stand,
>   Or we'll not get enough.
>
> That old familiar tree,
>   Whose glory fills the cup,
> And spreads o'er land and sea,
>   And would'st thou cut it up!
> Whitman, forbear thy stroke!
>   Cut not its park-bound ties;
> Oh! spare that aged oak
>   To rain us oyster-pies. . . .[7]

Refusing to be silenced, Whitman exhorted mercenary managers to improve repertoire, casts, and make-up. Why adorn every old man with white eyebrows and a "white hairy goaty tuft depending upon his chin"? Who

163

ever saw love made the way it was on the stage? The physical Forrest storming again through Lear, Spartacus, and Metamora reconfirmed his rank; but Whitman could not tolerate the "violent jerks, swings, screwing of the nerves" of imitators. Like Poe, who expounded the "infallible principles of a Natural Art" in the *Broadway Journal,* he offered nature as the one true model for player and dramatist. Anderson was exemplary; Mrs. Mowatt, more touching than Fanny Kemble, was another ideal performer; Charlotte Cushman merged physical and mental power into the "most intense acting ever *felt* on the Park boards."

Whitman made partial amends to the Keans in November by praising their *King John* produced at the cost of $12,000 with rare "truthfulness and appropriateness."[8] Kean's Edmund was indeed regal, his elocution good. Ellen Tree was perfection as the widow-mother of a boy imprisoned by executioners. When the saddened spectator returned to his desk he quoted her poignant lines that were the essence of loss:

> Grief fills the room up of my absent child,
> Lies in his bed, walks up and down with me.

Though Whitman knew that reformation of the theatre remained distant he did not wait disconsolate in the lobby. The world beyond the Park offered inimitable spectacles, from the beauty of sleighs in heavy snow to the Chinese junk that anchored off Staten Island and set Gotham agog, or the circus parade led by a bear that danced while the band played *La Fille du Régiment.* When Simpson painted and cushioned the Park for the 1847 season the editor blessed that "old favorite" and told of his love despite all its faults. He went there to hear *Linda de Chamounix* and sat next to Major Noah. But after one act the August heat abetted by the flaming decor of the refurbished boxes drove him out.

At first the literary scope given by the *Tribune* to Margaret Fuller and by the *News* to Bigelow seemed a possibility for Whitman, but the sequence of tariff, Treasury, Oregon, Mexico, and local crises imposed priority; he rationalized that the study of life was higher than that of books. Even so he wove literary allusions through his copy. When a girl drowned he talked of *Hamlet,* saddest of plays; he ended a summary of a sermon with a tribute to "Thanatopsis." A catalogue from Harper and Brothers, examined after

164

elections and the adjournment of Congress, led him to the opinion that "he who gets no inkling of any of the new developments constantly made, through books, (and he *will* get that inkling through honestly written book-notices) lives quite in the past." There were weeks when the county politician gave way to the urbane man of letters who paused whenever he walked on Cliff Street in wonderment that James Harper sought to be mayor: "The only office we should care about would be his printing office." He blessed Appleton, Monroe, Wiley and Putnam, Scribner, and other publishers for ample offerings.

He ransacked magazines including the *Dial* for verse and prose and asked *Eagle* subscribers to read a miscellany ranging from George Herbert's "Sunday" to "Kit Carson of the West" whose author he advised to delve often into this rich, original vein. To keep pace with presses that filled Wilder's bookshop in Fulton Street and Graham's in Manhattan, he crowded three or four reviews into one issue or gave each title a mere paragraph of description with the excuse that "the skimming tact which an editor gets after some experience, enables him to take out at a dash the meaning of a book—and his paper and his readers are invariably the gainers by it." By the first of September 1846, Lees of the *Advertiser* was telling Brooklyn that his rival intended "ere long, to abandon politics, theatricals, transcendentalism, and Leggett-ism for the higher and more dignified position of Literary Reviewer." Whitman answered that it was neither compliment nor service to townsmen to assume that they lacked interest in literature; an editor who surrounded himself "by thoughts and facts evolved from masterminds, as well as imitators—*cannot lag behind.*"[9]

To widen his critical horizons he followed Poe's *Marginalia*, Fuller's *Papers*, Simms' *Views*, then went beyond the East River to Europe. D'Israeli's *Amenities of Literature*, that "standard even of our bookish times," evoked an editorial. The *Biographia Literaria* was filled with "fascinating subtleties." Goethe, seen through Parke Godwin's translation of *Warheit und Dichtung* (which included a treatise on rhymeless verse), had thrown away all affectation. Hazlitt on style led the *Eagle* to suggest: "Don't attempt to be too fine in speaking. Use good honest English, and common words for common things. If you speak breeches, shirt, or petticoats, call them by their right names. The vulgarity is in avoiding them."

The "rapt, weird" *Heroes and Hero Worship* proved to Whitman that a writer achieved little by merely inventing a new style; but when he finished reading *Past and Present*, he found Carlyle's originality "strangely

165

agreeable." Returning to the first book Whitman re-examined the Hero as poet who penetrates into the divine mystery embodied in all appearance, "from the starry sky to the grass of the field." Carlyle also questioned traditional prosody and found rhyme "that had no inward necessity to be rhymed" a melancholy business. "It ought to have told us plainly, without any jingle, what it was aiming at. I would advise all men who *can* speak their thought, not to sing it."

W. A. Jones, a Knickerbocker essayist who would become the librarian of Columbia College, rated most newspaper notices no better than advertisements for Brandreth's pills. Their authors had but two tones: eulogium or detraction. Whitman recognized this addiction to superlatives and promised to lean to a "kindly vein"—as "it is not our province to 'cut up' authors." He would admire those who left the beaten track of fulsome adulation, scorn "small potato" critics, expose false sentiment, perverted taste, and erroneous opinion: Simms, in his judgment one of the most attractive writers of the age, had filled a scene in "Caloya" with coarseness. A female poetaster's silly "Crushed Heart" belonged to a class notorious for wounded hopes, deep despair, and withered affections: "We have an aversion to stuff of such a sort. It begets a morbid and most unhappy general result on its readers—opposite, as it is, to all wholesome and manly" writing. The fops and flirts of *Jessie's Flirtation* were his "especial detestation."

The number of lines the *Eagle* gave a book bore little relationship to its value in belles-lettres. Acknowledged masters shared inches with farm manuals, treatises on the water cure, and advice for a happy life in a boarding house. Whitman remembered Rousseau for "fascinating melancholy" and called Keats one of the pleasantest of poets, yet wrote at greater length about a cookbook in order to show Louisa Whitman's taste in pickling recipes. Responding to the new lyceum subjects he sent readers to Olmsted's *Astronomy* to learn that noble science. An illustrated botany text brought a rhapsody from him: "To take up the simplest flower—to examine it, its leaves, seeds, curious formation and beautiful colors—how well may the intelligent mind be impressed thereby, with the wisdom and vastness of God!" When he first witnessed a phrenological demonstration, Orson Fowler's singular pronunciation and odd manners reminded him of a farmer growing turnips. But a reading of Spurzheim convinced him to join Bryant, Mann, and Dr. Howe in granting phrenology a position among the sciences.

He chose Chambers' *Cyclopedia* above all other volumes in Graham's ample store because out of it came the immortal music of the great chorus

166

of English poets. What holiday tour so soothing as the meadows and woods of Thomson's *Seasons* illustrated by members of the Etching Club? A sumptuous edition of Milton commanded a new reading of "the great poet of heaven and hell" though one needed Milton's "own vast abruptness, (if we may use such a term)," to appreciate a writer who, "apparently conscious of his own gigantic proportions, disdains the usual graces and tricks of poets who are read more widely, and understood more easily." He may have paused over the preface to *Paradise Lost* where Milton stated that rime was "no necessary adjunct or true ornament of poem or good verse, in longer works especially, but the invention of a barbarous age, to set off wretched matter and lame metre."

Too many female versifiers did not know that words and rhymes were only "settlers to the real gem of thought contained within them." To stress the primacy of bold and startling figures he created one: "The Poet, like the electric rod, must reach from a point nearer to the sky than all surrounding objects down to the earth, and into the dark, wet soil." Coleridge ranked high for imagery, passion without morbidity, and an "Adamic lack of artificiality." Bryant continued to be one of the best poets in the world; Longfellow, "endorsed with the special faculty of clothing thoughts in beautiful words," gave Whitman "hours of pure religious, living tranquility of soul." The *Eagle* printed Poe's fiction, mentioned "The Raven," and followed the cycle of poverty, illness, and Virginia's death: "Her funeral will take place tomorrow at 2 o'clock P.M."

Because he thought the "august scope" of Martin Farquhar Tupper's *Probabilities* required pages rather than a squib, he promised to return to this popular treatise "of God and his attributes; of the fall of man, of heaven and hell." The Oxford man's earlier *Proverbial Philosophy* (1838), admired by Gladstone and Wordsworth, had become a passion here; after lying for a while unsaleable in America it had begun a spectacular progress, matching the demand for some fifty editions in England. (Twain found a copy in the library of a riverboat, "much pencilled.") Soon an international celebrity, Tupper would tour America in 1851, dine at the White House, and spend evenings with Irving, Prescott, and Longfellow. When he returned home to write his autobiography, he quoted none of his famous hosts but rather the review in the *Eagle*.[10]

There were readers on both sides of the Atlantic who thought that Tupper's five hundred pages of moralizing made Solomon seem like the author of a brochure; W. S. Gilbert parodied the "self-enobled Author." But Whitman ranked the writer who saw "the effaced signature of God" on all creation as one of the rare men of the era. Within a decade the London *Examiner* would call the American the Wild Tupper of the West. Henry James would also find reminders in his poetry of the thousands of long, un-rhymed lines, catalogues, and iterations of *Proverbial Philosophy*:

The river-horse browsing in the jungle, the plover screaming on the moor,
The cayman basking on a mud-bank, and the walrus anchored to an iceberg,
.   .   .   .

The horrid eye of murder scowling in the dark,
The bony hand of avarice filching from the poor,
The lurid fires of lust, the idiot face of folly,
The sickening deed of cruelty, the foul, figure orgies of the drunken . . .

With the novel almost as suspect morally as the theatre—Brownson would soon say that *The Scarlet Letter* should not have appeared—the author of *Franklin Evans* condemned fiction that lacked intrinsic merit. In an extended figure he warned of a current that carried mud, stone, and reptiles rather than health-giving drops; through the sluice came the affected sentimentality of Bulwer and the verbosity of G. P. R. James. He would filter out the unnatural "high-life-below stairs" romances of Ainsworth, the coarseness of Marryat, the "dish-water senility" of Lady Blessington, the "stuff, (there is no better word), of a long string of literary quacks, tapering down to the nastiness" of de Kock. "Shall Hawthorne get a paltry seventy-five dollars for a two-volume work—shall real American genius shiver with neglect—while the public run after this foreign trash?" Unlike other jour-nalists who continued to resent their caricaturist, he chose to remember Dickens as a compassionate Boz who even now tried to topple the scaffold. An eager reading of the first number of *Dombey and Son* promised "some-thing of the real Dickens sort—the Nickleby and Twist style," but only Little Paul and Edith fulfilled his hopes; the others were "all imitators—second-hand affairs."

The humanitarian subject always brought a warm response from him. Mary Howitt's *Ballads* were by a "most favored female" who wrote "for love, for peace, for forbearance, for practical Christianity, for the ground-work of all the great reforms of this age." He also gave superlatives to her thick octavo translation of Frederica Bremer whose *The Neighbors* and other expositions of model domesticity were "the best books the whole range of romance-writing can furnish"; rather than great intellectual merit they contained charity, love, and "a *good, gentle mother.*" Louisa's son vowed that if he had children they would read these tales right after the New Testament. (George Templeton Strong found Bremer less magnetic: "A full-blown angel darning a pair of pantaloons would make a very good frontispiece for any of her productions.")[11]

The revolt of serfs in Cracow and other signs of unrest in Europe led Whitman to see brightness in the political future of the Old World. While waiting for the advent of popular liberty there the editor defended an earlier Jacquerie: "When one takes in the whole scope of the French Revolution, the work done by the axe will be quite lost sight of in the expansion of far higher, wider, and deeper results." Lamartine's *History of the Girondists* seemed the most dramatic of books; Hazlitt's *Napoleon* was noble, democratic, and wholesome for the young, fresh life of the republic.

The social vision of two French novelists placed them, in Whitman's opinion, by the side of the early Dickens. In *Consuelo, La Comtesse de Rudolstadt,* and *The Journeyman Joiner,* George Sand proved that the world needed a preacher of the holy rights of women lest it "stagnate in wrongs merely from precedent." Reflecting her personal knowledge of Fourier and intimate collaboration with Pierre Leroux, the printer whose religious ideal included the founding of world democracy, she promised careers for emancipated women and encouraged workers to become writers. Her novels kindled hope—as Dostoevski noted—in Russia, as well as in Fulton Street.

When Whitman opened the *American Review* for March 1846 he saw that it did not share his enthusiasm for the current advocate of the rights of man, Eugène Sue, whose blue-covered novels were found on the dressing tables of ladies and the work benches of mechanics. Beginning with *Les Mystères de Paris* in 1840, Sue offered fictionalized Saint-Simonism as the panacea for the victims of an industrialization that consigned them to slums, prostitution, drunkenness, and violent crime. The *Review* rejected Sue's "finespun theories of social perfectability and universal benevolence," but the *Eagle* critic hailed *The Wandering Jew* for gratification of emotions higher than "mere romance-loving curiosity." As for *Martin the Foundling,*

no work has yet been written of what are called novels, which more fully exhibits the potency of the romancer, *to do good,* in a certain way than this. It cuts into the very heart—the sore,

169

gangrened, guilty heart—of that immense social evil which has accumulated for long and artificial ages over the states of Europe; exposes the monstrous effect of the undue distribution of wealth, by unnatural means.

He concluded with the highest accolade: "It is a democratic book." [12]

With swiftening tempo his generation tried to outmode de Tocqueville's judgment made after reading *Henry V* in a frontier cabin, that the literary genius of Great Britain continued to dart its rays into the forests of the New World. Duyckinck estimated that if all the excellent papers and dissertations on "this prolific text of a possible native authorship, could be brought together in one mass, they would constitute a very respectable library, and go a long way towards settling the question, by making a national literature themselves." Soon his *Literary World* would publish the essay in which Melville complained, "You must believe in Shakespeare's unapproachability, or quit the country. But what sort of belief is this for an American, a man who is bound to carry republican progressiveness into Literature, as well as into Life?" Paulding, who named his own greatest merit that of being an American writer addressing productions to his countrymen only, told Duyckinck in February 1847, "There is a noble Harvest to be reaped in this New World of boundless space, and unexhausted fertility. Why then should we starve ourselves with the miserable gleanings of a worn out soil which has been so overcultivated that it has become Pine Barren?" [13]

Scorning this chauvinism as madness, Poe refused to be placed in the paradoxical situation of "liking or pretending to like, a stupid book the better because (sure enough) its stupidity was of our growth, and discussed our own affairs." Whitman, also sensing the claptrap involved in promiscuous denunciation of imports or indiscriminate praise of "home" products, searched for a middle way. *Eagle* readers met French novelists, Scotch essayists, Persian poets, German autobiographers. If their editor retold the heroism of Washington and John Paul Jones, he also spoke his admiration for Madame Roland. Love of frontier and eagle alternated with English meadow and nightingale. Catlin's Indians deserved a safe posterity along with Gliddon's Egyptians, their hieroglyphics, cartouches, and symbolic animal worship. But Whitman refused space to those who advocated poisonous doctrines: Cowper taught loyalty to the divine right of kings; Johnson was a "burly" aristocrat who scorned commoners; Southey laughed at republican freedom.[14]

To censure Scott, as rooted in his youth as the elms of Brooklyn, was no easy matter. Though he could not excise memories of Jeanie Deans and Rebecca he agreed with Cooper that their creator was a tory, a high-church and state man; the impression that remained after reading his fictions "where monarchs or nobles compare with patriots or peasants, is dangerous to the latter and favorable to the former." The novelist had ignored warriors for liberty, misrepresented truth, placed the shadow on the wrong face. His Cromwell, "heroic champion of his countrymen's rights," emerged as a "blood-seeking hypocrite," while the "licentious, selfish, deceitful, and unprincipled" young Stuart became a pleasant gentleman. Such shameful truckling turned Scott's "brightest excellence murky."[15]

Americans who used new materials found Whitman their advocate. "All books have their office," he noted after reading *Omoo* and praised Melville for entertainment "not so light as to be tossed aside for its flippancy, nor so profound as to be tiresome." Brown's *Whaling Cruise* led the islander to ask why, with the exception of *Two Years before the Mast*, "we know hardly a work prepared by a competent eyewitness on the subject of the whale fishery," in all its "strange and varied scenes." Sailors come home to Greenport often talked of one of the strange scenes—a white whale. The need to fill other lacunae made the *Eagle* cite *Jack Long; or Shot in the Eye; a True Story of Texas Border Life* as the right sort of book for an American to write: "We wish we had more of them." Mrs. Kirkland's *Sketches* were fresh native specimens. In his preface to *The Half-Breed* (formerly *Arrow-Tip*) he pledged to save space in his paper for other precious indigenous material.

Because the debate over copyright had become exacerbated Whitman endured another Tree-like episode. On the evening of 11 January 1847 the Hamilton Literary Association of Brooklyn held its anniversary banquet. Among the guests was Cornelius Mathews, the secretary of the Authors Copyright Protection Club. He had followed *Puffer Hopkins* with *Big Abel and The Little Manhattan*, a novel of the Poor Scholar doomed to finish his masterpiece just as a famous book arrives from Europe and preempts the attention of bargain-hunting publishers. In *Big Abel* Mathews described the city that marked his early work—the butcher boys in lumbering carts, hard riders from Harlem, the funeral of a stage driver, oyster cellars and taverns, drinkers of Monongahela "hot-and-hot" and Newark cider. But

171

above all he embodied the plea for copyright within the thin frame of the Poor Scholar, who was the obvious key to the *roman à clef*.[16]

Turning to the lectern, Mathews in June 1845 addressed the Euclein Society of his alma mater, New York University. The theme he chose was the potential literary accomplishment of the new generation:

> I do take it for granted, Gentlemen, that there are some new influences to be represented by the authors of this country. I am foolish enough to believe that we are leading a life peculiar to ourselves; that we are a province to no other country on the face of the world. I therefore, in behalf of this young America of ours, insist on nationality and true Americanism in the books this country furnishes to itself and to the world: nationality in its purest, highest, broadest sense. . . . The writings of a great country should sound of the great voices of nature of which she is full. The march of a great people in literature should be majestic and assured as the action of their institutions is calm and secure. . . .

Under the caption "Young America" the *Mirror* printed the entire address, including the author's warning to tinkling rhymers to avoid attempting to represent the life of the continent with sparrows' quills.[17]

The *Knickerbocker* bitterly hostile to Mathews over the years because of his ridiculous imitations of Dickens and his cries of persecution for his copyright advocacy, now announced that *Big Abel* had the depth of a thimble and its author a screw loose in his head. In turn the *Morning News*, the *Democratic Review*, and the *Literary World* defended author, books, and program. In December 1846 the *Knickerbocker* retaliated by calling him a sapless mind trying to wet-nurse "that sturdy bantling, the National Literature."

When Mathews stood before the Hamiltonians the next month he struck back. As the *Eagle* reported the sequence, he retorted to a string of toasts "of a character the very opposite of American" by proposing "The United States of America, an independent country, not a suburb of London." Then someone at the table hissed.

"Is it too much to say," Whitman asked, "that this was a specimen of the monkeyism of literature?"[18] The *Yankee Doodle*, which "expected better things of the *Eagle*," promptly answered that Mathews deserved to be hooted for intruding his idiosyncrasies where they were obnoxious. The extreme of all monkeyism, concluded the weekly, is that which makes literary apes "attempt to chatter the world into recognizing them as men."

By now a veteran litigant Whitman used the *Yankee Doodle* "whose very foundation starts in the idea of nationality" as an exhibit in defense of Mathews. Then he scolded copiers of castoff British fashions and their converse, "solicitous thrusters forward of the claims, in every ridiculous connection, of writing that is merely American because it is not written abroad." His outrage soon subsided when he learned that another guest rather than a Hamiltonian had hissed. In a conciliatory tone he asked not to be listed with petty bigots, for he valued the writers of Great Britain more than kingly treasures. But "we are not content to live only on the strength of the aliment they have furnished."[19]

The issue remained open. That March the *Democratic Review* defended Mathews as the target of small critics and publishers who feared copyright would destroy them, and went on to quote from the "Young America" address. In 1850, after reading *Mosses from an Old Manse* while stretched on new-mown clover in a barn near Pittsfield, Melville sent an essay to Duyckinck with the imperative: "Let America then prize and cherish her writers; yea, let her glorify them. They are not so many in number, as to exhaust her good-will."

By the Saturday after the election in November 1846 that saw disaster overwhelm his Democrats the editor no longer despaired. Locally in 1844 Wright had a majority of 239 votes; now the count reached nearly 600. This increase made Whitman proclaim Kings the banner county, a spirit of light amidst ghosts, and he accepted praise for promulgating the great doctrines of the party—though regret at the shaming of an honored leader softened his crowing. Unlike other losers he refused to deny that Whiggery was having a great swing, for the returns from other states could not be nullified by willful myopia. But rather than concede permanent defeat, he chose to compare the victors to the consumptive whose friends mistake a climactic flush for the bloom of returning health. Changing his figure he prophesied that calm waters in 1848 would allow the passage into Port Inauguration of a Democratic president. Those who had "un-voted" would march to the polls and summon Wright from his Canton farm to the White House. Warmed by this vision Whitman scissored Whittier's "Reformer" and reprinted the paean to a world gray with morning light.

In the role of elder brother he soothed the timid with assurance that "he who takes large views, will see the greater necessity of unflinching adherence to his cause." By the time Congress convened that winter *Eagle* readers knew that their editor had made *his* cause the passage of the Wilmot Proviso, which he thought should carry Jefferson's name. Throughout the session he told the legislators that by marching forward they could bar slavery forever from annexed territory: "We must." The start of 1847 brought encouragement from Washington and Albany. When Congressman Preston King offered free-soil legislation and Albany passed similar resolutions Whitman hastened to claim priority for the *Eagle* as "the very first democratic paper which alluded to this subject in a decisive manner—expressing the conviction that it is the duty of its party to take an unalterable stand against the allowance of slavery in any new territory, under any circumstance, or in any way."

Despite his opposition to the spread of slavery he did not ally himself with the abolitionists; in fact he charged that their ultraism and officiousness hindered the cause of freedom. In the midst of a eulogy on Thomas Clarkson, he emphasized that this arch foe of the African traffic—"the most abominable of all man's schemes for making money"—was not an abolitionist. When Delaware ended slavery he accused "red-hot fanatics" of blocking similar "prodigious strides" by other states. But he did not imitate the bias of a metropolitan paper that reported a meeting attended by "white ladies and black wenches, fat niggers and spare white men." His strategy embodied the avoidance of agitation and a firm refusal to "tolerate building up the edifice of slavery any further."[20]

As the free-soil debate intensified he compared it to Aaron's rod that changed all it touched. Calhoun became an intellectual Saladin who with brazen logic tried to justify disunion. When dispatches from Charleston relayed the speech which jeopardized union ties the *Eagle* invoked the spirits of earlier Southerners, Washington and Jefferson, to guide true lovers of the republic and to safeguard God's blessings. When the Senate that March defeated the Proviso Whitman denounced Senator Dickinson who had voted with the opposition despite categorical instructions from Albany: "The *freemen* of the *North never* will consent to the making of slavery states of this new territory," he told the Hunker. Though northern apostates and southern

174

sophists continued to threaten free soil, he did not abandon hope for ultimate enactment of the Proviso, and created a maternal image of the West "with its great bosom spread so lovingly for resting spots to God's poor children, (ah, what a number there are!)." In this holy millenium the needy and the degraded of the Old World and the New would be transplanted to a richer destiny; the mechanic would not be shamed by the competition of slaves.

Turning to local politics he pleaded for harmony at the ward meetings, but the choice of a mayoralty candidate brought endless disputes and another decisive loss in the election. His jocular acceptance of the fact that the Democrats were a "golfizzled" party and his quip that "it varies the monotony, for *our side to be be beaten*" fooled no one. Soon he complained of the cold and backward spring.

New victories by American troops deep in Mexico again made the Wilmot issue paramount. After celebrating Buena Vista and Vera Cruz, Whitman demanded to know whether the new states were to be free or slave: "The voice of the north proclaims that *labor must not* be degraded." He joined those who sang

> Clear the way for General Taylor
> To lick the Mexicans he's a whaler.

But the hero outracing all candidates for 1848 with every stride of Old Whitey had not clarified his politics. "Is he for free territory?" the *Eagle* asked. A Whig national bank, government financed with paper? By May Benton had taken a high place in the editor's pantheon, and the *Eagle* carried columns of the Missourian's assaults on Calhoun and the "slavery propagandist" resolutions. Avoiding blatant sectional bias the paper congratulated Jefferson Davis on his promotion to brigadier, for "a braver man never wielded a sword."

Cannon and cheers welcomed President Polk to Brooklyn in late June 1847. Whitman stood close enough to admire his "massive intellectual face and marked courtesy." But after that hour he complained of the reign of dullness through mid-summer. No news emanated from a somnolent Common Council; no assault cases stirred the police office. When a raid on a brothel in Williamsburgh dispersed "black spirits and white," he assured readers that unlike the Gomorrah across the river Brooklyn had few places to cause shame. Because dysentery plagued many children he mentioned again that blackberry syrup would cure them. The "b-oys" went fishing for porgies and blackfish and prepared for the long day, as was their fashion,

175

by stopping at a tavern and laying a foundation. The one political row erupted when his friend, Samuel E. Johnson, elected to the county judgeship, became "non-elected" because commissioners voided four votes. The *Eagle* began a long and successful battle to preserve the integrity of the ballot and to seat the future financial backer of another Whitman paper.

Then came the day in August when Whitman asked his compositors to line the *Eagle* in black for Silas Wright dead of a heart attack. From Albany he had returned to the countryside to live his years as a farmer, pitching hay and hoeing corn, though admirers—a silver service from the merchants of New York City was ready for presentation—expected to move him to Washington in 1848. In the "Lost Statesman" Whittier asked

> Who now shall rally Freedom's scattering host?
> Who wear the mantle of the leader lost?
> Who stay the march of slavery?

While Whitman mourned he plunged deeper into the struggle to preserve the future of the republic; he now saw the issue as clearly drawn between "the *grand body* of *white workingmen*, the *millions* of *mechanics, farmers,* and *operatives*" on one side and "the interests of the few thousand rich, 'polished' and aristocratic owners of slaves at the south" on the other side. With Greeley and the local survivors of the National Reform Association, he remained adamant against "halfway work" in the matter of slavery in the new territory. "We must either have it there, or not."

To his chagrin Hunker and Barnburner estrangement deepened during the autumn campaign for state offices. He had preserved a precarious neutrality by avoiding "euphonious appelations" and insisting that he recognized neither faction—"*our* duty is to work for the good of the *Democratic* principle." But Hunkers outnumbered Barnburners in the convention convened at Syracuse on 29 September 1847, and their chairman ruled an endorsement of Wilmot out of order. Refusing to be silenced Barnburners in October convened in separate session at Herkimer where they picked their own slate. Blunting the horns of this dilemma by rationalizing that it was impossible for every member of a great party to have all his preferences gratified and that the majority must rule, the *Eagle* called the Syracuse candidates honest and capable. The party had weathered real tempests; no need to fear a squall. Later in the week in an analysis of the summary address of the Syracuse leaders the editor objected to their implied sanction of internal improvements and a revenue tariff.

176

By the last week of the campaign though he had hoped that all the vexatious divisions would "rest in oblivion"—until after the election—he saw them surface at the mass meeting held at the Brooklyn Gardens on 1 November. Acting as one of four secretaries he recorded the sentiments of one speaker who favored "the great truth that democracy teaches the universal equality and equal rights of the whole human race, without any distinction whatsoever"; but a second speaker doubted the need for the Proviso. The band then played "Hail Columbia," after which the crowd gave three "tremendous" cheers and adjourned apparently in the best of spirits.

Casting his vote the next day, Whitman seemed confident that his exhortation to "Rouse and Come Forth" would be heeded. After a time at his office he boarded a Fulton ferry whose bell tolled a warning through the dense fog. At the Park he heard Bishop sing the role of that high-placed traitor, Lucrezia Borgia.

Whig victory by "a prodigious majority" shocked him into open militancy. In the days after this latest debacle he charged that the Democrats deserved defeat for not being "sufficiently bold, open, and radical" in their avowals. The Syracuse leaders had ignored the Proviso and failed to understand that the electorate would honor "almost any draughts" upon radical ideas, and upon "those once derided, but now widely worshipped doctrines" which "the great Jefferson and the glorious Leggett promulgated." As key evidence of the discontent spread by "pestilential" conservatives he cited election returns from Manhattan which revealed that many eligible voters had avoided the polls:

> *We must plant ourselves firmly on the side of freedom and firmly espouse it.* The late election is a terrific warning of the folly of all half-way policy in such matters. . . . The party must be true to the memory of fathers who fought for freedom, and not for slavery.

Amidst an atmosphere poisoned by "spiteful talk" that called him bolter and traitor he followed a normal routine of saunters, visits, entertainment. Brooklyn now stretched seven miles. The white-pillared Dutch Reformed church and several other new buildings pleased him; so did the autumn flower show he attended as the guest of a florist. Hertz, the Emperor Pianist, played another set of variations on "Yankee Doodle." A dancer at the Broadway reminded Whitman of Elssler, but those tawdry figures that supported the chandelier! At Castle Garden he fondled local silver, flint glass, and Mundell's elegant book bindings and letterpress. Here he spoke with the authority of fifteen years as a printer. Whether on muslin, sheepskin, or morocco he liked liberal gilt; the ideal page showed clear large type with every hair-stroke sharp and every line well leaded on thick white paper.

The *Advertiser* and the *Star* had been as cordial to Whitman as financial and political rivalry allowed, alternating insult and compliment. On occasion Lees called him a prompter's devil, a posed and mincing genius, an obsequious writer of namby pambyisms whose ancestors were a tribe of aborigines, the Flat Heads; their offspring combined "the valor and modesty of Falstaff and the wisdom and learning of Dogberry." The *Eagle* then taunted the cockney from Nottingham who spurned the eighth letter of the alphabet. After these sallies came tokens of appreciation, Whitman thanking "Toots" for a "hugaceous" slice of cake or a basket of peaches. The *Star* sent cherries and so many roses and carnations that a third paper asked if he were an opera singer. When a Manhattan editor slurred the *Eagle* both the *Advertiser* and the *Star* came to Whitman's defense.

But the Brooklyn papers' exploitation of the current feud was inevitable and harmful. In that painful autumn of 1847 the *Star*, whose ailing Alden Spooner had retired, called Whitman weak and scoffed at "smoky paragraphs, which regularly throw his democratic friends into convulsions, and which have already done vast service to the Whig cause. We would not for the world unseat him!" When the *Star* went on to write of "the true scurrility" of his character as a school teacher he sighed for the kindly Spooner. Pressed again for a clear statement of allegiance to either Hunker or Barnburner he answered, "We are a democratic republican."

The dedication of a monument to Washington and the celebration of Evacuation Day allowed him to turn to an era beyond controversy. Visits to the Brooklyn Institute filled many hours; next to oils by local artists hung those of Doughty whose "Scene on the Tioga" proved him the best of American landscape painters. In Whitman's judgment Harper and Brothers' new catalogue ought to silence the common cry that the firm published only foreigners; he counted over three hundred titles by natives.

As the year ended he predicted unity within a few months; indeed, the unfolding presidential campaign mandated the closing of ranks. From Chapultepec and other battlefields news came of the death of neighbors whose selflessness could not be shunned. But Whitman did not counsel surrender to Hunkerism. A lecture by Dr. Giles on liberty, "one of the most powerful

178

we ever heard," inspired him to promise to remember its picture of slavery. Reading Emerson's "inimitable" *Essays*, he vouched for the truth of the "striking" paragraph that opened "Spiritual Laws":

> When the act of reflection takes place in the mind, when we look at ourselves in the light of thought, we discover that our life is emblossomed in beauty. . . . Not only things familiar and stale, but even the tragic and terrible are comely as they take their place in the pictures of memory. The river-bank, the week at the water-side, the old house, the foolish person, however neglected in the passing, have a grace in the past. Even the corpse that has lain in the chambers has added a solemn ornament to the house. The soul will not know either deformity or pain. If in the hours of clear reason we should speak the severest truth, we should say that we had never made a sacrifice.

Meditative on the last day of 1847, Whitman found comfort in lifting the religion of Christ above all others—"though it cannot make a man essentially different." Then he went to a fancy dress ball to celebrate the new year.

He started 1848 as though sensing the need to return to the prime source of his political faith. Once again he read Leggett's essays and marveled at their strength and clarity, their love of freedom. He thought too of Jackson whose fame would ever brighten because of the Bank veto that had aroused men to take a stand against corrupt bankers. In an expansive mood, Whitman enjoyed the theatre and a German band that played Strauss. A tour of the engine room of a new ferry brought from him a panegyric to the mighty machinery. He also scrutinized the dispatches from the Thirtieth Congress now in session and decided that it was time for him to obey a mandate beyond that of station and money. Week after week he had indulged himself on an undisclosed but obviously ample salary. At first a silver watch, a gold ring, a carnelian pin; then he clad his fine figure in a new frock coat, vest, trousers, and shoes. As always his family shared his affluence; he paid their house taxes and repair bills, bought his brothers boots and his mother furniture. To speak the severest truth in his editorials could end all this.

On 13 January the *Eagle* reported that Senator Dickinson "is against imposing conditions on territorial organization; in other words he is against Wilmot!" The rumor now spread through offices in Brooklyn and Manhattan that the publisher of the *Eagle*, Van Anden, as well as Senator Lott

179

and Congressman Murphy "determined to rule or ruin," had confronted Whitman. On 21 January, Van Anden admitted that he had "dispensed" with his editor and promised that the *Eagle* would continue to present a solid front to "the old bank, high tariff, federal and anti war party." But he omitted free soil from the list. Soon the paper called the Proviso a humbug fraught with mischief and applauded Congressman Murphy as Wilmot's foe.

Different versions of the leavetaking circulated. Friends insisted that Whitman had kicked a prominent politician down the stairs. Arnold, the new editor, answered that his predecessor was too indolent to kick a mosquito. Friends countered by asking who could believe a great grandson of Benedict. Whatever the manner of going, the *Atlas* gave the reasons:

> Mr. Walter Whitman, who has . . . ably conducted the Eagle . . . has been displaced by a clique . . . because of his bold denunciation of slavery, and advocacy of the Wilmot Proviso. He is a young man of fine literary attainments, fearless, energetic, and beyond the reach of corrupt political cliques. He is, however, in my humble opinion, much better capacitated for pursuits that have no connection with the strife of party, and which will not require him to prostitute his talents for the advancement of mendacious office-seekers and ambitious demagogues.[21]

When Whitman removed the mementos of the long tour in Fulton Street, he carried away the valentine sent by an admirer. Its last couplet remained apt:

> No praise of mine can e'er enhance the glory of your name,
> *In feelings* you deserve at least imperishable fame.[22]

13

CREOLES, COTTON, CALABOOSES

WITHIN THE WEEK after his dismissal rumors spread on both sides of the river that another paper was to be started for Whitman, but as the days passed it seemed that his friends could do no more than taunt the Hunkers with the suspect lineage of his replacement. On Thursday evening, 10 February 1848, the jobless journalist went to the Broadway to see Wallack act Byron's *Werner* as the embodiment of a broken-hearted and despairing man whose "agony, distraction, and listlessness of the soul" were engendered by misfortunes. In the white and gold lobby during intermission of this catharsis he met J. E. "Sam" McClure, a publisher from New Orleans.[1]

Trained in the circulation department of the *Picayune*, McClure had helped start the *Delta* whose war correspondents, "Mustang" and "Chaparral," made that paper famous. McClure had come to New York to equip and staff a new daily, the *Crescent*, for many Southern newspapermen remained with the army in Mexico. Impressed with recommendations from the Manhattan press, McClure offered Whitman "a handsome place." As further incentive he agreed to find chores in the shop for Jeff, the fifteen-year-old brother Whitman had helped to rear.

To accept meant regular income again and the promise of sharing in the current phase of the reconstruction which had turned New Orleans, according to observers, from pestilence, death, and destruction to prosperity, pleasure, and enjoyment. For a bachelor almost thirty, a stranger to most of America, here was the chance to encounter a legendary section. The *Yankee Doodle* listed all that New Orleans evoked by 1848:

> Odd the thoughts thy name induces,
> Creoles, Cotton, Calabooses,
> Coarse grain'd sugar, coarser niggers,
> Sweltering weather, fever's rigors,
> Ball-rooms, julaps, cobblers, punches,

181

> Various sorts of gen'rous lunches;
> Dark and melting-eyed quadroones,
> Racy "Deltas," "Picayunes"—
> Who can e'er forget the trip he
> Ends at mouth of Mississippi?

Europeans testified to the city's lures; Manhattan journalists sent titillating copy north. Theodore Gould, who seemed established there as a portrait painter, in recent letters to "Well-beloved Editor" Whitman had written of weather cool enough for cloaks, of brisk business in the crowded city, and of Camp and Royal Streets swarming in the afternoons "with beautiful women, those living flowers of creation, making earth so lovely by their presence. More poetry in the glances of their lustrous eyes than in columns of letter print, after all. Don't you agree with me?"[2]

McClure surmounted a final obstacle when he convinced the Barnburner that to work on the *Crescent* was not tantamount to surrendering to Hunkerism. The publishers would champion regional interests, but in national affairs they promised to abstain from the "party contests of the day, either *directly* or indirectly."[3] Whitman then accepted two hundred dollars for the trip and joined in drinking to the success of the venture. Some families (like George Templeton Strong's) believed that to send sons to so sensual a society turned them into roués. But Whitman's parents evidently gave their blessings.

Two days later at nine in the morning the brothers boarded a train at the foot of Liberty Street. They reached Philadelphia in five hours and Baltimore by evening. After a night there they left at seven the next morning for Cumberland. As they rode in the cars at thirty or forty miles an hour Whitman compared their pace with the lightning flight of the telegraph and concluded that railways were very slow and obsolete. At Harpers Ferry the two dined well for twenty-five cents; afterwards they walked half a mile to the scene Jefferson called one of the most stupendous in all nature. In Cumberland where the tracks ended, caravans of great Conestoga wagons with arched roofs of white canvas assembled before the gateway west.

The next phase of the journey overland to Wheeling started that evening when "nine precious souls" paid $13 for a seat and fifty pounds of baggage on a stage of the National Road and Good Intent Company. Exhilarated by pace and landscape one of the souls recorded the itinerary:

182

Night now falling down around us like a very large cloak of black broadcloth, (I fancy *that* figure, at least, hasn't been used up by the poets,) and the Alleghenies rearing themselves "some pumpkins," (as they say here,) right before our nasal members, we . . . dashed through the town and up the mountains.

Later, using a trope from dermatology rather than textiles, he called the mountains "mighty warts on the great breast of nature."[4]

Full gallop over the rutted, snow-covered pike led to accidents or, at best, head-thumping against the rough roof. "If there be any truth in phrenology," exclaimed one survivor, "what changes in character must be wrought during a journey across the Alleghenies!" Whitman did not allow the jostling or the intense cold to lessen his appreciation of the historic route or the conversation of companions which was more vital than that of cosmopolites on the Fulton ferry. An old farmer from Ohio repeated at least twenty-five times his experiences as a privateer in 1812, but had "sage and sound conclusions" about pensions. The stops made every ten miles to change horses also helped to pass the hours, for the long, low inns with gangs of drovers lounging before huge fires of bituminous coal deserved to be painted by a Doughty or Mount, "one who, not continually straining to be merely second or third best, in imitation, seizes original and really picturesque occasions of this sort for his pieces." The silent beauty of a station reached after midnight could convert an infidel.

At dawn the stage rolled into Uniontown but the passengers had no chance to rest their racked bones. They pressed on to Wheeling, the terminal of boats bound for New Orleans. When the brothers reached the wharf a few minutes after ten that evening, the *St. Cloud* had steam up. The tired pair spent little time examining the packet, but made certain they had a comfortable stateroom with separate beds. By the time they awoke the next morning the *St. Cloud* was on the way to Cincinnati.

As they moved through the Ohio, the *belle rivière* that Dickens found more opaque than gruel, the brothers marveled that it was possible to journey two thousand miles into a great continent on the same "clever little steamboat" and enjoy creature comforts as regal as at a Broadway hotel: "eatables, in the utmost freshness and profusion—*too* much profusion, indeed; good clean beds; a long saloon to promenade in; or, if you prefer it, in fine weather, the outside." The gaucheries of voyagers forced Mrs. Trollope to warn those who sought agreeable impressions of American manners to avoid

183

this mode of travel. Whitman also questioned the wisdom of gulping an entire meal in five minutes, but he was gratified all the way down the rivers to find little of that "crudeness and semi-barbarism which persons and papers at the northeast seem to take it for granted still exists at the west."

There were "dozens of places on Long Island within fifty miles of Manhattan," he told Major Noah in a letter, where ignorance and uncouth habits abounded more than among his shipmates from the valleys of the Ohio and the Mississippi. Even "the roughest shod and roughest clad" of the natives displayed "a sterling vein of common sense." A Dickens could find ample material in western ways, just as he had in fashionable eastern circles:

> I fully believe that in a comparison of actual manliness and what the Yankees call "gumption," the well-to-do *citizens* (for I am not speaking so much of the country), particularly the young men, of New York, Philadelphia, Boston, Brooklyn and so on, with the advantages of compact neighborhood, schools, etc.; are not up to the men of the West. Among the latter, probably, attention is turned more to the *realities* of life, and a habit formed of thinking for one's self; in the cities, frippery and artificial fashion are too much the ruling powers.[5]

The ports of call also brought comparisons with the East. Cincinnati startled him with the size of floating docks, markets, and cheap produce. The passage of the laden vessel through rapids and a narrow rocky channel below Louisville sent some frightened passengers to bed, but he remained on deck with Jeff and watched every maneuver. Cairo, the town Dickens called a detestable morass, made him wonder if it would ever be of any great shakes "except in the way of ague."

The landscape turned flat and monotonous but the Jefferson Proviso man knew that one side of the river was free, the other slave. He passed hours listening to the talk of Negro gangs as they "wooded up" by stretching a plank ashore and then, stripped to the waist and padded with empty salt sacks, moved cords to the deck and the furnaces. There were encounters with the *Diadem*, the *Saladin*, and other boats whose owners had turned to royalty and the Orient for names. When the *St. Cloud* stopped to load cargo from various wharves the captain proved entertaining as he bargained for bacon, lard, leather, candles, beef tongues, butter, and corn. The author of *Franklin*

Evans may not have been aware that the hold contained one hundred barrels of whiskey.

Soon in the main current of the Mississippi the *St. Cloud* swept past islands, bends, and dense forest that reached inland endlessly. On deck one murky night Whitman compared the "tireless waters" to

> Life's quick dream,
> Onward and onward ever hurrying—

Before long the boat passed the town where lived the boy two years younger than Jeff who would memorialize the river in magisterial prose.[6]

Toward the end of the week the land showed swampy with occasional sand hills or bluffs. Alligators lay on logs and snags. Then the brothers saw plantation houses and rows of slave huts. They passed clumps of cypress with pendant moss, palmetto, dark ilex, and fragrant groves of orange. By Thursday, 24 February, they had reached the levee that started 120 miles above the city. The next afternoon they sighted the famous landmark of New Orleans, the glittering dome of the St. Charles Hotel. For hours they watched the pilot nose the *St. Cloud* through a vast assemblage of ships and flatboats until she reached anchorage at nightfall.

Disembarking in the morning amidst a confusion of passengers, freight, carts, and mules that reminded them of Manhattan on the first day of May, the brothers walked through the rain in search of lodgings. Disillusioned by their inspection of the few places available and by encounters with landlords who made them feel that the wayfarer was "apt to be taken in, not scripturally," they sent word north that the crowded city of 125,000 needed "a score or so of cleanly, well-kept boarding houses. One of those nice places in Brooklyn, now, transposed to here, might make the owner's fortune in a very little time." Their first lodging proved to be so dirty that Jeff told his mother, "you could not only see the dirt, but could taste it, and you had to if you ate anything at all." Searching again they found a cleaner room with an excellent table near Lafayette Square. Mr. Irwin charged each of them $4.50 a week.[7]

From the window the two could see the levee where stevedores loaded bales of cotton and hogsheads of tobacco, and at night they strolled Lafayette Square whose delightful promenade, lawn, and flower beds the older brother thought would make a perfect set for the play now showing: "Would that Mercutio were alive to recount the very tender things said by beings whose hearts were inflamed by love." The French markets displayed food to tempt Augustus Graham. Negresses swathed in yellow and red turbans sold fruit, breads, and game, broiled pompano, terrapin eggs, asparagus, and coffee. Here were green peas, cucumbers, and other delicacies served daily at a time when Long Island farmers had not plowed their fields.

To his relief as custodian of a boy he loved, Whitman decided from the outset that New Orleans had been slandered by those who associated it only with dueling, bowie knives, yellow fever, and hogs. The North also suffered endemic diseases; by actual count he knew one hundred pens in Myrtle Street where pigs made "pork, manure and cholera." Here, moreover, women were treated with exemplary courtesy for the city had been spared that "abominable evil" prevalent in Manhattan—gangs at street corners insulting ladies and gentlemen with obscene talk and impudent gestures.

If New Orleans had a vice that could be called "*the* bad one of all," it was the obvious excessive drinking indulged in by males above Jeff's age. Bars were as large as the rotunda of the Merchants' Exchange in Wall Street, and from eleven to one every day they set out free lunch. But indulgence was not confined to those hours. The consumption of vast quantities of juleps and iced ale appalled Whitman. "Now you know," he told Major Noah, "I am not *ultra* in these matters, but it isn't good to drink spiritous compounds at this rate in hot climates."

He reserved comment on another social dilemma exposed by daily advertisements in the *Crescent* and all other papers. Dr. Watson, who "has obtained so great a reputation in the cure of Venereal Diseases," offered to aid the stricken if they called at 118 Canal Street. The physician also promised the ultimate salvation by treating "debility of the sexual organs" brought on by self-abuse and other unspecified causes: "It is impossible, I believe, for one to be placed in a more mortifying condition, cut off, as it were, from all allurements of female society, without hope of domestic happiness, and deprived of one half of the incentives of life."

The end of February brought a military armistice but New Orleans would not lapse into civilian ways for months. Meanwhile the brothers lived and worked in an armed camp, a staging area and hospital depot. Recruits continued to arrive from the interior and bivouacked in open fields or pitched tents in Lafayette Square until steamers carried them along with teamsters and quartermasters to Vera Cruz. Every ship returning from that port brought sick and wounded veterans who filled all hospital beds while healthy victors paraded and accepted honors and hospitality. Souvenirs and baggage—Mexican lances, sabres, saddles mounted with silver—all lay heaped at the St. Charles Hotel.

Though the campaigns that made generals famous—and Whig candidates—were over, analyses and anecdotes of their exploits from Matamoros to Chapultepec filled the city's newspapers and bulletin boards. One parade honored Twiggs; a second, Kearny who had marched from Independence to Sante Fe and across the wilderness to the Pacific. Then came Zachary Taylor. Like the rest of the electorate Whitman watched for the results of preliminary probes of the hero's political philosophy. The diagnosis that Taylor was a Whig revived Whitman's bitter memories of 1840, and prompted his agreement with those opposed to turning the White House into a sort of Persian palace, to which triumphant generals could retire. As long as New Orleans echoed to thirteen-gun salutes, he continued to deprecate the effort to force the nation to swallow the bearer of sword, plume, epaulettes, and spurs as president merely because of skill and courage in maneuvering men, horses, and cannon. The "Leonidas letter" court of inquiry ordered in New Orleans by the War Department to probe charges by General Scott against three ranking officers, lessened the prestige of military leaders after revelation of their squabbles over sharing the glory of battles like Contreras. (General Pillow, one of the accused, paced the streets of New Orleans followed by a black servant who carried his sword.)[8]

The response to the first edition of the *Crescent*, which appeared on Sunday, 5 March 1848, justified McClure's care in choosing his staff. The *Delta* called the new rival a beautiful sheet and the *Picayune* predicted that "without party bias of any sort" it would become a shining member of the fraternity. Acknowledging the flattery of these neighbors Whitman challenged anyone to name a city whose press corps was more courteous and liberal. (When a copy of the *Crescent* reached Brooklyn the *Eagle* found it printed with admirable taste and wished its publishers and editor would flourish like a green bay tree.) After two weeks more than two thousand subscribed; since McClure appeared to be fully responsible, the future of the shop seemed assured.

Aglow with pride and some of the contents of a complimentary bowl of punch "fit for Xerxes," Whitman went walking with Jeff after the office closed. The day seemed so idyllic he knew that Wordsworth would have loved it. First they toured the levee and watched the "gigantic" Mississippi; then the streets where every face "seemed redolent with joy." At last they reached the suburb of the Faubourg Ste. Marie where surrounded by high brick walls and live oaks they found the "silent abodes of the dead." The paths through this old Catholic cemetery were lined with white and red roses; the graves, unlike those at Greenwood, were above ground. Fascinated by his proximity to the exotic, Walt promised to send descriptions north of other cemeteries as well as of the vital French First Municipality; but other matters intervened.

From the moment of arrival he had sensed that here in New Orleans was "a willingness, at all times for peace, but a stern determination not to be played the fool with." Rather than accusations by Greeley and other Northerners of bloody intentions, one heard acclamation for the planting of republican government in Mexico by an army so gallant that señoritas would protest orders from Washington withdrawing "our good looking Yankee lads." (This in its way rephrased the *Herald*, which, arguing for annexation of Mexico, wrote, "Like the Sabine virgins, she will soon learn to love her ravisher.")

The *Crescent*, like the other papers of the city, from its first issue tried to guide this "right feeling about the war" into a policy of hostility toward the terms reached at Guadalupe Hidalgo on 2 February and sent to Washington by Trist through "Mustang" of the *Delta*. With Senate deliberations under way the local press questioned the authority of Trist (who had, indeed, been ordered home by President Polk), General Scott, and the Mexican negotiator who had replaced Santa Anna. Divested of verbiage, the treaty was only a sorry business transacted with bribes; a senseless compact that nullified the unparalleled conquest gained through expenditure of American lives and dollars. Neither honor nor logic justified surrender of the great military line of the Sierra Madre for a return to the lesser Rio Grande and perpetual border warfare.[9]

As rumors of imminent ratification reached New Orleans, the *Crescent*

188

asserted that peace between the two countries was impossible, assaulted Polk
in prose and doggerel for humbugging the Senate, and imputed this "*triste*
affair*" to British connivance and Mexican venality: "the power of gold is
great!" After many other advocates of annexation had become silent, the
Crescent still insisted that Mexico must be subdued. When its correspondent "Topaz" sent word that the Mexican government would accept the
"horrible joke," the paper wrote its postscript in language made famous by
O'Sullivan (now involved in the attempt to acquire Cuba): "We will, at
present, not enlarge upon our manifest destiny—it is self-evident." En-
largement came in later editorials that prophesied a second Punic War and
the extension of the United States to the Isthmus of Darien, "whatever
politicians may plan or parties resolve. The thing is decided on, and it is
useless to resist fate."

The *Crescent* staff member who trumpeted manifest destiny from its
columns was a slight, dignified native of Nashville who had earned his first
university degree at fourteen, studied medicine in Philadelphia, and become
a physician at nineteen. Then followed two years at the Sorbonne, Heidel-
berg, and Edinburgh where to Latin and Greek he added French and
German, while Victor Hugo joined Byron as his libertarian mentor. His
chief medical interest seemed to be in the potential of mesmerism. Home
again, he decided to change professions and cities, moved to New Orleans,
and became a lawyer. Now at twenty-four he closed his Canal Street office
and turned to journalism. By 1855 he would be famous as the Nicaraguan
filibuster, General William Walker. Then overtaken by disaster while
battling to win lands for slavery he would die before a firing squad.[10]

When Polk's Washington *Union* noticed the first *Crescent*, it exposed
the paradox in the paper's desire to "escape from the maelstrom of party
politics" while at the same time bearing "already to the side of the opposition." Whitman himself on sober reflection could not help concluding
that the paper's "All Mexico" policy negated free soil. But exulting in the
scope of the immense land he had begun to know since February he chose
at first to see the issue in the tolerant perspective of "a very true and very
profound" remark by de Tocqueville (whom he admired as the author of
one of the best works ever published on American institutions). Whatever
the course of things on minor points, the *Crescent* paraphrased, "no earthly
power can deprive our republic of the *facts* which make her grow so fast,
and have already made her become so great." The Mississippi and the limit-

189

less world beyond its banks, the promise in the western miles trekked by Kearny made all political issues petty: "Probably the error of those who bring such matters as the Mexican war, the tariff question, slavery, federal finance, and so on, to bear on the solidarity of our national future, is simple here: they do not rightfully estimate the greatness of what goes to make up that solidarity." [11]

The man who had caused controversy in Fulton Street turned discreet in Charles Street. The *Picayune* denounced Wilmot and the *Crescent* branded his legislation a gigantic phantom that disturbed repose, but Whitman did not attempt to refute the local Dickinsons. In silence he read copy of advertisements of auctions to be held by Beard, Calhoun, and other dealers at Banks' Arcade where "very likely" merchandise just received from Virginia or North Carolina would be put on the block:

> Jerry, aged 26, a superior cotton picker and leader in the field, fully guaranted;
> Sarah Ann, 17 years, house girl, and her infant girl, fully guaranteed;
> Etty, 30 years, an excellent cook and washer, fully guaranteed excepting sometimes drinks.

Because the Arcade served as a newsgathering center, he was there to watch the spectacle. Sales began at noon after inspection by prospective buyers of the chattels who filled benches and small rooms. A waiter with a tray of brandy and water stood ready to refresh the auctioneers; planters lounged at the huge bar that filled an entire side wall of the Arcade and, abolitionists charged, became drunk while their neighbors bought themselves rich in Negroes. When Frederica Bremer came to New Orleans the next year, a tour of the Arcade shocked her into declaring that no orator could indict the institution of slavery with the power of an hour spent at this auction.

The *Crescent*, like other southern papers—and Twain's Duke—printed the classic woodcut of the runaway and its promise of reward for his capture. It listed those arrested for sheltering fugitives and in the daily summary of crime branded accused thieves with the divisive letters f. w. c.—free woman of color. Each evening at eight the brothers heard the bell in the Market House warn all slaves to leave the streets. The treatment of blacks imprisoned for breaking the curfew law—or any other—made the visiting Dr. Howe blush that he was a white man.

190

In his assignment as exchange editor Whitman used pen, scissors, and paste on papers received from all over the country. The work was easy except when an "extremely intemperate" colleague failed to reach the office. In these emergencies he turned to his travel diary or scrapbook and reset an old column: on All Fool's Day readers met the admonition he had given Brooklynites—avoid worshipping the Dollar God. Another day he repeated the reasons for a park on Fort Greene.

Some of his original pieces for the *Crescent* were those of a sightseer, a fascinated spectator come to a foreign capital where it was possible to go through the whole alphabet of enjoyment and "not miss a letter from A to Izzard." In Brooklyn Shrove Tuesday was merely another day; in New Orleans crowds in grotesque costumes celebrated the Mardi Gras with frenzied revels. Women impersonated Amazons, but "bestrode their horses with the grace of Jean d'Arc." Men threw handfuls of flour upon every stranger, to the amusement of native bystanders; Whitman received his share of flour and laughter. The festival culminated in a series of masked balls.

With Jeff he stopped to applaud the eleventh anniversary celebration of the volunteer fire department. In the parade were firemen of hook and ladder companies in red shirts, blue collars, and white trousers; their burnished equipment and matched teams of roan, bay, and black were bedecked with flowers. The proper end to all this was a spread in the rotunda of the St. Charles, "with something to wash down the edibles." The brothers wasted fifty cents a ticket to watch a balloon that never ascended; after the third failure angry native "b-oys" littered Poydras Street with pieces of the balloon. Another time, the Whitmans joined a huge crowd at the Jockey Club across the river for the long-awaited match between Colonel Johnson's famous Orator and a chestnut mare, Quadrille. In an upset the mare won two three-mile heats, and the crowd filled with dollars the cap of the victorious rider, a slave boy who had survived a near fall.

The relaxed Sunday tolerated saunters along the levee and visits to the barber and the many clothing shops. One could watch cockfights or see an "artiste" spear bulls imported from Havana. In the evening there were theatres, ice cream saloons, processions of dandies, war volunteers clad in indigo uniforms, sailors in blue blouses and tarry breeches. Thronged around the St. Charles were swindlers, faro cheats, and Peter Funks who decoyed rustics to mock auctions. A lover of flowers—he cautioned sister Hannah to water his recent plantings—Whitman walked under the white buds of the magnolia. Who in Brooklyn knew the live oaks of Carrolltown gardens and the beautiful green of orange trees, or could buy bouquets at every street corner for a dime? But in this sense-quickening season Miss Dusky Grisette, the flower vendor stationed across from the St. Charles, drew his patronage for another reason: "The em bon point of her form is full of attraction."

Responding to all beauty the bachelor spent an evening "superb beyond compare" at the Hebrew Benevolent Association ball among "lovely Daughters of Israel" and "elegant Christian maids." But those who frequented the ballrooms reserved for the f. w. c. and white men often met violence rather than romance. The *Crescent* reported the murder at one of a Californian carrying $900; bloody brawls between drovers and flatboatmen were common. Testimony to the beauty of the quadroon came from observers as different as Mrs. Trollope and de Tocqueville. Whitman may have pondered the sociologist's comment that immorality between the two races had tightened local custom into a virtual law that doomed the quadroon to concubinage.

The streets and the courtrooms of the municipalities showed him the opposite faces of the city. In an afternoon's walk he passed hundreds of modest, graceful ladies who "moved along like swans upon the surface of a calm river." Six harlots in Recorder Baldin's dock evoked his compassion for they ranged from a young girl to "an old gray haired inebriate (and yet she was a woman)." After they were sentenced, he mused that the poor Magdalenes might have known a mother's love but "never had they knelt at the Savior's feet." Where in the North could a reporter's lead describe a trial like that of Senator Pierre Soulé, who acted as his own defense counsel. When a judge resented Soulé's histrionics and ordered him held for contempt, partisans of the senator formed at the calaboose, serenaded him, and after his liberation followed his coach and four white horses with a band.

Prayer also had its pageant. During Easter the brothers pushed their way through the Place d'Armes into the small brick Cathedral of St. Louis hallowed for Whitman because Jackson had given thanks in it for the victory against the British. The cathedral claimed another distinction: here only could men and women of every shade and color meet side by side. On Holy Thursday the brothers saw that many of the supplicants were Creole girls who carried gilt-edged missals. The altar was heaped with flowers and lighted by candles set in silver, the cross was draped with purple silk. The service seemed to Walt to show "reverence and respect for the tortures endured by the God-like Hero of Calvary, for the benefit of a sinful world," and endowed his soul "with full reliance in the power of Him who rules alone." Jeff's description was less pious: "Everyone would go up and dip their fingers in the holy water and then go home and *whip* their *slaves*. One old black took a bottle full home to wash the sins out of her family."[12]

The city's many playgoers found incomprehensible the gossip sent from Manhattan by "Figaro," correspondent of the *Picayune*, that legitimate drama was in its last days there; or that Bennett, as Max Maretzek testified, "consecrated a certain amount of space, in his columns daily, to the abuse of the opera." Here, where a golden curtain bore an embroidered allegory of an American eagle carrying Shakespeare, the theatres managed by James Caldwell, Noah Ludlow, and Sol Smith prospered. French opera directed by a graduate of the Paris Conservatory enjoyed regular patronage. Nor were composers and singers from other nations ignored. The night the *St. Cloud* docked, Madame Bishop sang *Linda de Chamounix*. (Some of the Creole audience found her English lower register poor.) Whitman soon sensed that all music gained a hearing, from the tooting of a penny whistle to the call of soul-entrancing silver bugle, a blind harpist, Sable Methodists, and the eighteen Austrian Steyermarkers whose "Sounds of Home" made him so melancholy he shed tears.

A fortunate association deepened Whitman's enjoyment of a sequence of Bellini and Donizetti. The language translator of the *Crescent* was Durant da Ponte, grandson of the librettist of *Don Giovanni* and *The Marriage of Figaro*, and the son of the late Professor of Italian at New York University. Knowing da Ponte and his wife, an artist-poet, made performances of *I Puritani*, *Norma*, and *Lucia* meaningful. The rest of the audience had its own enticement; planters from Lafourche, scions of merchants, and leaders in the professions were all served in the upstairs wine saloon between acts. "Nowhere in this country," wrote a columnist in the *Literary World*, "could I satisfiedly listen to operatic performances after wearing out a brace of coats at the Orleans theatre, and preserving in memory the uniformly good music there listened to, or the attentive and animated faces there looked upon."[13]

Actors and other entertainers from the North seemed to converge on New Orleans that spring. The equestrian Levi North, a boyhood friend from Brooklyn, was at the National with his horse, Tammany. Forrest held sway for weeks at the refurbished American, the native "Talma," as the *Crescent* called him, giving in his robust manner *Jack Cade*, the *Broker of*

Bogata, and *Hamlet*. A company from New York led by Placide included Mrs. Hunt whose "graceful and Hebeish" figure Whitman admired. Then came Julia Dean, whose debut at the Bowery he had attended two years ago; he found her beautiful and talented. Relishing her in *Evadne*, *The Lady of Lyons*, *The Wrecker's Daughter*, and *The Wife*, he felt certain that the girl who had leaped from boarding school to the boards would become "the bright particular star of the American stage." (But the *Picayune* objected to her "redundancy of action and too majestic a walk"; and when she did Juliet to Mrs. Hunt's Romeo the next month the audience found humor Shakespeare never intended in a lover who was not only much smaller than his beloved but who was "sporting inexpressibles.")[14]

Jeff wrote home that he expected "some fun" from John Collins, the Irish comedian whose Rory O'More and Paddy Murphy made him the successor to the late Tyrone Power. But the boy evidently did not receive a brotherly invitation to see the sensation of the season, Dr. Collyer and his Living Models—twenty specialists in nude posturing. Greeley called these displays seminaries in vice for the young; they also lured "gray-headed roués." Before the troupe reached New Orleans, Whitman told the Mobile *Herald*, which also charged lewdness, that the undraped figure was a divine masterpiece, that few subjects were more important and less understood than physiology, and that "sickly prudishness" beheld "only the indelicacy of such things." He gave a simpler reason to Major Noah for buying a ticket: "Everyone is anxious to see *the one whom Mr. Clay kissed*— 'Psyche.' "

He hurried to report after the first viewing that "modesty of actions and posture was not violated." The real danger was suffocation in the crush of patrons of the fine arts and mythology who at a dollar a ticket filled the St. Charles to watch poses based upon paintings by Titian and Rubens, sculptures of Zeus and his heavenly court. As an encore the models danced an Olympian polka. To celebrate the anniversary of Palo Alto and Resaca de la Palma, they gave Venus rising from the sea and Eve when first sighted by Adam. General Taylor was in the audience and Whitman thought he looked like James Fenimore Cooper. In the entire series that spring the *Crescent* questioned only one lapse from taste: during a curtain bow Collyer wore a pea-green vest.

Attendance at Gliddon's nine lectures on Egypt was understandably sparse, for he competed with Collyer and a second troupe of "exhibitionists" who had been heralded by the notoriety of arrest in a groggery brawl. Eager

194

for press notices the lecturer visited the printshop and "astonished"[15] Whitman with a wealth of material on hieroglyphics, animal worship, and the pharoahs. When Gliddon, who had literally pitched his tent in the shadow of the pyramids as a boy of thirteen, published the series of lectures he used the blurb Whitman had placed in the *Crescent* in an attempt to fill the seats at the National Gallery. But citizens of New Orleans preferred undraped living bodies to mummies, the *Book of the Dead*, and "a sublime definition of the Godhead, under the Hindoo name of Brahma." Knowing the Mississippi, as one wag had it, they would not walk ten paces to hear about the Nile. They also cared little about the Styx for few attended the Reverend Mr. Campbell's sermon on Hell.

Literature and taverns, a traveller noted, "touched noses in cosy friendship in New Orleans." Morgan's, the largest of the four book depots, had space in the Exchange near a fifty-foot bar and the post office. After seeking letters from home or sending them, the brothers moved through the aroma of mint and lemon, beyond splendid pier glass and marine paintings, into a room where tables held imported papers and magazines. *Yankee Doodle* and the *Literary World* lay near *Punch* and *Blackwood's*. The stock of English novels had to be measured by yardstick; yellow- and blue-covered translations of French fiction filled an entire counter. Patrons or loungers who read there by the hour, rather than in the city's one small library, were welcomed by the proprietor known for his good humor as well as catholic taste. Whitman also sampled Rusconi's depot across the street from the St. Charles, and White's, which sent him a gift copy of Walker's *Dictionary*.

Jeff proved to be a severe judge of his brother's selections: "he gets a few books most every day but none of them worth much." Fiction helped pass evenings too rainy to walk streets ankle-deep in mud; Whitman recommended Cooper's *Jack Tier* for its romantic interest, and C. W. Webber's *Old Hicks, the Guide*, "a true sort of American book" of adventure in Texas during the thirties. But he scoffed at the Mobile *Herald* for praising *Dombey and Son* which he found a motley jumble with an "inartistical" plot and hurried ending. The reviewer's enthusiasm went instead to a treatise on prosody just published by Appleton.

He told versifiers and those aspiring to read poetry with a full perception of its beauty to buy Erastus Everett's *System of Versification*. If prose like Addison's was the product of consummate art, why should good poetry be considered the result of inspiration "utterly unaided by art? The idea is preposterous." Everett had moved methodically from Gascoigne through

Hallam and had chosen illustrations from that wide range; but the *Crescent* suggested that the next edition include the hexameter used in *Evangeline* and the *Vision of Judgment*. Southey's preface like that of *Paradise Lost* contained a justification of long lines that "have none of the customary characteristics of English versification, being neither marked by rhyme, nor by any certain number of syllables, nor by any regular recurrence of emphasis through verse."

Later that spring Whitman returned again to question the source of the greatest beauty of poetry and concluded that it lay "in a faithful adherence to nature and truth." Knowing an unemployed poet who was "gnawed by an ambitious vulture in his heart," he pondered why those assured of income perpetrated sententious pieces. Meanwhile he scissored "Love! though ye clasp a phantom to the heart!" [16]

There were sessions at Gould's studio in Camp Street where New Yorkers talked of home, of this southern life, and of the letter sent from Rome by the painter Thomas Hicks and reprinted in the *Crescent*. ("When I came here," Hicks wrote, "the meaning of art burst upon me. I saw . . . that what we call Art in America was only the faint imitations and decaying branches of a goodly tree.") After Whitman told subscribers to place in their rooms a print—no matter how cheap or costly "provided they *see something* in *it*," —Gould brought a portrait of Schiller to the office in keeping with his friend's belief that "the companionship of anything greater or better than ourselves must do us good."

Nothing Whitman read that spring stirred him as deeply as Lamartine's "almost painful" *The Girondists*. Now available in its impassioned entirety the three-volume work on Brissot, Vergniaud, Madame Roland, and compatriots confirmed his first impressions that as a history of "that wonderful era—when the works and changes that at an ordinary time required hundreds of years, were done in so many days (we may almost say hours) *The Girondists* is, beyond comparison, the best book ever written." Guided by the Breton priest, Lamennais, whose doctrines urged evangelical charity and Christian idealism rather than frivolous class distinction and political selfishness, Lamartine had transformed the deputies from Bordeaux into apostles preaching the gospel of democracy as an emanation of profound faith. Attempting to make the Constitutional Assembly an "ecumenical

196

council of modern reason and philosophy," the deputies were martyred while proclaiming liberty, equality, and fraternity. Other critics would call Lamartine a rhetorician rather than an accurate historian; de Tocqueville found him an ambitious egotist who never honored truth. But many Americans shared Whitman's response to *The Girondists*; Lowell composed an ode of gratitude. That spring, events across the Atlantic made the volumes a preface to a new revolution and turned Lamartine into a statesman soon to be compared with Washington.

Like all American journalists Whitman prized news from the capitals of Europe. In the first *Crescent* he itemized the antics of Leopold, King of Bavaria, and the woman from Scotland now called Lola Montez. The next week he gave space to Pius IX, who after his election in 1846 had walked the streets of Rome, pardoned political prisoners, given audiences without ceremony, and appointed commissions to remedy abuses. The Pope, in the view of the one-time antagonist of Bishop Hughes, "seems fitted, in an extraordinary manner, for the work that is to be done in Italy—the work of freedom. His heart is right, and his motives are pure!"

Throughout March 1848 the exchange papers kept Whitman aware of growing tension abroad. Ik Marvel in Paris for the *Courier and Enquirer*, described heated sessions in the Chamber of Deputies; a steamship brought news on 15 March of uprisings in Naples. The next days in New Orleans seemed to belong to the Model Artists and to Forrest who gave a farewell *Hamlet*. A Dr. Nott of Mobile gained passing attention with his hypothesis that yellow fever was of "animalicular origin"—the result of attack by some invisible species of insect. Then on 24 March the city learned of revolution in France.

The news relayed by "special and extraordinary messenger" from eastern ports provided bare outlines of the forbidding of political banquets, the fatal street fighting, the deposition of Guizot, and the abdication of Louis Philippe. The *Crescent* at first followed a policy of cautious acceptance: "All these things may be. And if they are, the world is about to see stirring times!" Additional bulletins obtained after the docking of later ships provided enough details to fill three columns, and the staff left 95 Charles Street to join the throngs rejoicing around the Exchange. Sunday night the city officially celebrated the birth of the French Republic in the hope that "its future be glorious and happy as its past has been brave but unfortunate." At the end of the first week when Whitman heard that Lamartine was now minister for foreign affairs and that the new government had decreed universal male suffrage and abolished the death penalty, he exclaimed, "One's blood rushes and grows hot within him the more he learns or thinks of this news from the continent of Europe! *This* time, the advent of Human Rights, though amid unavoidable agitation, is also amid comparative peace."

Every ship and every dispatch over the telegraph—available to the city through Mobile since the end of March—added to the virtual frenzy. "Editors are making all they possibly can out of that perfect God-send," explained the correspondent of the *Atlas*. Compositors set heavy leaders and whole columns in minion type to follow the "Progress of Liberty." Rivalry grew over the sponsorship of banquets: the one at the St. Louis ballroom charged two dollars, one at a modest place only a dollar; at both toasts were offered to the freedom of the whole world. The military fired a hundred-gun salute, citizens sang the Girondist hymn, "Mourir pour la Patrie," the *Crescent* printed the "Marseillaise." Whitman rejoiced when he learned of sympathetic demonstrations in New York where "our esteemed friend Major Noah" aided by Bryant, Greeley, and Sedgwick, had chaired a vast assemblage.[17]

On Monday when a ship docked with sixty-nine followers of Étienne Cabet, author of the utopian novel *Voyage en Icarie* and coiner of the word "communist," they met festive throngs eager to welcome all refugees. Whitman watched them embark on an inland steamer in search of a home in Texas and found them "comely" men and women: "We never saw a more cleanly, tidy party than the Communists. They stepped from the wharf to the sides of the steamboat, with all the energy of those who knew and felt that 'Freedom's land was theirs.'"

Confirmation that Minister Rush had addressed the Provisional Government and proceeded to the Hotel de Ville in formal recognition of it, brought praise from the *Crescent* for prompt, manly conduct in the tradition of Jefferson. President Polk's message backed by congressional support—both Abraham Lincoln and Jefferson Davis in accord—offered reason for every American bosom to fill with unalloyed optimism for the revolution of '76 extended across the sea.

The first serious questioning of the nature of the Republic came after the analysis of a circular distributed by the minister of the interior, the lawyer Ledru Rollin, who advised by George Sand attempted to secure an Assembly "animated by a revolutionary spirit." The *Picayune*, whose Kendall was in Europe, thought this an attempt to promulgate a doctrine of unlimited governmental power. Elsewhere in the South the edict freeing slaves in all French possessions was received with hostility. In New York the *Courier and Enquirer* charged that the new leaders went far beyond simple republicanism and embodied many of the principles of communism and socialism: they favored national workshops and had plans to nationalize insurance companies, railroads, mines, canals, and the Bank of France. The *Tribune* countered by praising the "social science" of a sister republic whose birth seemed the "grandest spectacle of modern times." The *Crescent* echoed Greeley: "People will know something more about this Fourierism, of which so much is said, and so little understood!" When the Senate of the United States by one vote withheld a resolution of sympathy, Whitman printed Gould's sonnet to France that ended with "à bas le Senate!" As days passed without news of violence or the replacement of the tricolor by the red flag, Whitman found evidence that local support had intensified. The *Picayune* now felt confident that the work of destruction had ended and the labor of reconstruction begun. The merchants of New Orleans showed admirable restraint despite the lists of bankruptcies among international traders; the *Crescent* assured them of the great benefit a new, vigorous Europe would bestow on them.

With few exceptions little else seemed to occupy Whitman. He joined local ladies and gentlemen for an inspection tour of the Lafayette schools and found them delightful: "They do not trammel the mind of pupils by fixed rules—here it is no heresy to express doubt as to the infallibility of Lindley Murray's grammar." The razor-strop man, stationed for years on the corner of Nassau and Spruce Streets in Manhattan, stopped by and gave Whitman one of his 25-cent items; they talked of the death of the wealthiest New Yorker, John Jacob Astor.

Ships arriving with further news from France kept the populace "in a perfect ferment." Whitman scissored from a Dublin paper the account of the funeral of Louis Philippe's victims, then attended services at the cathedral for the heroes who had died in the assault on the Tuileries. Each night the crowds in the square and the Exchange grew larger, the banquets more elaborate. Three hundred "gratified" appetites and enthusiasm for the republic at the Orleans, which was decorated by a transparency of the Goddess of Liberty bearing the holy script: Liberty, Equality, and Fraternity.

By mid-April Whitman believed that Europe, with the example of

199

France as the spark to the gunpowder, was undergoing the reconstruction of an entire social and political system: "The whole civilized world is in commotion. . . . Everywhere the people have risen against the tyrannies which oppress them." Other ministers and kings had joined Guizot and Louis Philippe in exile. The aged Metternich fled riots in Vienna; Ludwig and Lola Montez went their separate ways out of Bavaria; Berlin and other German cities knew fighting; citizens of Milan ousted Austrian troops. The *Crescent* now printed Bryant's translation of the song of Italian patriots, a German ode to liberty, the Irish "Fall, Flag of Tyrants!" and "Vive le Tricolore." As dispatches reported details of revolution from Lombardy to Poland, from Dublin to Budapest, Whitman assumed that the democratic principle had at last triumphed and that war, desolation, "and furious hate, must sink away as blood of slain men into the soil." He offered the new electorates a formula for permanent success: that government is best which governs least. (He had enjoyed a recent series about Paine in Noah's *Sunday Times*.)

By his eager reckoning social reform would come first to Germany, then to England and Ireland where "the Chartists only ask for universal suffrage —and some among us are foolish enough to think that the Government will give it to them!" Americans in England that spring found Chartist agitation growing, as leaders like Fergus O'Connor exploited the desperate condition of the unemployed. Emerson in London attended a meeting where the sentiment was, "Every man a ballot and every man a musket"; at teas, his hosts and other guests confessed they expected revolution. Kendall sent letters to New Orleans so graphic they merited the boast of the *Picayune* that they gave a more satisfactory account of the demonstrations than did any other witness. In them Whitman read of Chartist preparation for the march by half a million from Kennington Common to Parliament, to present the giant petition signed by six million; then of the demonstration's "perfect failure" on 10 April thanks to the overwhelming strength of 175,000 special constables deployed by the Duke of Wellington. One of the constables, Louis Napoleon, would soon rule France. (Amid all this, Kendall went to Covent Garden to hear a *Barber of Seville* he rated far inferior to productions at home; the next night, he admired *Don Giovanni* sung by the great Mario.)

Puzzled by the Chartist fiasco Whitman wondered why the fiery cross of freedom, which had passed from hand to hand and nation to nation throughout Europe, had failed to cross the channel. After reading the exchange papers he attempted to explain the "retrograde" movement:

> Words cannot hardly describe the fierceness which the "better off" portion of Englishmen feel towards the English Chartists and Irish Repealers. Nearly all the London and Liverpool prints develop this hatred—sometimes quite painfully so. They forget everything in the griefs, wrongs, oppressions, destitutions, and frequent starvation of the "lower orders" in England and Ireland, and think only of the presumption of poor starving men in daring to ask *anything* from the government. The truth is, the body of English believe in the superiority of their lordlings and gentry, and think it right that the latter should ride "booted and spurred" over all who stand in the way of their dignity.[18]

Other dispiriting news followed. Late in April a papal encyclical announced neutrality in the war of independence Italy was waging against Austria, and Pius IX then withdrew his troops from the Italian army. Kendall's letters from Paris were as foreboding as the earlier ones from London. National workshops had burgeoned from six thousand to a hundred thousand; there was danger of conflict between Paris and the countryside, between the clubs and members of the National Guard who shouted, "Down with the Communists!" Ledru Rollin was believed to be in open disagreement with Lamartine; many feared a new Jacobinism.

New Orleans learned of the elections to the French Assembly by 24 May; Lamartine was quoted as believing the country was safe. Kendall described a triumphant fete with at least a million citizens, many carrying the tricolor and banners with their egalitarian motto embroidered in gold letters. Whitman was gone from New Orleans by June when Paris endured three days of street fighting in which cannon were fired pointblank by troops into the barricades built and manned by their countrymen—among them Baudelaire. General Cavaignac emerged victorious over the insurgents, but Lamartine mourned the death of the Republic. It seemed that Emerson would not have to wait until the end of the year to know if the revolution was worth the fine trees cut from the boulevards for the barricades.

At four in the afternoon on Friday, 26 May 1848, the brothers boarded the St. Louis-bound *Pride of the West*; at dusk the packet cleared port. A congeries of reasons had ended their stay, though the *Eagle* a year later in an analysis of Whitman's character had a simple explanation: "How long did he remain there? Until they could decently get rid of him."[19]

The climate seemed intolerable. "Literally we have no spring here," wrote the *Atlas* correspondent. "The end of April brings with it a scorching sun, and a dull, heavy oppressive atmosphere—enough to make an ordinary person commit suicide—despite nankeens, straw hats, cold baths, iced rum, punches, juleps." Rains that made "the very umbrellas shiver with cold" flooded streets, with the result that ladies refused to risk splashing their white stockings. When north winds dried the mud, dust filled the air and covered trees and grass. Water carts sprinkled the streets but filth from the gutters was then raked toward the middle and remained there to nauseate natives and strangers. Whitman's exhilaration over beautiful days when "the roof of the world—the clear blue sky—seemed to have been newly shingled" was replaced by complaints that "the caloric of our New Orleans atmosphere is approaching some!" Humid vapor out of the great swamps turned the city into a vast furnace and made breathing difficult. As a humanitarian gesture Whitman asked that a fountain for parched passersby be placed in Lafayette Square and that those "children of the soil"—flowers, shrubs, and trees—be planted in Canal Street. On 12 May he wrote Noah that the city was getting "too hot to hold us much longer. . . . There is little of interest stirring here just now. The revolutions of Europe absorb everything else."[20]

Opera and theatre curtains lowered until autumn. Julia Dean no longer showed her "fine figure, good—nay, handsome and expressive features." The race track closed; no one sponsored masquerades; traffic thickened on the shell road to Lake Pontchartrain and other resorts. "Strangers from the rocky North," wrote the *Picayune*, "are breaking up and wending their way, by various routes, to their homes." Those who remained inevitably worried about their chances of escaping contagion. Visitors had always found summer in New Orleans and yellow fever as inseparably connected as ham and chicken; the writer who recorded impressions of one had to mention the other. Though the *Crescent* and other papers advertised Townsend's Sarsaparilla as a cure for fever and ague no real faith existed in its efficacy; Dr. Nott's animalicular idea would remain unproved for half a century. Meanwhile the city had the highest death rate in the country with Northerners seemingly most susceptible. The brothers assured Louisa Whitman that they were in perfect health; in fact Walt thought he had never felt better. But after the homesick Jeff contracted "disentery," early bravado turned to apprehension. McClure also seemed to demand that the boy work harder than Walt thought he should.

At one time in March, Walt estimated "prospects in the money line" so bright that he confided to his mother, "O how I long for the day when we can have our quiet little farm, and be together again." Whatever agreement existed with McClure about the duration of their contract, by 23 April Jeff told the family that they would come north as soon as Walt had saved a thousand dollars, "and already he has quite a sum." But the goal may have proved elusive, for expenses were far greater than in Brooklyn. Hours had to be spent in hotel bars, the sites of bulletin boards, telegraphs, and other news sources; their sherry cobblers cost ten cents and so did apples sold in Suffolk for a penny. An extremely low price for cotton, tight money, the impact of Senate ratification of the treaty of Guadalupe Hidalgo, chaos in Europe—all slowed business and made bankers cautious. Many small shops closed; soldiers sold their discharge notes, worth $100 or 160 acres of government land, for a little as $40 to speculators. Whitman's attempt to get a salary advance at this time led only to irritation.[21]

The expansionist policy of the *Crescent*—"Mexico must be subdued"— negated the early promise of the publishers to "keep clear from the maelstrom of party politics"; in fact by April they announced, "we shall never hesitate to put in a word—many words sometimes—upon these questions." With doggerel and epithet Walker ridiculed the Trist treaty as a budget of fun and the Proviso as a laughingstock. For Whitman to remain silent the next months in New Orleans during the campaign debates over these issues would amount to willful surrender of franchise.

In a letter sent to him after New York's April elections (the Whigs victorious in Brooklyn, the Barnburners in Manhattan), an *Eagle* printer told him:

> Now and then a negro might be seen stepping up to the ballot box to deposit his vote. How would such a maneuver suit the people of the "Crescent city?"—not only allowing them to vote, but carrying them to and from the polls at the expense of the party.[22]

Issues of the *Crescent* gave the answer. Insisting that the 60,000 blacks of the city were allowed "too much latitude in the way of vice and amusement," the paper asked the police to arrest those found in grogshops; thirty-three were jailed for unlawful assembly. It reprinted the "able" report of

203

Senator Butler of South Carolina on the enforcement of fugitive-slave laws, and on 20 May itemized the results of "ill-judged philanthropy" in the West Indies where, the *Crescent* claimed, abolition had ruined planters and turned contented field hands into idle hordes of drunken, savage freemen.[22]

Exchange papers from New York, letters from Judge Johnson and other friends, told Whitman of political affairs. The Barnburners had "taken the reins in their hands, and right or wrong, . . . thrown off everything like a wish to harmonize with the Hunkers." All intraparty skirmishes now led to the climactic battle at the national convention in Baltimore, where each faction sought to be seated as the official New York delegation. By 24 May after compromise failed, the Barnburners departed, taunting the victorious Hunkers that the lash resounded through the hall. General Cass became the candidate of those who remained. He had published his hostility to the Proviso and branded anything less than annexation of vast Mexican territory "metaphysical magnanimity."

The Whig convention in June also promised to be bitterly divisive. The *Tribune* called the supporters of General Taylor political Model Artists for having stripped themselves of all principles "and standing before the world to be laughed at in their naked imperfections." Those who found it anathema to vote for a slaveholder talked of joining disaffected Democrats and forming a third party. A young Conscience Whig in Massachusetts, Charles Sumner, thought this campaign would become the American counterpart of the European revolution.

On Wednesday, 24 May, Whitman quoted in the *Crescent* a letter from Brooklyn boasting of urban progress: the city of eighty thousand was about to emerge from "oil darkness to brilliant gas light"; the seventieth church had been built; spring business was brisk; the streets were shaded for miles by lush trees. On Thursday he printed an anonymous verse, "Brother, Come Home." The humidity that morning became so oppressive that it seemed his lungs almost refused to function. He then settled his accounts, cleared his desk, and brought two tickets on the *Pride of the West* sailing late the next afternoon, 26 May.

The journey "up country" and through the Great Lakes lasted twenty-one days, its monotony relieved by the talk of deck hands and a race with the

Grand Turk. Some of the passengers were on their way to Philadelphia and the Whig convention, where they would hurrah for the victorious soldier who remained humble enough, according to his managers, to share with anyone a glass of buttermilk, a slice of bread, and a yam potato. When the *Pride of the West* reached St. Louis, Whitman learned that the Baltimore convention had indeed named Cass. This terminated his allegiance to the Democratic party.

Somewhere along the way he knew a moment of gratification when he came upon the June issue of Mrs. Kirkland's handsome *Union Magazine* which contained his familial homily, "The Shadow and the Light of a Young Man's Soul."[23] Its Archie Dean, aimless and "unstable as water," has saddened his widowed mother. Forced from the city to work as a country schoolmaster Archie at first writes her of his misery—"strange as it may seem to most men, she was his confidential friend." Then the untainted air, hospitable folk, and new habits of work transform the loafer into a plentiful provider for the widow. The adjacent pages of the *Union* reviewed *Wuthering Heights.*

A Hudson River steamboat brought the brothers home on the afternoon of 15 June, a day of 97° heat. "Arrived about 5 o'clock in Brooklyn. Found all well." The crowd at City Hall was not for them but for General Cass. The candidate was gracious to the aged, the hard-handed, and the children. While he spoke a rainbow spanned the arch of heaven. Whitman was one of the disenchanted electorate who made certain that it did not point to the White House.

14

ABDIEL

LEES OF THE *ADVERTISER* in a proper phrase for a year of revolution announced that "Rienzi hath returned." The wry chronicler of local events had met his erstwhile colleague in Fulton Street where, "brown face smiling like a wicker basket filled with wooden particles cleft from timber," Whitman disclosed plans for a paper in which he would handle Hunkerism without gloves. Lees went on to predict a dead certainty: if "our Barnburner friend does put forth a daily here in Brooklyn there'll be fun. No bulldog ever clutched determinedly on cattle's nasal membrane (that tender spot)—no grimalkin ever worried horror-stricken mice—more than our amiable locofoco friend will be likely to clutch and worry old Hunkerism in King's County." Early the next month Greeley also talked of the forthcoming paper.[1]

The traveller had survived 3000 miles of rough road, river, and yellow jack—to the regret of a few politicians. Now in the phrase of the *Advertiser* "large as life, but quite as vain, and more radical than ever," motivated by principle and a desire for revenge, he plunged into activity that seemed as intense as the summer's frequent lightning storms, torrential rains, and mad-dog scares. His preparation for publication alternated with public demonstrations of sympathy for Europe in chaos; Ireland now leaderless after the deportation of John Mitchell; Paris, according to Dana of the *Tribune*, flooded with blood during the unparalleled three days of slaughter.

The thirty-six Barnburner delegates who had bolted the convention rather than allow Hunkers to sit in their laps returned from Baltimore to address thousands in the park; on the platform were the leaders Whitman had admired through the years—his Long Island neighbor Cambreleng, Butler, and Tilden. The entire state soon resounded to their summons for a convention to be held in Utica on 22 June; there the Barnburners made Van Buren their presidential nominee and adopted a Wilmot platform.

206

Polk branded their strategy more threatening to the Union than any other episode since the Hartford Convention in 1814: "Mr. Van Buren's course is selfish, unpatriotic, and wholly inexcusable." Nevertheless, forty-nine papers in various parts of New York pledged their support to Van Buren and repudiated the Cass ticket. Adding to Whitman's gratification, exchange papers brought evidence that throughout the nation Liberty Men and Whigs unwilling to accept General Taylor were beginning to talk of joining the Barnburners in a Free Soil convocation at Buffalo, whose vital breath according to the *Tribune*, would be the assumption that the question of slavery extension ought to override and dwarf all others. At Worcester Charles Sumner called upon the Whigs of New England to revolt from the domination of the "lords of the lash and the lords of the loom"; seeking to widen the base of the revolution he wrote to Bryant, Joshua Giddings of Ohio, and Gamaliel Bailey, editor of the Washington *National Era*. Salmon P. Chase began to consult with John Van Buren and Tilden about possible nominees at Bufflalo. During the summer a sense of outrage spread —at a time when all of Europe had risen to end tyranny forever, Whigs wanted to elect a planter whose slaves worked in sugar fields ruled by overseers, "the dregs and refuse of mankind," and Democrats a candidate pledged to extend those sugar fields.[2]

On Saturday evening, 5 August, one hundred Barnburners met in Washington Hall to apoint fourteen delegates to represent Brooklyn at Buffalo. Whitman was one of the speakers, a fact the *Eagle* interpreted as proof that the meeting was "hard pushed," for the Hunker sheet stamped the political philosophy of its former editor as "not much of anything."[3] The Barnburners, however, were more impressed and chose him along with Judge Johnson, Alden Spooner, C. Edwards Lester (an art critic and playwright who had recently come home after years in Italy), and Marcus Spring (a socialist-transcendentalist friend of Emerson). All agreed to campaign against Cass because he would veto the Proviso, and against Taylor because his principles—"if he have any—are unknown."

On the boat to Buffalo early the next week—transportation at half fare to delegates—Whitman and the other "soreheads," as the regulars called them, were joined by the Manhattan contingent which included Bryant, Tilden, and Bigelow. When they reached Buffalo they found over thirty thousand representatives of states ranging from Iowa to Maine who made the streets a moving mass of humanity and filled temporary stands in the park, a mammoth tent pitched on the shore of Lake Erie, and the Universalist church where the policy makers of the Committee of Conference held their sessions.

Day after day Whitman sat among Liberty Men, Conscience Whigs, and abolitionists. He joined in three cheers for the former Tuckahoe slave, Frederick Douglass, also there in search of "free soil for a free people." Now editor of the Rochester *North Star*, Douglass was living testimony to the conflict between black slave and free white labor, for he carried the scars of beatings by white apprentices at a Baltimore shipyard and the memory of ostracism by the calkers of New Bedford. He may have told the Brooklynite—if they met during the social intervals over ice cream and mint juleps—that he shared Whitman's admiration for the Hicksite Friends from Long Island, the British humanitarians, William and Mary Howitt, and that sweet-singing band of young apostles, the Hutchinsons.

Heat taxed the skill of the speakers and the endurance of the audience, but could not silence Stanton, Chase, and Samuel R. Ward, a black man whose oratory equaled the most eloquent of the Caucasians'. The flow of evangelical fervor turned the site into a Bethel; the congregation became a Parisian General Assembly, with Stanton suggesting that they also take as their motto "Liberty, Equality, Fraternity." Many rose at five in the morning to attend prayers and chant

> Come Holy Spirit, Heavenly dove
> With all Thy quickening power.

The evening sessions lighted by oil torches lasted beyond midnight. When Charles Francis Adams wearing a band of crepe was chosen president of the convention, the spirit of his late father seemed within the tent. To Whitman's gratification, Brinkerhoff of Ohio, who in 1846 had been one of the first to attempt to secure territorial restrictions, glorified another departed leader:

> I heard a remark on this stand today—made innocently, no doubt—but being made without reflection, it did injustice to the subject. I heard the name of Locofoco used with reproach. Now, gentlemen, I have glorified in that name. Who was it that first gave that name to any political organization? William Leggett, of the city of New York, and I will ask your chairman if that man ever breathed who advocated, with more intense zeal, with more

208

glowing eloquence, and in a style which genius may have envied, the cause of freedom better than William Leggett? . . . Would to God that he were alive now! He would be with us—his voice, calling us to combat the influences of slavery, would be heard, eloquent as of yore.[4]

Others mined the Bible for tribute to Wilmot who like an earlier David "with the sling of freedom and the smooth stone of truth struck the giant slavery between the eyes—he reels—let us push him over!" Adams devoted part of his address to raising the Proviso to the eminence of the Magna Carta and the Declaration of Independence. When Butler's turn came he used his Cabinet experience to review constitutional issues and to exhort legislators to abstain from compromise; he was confident that a free, Christian electorate would refuse to abolish liberty in New Mexico and California. Whitman joined in the applause when Butler concluded by telling the assemblage that free labor could not survive where slavery held sway.

Around the central Wilmot plank the committee built a platform wide enough to hold everyone who wanted homesteads, cheap postage, a revenue tariff, river and harbor improvements, and economy in government. As one of the keynoters explained, "If we are wrong on the Tariff, it can be righted in twelve hours. If we are wrong on Banks, it can be righted by legislation. But if we are wrong on the subject of slavery, it never can be righted. It will reach down to posterity, inflicting curses and misery upon generations yet to come." (When a Whig congressman from Illinois read the platform, he compared its promises to those of a Yankee peddling pantaloons "large enough for any man, small enough for a boy." Twelve years later Lincoln welcomed two of the Buffalo veterans into his Cabinet.)

The choice of a presidential candidate narrowed to a contest between Van Buren, professing now to be imbued with the spirit of the Ordinance of 1787 and the Proviso; and the hero of the Liberty party, "Hale-storm" of New Hampshire, who in his short time in the Senate had been threatened with hanging if he dared visit Mississippi. But Hale's friends lacked organizational strength. One of them, Joshua Leavitt, brought tears from the audience when he asked other Hale supporters to comply with the wishes of the majority as a sign that their fifteen-year labors were completed.[5] Adams was nominated vice president to placate those who remembered that ten years ago Van Buren had not barred southern postmasters from destroying abolitionist mail, or ended slavery in the District of Columbia where one could still see slaves auctioned as openly as in New Orleans. This "codfish and cabbage" ticket brought dissent from Lowell's Hosea Biglow, who charged that Van Buren "ain't half antislav'ry enough." Webster scoffed that the free-spoiler had turned free-soiler.

After "O, Liberate the Bondsmen" by the Hutchinsons the delegates shook hands, cheered, and adjourned. With banners streaming and drums beating, they marched through the streets and chanted for Van Buren and Free Soil, Adams and Liberty. Douglass, who had met John Brown the year before and had listened to his plan for guerilla war upon plantation owners, thought that these three days signaled a dynamic change in the strategy of resistance: "Anti-slavery thus far had only been sheet lightning; the Buffalo convention sought to make it a thunderbolt."

In the little time remaining for the campaign Whitman readied the essential newspaper. (Douglass could have told him that 3000 copies of a weekly cost $80.) Since early July local Free Soilers had begun to assemble a list of subscribers for the *Banner of Freedom* "which shall oppose the extension of slavery, and support for election offices persons who will advocate the same." Promised financial aid by the Johnsons if he agreed to edit the paper, Whitman obtained the list and changed the name to the *Freeman*.[6]

The Reverend E. M. Johnson, now in his seventies, had for years officiated without fee as Episcopal pastor in a church built with his own funds. (Some of his wealth came from the sale of building lots, including one to Walter Whitman). As a theologian "Dominie" was known for tractarian strictures which classed dissenters as heretic wanderers; as a politician, he was a long-time Democrat whose position and wealth placed him high among the county's leaders. In recent years he had become a "strong and persevering advocate" of the Proviso. His son, Judge Johnson, member of the Hamilton Literary Society, had befriended Whitman as far back as the 1841 debut in Manhattan, entertained him at the mansion and garden in Clinton Avenue, one of the showplaces of the expanding city, and written to him in New Orleans. Because of his zealous aid to fugitive slaves the Judge's enemies had begun to call him the "nigger catcher." That August he invested enough money to help equip a modest shop in the basement of the Franklin Building, under the offices of an architect, a daguerreotypist, and a bookseller.

For the present Whitman planned to publish every Saturday at two cents a copy. By October, in time to "wake up Brooklyn to radical sentiments," he envisioned changing the *Freeman* to a penny daily. Convinced of public support for a journal "favorable to the genial and enlightened doctrines of the Free Soil" party, he promised to continue after November with clear type and good paper. Meanwhile he asked indulgence for broken letters, misplaced words, and other "awkwardnesses," and exhorted:

> Free Soilers! Radicals! Liberty Men! all whose throats are not quite tough enough to swallow Taylor or Cass! come up and subscribe for the *Daily Freeman*! It will be chock full of the right sort of matter. Let us see whether we can't make both Whig and Democratic Old Hunkerism reel in Kings county.[7]

He made certain that readers of the first *Freeman* on 9 September understood his program:

> Hardly any one who takes the trouble to look two minutes at our paper will need being told, at any length, what objects we have in view. That our doctrine is the doctrine laid down in the Buffalo Convention, and expounded in the letters of Van Buren and Adams—that we shall do what we can to help the election of these candidates—that we shall oppose, under all circumstances, the addition to the Union, in the future, of a single inch of *slave land*, whether in the form of state or territory—these are our first objects.

To justify a policy whose essence was that future generations must not be visited with a "wicked and most dangerous curse," he pointed to the serene light shed by Jefferson:

> How he hated slavery! He hated it in all its forms—over the mind as well as the body of man. He was, in the literal sense of the word, an *abolitionist*; and properly and usefully so, because he was a Southerner, and the evil lay at his own door.

Had the South followed Jefferson's teachings, how much better for the nation. Congress must recognize that below the Mason and Dixon line

211

now, as in his time, white farmers, mechanics, clerks, and professionals entertained "anti-slavery and emancipation doctrines." For lawmakers to defer only to slavers, agents, and breeders was to perpetuate a "cunning trick."

The *Freeman* reprinted Van Buren's endorsement of the Buffalo platform and advised readers to press home upon old Hunkers that it covered the whole ground "and is as much ahead of the hid-in-a-cloud, water-and-molasses letters of Gen. Taylor and Gen. Cass, as daylight is of candlelight." The editor ridiculed the doctrine of popular sovereignty for the new territories. "What we call the extension of slavery Mr. Cass speaks of by a softer appellation . . . the diffusion of slavery." Though he pleaded for civility from other papers, he abused the *Eagle*. Murphy and Lott were political Jesuits who had poisoned Kings County; their clique had reduced government to a game of cunning, of fishing for votes by any means; since Baltimore they had banned the free sentiments vital to citizens of a republic. In short, they lacked regard "for the dictates of men's consciences." Under ordinary circumstances these crimes might be tolerated, but not when they placed in jeopardy "a Great Truth, as holy as any in the Declaration of Independence."

There were a few routine items in that first *Freeman*. Mr. Nivin at his new shop in Fulton Street carried books and periodicals; Mr. Kidder built sturdy frames and mirrors. Fire early Friday had destroyed Nostrand's tannery; citizens pleaded with the mayor to offer a reward for the capture of a gang of arsonists operating almost nightly.

A stroke of fate—or arsonists—that Saturday made the luckless editor wonder if he had been abandoned by the goddess of justice atop the ninety-foot cupola of the new City Hall. Just before midnight a camphene lamp exploded in Riley's crockery store in Fulton Street. Flames soon leaped from its windows into an adjacent factory and combined with strong wind and dry pine buildings to turn the next hours into a holocaust. When the cisterns, low because of drought had been emptied, hundreds of men with buckets built little dams in the gutters to save water. (Three years earlier Whitman had explained in a note to the *Star* that the one way to avoid wide conflagration was to ensure a plentiful reservoir.) No one established a hose line to the river until three in the morning. Twenty engines came from Manhattan, but at the height of the conflagration rival companies of firemen and their rowdy allies brawled; looters had free reign until the Columbia Rifles and City Guard began to patrol the streets.

The fire ended only after marines from the Navy Yard blew up some of the houses in its path to create a break; by then twenty acres of the lower section of the city lay ruined. The melancholy inventory included hundreds of dwellings, dozens of stores, four churches, and the shops of the *Star* and the *Freeman*. "We had not much to lose," Whitman wrote later, "but of what we had not a shred was saved—no insurance." Further calamity threatened the Whitmans, for on Thursday morning despite a patrol of volunteers, Myrtle Avenue was ablaze. This time "salvation came by the stout arms" of Number 5 Company who saved the house and family. In praise of their honorable conduct the son published a "due and heartfelt tribute" in the *Advertiser*.[8]

Always an avid reader of periodicals—he had written to Noah of an impressive pair published in New Orleans—Whitman had time now for the September *Massachusetts Quarterly Review* with its study of "The Philosophy of the Ancient Hindus." Based on Wilkins' translation of the *Bhagavad-Gita* (London, 1785) and Colebrooke's *Miscellaneous Essays* (London, 1837), the paper defined the essence of Hindu metaphysics as the reduction of all reality to pure, abstract soul or thought unified in Brahma. Confessing that a methodical exposition was as difficult as a topographical survey of a wreath of mist, the author used passages from the *Bhagavad-Gita* and the *Vishnupurana* to illustrate that the ideal end of all is soul possessed of the self-knowledge to contemplate nature at leisure and with ease:

> The wise neither grieve for the dead nor for the living. I myself never *was not*, nor thou, nor all the princes of the earth; nor shall we ever cease to be. . . . Death is certain to all things which are subject to birth, and regeneration to all things which are mortal.

In this calamitous season Whitman could test the Vedantic concept that a properly disposed man "having received good or evil, neither rejoiceth at the one, nor is cast down by the other."[9]

Continuing the campaign without the *Freeman*, the Free Soilers held rallies in Brooklyn and joined New Yorkers in vainly battling Mike Walsh and Dan Sickles for control of Tammany whose General Committee soon resolved that it detested "those who supported the infamous coalition formed at Buffalo by Whigs, negroes and the so-called leaders of the Van Buren faction." A hostile press taunted the Free Soilers as broken-down politicians and disappointed office seekers, "all brag and gas, banded into a mongrel party for an unholy purpose." When firecrackers thrown by hoodlums of the Empire Club drove the Free Soilers from assembly halls, they adjourned to the park where "Prince John," Van Buren's eloquent—and elegant— son, blamed the Hunkers for allowing South Carolina to wield at cat-o'- nine-tails on the back of New York democracy. Then they sang:

> And he who still for Cass can be
> He is a Cass without the C.

Racing to publish at least once more before the election, Whitman spent the next few weeks remodeling the ground floor of the Myrtle Avenue house into a shop; on 1 November he issued a *Freeman* larger than the first one. His editorial acknowledged the numerical superiority of the Hunkers whose leaders had grown rich and would not yield without a long struggle:

> But though the conservatives are strong here, that's no reason why the Radical Democracy shouldn't have their say. Indeed the fact that they are powerful is reason enough, without any other. We want folks to hear what our side has to offer. We want a press which can promulgate something more than the mere edicts of caucuses and packed conventions.

He repeated his September pledge to make the *Freeman* permanent and to continue "expounding the most liberal principles in politics, Radically Democratic, and opposed to Slavery and all other infringements on the rights of man to life, liberty, and a comfortable existence." [10]

After examining a copy of the "remarkably handsome" *Freeman*, the Long Island *Democrat* thought its future safe; no other Free Soil organ existed in the county and the editor had many friends. Within the month the *Star* reprimanded him for borrowing columns of statistics without acknowledgment.

Too experienced to be swayed by rallies, songs, and other emotional aspects of the campaign, Whitman conceded victory to Taylor or Cass, but looked to the large future when the contest for "freedom and other radical rights" would be settled. Marcy, the Hunker leader, pained by the prospect of defeat for the party he had served since youth, also rationalized about the "usefulness of our future services." Those whose memories went back to the turn of the century thought that they had never seen a brighter election day. It was—for the Whigs in city, state, and nation. The Free Soilers lost every electoral vote though they did capture thirteen congressional districts. But their ballots in New York added to those for Cass would have carried the state by sixteen thousand and sent a Democrat to the White House. Leaders of both factions used this arithmetical fact as a parallel to the prophecy seen on the wall by Daniel.

The lull in politics after the election allowed Whitman to indulge other interests. Common Council's "parsimony in the great concerns of humanity" continued to vex the advocate of lungs for the citizenry. Crowded Sabbath evenings at the Plymouth Church indicated a religious revival, especially among young men who had heard Henry Ward Beecher discourse on the theme that mere curiosity led thousands into vice: "To *see*, only, was their *first* motive and that was all that Satan wanted to entrap them." Local literati were productive. Lester finished a play honoring the "Achilles of Long Island," General Nathaniel Woodhull. Theodore Gould, back from New Orleans, had a volume of verse in press. Dutton published *Gathered Leaves* by Mrs. Spooner, a title appropriate to a family long associated with printing. Her pleasure in that accomplishment became clouded in late November by the death of Alden Spooner. Obituaries cited his championship of the Fort Greene park and free schools; they could have included his guidance of young associates.

A lover of music could feast on both sacred and secular fare. The Mendelssohn Association of Brooklyn sang Mozart and Rossini requiems. Ethiopian minstrels entertained earthier patrons, with Christy featuring his bones player, Julius, by now a celebrated virtuoso. In private parlors one danced to a sheaf of Free Soil waltzes dedicated to Charles Sumner. With a fresh memory of the place given opera in New Orleans the dilettante Whitman hoped Edward Fry would succeed as an impresario in Manhattan. Fry hired the "Napoleon of Conductors," Max Maretzek, who with his gold-tipped baton drilled orchestra, full chorus, and lead singers. The troupe started auspiciously with *Linda de Chamounix* and then the new *Ernani*, "the most brilliant night of this or any other season," according to the *Tribune*. Madame Truffi, doubly blessed with an elegant figure and a voice with a superb middle register, sang Elvira, a role that at once became a Whitman favorite. Performances of *I Lombardi* and *Nabucco* made audiences recognize that Verdi's dramatico-musical power ushered him into the domain hitherto ruled by Bellini, Rossini, and Donizetti. But the dream

215

of a stable operatic company proved elusive. Gossips reported that in a squabble over Benedetti's refusal to be cast with one of the sopranos, Fry "planted a right hander" in the handsome face of the tenor. (This was the winter of the Yankee Sullivan–Hyer prizefight.)

The theatrical critic of the *Atlas* summarized a meager season by noting that "the two-legged legitimates have absquatulated and the four-legged legitimates have taken their place." In December the Park burned but surviving houses did well with Shakespeare, first by Macready and then by Fanny Kemble Butler. Tickets for her readings that started with *Macbeth* were sold days before she appeared in white poplin, her hair "rather low on her temples but without disturbing the classic outline of her head." Aware that here was the type of the suffering woman married to a notorious slaver and adulterer, the press detailed each gown and ornament; Brooklyn saw the lavender silk whose low neck was secured with a diamond brooch. She earned Whitman's unqualified enthusiasm, but Melville thought her Desdemona seemed like a boarding-school miss. Her Lady Macbeth was glorious but "She's so unfemininely masculine that had she not, on unimpeachable authority, borne children, I should be curious to learn the result of a surgical examination of her person in private. The Lord help Butler." [11]

The elderly recluse, Richard Henry Dana, Sr., emerged from self-imposed retirement to give the papers that represented years of labor; Margaret Fuller thought they contained wiser criticism of Shakespeare than Emerson's. Invited to Brooklyn after a successful lecture series in New York, Dana was shocked into contemplating a second retirement by the warning to infuse more life into his delivery or lose the audience.

That winter the rising membership in art unions and the attendance at their exhibitions (so many women that wits called them gal-eries) seemed to presage the arrival of permanent patronage. Whitman crossed to Manhattan to see Rembrandt Peale's allegorical "Court of Death" but stood transfixed when before Ary Sheffer's "Dead Christ." Unlike other connoisseurs he spent little time with the popular imports from Düsseldorf studios.

Heavy snow allowed weeks of splendid sleighing when parties drove the pike to dance at Snedeker's where almost a decade ago Webster had failed to convert a young Locofoco. Though city streets were treacherous, the churchgoers who complained of falling on the way to worship were answered with reference to the wicked standing in slippery places.

But no lecturer, opera, or sport surpassed the drama reported by the daily press from the gold fields of California. Stories of sixteen-pound nuggets were topped by that of two miners who had panned ten thousand dollars in one week; the Philadelphia mint whetted appetites by certifying the high quality of all samples. Brooklynites, like other Easterners, tried to form overland trains or to provision ships for passage around the Cape. Wall Streeters wondered if the nation faced another South Sea bubble. Clergymen began to sermonize on the duties of Christians in relation to California, and warned that golden fleece often dazzled vision. Letters sent from the diggings told of hard times for green hands in a lawless land; in addition to beds, boots, pans, pills, and other "fixins," they advised would-be prospectors to include a coffin.

Whitman saw little need to join the Argonauts. After the great fire, now accepted as a blessing, the rebuilding of the city brought steady work to mechanics and profits to speculators; within the year two thousand buildings were under construction—a rate unsurpassed in the nation. Whitman attended the forced sales of lots whose assessments were unpaid, and using the money earned from one bargain as well as a $400 loan from Judge Johnson (at seven per cent) he improved the print shop, ordered a Napier press, hired a young law reader as a helper, and converted the *Freeman* into a daily.

While he was in the midst of these activities, the local Democrats endured another debacle, for the Whigs routed both factions in the spring elections of 1849. But the Free Soiler rationalized that "The Cause of Freedom and Liberal Principles derived more good from the bitter quarrel, the past two years . . . than it could have derived from the closest party harmony." Faith in the large future unshaken, this "able man," as the Williamsburgh *Times* described him, published a specimen "good looking" daily *Freeman* on 25 April. His editorial assaulted Hunkerism, its leaders, and its tactics: "We have very close at heart the desire to prevent them from ever taking their seats in high places again; and we would resuscitate the Democrats of Brooklyn from their palsying influence."[12]

This flinging of "his gage of battle" made Lees ask, "Walter, have you not the fear of No. 3 before your eyes?" For the moment the reprisal from Hunker headquarters was brief. After hearing the editor of the new daily called "well known," the *Eagle* jibed, "Well, he ain't nothin' else."

217

Regular publication started on Tuesday, 8 May 1849, the morning after the first of the Forrest–Macready riots. Smaller than its three rivals, the paper sold for only a penny; but there was no direct ratio between its size and its editor's aplomb, for he soon boasted of having the second-largest circulation in Brooklyn and of capturing all the municipal advertising. "If Mr. Whitman will tell us how many papers he has given away," retorted the *Star*, "we will tell him within twenty the amount of his subscription." The veteran reminded the newcomer that it took time to gain circulation. "Six days won't do! We wish Mr. Whitman well, but *humbug* is of no use."

He resorted to more than humbug. His newsboys hawked the sheet under the windows of the other shops until they countered by reducing their prices; then he switched to evening publication. To curtail his income the *Eagle* offered to do the corporation printing gratis, but he nevertheless obtained a quarter share at standard rates. "This we are right glad of," Brenton noted in Jamaica, as he ran "A Legend of Life and Love" in the *Democrat*. But Lees warned his new competitor that he had met a man with a green cowhide in hand seeking the editor of the *Freeman*.

The struggle for financial success did not dull Whitman's civic sense. For the sake of oncoming generations he asked for the preservation of open space on the Heights where he often stood and surveyed the roadstead: "You hear the hum of voices, the single and double stroke of the ferry-boat bell, the rattle of its chain, and perhaps the booming cannon, which for an instant silences the steady roar proceeding from behind the forest of masts, and from the midst of the immense pile of bricks before you." Always the elder brother, he urged young idlers to heed Beecher's sermons, and he welcomed another tour by Father Mathews, who administered the pledge to Brooklyn councilmen. (Rum shops and pickpockets did well that day.)

With twenty-nine other "distinguished citizens" he spent an afternoon at the Kings County Poor House and Lunatic Asylum. In one crowded building he walked among rows of iron beds that held aged paupers. In another across the road he observed seventy-four mental patients. A stout woman danced and told secrets; a girl spoke disjointed sounds; one of the men told of a place called Hallelujah. Others laughed, wept, or stared silent at the walls. The superintendent then brought the visitors back to the dining room where he served dinner "on the temperance principle" of meat, vegetables, fruit, and dessert. Whitman thought it obvious that while "economy, humanity, and Christianity" were the "palpable" features of the

218

Asylum, gross overcrowding and the lack of a fire engine imperiled the inmates.[13]

When cholera came in the summer the *Freeman* demanded that Dr. Goodrich, the health officer, remain on constant duty at the emergency hospital. Appalled by the hourly fatalities the editor urged the cleansing of miserable tenements and the closing of slaughterhouses—wiser preventives than ten drops of camphor in cistern water. Charged a dollar for a bushel of lime to purify the family privy, he noted "We were not sorry to hear that the great demand had 'run up' the price in that way." For days the city seemed like a vast charnel house as it endured a procession of caskets on the way to Greenwood.[14]

The cholera had spread westward from Europe. Spring and summer brought details of another sort of suffering, inflicted there by despotism. Restoration of the guillotine in France by the "double-faced dynasty of stock-jobbers" became the grisly symbol of the doom that awaited those seduced by the love of liberty. Charles Dana dispatched to the *Tribune* a series of laments for Italy and Hungary; when French troops entered Rome, Greeley banded the paper in black and Whittier rued the Eternal City's "fresh young life . . . bled in vain." Short months ago Whitman had hailed the promise of reform; now he counted the rising toll of martyrs and watched each ship debark fugitives from betrayed or conquered lands.

But not even the epidemic or the dismaying European news curtailed his saunterings. In Nassau Street one July day after hearing Orson Fowler on "Man," he visited Clinton Hall modeled upon the phrenological museum in Edinburgh with cabinets of skulls and Peale's portrait of George Combe. An occasional lampoon bespoke the hostility of sceptics to the practitioners:

> Hail! glorious science, which all men should foster:
> That would roughen a scull like the shell of an oyster;
> That would think a great head, incomparably greater,
> Stuck over with knobs like a mercer potatoe.

But like many of his credulous contemporaries he submitted to a cranial survey. Lorenzo Fowler found that his dominant traits were friendship, sympathy, sublimity, and self-esteem. At times too open, he lacked restraint in speech and could be sarcastic. If Whitman sought further explanation for amativeness that scored higher than his language, the phrenologists sold a fifteen-cent pamphlet on *Amativeness, or, Evils and Remedies of Excessive and Perverted Sexuality, with Advice to the Married and Single.* The subject gave his occupation as printer, but Fowler suggested another career: "By practice might make a good accountant."[15]

Like other doctrinaires who envisioned victory in 1852, Whitman sought a leader stronger than Van Buren. On 1 June 1849, in his dual capacity as editor and vice president of the seventh ward Free Soil party, he placed the name of Senator Benton on the office flag and the masthead of the *Freeman* as a candidate for the presidency. Whitman had long admired this enemy of the Bank, paper currency, high tariffs, who was an advocate of homesteads and a transcontinental railroad. In the past months the veteran of thirty years in Washington had added another claim to support: he had built "a high wall and a deep ditch" between himself and slavery. Though he represented a slaveholding state, Benton had refused to sign a manifesto devised by southern members of Congress against Wilmot. After the Missouri Assembly instructed him to obey a set of "Calhouniac" resolutions he had taken to the stump and written pamphlets to deny the authority and philosophy of these new nullifiers. At his state capital in May he cited the Northwest Ordinance as an authoritative precedent and praised the Proviso for its Jeffersonian spirit: "It should bear his name, and not Davy's."[16]

Flushed by the acquisition of an ally as renownned as the "Great Missouri Barnburner," Whitman was the first editor in the nation, according to the *Advertiser*, to "nominate" Benton. Soon the editor filled the *Freeman* with exultations over the brilliant prospects that awaited him after the election. In addition to a salary of four thousand dollars he would have one of the most profitable newspaper establishments in the land—"which will enable us to sell out for enough to buy a good farm, to retire to, when we get too much vexed with our official duties." His benevolence—a trait that scored high on Fowler's probe—manifested itself with the promise that in the good time coming he would bestow offices "that don't require great capacity" on men like Van Anden of the *Eagle*. "We will indeed."[17]

His good spirits showed in pleasantries with a neighboring paper which, after an informal survey, had awarded the palm to the ladies of its own district. "Audacious *Times*! The little alleys of Brooklyn have more feminine beauty than Williamsburgh's fashionablest avenues!" "If ye philosopher of ye *Freeman* searcheth for beauty in alleys," answered the *Times*, "we have done. Alley beauty, eh! 'Sally, Sally, Sally in our alley.' "[18] The bachelor's search extended to the annual ball of the Young Men's Association held one hot night in Gothic Hall. Here dresses of white book muslin and hair twined with colored wreaths complemented black coats and pants, white marseille vests, japanned leathers, and white kids. An observant reporter counted only three bustles.

While Whitman furbished the future with sinecures and farms, a major political realignment impended. Throughout the state disgruntled Democrats asked for an end to dissension. Those Barnburners motivated by personal pique had executed their plan by defeating Cass and other Hunkers. The moderates of both groups, the county "fuglemen"—would-be sheriffs and clerks—balked at a feud that brought defeat and humiliation. The *Eagle* added its voice to those in Kings County which sought accord and, like the *Freeman*, began to praise Benton. This turn brought Lee to conjecture about the shape of a union headed by a Barnburner: "Our friend Whitman will then be in his glory, for he will take precedence as the leader of the party in Kings county, and will hang his banner on the outward walls in triumphant exultation over the clique which ejected him from the position he once held, because he would not complacently yield to their intolerant dictation."

But the Hunkers of Kings promptly indicated that they would not extend amnesty to Whitman. The *Eagle* in mid-July reviewed his career, heaped calumny on every phase, and once again insisted that he had been dismissed for incompetence: "Slow, indolent, heavy, discourteous . . . Mr. W. has no political principles, nor, for that matter, principles of any sort." The *Times* came to his defense: "Now, every reader of the *Freeman* must know, that Mr. Whitman, its editor, is a writer of undoubted ability, and furnishes a very excellent journal. We have no paper on our exchange list with which we are better pleased." All antagonists became silent when the *Star* chided them for pettiness while friends and neighbors were dying of cholera.

In August "Union and Harmony" delegates from each faction met for three days in Rome, but the qualified resolutions on the extension of slavery sent from Hunker headquarters at the Presbyterian church to the Barnburners at the Baptist church failed to bridge the gulf. Whitman remained confident that so long as the Hunkers were led by Senator Dickinson and Marcy there would be neither union nor harmony. His judgment seemed confirmed at a meeting in Brooklyn where to his delight Barnburners refused to be fascinated by "the old snakes."

But he misjudged the skill of the Hunker leaders and the desire in both camps to taste the sweets of pap. At Syracuse on 5 September the Hunkers chose a full slate of anti-Wilmot candidates for the fall elections, but announced that for the sake of unity they would allow Barnburners to replace four of these. All that week Whitman waited to hear that his allies had rejected the conciliatory proposal. To his outrage he learned that at their forthcoming meeting in Utica on 12 September they would accept the joint ticket that included Senator Lott, an implacable foe responsible in large part for his loss of the *Eagle* editorship.

The rhetoric of Barnburner leaders failed to convince the editor that merger with the Hunkers would create the "great anti-slavery party" of New York and the nation. Utica became his symbol for the betrayal of Free Soil ideals by ambitious ex-officeholders, a place to be linked with surrendered cities like Paris and Venice. Once again he faced the need to abandon his principles or his post. On 11 September he published his resignation and with his Benton flag held high marched away from another editorship:

> After the present date, I withdraw entirely from the Brooklyn Daily Freeman. To those who have been my friends, I take occasion to proffer the warmest thanks of a grateful heart. My enemies—and old hunkers generally—I disdain and defy just the same as ever.

The *Eagle* rejoiced at further proof that his obvious talents could not compensate for the "low tone of his mind and morals. . . . He lacks, besides, the industry and tact so necessary to the conduct of a political paper; and is more gifted in alienating friends that in making them." But the *Star* saluted the defiant politician: "One man among the Free Soilers rejects the alliance of the Hunkers and holds out—the Abdiel of his party. This man is Mr. Whitman."[19]

15

A TRAVELLING BACHELOR

WHEN BRENTON of the *Democrat* announced to Long Islanders Whitman's severance from the *Freeman*, he added an avuncular blessing: "May the smiles of fortune ever attend Walter in all his peregrinations."[1] Whatever Walter's first impulse he did not journey south or west. For a while he remained at home, the butt of derisive analysis.

On 22 September 1849, the anonymous author of "Sketches of Distinguished Animals" promised to devote an entire piece in the *Advertiser* to "Editor Whitman, that transcendentally fast politician, far ahead of his day and generation, at whose coat tails time and events must keep pulling." By 4 October the sketcher had completed his rendering of the most distinguished of all editorial bipeds of Brooklyn who, "full of egotism" as the first block of Fulton Street was of politicians, assumed "to be a literary genius—one of the shining lights" of the century:

> In person as well as in feeling, our biped is a pretty fair specimen of the "native raw material," what you call a civilized but not a polished *Aborigine*. And, by the way, it has been asserted by one of his brother Editors that he is a lineal descendant from some Indian tribe, with what truth we will not venture to say. In dress and gait he apes in some degree the gravity of the student, with inverted shirt collar, of course, after the manner of "Childe Harold." His face, good looking but remarkably indolent in expression, is sometimes "bearded like the pard," and at other times, probably to suit the season, as free from hair as the fair cheek of "Justice". . . . From the South he brings the French motto "Liberty, equality, fraternity," and he stands before us as a "Freeman." But, like all hot-headed ultras, he awards no "liberty" unless they belong to the "spirit of progress"; as for "equality" . . . 'twould be ridiculous for foreigners to claim such a privilege;

223

as for "fraternity" the old hunkers would not, by any manner of means, take him again into their brotherly embraces, and so our motto and our little sheet are gone, or, which is the same thing, our distinguished biped is gone from it, and is again "on the town."[2]

Free Soilers elsewhere also suffered the aftermath of their third-party heresy. In Boston Charles Sumner, who had journeyed to Buffalo as an observer, found many doors shut on Beacon Hill. Charles Francis Adams sought relief from similar ostracism by editing his grandfather's papers. Whitman chose exile in ancestral Paumanok. Based at Greenport where his sister Mary,[3] the onetime "child of light and loveliness," and her husband had their home, he would record impressions of the area in the format of weekly "Letters from a Travelling Bachelor" (reprinted as an appendix to this volume). He would send them to the Sunday *Dispatch*, a paper identified with progressive ideas. Two years earlier after a one-day excursion to the Greenport area he had noted, "It is a pity that the eastern extremity of our island—the good honest, democratic, agricultural hard-working, old-fashioned, hospitable, well-to-do county of Suffolk—lies aside from the path of literary chronicles."[4]

On the day he left for Greenport he reached the depot of the Long Island railroad at the South Ferry in time for the scheduled nine-thirty departure —which always came five minutes later, an allowance of grace he appreciated since he hated to choose between losing his breath and missing the trip. It seemed to him that there was nothing more ridiculous than a red-faced, sweaty man running after the cars or the ferry, shrieking to the engineer or pilot to hold on "and they heed him no more than the dead—and the passengers all look back and smile!" The occupants of the car next to the locomotive had suffered heavy casualties in a recent crash so he picked a safer rear seat and looked through the window at the women vending oranges, the newsboys, and a limping young man who sold "long-lived cakes." Then the final bell, heavy greasy smoke, and the train began to move.[5]

The half-mile tunnel under Atlantic Street, "dark as the grave, cold, damp, and silent," evoked musings on his own plight: "How beautiful look Earth and Heaven again, as we emerge from the gloom! It might not be unprofitable, now and then, to send us mortals—the dissatisfied ones, at least, and that's a large proportion—into some tunnel of several days' journey. We'd perhaps grumble less, afterward, at God's handiwork."

The first furlongs of the surface route renewed his pride in the city. From the tracks he could see the lines of the new avenues, knolls and sedgy places, the hills of Greenwood, and the land sloping toward Gowanus. Its powerful men had treated him shamefully, but even in this time of exile he remained the admirer and adviser: "Brooklyn! Brooklyn! thou art indeed a Dame Beautiful! But thou canst never have a fresh face, and clean stockings, till those Water Commissioners are appointed, and have done their duty."

Near Bedford station, the first stop, parcels of building lots for sale excited a gentleman who "showed speculation in his eyes as sure as ever an auctioneer bawled in Wall street." The rich, moist soil there had enabled gardeners to smother houses with trees and shrubbery, and Whitman sensed that, as in New Orleans, fever and ague seemed to taint the air. Rising above the flat land was the white tower of Cypress Hills Cemetery "looking like some solitary bachelor."

Among the many who debarked at the Union race track to spend the afternoon cheering the horses he spotted blackleg gamblers unmistakable in their colored broadcloth and showy jewelry. The oncoming farms ready for harvest proved the blessings of fine weather, for everywhere they showed tall corn, buckwheat, cabbages, turnips, potatoes (the healthiest yield since the onslaught of blight), orchards with yellowing apples, pastures with heavy cattle. Had he time to walk down the one street of Jamaica he would have paid his respects to Brenton, "a good soul," and to Onderdonk, master of Union Hall Academy whose history of the Revolution belonged in all libraries. The train passed the house once owned by the actor, "Nimrod Wildfire" Hackett, and the new church of Dominie Schoonmaker who preached oftener in Dutch than in English and after forty years in the pulpit continued to toss off jokes and an occasional glass of wine. Once again the heavy foliage that obstructed sunshine warned of the danger of disease too virulent for quinine.

When the train began to traverse the extensive plains owned by Hempstead, a town of 1400 with "a Presbyterian tinge, of the deepest cerulean," he inveighed like a homestead disciple of George Evans against the selfishness that barred regional betterment and kept cities crowded:

> *Land Monopoly* shows one of its beauties, most pointed, in this matter. I don't know, indeed, where one could go for a more glaring and unanswerable argument of its evils. Here is good

225

land, capable of ministering to the existence and happiness of thousands upon thousands of human beings, all lying unproductive, *within thirty miles of New York city*, because it is monopolised by one principal owner! I know the people have the right of pasturing their cattle, horses, and sheep, on the plains—but that privilege, however widely used, does not develope one twentieth of the natural resources of the land.

Jericho, home of Elias Hicks, remained Quaker. While the other passengers bought sandwiches, pie, and coffee at Farmingdale, once known as Hardscrabble, Whitman thought of the station as the point of entry into an area populated by "the more peculiar specimens of humanity." Soon he suspended all judgment upon towns and stiff old farmers in order to praise the scarlet and yellow stretches of sumac, scrub oak, hickory, and birch:

> I have often thought that those who make designs for carpets could get most excellent hints from these autumn garnishings. How pleasing and graceful would be a carpet pattern, richly covered with figures and colors, closely imitated from what one sees here—how much better than the tasteless, meaningless, and every way unartistical diagrams that we walk over, now, in the most fashionably carpeted parlors.

Sighting an isolated hut brought to mind an adventure he assigned to a crony rather than to himself and prefaced with *honi soit qui mal y pense*. Here on the plains ten years ago a tolerable morning had turned into drizzle and fog, and a hunter from the city had spent the rest of the day vainly circling in his own tracks. At last a light led him to a clearing and the one-room home of a young couple married but a few months. Sukey was already in the only bed under the few covers, and Derrick half-dressed ready to join her. After welcoming the wet hunter and giving him supper Derrick refused to allow him to sleep cold on the bare floor: "Na' theless, we can 'commodate ye, if ye'll sleep with us. Sukey is not much of a body, and the bed is big and strong, and I dare say you are tired out like. Come in; come in." With the nearest shelter miles away the hunter accepted and spent a surprisingly restful night. In the morning, Derrick left the two in bed while he went out to capture a cow loose in the buckwheat:

> My friend, be it known, is the most modest of men—and now what the deuce to do, was the question. His perplexities were cut

short by the loud clear voice of the young man outside:
"Suke! Suke! for God's sake come here. I can't get the darned
cow out, except you help me."

While Sukey put on her gown the modest man closed his eyes, but as soon
as she joined Derrick he dressed in haste. Whitman ended this testimonial
to "simplicity, unsuspiciousness, and goodness" by revealing that the three
remained friends and that on occasional visits to what in time became a
large family the "hunter" rejoiced that Derrick and Sukey had prospered.

Whitman knew other families within the forty miles of brush, half-
grown trees, blackened stumps, and kill-calf who by hard work had cleared
cheap land and built fertile farms. In the West poverty was universal; here
prosperous homesteads adjacent to the crude huts of charcoal burners made
annoying contrasts. "It is a perplexing paradox," observed the traveller,
"that where all are poor nobody is poor."

The train moved through the pine barrens east of the cluster of houses
called Deer Park, though the area rarely yielded a buck or doe—but we
Americans "seem to christen new localities according to contraries, like
the way dreams go." At the village's shabby inn Madame Dodd, wearing
a prodigious turban, dispensed gin and gingerbread with the grace of a
French hostess. Babylon, five miles south, produced the largest "musketos
and the most tiplers, of any known community of its size." In the hilly
north, adjacent to the Sound, was the Democratic banner town of Huntington, whose voters always gave a five to eight hundred majority. (But
party solidarity now lacked the virtue of happier years.) At Oyster Bay
lived the Reverend Marmaduke Earle, for more than fifty years both pastor
and schoolteacher. Nearby natives could point out the rock on which George
Fox had stood when he gave the sermons that turned many sinners in the
way of getting "born again."

As the train steamed deeper into Suffolk, it passed the domain of those
scoundrels who had opposed the building of the railroad and then after its
completion had cut or blocked the tracks. By the time of the train's arrival
at Riverhead, a "sober, quiet, old place" seventy-five miles from Brooklyn,
Whitman was ready to stop for a day or so. In the morning he walked to
the wooden courthouse where relatives of those killed in a wreck were suing
the railroad for damages. The jail built in 1725 was so flimsy that the police
reporter who knew the Tombs thought that any city criminal held there
would easily show it his heels. The militia had assembled for general train-

ing, but as the consequence of commutation (the substitution of a cash payment for militia service) the affair lacked its original pomp. Whitman remembered when the annual muster had turned Riverhead into a military bivouac, a beleaguered town:

> Eatables, drinkables, and frolic, were the accompaniments; the girls came from far and near, and many nigger fiddlers, and there was dancing and making merry, and no going to bed. All the young fellows of the county had to be there present, "armed and equipped as the law directs," and they *were* there. But O what a falling off this last training presented! Some forlorn looking youths, and poor middle-aged men, with rusty guns—and the officers, almost as numerous as the men! It was a very melancholy sight, the way those disconsolate ones were marched around, and occasionally stopped and put through the motions.

A while ago he had compared the map of Brooklyn to the human heart. The eastern end of Long Island now animated into the jaws of a prodigious alligator enclosing Peconic Bay with Montauk peninsula on the south, and Greenport, the harbor town he preferred to Saratoga and Newport on the north. In warmer weather he loved to "souse" in Greenport's clear salt water twice a day, but now in the cool October mornings he fished from one of its docks and within the hour—though he by no means claimed great skill—caught a mess of blackfish that would cost more than a dollar in a New York market. Split and broiled over coals the sweet, firm meat was as unlike the dish served by Broadway cooks "as the pure breath of some whole-toothed country girl" compared to "the scent of almond-paste which the perfumer had furnished for the mouth of perhaps the most lovely metropolitan belle."

Seeking like de Tocqueville or von Raumer to penetrate the surface of an enclave, Whitman pointed to the easy availability of fish as evidence for his belief in the intertwining of the physical characteristics of a locality and its people. Certain that bay and ocean would keep them from starvation, hundreds of families "rubbed" on year after year and indulged in the pride of poverty—"the costliest in the world." But their way of life also showed a "golden side," for the land they fertilized with mossbunkers gave body to grain and their diet of fish tempered the blood:

228

Imagine a community of straggle-limbed, yellow-faced, hard-fleshed sea-dogs—or a goodly infusion of such communities in the nation; do you suppose such a nation could ever degenerate and decay, as old Rome did with her Sybarites? No, indeed. And though my compound adjectives above do not describe the ideal of masculine good looks, there is something surpassingly welcome in the sight of these sinewy and huge-pawed fellows.

The maritime settlements reached by sailing out of Greenport had their "briny cast." One morning while trying for blackfish, Whitman moved his line and fiddler-crab bait to avoid fouling a sloop ready to leave the dock with "a party of lively girls, conveyed by a clerical looking personage, and one or two young fellows." Invited to accompany them to Montauk Point, he boarded the sloop and soon blessed his lucky stars at the chance to sail with pleasant acquaintances through sweet air and sunlight. Near Gardiner's Island he reminisced of the first settler, "one of those massive old characters of the English commonwealth—belonging to the republican party of the early portion of the 17th century, with Hampden, Cromwell, and other hearts of oak." As they sailed along the Montauk peninsula, they passed the cave of an old Indian hermit, and from the description given by one of the sailors Whitman concluded he was another Chingachgook.[6]

At Montauk, where the keeper of the lighthouse offered board and lodging in a sheltered cottage, Whitman found that the juncture of ocean and land, waves and wind that forced a man to hold tight to his "sea-weed" hair, had bred a race never seen in New York—"where you see almost everything." The Montaukers were "great unshaved, gigantic-chested beings, with eyes as clear as coals, and flesh whose freedom from the gross humors of artificial life told its tale in the dark and unpimpled brown of their faces and necks." Ignoring dietetic oracles, never lanceted or calomeled, they worked half-stripped up to their waists in water, ate raw pork seasoned in vinegar or bad rum, and bedded down on hay or sails. After many seasons of this harsh routine they died of old age rather than of sickness. Their natural toughness—every baby seemed guided by instinct to crawl into the whitecaps—led the visitor to confess his shame "to be so particular against sleeping in a lately scrubbed room, or a draught of wind from some chink in the window."

The eyes of the fisher folk seemed as sharp and piercing as those of hawks. While Whitman gossiped with the master of a fine young New-foundland retriever and watched its antics in the surf, the Montauker—whose "brilliant (I really cannot find the right word,) vitreous eyes were vibrating from mine to the surface of the sea"—whistled the dog back to shore. Then he pointed to a small black chip moving over the surface of the waves. It was a shark's fin.

Here Whitman watched a marine exhibition that surpassed the yacht races in New York harbor. Two hundred men, bearded like sons of Esau, "trailed" for bluefish from a hundred skiffs:

> Imagine the skiffs, real beauties, too, darting like swallows, and managed by five-score bold and expert water-dogs, each ambitious of doing some dare-devil maneuver that would eclipse his fellows —the sails bulging like the puffed cheeks of an alderman, and anon dipping in the water, or making the boat turn sharper corners than I ever saw boat turn before—a hundred men cease-lessly employed in hauling in the lines, taking off the fish, and casting out again—and then such a casting out! Such a length as they made the bones fly! such a twirl of the rope! no twisting, although the coils be many! such superb attitudes, equal to any thing in Greek statues! such ready expedients to avoid any ob-stacle to the incessant hauling in, and throwing out of those lines, and the rapid depositing of fish in the boats, which seemed, to my eyes, to rival the celerity with which a "fast compositor" deposits type in his stick!

The spectator was amused to learn that sea-bass fishermen thought it de-meaning to go after the blues and preferred to buy a basket rather than waste time catching them.

He took pains to dispel the belief of Manhattan sophisticates that Mon-tauk was so grim that Columbus would have turned back had he touched there. Rich soil reached close to the beach and grew crops of Indian corn within gunshot of the Atlantic. The lighthouse with a beacon 200 feet above sea level stood on Turtle Hill—a "verdant wart." Whitman climbed here one day after admiring the keeper's garden and lush lawn:

> I went out to the very edge of the cliff, and threw myself down on the grass, and tossed aside my slouchy hat, and looked to the eastward. The sea was in one of its calmest phases. A hoarse low

roar, only, gave some token of its fiercer vitality—a sort of *living roar*, it seemed to me, for it made me think of great storms, and wrecks; and the despairing and dying who had groaned erewhile upon those waters.

The discovery that he was to share the hill ended the reverie. A stranger whose emaciated face and cough revealed him an invalid moved slowly up the slope and looked "curiously and half-bashfully" toward Whitman who called to him. Grateful for a sympathetic ear the stranger identified himself as a fisherman from Sag Harbor who could not keep pace with his mates because of the pain brought on by the wet and cold. Soon he confessed that for years he had eaten opium, and as proof showed a globule that was his daily dose. "It was frightfully large!"[7]

Whitman hesitated to enjoin the use of opium but "laying before the poor frightened fellow the plain condition and probabilities" advised him to abandon fishing, return to his mother's care, and seek the advice of a physician. At Southold several days earlier the traveller had met another addict; the habit of using the drug undiluted in laudanum or in Godfrey's Cordial was prevalent in country districts, and in the city every druggist sold unlimited quantities of opiates without question. "We talk a great deal about 'the intelligence of the age,'" he concluded, "but truly there is ignorance enough yet among the masses to grow up in mountains of sickness, destitution and vice."

Alone again and with hours until dinner he walked for several miles and wondered at the mineralogical riches along the cliff edges and the shore. Everywhere were stones of different shapes and density, colored earth, shells, white boulders, pebbles the country children called milk stones, and others of yellow, blue, and green. Then he joined his friends:

> We rambled up the hills to the top of the highest—we ran races down—we scampered along the shore, jumping from rock to rock—we declaimed all the violent appeals and defiances we could remember, commencing with "Celestial states, immortal powers, give ear!" away on the ending which announced that Richard had almost lost his wind by dint of calling Richmond to arms. I doubt whether those astonished echos ever before vibrated with such terrible ado. Then we pranced forth again, like mad kine—we threw our hats in the air—aimed stones at the shrieking sea-gulls, mocked the wind, and imitated the cries of

various animals in a style that beat nature all out! We challenged each other to the most deadly combats—we tore various passions into tatters—made love to the girls, in the divine words of Shake-speare and other poets, whereas the said girls had the rudeness to laugh till the tears ran down their cheeks in great torrents. We indulged in some impromptu quadrilles, of which the "chasez" took each participant couple so far away from the other that they were like never to get back. We hopped like crows; we pivoted like Indian dervishes; we went through the trial dance of *La Bayadère* with wonderful vigor; and some one of our party came nigh dislocating his neck through volunteering to turn somersets like a circus fellow. Every body caught the contagion, and there was not a sensible behaved creature among us, to rebuke our mad antics by comparison.[8]

Returning from "this nice exercise," the hungry man and his companions heard "appalling" news—the master of the revels had failed to arrange for dinner at the lighthouse keeper's cottage. An improvised chowder of sea bass, six pullets from the flock feeding at the door, potatoes, cabbage—"I and the fat girl cried bitterly, peeling onions"—with bread and butter, eaten in sight of ocean and setting sun, became a miraculous feast that Whitman hoped to remember to his dying day.

By the time they boarded the sloop that night for the move to one of the nearby islands the tide had shifted. Spreading a bearskin rug on the deck, Whitman lay flat and in silence looked up at the stars "and the delicate figure" of the new moon moving down the west "like a timid bride." His companions told stories of lovers and ghosts, then sang country ditties. "The night and the scene mellowed all, and it came to my ears through a sort of moral distillation." After a while he made his bed in the furled sail but remained awake watching the sky:

Not a sound, not an insect, interrupted the exquisite silence,— nothing but the ripple of the water against the sides of the vessel. An indescribable serenity pervaded my mind—a delicious abnegation of the ties of the body. I fancied myself leaping forward into the extent of the space, springing as it were from star to star. Thoughts of the boundless Creation must have expanded my mind, for it certainly played the most unconscionable pranks from its tabernacle lying there in those fields of hempen duck.

232

They reached the island after sunrise and searched its creeks for wild birds. Then on the sands "we issued a second edition of the proceedings on the hills and shores of Montauk. But, owing to the absence of the terraqueous girls, we didn't have as good a time. After all, what a place this wretched earth would be without the petticoats!"

When they sailed back to Greenport after breakfast Whitman sensed the fresh vitality of the party: "Fast and loud rose the voices again, the clear upper notes of the girls, and laughter and singing. We knew we should soon be home—down amid the clouds and commonplaces—and we determined to make the most of it. And we *did*!" All this without a drop of brandy aboard. But when the steeples and white houses of Greenport came into view, the spirit of these "wonderful hours" fled: "We landed at the dock, and went up to the village, and felt the tameness of respectable society setting around us again. Doubtless it was all right; but as for me, I fancied I felt the mercury dwindling down, down, down into the very calves of my legs."

At times on the extended holiday he found so much "real enjoyment" in exploring ancient cemeteries that he wondered if he had inherited "tatters . . . of Old Mortality." After a long walk to Oysterponds Point on the northern jaw of the alligator, he turned off the road to try the bleak hills near the Sound. Between two of them, where the wind "piped its thousand trebles" and a "sullen base" came from the shore, he saw hundreds of abandoned graves whose crumbling stones were moss-covered. He tried to decipher the inscriptions but realized it would take days. The cemetery at Southold held further proof of the antiquity of the area; here someone had reset the stones so that the visitor could read and copy inscriptions like the one carved for a "Lestershire" man:

> Here sleeps the Body tombed in its Dust
> Till Christ shall come & raise it with the Just.

Mrs. Mary Hobart, born in Boston, lay nearby:

> Desir'd she Liv'd
> Lamented she did
> Dye   yet still she
> Lives in precious memory.

The grave of Colonel John Youngs, who departed this life on 12 April 1698 made Whitman pause in wonder at finding on republican soil tangible evidence of the presence of an officer of the Crown.

233

After these sorties he complained that country funerals were chilly and depressing. Rather than choosing a warm site and building a Greenwood, rural folk placed their dead on a barren knoll useless for any crop. "Must we say the choice is from that sort of 'thrift, thrift,' which served up certain meats at the wedding-table of Hamlet's step-father?"

To one who remembered Elias Hicks and had sat before Cox, Thayer, and the other eloquent divines of Brooklyn, Sunday night at a Greenport meeting became a parody:

> The regular preacher was absent, and his place was supplied by certainly one of the oddest of human specimens. (I saw him the next morning cheapening a gun in a neighboring shop). If he was a wag, he succeeded to perfection in burlesquing the sermon: if serious, it was a seriousness as funny as Mitchell's or Placide's in their dreadful travesties. You may imagine something of the gentleman's style when you know that he earnestly demanded of the audience, "Do you imagine Christ was such *hypocricat* as that?" Shade of Mrs. Malaprop! *"Hypocricat"*! About every third or fourth attempt at rolling off a sentence would stick him in the mud; whereupon he would extricate himself by an unintelligible jabber, containing no distinct words—a decidedly "unknown tongue." One of the contingencies he put before the audience was the being "as rich as *Zeros*"! And as to moods and tenses, and the good old rule of "a verb must agree with its nominative," &c., the work was a slaughter beyond precedent. My poor handkerchief, when I pulled it from my pocket the next morning, was what the wolverines might call "tetotaciously chawed up." I had done it in the agonies between my laughter and attempted decorum.[9]

Nothing humorous occurred at the dock when he joined the Greenporters in saying farewell to a whaler whose two recent voyages had failed to fill many oil barrels. Chandlers had once kept busy outfitting and unloading the ships which, with the apparent scarcity of whales in recent years, returned "weary enough, but not heavy laden." Each captain continued to get his sixteenth or twentieth "lay," but most of the hands earned barely enough to pay for their clothes. Lacking Melville's experience with monomania, Whitman wondered why the owners did not try the California gold fields.

Throughout the autumn tour, as though seeking to decide once and for all whether he should buy the long-desired farm, Whitman indulged in what he called poetical comparisons between country and city. He yearned for pastoral freshness and quiet, and for freedom from metropolitan "ligatures and ceremonies." But

> to be born and "brought up" in an out of the way country place, and so continue there through all the stages of middle life—and eat and drink there only, and "dress up" of a Sunday and go to church there—and at last die and be buried there—is that an enviable lot in life? No, it is not. The burying part may be well enough, but the living is much such living as a tree in the farmer's door-yard.

Many villagers never visited New York, never entered a theatre, read a play, heard a piano, or saw sculpture or painting. Few subscribed to newspapers; the books on their tables were *Rinaldo Rinaldini, Alonzo and Melissa,* or "those interesting horrors of Calvinism by Masters Fox and Baxter." Meanwhile, that October at the Broaday theatre Charlotte Cushman at the peak of her form, inspired a sonnet "Upon Her Shakespearian Performances."

Varied experience had taught Whitman one precept: *"Let every one mix for at least some part of his earlier life with the bustling world of the great towns."* The isolated life kept the husk on manners, dulled the power of conversation, rarely developed the intellect, and generally left the man raw; its advantages were "preserved on the same principle as the father's who, fearing his son *may* be drowned, lets him never go in the water to learn to swim."

Avarice also bred here. Montauk hosts refused all payment except some plug tobacco and the latest political news in two old copies of the *Tribune* he found in his jacket, but on Shelter Island a miserly couple resembled a "sadly large number of Long Island and New England country people." Tired after a day in the woods he had missed the ferry to Greenport. Seeking food and lodging, he followed a creek whose water was as clear as plate glass to a knoll where he saw a large two-story house, barns, and outbuildings. While the farmer's wife prepared a meager supper she told him that the produce of three hundred acres, the poultry flocks, and the daily eggs all went to market. When the farmer came into the kitchen Whitman saw that

235

he carried small quantities of butter, bread, candles, and salt fish purchased at a store, as though he were a laborer in New York rather than a wealthy landowner with money out at interest. "I really could not eat the thin milk and coarse burnt corn; but, as I rose, I put down a shilling on the table. The fierce clutching look of the woman's eyes, as she sidled toward the money, made me sick."

Those who wrote about the virtues of solitude had never encountered the hermitess whose short blanket-coat, horn spectacles, and hickory staff reminded him of the women in Scott's novels. He had befriended her some years ago with a small gift; now her hut was empty and a wild black cat scampered around it. In Southold he learned that the "half-deranged old creature" had died six months ago. North of that village he passed another recluse, an old man on whose skullcap "benevolence and philoprogenitiveness" had made themselves scarce. Anyone who walked these woods or the barren plains met many other isolated souls.

Whitman also refuted the idealistic tenet that the country "surely" produced innocent characters and healthy bodies. In proportion there was as much crime and illness as in the city. Suffolk contained some 40,000 inhabitants, New York eight to ten times that number: "Does any one suppose that any fair average eighth part of the city generates more vice, or contains more, than Suffolk county?" Granted, the children breathed wholesome air, but they started heavy chores too early and lost their elasticity, became round-shouldered and clumsy, learned to smoke, chew, and drink as soon as their urban prototypes, ate "pork and grease, doughy bread, and other equally indigestible dishes." The hard work of a hurried harvest during the hottest season of the year broke many a boy and young man.

Totaling the evidence, he concluded that he would not rear his child in the "barbarous ignorance" of so many country families. Whatever the teachings of metaphysicians, "the human race away from cities does not expand and improve so well morally, intellectually, or physically." But he did not advise boys to betake themselves to Manhattan right off: "God forgive me, if it should tend that way: no! The city hath its perils, too, and very likely the novice would find them great ones." (At the National the burlesque *Female Forty Thieves* was "spiced with a liberal display of female legs and loveliness." And a police raid one Friday night that October saved visiting young farmers from exposure to "three white graces and a Hottentot venus"—all naked.)

The results of the November election—defeat for Lott and most of the Democratic slate whose creation had cost him the *Freeman*—encouraged Whitman to board the train at Greenport and return to this quickening world. Eight years ago in the *Aurora* he had fought Governor Seward's plan to educate the children of Catholic immigrants and had ignored the parallel proposal for Negroes; now his sympathy turned to Seward, currently a Whig senator, who had been assaulted for his Wilmot stand by Jefferson Davis and other Southerners in Washington and by the northern foes of abolition and enfranchisement in Albany. Lacking an editorial page in this critical season of political flux, realignment, and threat of dissolution of the union, Whitman filled his letters to the *Dispatch* with saunters and rambles in the metropolis.

Ever since the completion of the Croton system he had come often in the afternoons to the Murray Hill reservoir at 40th Street where he climbed the hollow-echoing stone stairs to the broad walk 45 feet above the ground. The monumental engineering overwhelmed him. Here a four-acre lake held 20 million gallons of pure river water; at 86th Street 35 acres held 150 million gallons. Every drop had moved 38 miles from the Croton dam through rock tunnels, embankments, culverts, and aqueducts, and across the Harlem River on a magnificent bridge. Sunset viewed from this promontory built by men more expert than the Romans induced in him a mood of prophecy for the next century:

> You and I, reader, and quite all the people who are now alive, won't be much thought of then; but the world will be just as jolly, and the sun will shine as bright, and the rivers off there— the Hudson on one side and the East on the other—will slap along their green waves, precisely as now; and other eyes will look upon them about the same as we do.
>
> The walks on the battlements of the Croton Reservoir, a hundred years hence! *Then* these immense stretches of vacant ground below, will be covered with houses; the paved streets will clatter with innumerable carts and resound to deafening cries; and the promenaders here will look down upon them, perhaps, and away "up town," toward the quieter and more fashionable quarters, and see great changes—but off to the rivers and shores their eyes will go oftenest, and see not much difference from what we see

237

now. *Then* New York will be more populous than London or Paris, and, it is to be hoped, as *great* a city as either of them—great in treasures of art and science, I mean, and in educational and charitable establishments.[10]

Descending to ground level, the lover of hills and slopes wondered why most American cities required flat grades and streets cut into each other at right angles—"certainly the last things in the world consistent with beauty of situation." The elevations of upper Manhattan merited preservation by Council rather than ordinances imposing conformity. What romance was there in the "checker-board principle" compared with following a curve and beholding something fresh? "Uniformity! Why it's the taste of the vulgar. Nature hath nought of it."

After walking one of the avenues, Whitman entered Union Square, the "aristocratic neighborhood" of the "upper ten" with its fountain, spotless park, delicate floral and shrubbery plantings, stately houses fronted by high marble stoops and iron balconies, and carriages waiting at the doors. Unfortunately this external opulence lacked any inner correspondence:

> Perhaps you fancy that this elevatedness of wealth and furniture, is significant of a like elevatedness of intellect, purpose, and heart, in the people. By no means. Here and there, among them, you find beautiful and sweet-souled women, and learned and chivalrous men; so you do among common people. But the great body of "fashionables" are vulgar, flippant and overweeningly selfish. Nine-tenths of the families residing in these noble dwellings, have "sprung from nothing," as the phrase is—by which is intended that their parents were hucksters, laborers, waiters, and so on; which made the said parents not a whit the worse, but, on the contrary, they were perhaps more sensible and respectable than the children who would burn with shame if their daddies or granddaddies were to start up before them, like Hamlet's, in their habits as they lived.

Their Grace Church seemed to symbolize money rather than piety. After three years the spires, the tracery, and the fretwork continued to flaunt a garish air that made a passerby wonder about cost rather than satisfying "the subtle sense of the beautiful"; the congregation emerged rich, showy, tasteless. "The mellowing and sanctifying influence of time, *may* perhaps do

238

something for this church. We hope so." In his judgment, the ideal theological organization centered on two essentials—God and immortality, all
else being so irrelevant that he saw no reason for exempting church property
from taxation.

On Broadway the galleries of art unions gave the saunterer the chance
to turn from scoring vulgar display to praising painters who transmitted
"the seeds of a love for beauty" to the masses. His column this time went to
the International, sprung like Minerva into mature excellence with a show
he thought superior to any ever hung in America. Some critics called one of
the exhibitors an imitation Rembrandt with little color and less chiaroscuro,
but Whitman waved these quibbles aside:

> Long, long half hours have I passed looking at "The Dead
> Christ" by Ary Sheffer. It has grown into my very soul. The face
> and breast of the Saviour are exhibited, with the grave clothes
> raised from them, and the prostrate head of his mother resting on
> his breast. There are three other female figures, whose faces ex-
> hibit different developments of grief. The countenance of the
> Sacred Corpse is beyond all description; he or she who can look
> upon it without the deepest emotion must be insensible to the
> great achievements of art. Yet the painting is entirely free from
> any strained effect, any daring attempt at wonderful things: it
> is after the severest forms of simplicity and spirituality. The serene
> grief, too great for words, of the female at the left is beautifully
> expressed—and the bitter wailing of the aged woman more in
> the background almost touches the ear—but the face of the
> mother is too intense for depicting, and it is bowed and hidden on
> the cold bosom of Christ. No tricks of ambitious color, or "warm
> light," or any thing of that sort, mar this great picture.[11]

Other choice canvases were by Court, Delaroche, and Waldmuller whose
"Children Leaving the School" was incomparable for the variety of scene
and expression. Whitman also liked his "Convalescence," picturing an old
man warming himself in the sun near a blossoming cherry.

On the way to the ferry this veteran of hundreds of crossings of the East
River wondered why Harper, Appleton, and other firms issued many books
of journeys between the Old and New World but never published a description of this voyage taken every day by myriads. Since early childhood
he and countless others had responded to the three strokes that announced

departure and the six strokes of arrival. "Besides, we have ourself seen authors, editors, reporters and all departments of the 'press-gang' go aboard the boats of the Fulton Ferry Company, (after depositing two cents with the gentleman at the gate,) and cross over—sometimes even coming back again on the same boat. (This latter, doubtless, to get the pure air, at the economical price of a penny a trip.)" Until one of these authors filled the lacuna he offered his own column of observations on what was a fact of urban life rather than a mere mode of travel.

The access route, ugly and crooked, crowded with carts, omnibuses, and other "wheeled horrors" reminded him of "things Milton describes." The one impressive structure was the United States Hotel built by a Mr. Holt who had made a hundred thousand dollars in cheap eating houses and lost all of it here. Whitman commiserated the owner for his bankruptcy by adapting lines from *Macbeth*: "The 'days of the speculation' passed like a dream, after having lighted many fools the way to dusky death."

The flimsy pine canopy and walls of the terminal prompted his suggestion that the owners erect a stone and iron building with large entrances— a better investment than stocks in Wall Street. In the waiting room he did not imitate the young clerks who stamped impatiently "as if Time didn't fly fast enough without wanting to hurry it." Nor did he rush after them to the edge of the wharf and spring to the deck of the incoming boat, for a foolhardy passenger could become wedged between the wharf timbers and the bow.

When the bell tapped the new *Manhattan* got under way. The high-ceilinged interior with colored glass windows and comfortable cushions was heated these winter days; it provided an escape from the cigar smokers and spitters:

> The ladies, too, *they* form not the least part of the pleasantness. When the cabin is full, and they are seated in close rows all along from one end of the cabin to the other, it takes a fellow of some nerve to run the gauntlet through that cabin. For our part, we always feel our heart beat quicker when we attempt it—and are fain to pop down in a seat before we get half way. But then every body knows we have an unusual amount of modesty.

From midstream he surveyed the ever-wonderful scene: forests of masts, the dominant spire of Trinity, and the trees of the Battery; on the other shore the Heights lined with buildings though space remained for a prome-

240

nade "if it be applied to that purpose *soon*." Through the open end of one street stood the squat tower of St. Ann's; to the left were the Navy Yard and the great Dry Dock. Then the high banks of Williamsburg, the poplars of Governor's Island; in the distance Staten Island and the Jersey shore. The pilot of the *Manhattan*, in control like the rider of a trained horse, plied between sailcraft and steamers, shaving some of them "to the verge of a hair," adjusting for the strength of the tide in order to keep his schedule. In a few weeks cakes of ice would form, but Whitman admitted enjoying the extended journey they sometimes forced. Several winters back when the river had frozen he had tried to cross on foot, but the dislodged ice began to move "leaving us just time, by hard 'scrouging,' to hop on the end of a certain pier, with the determination never again to trust our flesh on a mass of congealed water." Fog also added to the pleasure of the passage, for then he could listen to the muffled tolling of bells and join in the lookout for breakers. "We are not sure but we enjoy a bit—just a *little bit*, of danger— nothing, of course, that would give us the chance of taking to the cold water, but just a spice of excitement." On clear nights he wished that he could ride ten times longer under the sky. "Yes, yes; for some of the nicest of the 'happy ten minutes' that glitter in one's experience, have we been indebted to the Fulton Ferry."

No wonder he attempted to scotch a proposal by entrepreneurs to span the river with a bridge. This was as chimerical as balloon transportation between the Battery and Harlem or a tunnel under the Thames:

> Nonsense. There is no need of a bridge, while there are incessantly plying such boats as the Manhattan, the Wyandance, and the Montauk. If there be any spare energy, let it be applied to improving the indifferent accommodations at Catherine ferry, and the wretchedness of that at Jackson street. Also, to completing the proposed lines from the bottoms of Montague street and Bridge street.

He continued to side with those who thought it sheer folly to believe that a pedestrian would choose to toil in winter over a mile-long span when a ferry offered warm shelter and quick passage.[12]

The "little dab" Manhattan editors allotted for Brooklyn coverage reminded Whitman of the Chinese proverb of a lantern hung on a high pole

241

and casting a far light but leaving darkness near the pole. Many pains were taken to cover foreign localities; but the city which had become as much a part of New York as a central ward was delegated to one man who usually collected two or three dollars a week from several dailies for naming drunkards and brawlers. In "Pickings-up about Brooklyn" published in the *Dispatch* in the interval between two of his Manhattan letters, Whitman tried to show that it was possible to describe the civic affairs of a population of 100,000 in a "zesty," sensible column.

He began by remarking that at the corner of Fulton and Concord stood the new building of the Savings Bank, symbol of one of the richest sections of the city. This area also boasted more handsome churches than any other part of the nation; and the "vainglory and speculation" of Dominie Johnson had reared a splendid new one of stone, colored glass, velvet, and "similar pious adjuncts." No "shabby dressed sinners ever put their noses in these elegant sanctuaries, of course." Beautiful City Hall cost $200,000, but what a pity that a cheap fence rather than an "artistical" one surrounded the triangular grounds. The correspondant found the view from the building's cupola worth the tiresome ninety-foot climb. The Dry Dock was as impressive as Croton but the brilliant engineer who had supervised its building had been replaced by a party hack, despite the protest of Whitman's *Freeman.* The expanding Navy Yard with a free exhibition honoring John Paul Jones and other heroes also deserved a visit, but a disquieting rumor about its operations merited inquiry to determine "whether many of these ponderous and costly projects are not with a view to the navy as it has been, instead of the *steam navy,* which undoubtedly will soon supersede the old fashioned sort." At Monday evening meetings in a luxurious room in City Hall the "miserable politicians" on Common Council dominated by ten or twelve bickering Whigs had nullified the law passed last winter for the appointment of a commission to supply Brooklyn at last with pure water. Meanwhile the pumps spilled "partially filtrated nastiness." Visiting the schools again Whitman judged only two or three well-conducted, for the faculty of the others continued to instruct by rote. Until principals hired competent teachers, most of the "fat bags" of money appropriated to them would be wasted. Half a dozen free evening schools were as vital as fresh water, for the boys he saw loafing in the streets learned nothing there but evil; false economy withheld the modest sum that would prevent the crimes caused by idleness and ignorance.

Wherever he could he praised or prodded. Paving Fulton Street had created a handsome thoroughfare and a short cut to Jamaica, but why not continue two blocks farther to City Hall? Everyone rejoiced at the lighting of streets with gas, but when he walked late at night near his home where some of the dim oil lamps remained Whitman wished the conversion hastened. The arches built at the end of Montague Street in anticipation of a ferry created a glorious promenade; the friend to all public breathing places suggested that neighbors develop a little park there.

Searching to add to the income from these paragraphs he began to consider giving lectures on health; indeed he needed only to turn to his editorial files and use their many pleas for exercise and diet. Then came the day in December when the ferry carried him to Manhattan and a new assignment.

16

RESURGEMUS

FATE seemed willing to end the year of 1849 by showing Whitman two signs of favor. First Brenton included the early panegyric to love and death, "Tomb Blossoms," in *Voices from the Press*. The Jamaica publisher hoped to honor "practical printers" and ornament American literature with this octavo volume of specimen writings ranging from Franklin to contemporary craftsmen.[1]

Then after visiting 86 Nassau Street in Manhattan at the invitation of Walter R. Janes who had begun to staff a penny paper, Whitman accepted a "handsome" salary to become the principal editor of the *Daily News*. Along with a regular income, what he called the collateral advantages of the post were his again: the consciousness of power, the veneration and gratitude of the public, and an open road to political office—"if a change from the editorial stool to the legislative desk is a preferment, which we doubt." Flagrant deadheadism imposed obligations but free theatre tickets and books were welcome. After twenty years in a shop he was aware of the exhaustion and worry required to place an edition on the streets and the utter lack of tenure. But he entreated those who offered commiseration not to waste it on journalists, "the most self-reliant, the most contented and most useful of mortals."[2]

To Whitman's delight, the publisher spent freely to build a solid, dignified organization. He paid $2000 for type and fixings, $1200 for sundries, ordered steam presses, joined the Telegraphic News Agency, hired reporters, compositors, and carriers, and published a prospectus which indicated that the *News*, unlike its competitors, would not cover pages with offensive advertisements, love stories, and "sickening tales of Revenge and Plots." Politically, in this momentous opening session of the Thirty-First Congress, assembled since the first Monday of the month, the daily promised to be independent.

"Pretty with its clean-lined type," the *News* appeared on 19 December in time to share in the sensation caused by the arrest of Dr. Webster for the murder in Boston of Professor Parkman. Another boon to circulation was close at hand, for occult rappings seemed to prove the Fox sisters capable of "spiritual intercourse" during their seances. By the start of 1850 Janes had announced publication of an ambitious weekly edition, to contain twenty-eight columns of wholesome, reliable items rather than the customary "nonsensical stuff." Here would be space for Whitman's critiques of new books like Macaulay's *History of England,* with its pertinent description of the struggle between Parliament and Charles I, and Melville's *Redburn,* that was regaining the author's reputation damaged by what a local reader called the "gaseous nothingness" of *Mardi.*

Then, according to a rival reporter, as the days passed a faint suspicion began to be entertained at 86 Nassau Street that "there was a little, just a very little chance of some difficulty in establishing a daily paper." Through-out January the suspicion grew as subscribers refused to make the anticipated move from the *Morning Star* and the *Sun* to the chaste *News.* At last on 23 February the publisher reached the end of his resources and closed shop. Approbation for the sound morality and pure taste of the *News* could not compensate for the lack of revenue. Janes lost about $10,000; the entire staff their jobs. Whitman recalled the cynical anecdote of the bankrupt printer who became a wealthy brewer—proof that the populace valued their stomachs more than their minds.[3]

Although the few issues of the *News* vanished along with the investment, hardy contemporaries at times repeated the editor's comments. In this season of Kossuth fever, Whitman approved Senator Seward's bill to give tracts of public land to Hungarian refugees, but wanted the same bounty extended to Mexican War volunteers. The *News* objected to carriages' forcing omni-buses off Broadway, for the street belonged to all classes and it was a gross injustice to surrender to a monopoly of the aristocracy; a laundress or seam-stress laden with bundles had as much right to walk there as the lady driving home with a thousand-dollar shawl purchased from Stewart's or Beck's. The editor paused to lament the fate of Cabet's Icarian communists, decimated since their landing in New Orleans. The trek in search of a home through the wilderness to the Red River had brought them to land owned by others; less than fifty at last reached Nauvoo, where they purchased a few acres and the abandoned Mormon temple.[4]

The dedicated bloc of thirteen Free Soilers in Congress drew columns of praise from the *News,* for these Ishmaelites revealed power beyond their numbers in the extended contest for the speakership. As the session began its fateful business, an unexpected ally emerged from the White House. During the first months of the new Administration Whitman had scoffed at Whig papers for "singing out how great and glorious a man General Taylor is! only he puts himself in the hands of weak and wicked advisers!" Choice of advisers was "the true test of the man's gumption, my hearties!" But this Christmas when the Proviso editor read the first—and last—annual message he revised his judgment, for the president recommended that statehood be granted to California and that its self-determined, antislavery constitution be accepted. Because national rather than sectional fervor flooded the message, southern ultras and their northern friends—in anger that reminded Whitman of the Whig response in an earlier regime when Tyler had vetoed Bank legislation—branded the president an apostate. Nor did the special message he sent to Congress in January mollify advocates of slavery who feared they were to become shorn Samsons through a policy they identified as one shaped by Seward to assure the dominion of free-soil interests.

No more than three weeks of publication remained for the *News* when the Telegraphic Agency reported that Clay, desperate to end the threats to the Union, had come to the Senate and offered eight of what he hoped were conciliatory resolutions. Whitman judged at least three repugnant to Free Soilers: continuation of slavery in the District of Columbia, a firm law for the rendition of thousands of fugitives, and the declaration that Congress lacked authority to regulate interstate traffic in slavery.

Whitman's candidate for 1852, Benton, who had recently offered legislation to carve several states out of Texas, at once labeled Clay's compromises a capitulation to those who threatened secession. Sam Houston turned to the Gospel of Matthew for the text, "A nation divided against itself cannot stand." Jefferson Davis, the soldier the *Eagle* had praised for heroism at Buena Vista, asked justice for the South and contrasted the happy slaves at his patriarchal Brierfield with the scorned and excluded Negroes in the North. Less renowned senators also stood on the red carpet of the semicircular chamber and added their oratory, but the portentous responses of Calhoun, Webster, and Seward came in March after the suspension of the *News*.

Reports carried by the surviving papers of acrimony in Washington—Foote had called Benton a degenerate Roman and then threatened him with a revolver—were matched by violence in New York. Whitman witnessed cohorts of the Empire Club raid Free Soil assemblies and deluge the speakers' platforms with garbage. He heard Isaiah Rynders and Dan Sickles heckle the Reverend Henry Beecher and Frederick Douglass at the Tabernacle. Rynders told Douglass, "O, you are not a nigger! You are half-blooded; a real nigger can't reason." Then a Presbyterian pastor, Samuel Ward, "black as the ace of spades in a deep cellar on a rainy night," with superior logic and learning proved the white bully to be a nephew of a "rather dull orang-outang."

Literati Whitman had once admired and emulated also lapsed into invective as the debate widened. To Paulding the Proviso unjustly declared war against the South; he called Seward "one of the most dangerous insects that ever crawled about in the political atmosphere," and the abolitionists conspiratorial fanatics. When O'Sullivan had managed the *Democratic Review* it avoided all phases of the issue, but the new publisher made the magazine a virulent foe of free soil.

One night at the seventh ward headquarters in Brooklyn, the local Hunkers charged Whitman and eight others there with attempting to create a rebellion against the "leaders and usages" of the Democratic party. When the room resounded to repeated cries of "Down with the traitors!" the outnumbered recusants had no choice but to leave. Soon Whitman could not walk from the ferry up Fulton Street without provoking taunts in the *Eagle* about a grim "shirt collar man" whose "eye like a furnace glows."[5]

Unable to counter with editorials he wrote occasional verse. On 2 March 1850 the *Evening Post*, which had recently referred to the brief but brilliant career of the *News*, printed his "Song for Certain Congressmen." A dictionary definition of "dough-face" used as an epigraph established the key for the seventy-two lines: "Like dough; soft; yielding to pressure; pale."

In the poet's judgment, based on first-hand knowledge of political maneuvering since 1846, Webster, "Scripture Dick" Dickinson, the editor of the *Express*, and the Democratic and Whig senators from Pennsylvania and Wisconsin were docile doughfaces who obliged southern lords by howling against free soil and abolitionism. One of the stanzas reported the hostile actions of petty henchmen at the seventh ward session:

> To put down "agitation," now,
> We think the most judicious;

> To damn all "northern fanatics,"
> Those "traitors" black and vicious;
> The "reg'lar party usages"
> For us, and no "new issues."

The doughfaces had been twisted by chicane pressure to believe that

> Things have come to a pretty pass,
> When a trifle small as this,
> Moving and bartering nigger slaves,
> Can open an abyss,
> With jaws a-gape for "the two great parties."

They shouted "fiddlesticks" and "bah" at those who urged freedom and progress for the masses. "Compromise" was the one word that charmed their ears and eyes; with it as a weapon they planned to stab young Freedom.

Whitman identified the motive for their servility as the greed of daws to feather their nests, for doughfaces rather than Free Soilers received patronage. In his coda these "practical men" in Congress chorused for the Clay resolutions:

> We do not ask a bold brave front;
> We never try that game;
> 'Twould bring the storm upon our heads,
> A huge mad storm of shame;
> Evade it, brothers—"compromise"
> Will answer just the same.

Two days after the printing of the "Song for Certain Congressmen," the poet read the testimony of the dying Calhoun, spoken by Mason of Virginia, that the admission of free western states would destroy sectional equilibrium: "We would be blind not to perceive in that case, that your real objects are power and aggrandizement, and infatuated not to act accordingly." Recognizing the threat of secession, Whitman may have recalled the earlier figure in which Calhoun had compared slavery to Aaron's rod. The next day dispatches from Washington told that Hannibal Hamlin (who would become vice president in 1860) defended the Administration's plan for the admission of California. Then on 7 March, after Walker of Wisconsin (named as one of the doughface singers) yielded the floor, Webster spoke.

In 1840 when the young Locofoco heard the famous Whig, he accused

248

RESURGEMUS

the defender of Biddle's Bank of showing the effects of a queasy stomach. Now in relaying southern demands for the guaranteed return of fugitives, Webster seemed to display a malignant conscience, for he sanctioned Clay's venal covenant. Refusing to concede a patriotic motive in his arch-foe's dramatic plea, Whitman joined other outraged men in searching for bitter allusions. In the Bible he found one harsher than Ichabod.

Over the years in places as different as a Manhattan synagogue or a Brooklyn church or his room with Eddy, he had visions of the last earthly days of Christ. In "Blood-Money" printed in the *Tribune* supplement of 22 March 1850, he wrote about the selling of "the divine youth" and the doom of Judas thrown from earth and refused by heaven. To the poet who equated democracy with Christianity, the proposed legislation ensured another Calvary:

> The cycles, with their long shadows, have stalk'd silently forward,
> Since those ancient days—many a pouch enwrapping meanwhile
> Its fee, like that paid for the son of Mary.

He omitted the names of doughfaces and ultras but *Tribune* readers understood that Christ, the "brother of slaves," was again reviled and scourged because a betrayer plied his trade in Congress. (When Stephen A. Douglas returned to Chicago after the end of the session, the City Council called him and the others who had voted for the bill Iscariots.)

On 11 March the speech of Seward provided a positive sensation relished by his former adversary of the *Aurora*. To those politicians who based their support of the resolutions on the fact that they could not find condemnation of slavery in the Constitution, the senator who had recently shared a platform with Lincoln announced, "There is a higher law than the Constitution, which regulates our authority over the domain." Within weeks 100,000 copies circulated, and according to phrasemakers, brought honey to abolitionists and wormwood to their opposites. Those New York doughfaces who urged Seward's impeachment aroused Whitman's ire, and he filed a note to be used as refutation: "I tell you Americans the earth holds on her huge bosom not a creature more base and abject than that man who takes all that is dictated to him by superior power, whatever it may be, and having no other text for his obedience than political laws, then obeys."

As late as mid-April Free Soilers saw no need to despair over the flow of battle. President Taylor continued to indicate that his territorial policy was neither sectional nor selfish; he acted with the rectitude proper to an

249

occupant of the White House sworn to preserve the nation, rather than as the owner of the Cypress Garden sugar plantation in Louisiana concerned about the safety of his investment. Supported by Seward, Benton, Hale, Hamlin, Chase, and others, the soldier seemed immovable. Then on 19 April the Senate over Benton's objection authorized a select committee of thirteen to handle Clay's program. Elected chairman, the Kentuckian recruited Cass, Bright, and Dickinson from the northern Democrats; Webster, Phelps, and Cooper from the northern Whigs; and combined all resolutions into an omnibus bill.

This tactic goaded Whitman to write a third editorial verse. He could sympathize with the monomania of Calhoun that had endured until the senator's death on 31 March; he could attempt to understand the source of the anger that drove Foote to the verge of homicide. But Northerners abetting the passage of this legislation! (Michigan had gone so far as to rescind its instructions to Cass to support the Proviso.) "The House of Friends" appeared in the *Tribune* on 14 June, four days after another onslaught by Benton was printed in a fifteen-page pamphlet and sent north, and after the correspondent of the *Tribune* telegraphed that the omnibus would pass or fail within a week: "The chances are rather in its favor."

Once again the Bible yielded the furious poet an appropriate text, this time from Zachariah:

> And one shall say unto him, What are those wounds in thy hands?
> Then he shall answer, Those with which I was wounded in the
> house of my friends."

Like Emerson in the "Ode to Channing," but with harsher epithets, he ordered the North to sweep its own doorsteps; Massachusetts, New York, and Pennsylvania contained the lice of humanity, crawlers and muckworms lower than Carolina bondsmen. He repeated the earlier indictment against those who valued a dollar more than Christ's blessing. These mercenaries walked shrouded through life, insensate to all but the pocket. The one chance for the nation lay in repudiating congressional cowards who "would quench the hope of the ages for a drink," and in following the leadership of Seward, Benton, Hale, and Wilmot. These Spartans would fight, fearless of southern anger, though he refused to slight the peril that might lie in

> ... the still and forked fang
> That starts from the grass at your feet.

250

The *Advertiser* on 22 June quoted one of the vituperative stanzas and added a factional explication of the "queer little poem." It was a "specimen of the way one of the young democracy, Master Walter Whitman, lays it on the members of 'the party' whom he has had the pleasure of knowing. . . . See how he talks to 'em."

For Americans like Sumner the wave that threatened to drown the land in slave legislation seemed to have found some of its tidal force in a Europe now ruled by the twin aristocracies of musketry and money. The patriot poet of Germany, Freiligrath, whose "The Dead to the Living" had stirred lovers of liberty everywhere, was now in prison. A sequence of calamities had forced Kossuth to flee Hungary. Mazzini's ideal of a free young Italy had ended in April when Pius IX returned to Rome escorted by a French army. This time the Romans did not shout "Viva Pio Nono!" Whittier hurried into print his anger at this "Scandal of the World":

> Go, bind on Rome her cast-off weight,
>   The double curse of crook and crown,
> Though woman's scorn and manhood's hate
>   From wall and roof flash down![6]

In the midst of this bitter season Whitman wrote a verse history of the dismal trend of the revolution. His "Resurgemus," printed in the *Tribune* on 21 June,[7] used an image from Gliddon's lectures on Egypt to tell his sorrow at the loosening of the brief, tight, glorious grip of Ahimoth, "brother of Death," on the throats of kings. The revolutionists had failed because their "sweetness of mercy brewed bitter destruction." Scorning personal revenge they allowed monarchical conspirators with trains of "priest, and tax-gatherer, Soldier, lawyer, and sycophant" to return. General Cavaignac, Louis Napoleon, and Pope Pius aroused false hopes, gave false promises, and then imposed arbitrary laws against the press, abolished universal suffrage, and wormed the wages out of poor mechanics. Kings strutted now through an entire continent while "bloody corpses of young men" lay in new graves. Though the gloom seemed impenetrable, the poet refused to abandon faith in a resurrection:

Not a grave of those slaughtered ones,
But is growing its seed of freedom,
In its turn to bear seed,
Which the winds shall carry afar and resow,
And the rain nourish.

The next day the *Tribune* agreed that the misery would not last forever.[8]

"Resurgemus" marked the third "queer poem" Whitman had printed that spring. As in "The House of Friends" and "Blood-Money" the lines in the unrhymed irregular stanzas varied from two or three beats to hexameters like those of Southey and Longfellow. His prosody brought approval from the *Eagle* which had refused to tolerate similar political freedom: "Many associate the idea of rhyme so intimately with poetry that they both seem inseparable, but this is a mistaken idea." Brownson that January had also voiced contempt for the artificial suggestiveness and "gilt fetters" of rhyme "that conditioned the rejection of the first spontaneous idea for a secondary thing adapted to 'tinkling bells.' "[9]

On 9 July 1850 the soldier who had survived thirty years in the field succumbed to an enteric illness possibly induced by the contaminated water of a capital that lacked a Croton aqueduct. Brooklyn joined the nation in memorial services with Dodworth's Band playing "Rest, Spirit, Rest." In the midst of the eulogies a hurricane scattered the mourners, destroyed the funereal drapings, and uprooted trees. Whitman soon heard that off Fire Island the same winds had wrecked the *Elizabeth* carrying Margaret Fuller, her husband and child home from hostile Rome. The next day Thoreau joined in the search for their bodies.

For the remnant of the summer the Free Soiler sought refuge at Greenport. News reached him there early in August that Seward, Benton, and their allies had defeated the omnibus bill, but there was little time for rejoicing. The next weeks saw the Spartans overwhelmed by the new alliance of President Fillmore, an intrastate foe of Seward, and Senator Douglas. By September, Douglas with managerial energy beyond that of the feeble Clay and a superior strategy of piecemeal presentation, had guided the omnibus into law. The saddened libertarian then knew that resurrection would be delayed.

17

LITTLE RUSKIN

IF WHITMAN paused for a personal inventory now that he had reached his thirties he found cause to hide in the pine barrens of Hempstead or ship aboard a Greenport whaler. Illness, drunkenness, and subnormality depressed the family; the son bought clothing for the father partially paralyzed and subject to what Louisa called bad spells. Eddy, now fifteen, had not responded to tender fraternal care. Dr. Howe, chairman of a Massachusetts group studying retardation with the aim of transforming brutes into human beings, examined hundreds of children ignored by parents or dosed with poultices of oak bark to tan the brain and toughen it so that it would retain lessons; some had been given mercury to solder neural openings. After Dr. Howe admitted ten of these victims to his hospital, bathed, exercised, and instructed them, he reported that all made miraculous progress.[1] But Brooklyn could not provide comparable professional skill. In two years a tripled census had turned the local asylum, where another Whitman brother, Jesse, would be confined, into what the press called a monument to the cruelty of civilization. Inmates attacked each other in the crowded common room; passersby, unchecked by custodians or compassion, taunted them. Even the kindliest of supervisors lacked the vision of another pioneer, Dr. John Conolly of Middlesex, whose technique of nonrestraint purged manacles, hobbles, and strait jackets from Hanwell and substituted gardening, music, and embroidery.

Slurs on the literary aspirations of the man with the "high heeled" Byronic blouse rankled Whitman, but he had not silenced critics with his "queer" poetry or fiction. He passed Bixby's, where sometimes he could see the aging Cooper, Halleck, Whipple, and other literati, but he could not join them in the lobby or at Friday evening sessions of the Sketch Club; Anne Lynch did not invite editors of defunct papers or occasional columnists of the Sunday press to her salon at Waverly Place. Nor did Duyckinck have him in to eat brandied peaches side by side with Melville, Mathews, and

Dana, and afterwards entrain with them for Olympian weekends in the Berkshires.

He had prepared a series of "Paragraph Sketches of Brooklynites" for Lees of the *Advertiser*, but almost all were so perfunctory that he apologized for the limitations of these "humble" notes on preachers, printers, and other citizens.[2] The warmth of his long friendship with the jour Hartshorne and admiration for the Presbyterian minister, Dr. Cox, made one paragraph exceptional:

> Though an old man, his style of preaching has all the warmth and vigor of youth or early manhood. His language is almost oriental in the splendor of its scope, and in its figures and similes. ... Going along the street you may see a rather full, Pickwickian figure of a man, dressed in black, with a stout cane. He has his white hair combed behind his ears, exposing the finest sort of phrenological development.

Lees had little time left for other favors. Within the year, a heart attack killed him at age forty.

In politics all of Whitman's rage had not prevented Herod and Pilate from kissing and embracing—as the surviving "soreheads" described the compromisers. With antislavery hopes at the nadir, the Kings County Free Soil party disbanded. Its Benton flag would never fly again, for Missouri planters angered by his opposition to the "humbug compromise" stripped the veteran of the Senate seat he had held for thirty years; he would return as a congressman but refuse to seek the presidency.

By 1850 there were literally scores of papers that could be called abolitionist, but none had the wide appeal of the Washington *National Era*. Editor Bailey, who described it as an antislavery, political, and literary weekly, mailed over 25,000 copies of each issue. His home served as a gathering place for Whittier, Gerrit Smith, and other advocates of abolition.

That autumn Whitman over the signature of "Paumanok" sent three letters to the *National Era*. In the first he described the Manhattan phase of a struggle he found as fierce as though fought with gunpowder and bayonet. Attempting to counter the would-be nullifiers of the Fugitive Slave Law, sixty businessmen formed a Union committee and sallied from their command post in a Fifth Avenue mansion to Castle Garden where they led some twenty thousand in honoring Webster, Dickinson, Fillmore, Clay, and Foote for gaining glory for themselves and an imperishable future for the nation. They condemned Seward firebrands and Free Soilers for championing "blackey" and picked a ticket for the upcoming elections that combined Hunker Democrats and Compromise Whigs. Merchants in Broadway nailed Union campaign posters on their shop doors to ensure trade. "Blessed Union!" exclaimed Whitman, "how much cloaks itself under your name!" As he turned away from the paradoxical spectacle of agitation for calm and quiet, he comforted himself and *National Era* readers with the apocalyptic utterance that "the cause of Hunkerism and Slavery must go down. It may be years yet; but it *must* go."[3]

Paumanok filled the letters with the same dioramic formula he had first used on the *Aurora* and then on the *Dispatch*. After reporting the tactics of the Dickinson militants, he visited the Art Union, where Woodville's "Old '76 and Young '48" portrayed a veteran of the Revolution and his grandson returned from Mexico with an arm in a sling: "The mother and the old '76er are beautifully done; the whole picture is good." Nahl's "Death of Bayard" might enrapture the wife of an upholsterer, but a worldly viewer thought it false to the pink of chivalry.

On a sunny Saturday in November Paumanok strolled Broadway as he had these many years, and beginning at the iron gates of the Battery that glistened with fresh lampblack pointed out the sites to distant readers of the *National Era*. The new "Frenchified baby-house" fountain on Bowling Green had turned dirty green; he preferred the original rocks down which water had coursed. The fire-damaged trees were dying, a great pity, "for they acted as a sort of link between us of the present and the people of eighty years since." The original iron posts along the street stood topless, a memento of the night when Liberty Boys celebrated the skirmish at Lexington and chiseled away the royal crown and arms. The brick mansions of the Knickerbockers now served as warehouses; new places like Delmonico's were superb with palatial furniture, velvets, and gold wallpaper. Trinity and St. Paul's deserved moments of devotion, but the writer snubbed Barnum's Museum with its garish flags, its weird bipeds and quadrupeds.

Some of the older residents resented the virtual mania for converting Broadway into rows of shops, but Whitman found every window a rich mine of patterned fabrics, gutta-percha, bowie knives, gallipots of drugs, Parisian hats. A depot displayed books bound in Russia, Morocco, and calf; one of the quartos had splendid illustrations of Scotch costumes, another of Egyptian antiquities. Above street level on the third floor or high enough for sky light, dozens of daguerreotypists had their parlors: "Whatever artistical objections may be brought against this sort of picture, it is not the less true, that some of the Broadway operators do produce the form and spirit of the face to a degree that defies criticism." The plates of Gabriel Harrison, an operator at Lawrence's, were "perfect works of truth and art."

The ruins of the Park had been carted away; shops and taverns filled its place. Playgoers now patronized Chambers Street or the Metropolitan, where W. E. Burton as Toodles and Micawber seemed the funniest man that had ever lived. But Whitman could not pass by the site of the old Park without a word of gratitude for memorable evenings that began when "as a fat-cheeked boy, in round jacket and broad shirt-collar, there, trembling with expectation and excitement, I received my first ideas of the drama." When the curtain rose on the *School for Scandal* it seemed to the boy that the walls of an adjoining house had vanished. (Jonathan in Tyler's *Contrast* knew the same sensation.) When Clarke as Banquo came on stage and pointed to his bloody throat the boy quivered; that midnight he lay awake frightened by witches. Fanny Kemble, "passionate as a volcano, voluptuous as the spirit of wine," the Fishers, Placide, "best of comedians," Mrs. Vernon, Mrs. Chapman "with the well-shaped legs," Richings, the husky-voiced ruffian, handsome Mrs. Wheatley, Hackett burlesquing countrymen and irritable Frenchmen—all "strutted their hour" upon that stage. Remembered at their best, they made the performances at the new theatres seem flat, flippant, crude. "Good bye, old Park."

Partly because Jenny Lind followed a season of Bettini, Badiali, and others called by impresario Maretzek the finest cast in American operatic history, Whitman never succumbed to the "'Lind lunacy" that seized New York in September. There were other reasons for his aloofness. The unprecedented publicity, typified by carpets spread at the pier and an auction before the first concert with tickets bringing $225 from a hatter, made him suspicious. All the witticisms about the performance seemed to deal with the financial arrangements: notes exchanged for gold; every syllable worth five dollars. When the singer came on stage dressed in pink satin with black lace flounces and a green cape, Whitman noticed cockades in her hair, rouged cheeks, and a bad walk, but after a while he warmed to a facial expression that was "a sort of moral milk and honey, lighted up by intellectual sunshine." Her voice in a series of brilliant show pieces, although clear and "of wonderful fluency," was like plate glass rather than Amphion's lyre. A sea of handkerchiefs and ecstatic applause followed all her technical displays, but her "ventriloquistic" dexterity in the celebrated Meyerbeer trio with two flutes or in the Swedish echo songs failed to move Paumanok. When the coloratura turned to excerpts from oratorios he also found her overpraised. Granted, a scientific style had beauty, but it was "the beauty of Adam before God breathed into his nostrils." Rather than join in acclaiming her rendition of Handel's "Come Unto Me" to be as supreme as the Parthenon, he charged that most of the praise was "no doubt paid for" and that Barnum had trafficked Lind as though she were a Feejee maiden. As a result of this humbuggery eulogists, like commentators on the Bible and Shakespeare, found more in the songs than the singer dreamed of. Furthermore acceptance of all of her trills and shakes led to a musical taste as artificial as that for turtle soup and spiced dishes or the stunts of tumblers and India rubber men. He advised concert-goers to remember, "Music, in the legitimate sense of that term, exists independently of technical music, as much as language exists independently of grammar—or, perhaps, I might say, just as poetry exists independently of rhyme."

The Manhattan press had taken him to task four years ago when he charged critics with puffing the Keans; now the *Evening Post* challenged Paumanok to name the venal papers. "I wish all questions were susceptible of such an easy answer," he wrote in the third letter. "The answer is— omnes, or all!" The *Post* and the *Tribune* could not be bought for fifty dollars, but the *Herald*, the *Sun*, all the Sunday papers, and a large majority of the others were "by no means difficult to be 'had' " for they were commodities like paper, type, ink, and presses. Now and then God vouchsafed to the world men who refused to be silenced by promise of wealth and popularity or threat of poverty and death. "Well, a few of these characters stray into the editorial profession. Leggett was one of them. Whom shall I mention after him?"

Dr. Bailey placed a note under this indictment: "Our lively correspondent must not be too sweeping. The exceptions he subsequently makes are all well made." The next issues of the *National Era* did not carry Paumanok's views or "bits of philosophy."[4]

An admirer of Scandinavian literature ever since his first reading of Bremer —a recent visitor to Brooklyn—Whitman came upon a London translation of Bernhard Ingemann's *The Childhood of King Erik Menved*. After finishing the four hundred double-columned pages he proclaimed the Dane a better writer than the Swedish woman. In fact he had not been so stirred by fiction since *Consuelo* or *St. Giles and St. James*, in which Jerrold had voiced the social claims of the "governed million upon the governing few."

The Dane's use of medieval chronicles, customs, and fables meant little to Whitman. But in the political conflict that marred the last years of the reign of Erik's father and the ascendancy of the young king, the Free Soiler found parallels to the furor over the Fugitive Slave Act. The refusal by the principled Duke Waldemar to renounce his honor by signing a repugnant petition was uttered in a Danish castle in 1285, but similar emotion welled in 1850 from the Spartans in the Senate chamber or from the poet of "Blood-Money." The Brooklyn partisan could salute the nobleman who, rather than compromise with usurpers, chose a dungeon—and in it found a bird whose death carol sounded pleasant.

In another novel from the tetralogy, *King Erik and the Outlaws*,[5] Whitman may have come upon the alchemist's speech:

> Nothing is small in science and in nature . . . the least may here lead to the greatest; in every blade of grass there lies a world. How long will men shut their eyes on the great and only true revelation of the Deity, through the miracles and holy wit of nature!

In Copenhagen Ingemann's writings had been collected in forty-one volumes; in England his champions had begun translations. In America, though Longfellow knew the poetry, the fiction, especially the tetralogy formed of episodes in Denmark's early struggles, remained unread. Convinced that a reprint would be profitable, Whitman replaced with a few paragraphs many prolix pages of historical narration that filled the latter part of *The Childhood of King Erik Menved*, and named the shortened redaction *The Sleeptalker* because of the habit of one of the main characters.[6]

Having cut the original text by half, he offered *The Sleeptalker* to the *Sun* at a "moderate price." In its new form he estimated that the novel would fill three columns for twenty-one days, and then printed in a 25-cent book format "would pay handsomely." Neither the novel nor the promotional plan impressed the *Sun* or a second paper he approached that year, the *New Yorker*. Dr. Bailey serialized fiction, but rather than give further space to Paumanok, on 5 June 1851 he printed the first installment of *Uncle Tom's Cabin*.

The sequence of debacles did not end Whitman's pleasures. A reporter saw the handsome bachelor at another soirée of the Young Men's Association, where "he made himself conspicuous with the Ladies." On open days he visited galleries and rejoiced that these "noble establishments" attempted to satisfy the hunger for beauty that typified the nation. When heirs dispersed Colman's Emporium he recalled the late owner's unique efforts a decade ago to edify strollers with prints in the window. Now he could view the Art Union, the International, the gallery of Düsseldorf paintings, and other rich collections. Manhattan auctioneers fleeced the gullible, but the man who boasted that he had cut his eyeteeth on Broadway found their picture sales "a great treat," though he ensured his enjoyment by leaving all his money home—"Not but that some of the pieces may be good, too."

The Smithtown debater who had affirmed the prospects for the growth of the arts in America despite a citizenry prone to cupidity, knew that merchants spent their profits ostentatiously on French porcelain, buhl cabinets, and matched trotters. Politicians gave priority to tariffs and charters. But the grocer Luman Reed commissioned Cole and Mount; Congressman Gulian Verplanck sponsored Vanderlyn and Weir. Whitman agreed with Harriet Martineau that national receptiveness went beyond patronage of painters and sculptors, or subscriptions to engraved magazines and folio Bibles. Anyone who walked the docks marked the delight with which importers examined the curios brought from exotic ports.

Years as a newsman had taught him that artists commanded space by the side of soldiers and senators. The entire press mourned Allston and the unfinished "Belshazzar's Feast," and Cole dead soon after the paint dried on his masterpiece. Gould eulogized Inman with a sonnet, "We miss thy presence mid the gifted band." Bingham in town to show "Fur Traders Descending the Missouri" and other records of western life received prompt mention, while letters from the Kenyans and Hildas made the Caffè Grèco on the Via Condotti in Rome as familiar as a Manhattan oyster cellar painted by Woodville. Editors kept pace with Crawford's work in progress and debated the placement of the three heads of Cerberus in his "Orpheus" after subscribers had bought the sculpture for $25,000. Paragraphers sympathized with Leutze when his portrait of Washington burned, rejoiced at the recovery of the bust of Calhoun from the *Elizabeth*, welcomed Delaroche's "Napoleon Crossing the Alps," and joined Bryant in petitioning for a retrospective showing of Huntington portraits. The tour of Powers'

"Greek Slave" led to quarrels between those like Whitman who thought the white marble nude the sculptor's major work, and dissenters who called it a lesser Venus, an affront to modesty. (President Polk became furious when he overheard two young officers of the state department discussing Powers rather than their duties.)[7]

Returning home after years in Europe, Cooper (who was Horatio Greenough's patron) complained that his countrymen were so eager to beautify the nation that they filled it with Grecian temples which served as banks, courthouses, churches, taverns, and dwellings. This obsession as widespread as speculation led to children trundling hoops before classic entablatures and butchers carrying sides of beef into markets modeled after Athenian shrines. Consulting imported books rather than trusting to invention and logic, architects and builders ignored climate, site, and utility. "Nothing can be uglier, *per se*," admonished Cooper's Mr. John Effingham, "than a Swiss cottage, or anything more beautiful under its prime circumstances." But Effingham remained hopeful for in New Haven, along with "abortions," he saw "little jewels" that proved the commencement of a taste.[8]

Any critic capable of nurturing that taste found a waiting public. As a reader of the *Democratic Review*, Whitman knew the Greenough doctrine that beauty is the promise of function. In the summer of 1843 the sculptor home on a visit from his beloved Florence asked in the *Review* why civil architects failed to carry the responsibility imposed upon ship builders. When Whitman scorned Grace Church or wanted to know if John Wesley could worship at ease in the Gothic pile erected by the Methodists of Williamsburgh, he spoke with the supporting authority of this ranking professional. Greenough had also walked Broadway and found there a cathedral whose designers had sought sublimity but wrought a structure so puny it seemed an elephant dwindled to a dog. Greenough succeeded in transferring his scorn for the carving of rhetoric into stone, the imitation of outlandish styles rather than the spirit of nature, and gingerbread embellishment rather than simplicity.

On rambles in secular Wall Street Whitman saw places where designers had ignored the law of natural adaptation obvious in the shanks of a horse or the chest of a greyhound, forced buildings of all functions into one general form rather than working from the heart of the structure outward, and then masked ill arranged and ill lighted rooms with a façade of marble tracery and columns. After the consecration of the multispired Church of the Savior built for the Unitarians of Brooklyn, he clipped an article that asked why so many places of worship in a democratic land in this nineteenth century had to be *moyen âge*. The sensible Reformed Dutch congregations of Long Island refused to attempt to unite Catholic splendor with Protestant plainness and as a result churches like the one in Jamaica emerged as substantial religious instruments. Furthermore, to be Gothic without solidity and amplitude was like a frog trying to inflate itself to the bulk of an ox.

The son of a carpenter who had built small wooden houses for mechanics could wonder at the plans in *A Home for All* by O. S. Fowler. The phrenologist illustrated his theories of economy and utility by showing how to fashion gravel-concrete into an octagon castle with sixty-five rooms and a gymnasium for females.

As the topic of art gained popularity, lyceums in their function as halfway houses between pulpit and stage billed lectures. Emerson told Brooklyn audiences of the glories of British art—though chauvinists in the room were audibly hostile—and also talked of Germans who taught that a building designed to answer its purpose became beautiful even though beauty had not been intended. Whitman heard his friend Godwin survey the history of aesthetics from Baumgarten through Hegel, with a memorable dictum from Goethe: "Our aesthetics speak of a great deal of poetical or antipoetical subjects; fundamentally there is no subject that has not its poetry; it is for the poet to find it there." (Visiting Nashville, William Walker addressed students on "The Unity of Art.")

A sequence of books and essays supplemented the lyceums. Lester in *The Artist, the Merchant, and the Statesman* reminded Whitman of Pericles and the Medici. Tuckerman in *Artist-Life, or Sketches of American Painters* wrote of contemporaries. The younger Dana at last completed editing Allston's *Lectures on Art* with their evocation of strolls under the pines of the Villa Borghese with Coleridge. Robert Dale Owen published *Hints on Public Architecture*, which included specifications for ornament derived from native flora rather than from Greece. Greenough, after sending the manuscript to Emerson, published his *Yankee Stonecutter*. (In 1855 Whitman would write of himself, "Here comes one among the wellbeloved stonecutters.") Charles Deland's "The Philosophy of Art" in *Sartain's Magazine* contained another idea that Whitman later rephrased: Deland wrote, "The appreciation and admiration of a work of art is, more or less, an act of creation, on the part of the observer."[9]

Whitman first read *Modern Painters* during his *Eagle* editorship and like other sensitive men responded to Ruskin's vision of nature as God's truth. In superb prose the evangel wedded art to humanity, and as a benediction announced that perception is quickened by love and judgment by veneration. *The Seven Lamps of Architecture,* along with its own organic concept, documented Ruskin's scorn for the users of the false and the functionless that cankered national roots. But by the 1850s his emulators had begun to be derided as "little Ruskins" who lacked their master's profundity but persisted in firing salvos of "four-pounder" criticism. They must somehow, complained the New York *Daily Times,* "have their one, two, or three Turners to laud, and their living Salvators to execrate." [10]

Because painters and sculptors seemed to sprout as naturally as Indian corn, private citizens and public agencies added gallery space. After a collation to celebrate the new quarters of the National Academy of Design, Mayor Hone, who owned a Ruysdael, entered a felicitous phrase in his diary about the conversion of a stable into a temple of the muse. Thomas J. Bryan showed Mantegna, Watteau, Poussin, and other treasures gathered during his years in Europe. The vision of a few friends who met in a bookstore in 1840 led to the incorporation of the American Art Union which they intended to "adapt to the feelings, tastes, and circumstances of the people, and appealing to their national pride and sympathies." By the end of the decade 18,000 paid five dollars for membership, received the *Bulletin,* engravings, and, with luck, originals chosen at an annual raffle presided over by Lind or other celebrities. The expanding market for imported work led Goupil, Vibert of Paris to open the International Union uptown where Whitman saw Sheffer's "Christ" and other "chef d'oeuvres." The popularity of "lovely" Düsseldorf paintings—as George Templeton Strong called them —brought a display to Broadway where the lawyer could pass evenings tutored in their virtues by a friend who had once been a student in the German center.

In his columns Whitman often advised readers to visit Manhattan galleries to see the good things always there. For example, Mount's "Right and Left," a Negro fiddler calling a figure at a dance, brought back the nights of the Riverhead militia muster. The Long Islander's use of the offspring of Suffolk slaves as models led critics to call him the one American able to delineate God's image in ebony or mahogany. The editor rejoiced when Brooklyn, at last refusing to remain dependent upon that "great whirlpool of a city that swallows up everything in its vicinity," converted the Apprentices' Library into an Institute with gallery and lecture space. In 1850 he helped local artists form their own union in Fulton Street.

Attracted by these "warm impulsive souls" who were instinctively generous, he delighted in visiting their studios. He watched Henry Kirke Brown work on a ten-foot olive bronze of De Witt Clinton for Greenwood Cemetery. The sculptor, once a surveyor in the West, then carved a series of Indian figures; the young hunter in "Choosing an Arrow" seemed to be Arrow-Tip.

A modest landscape painter, Jesse Talbot, now in his mid-forties, became Whitman's frequent host and aesthetic tutor. Some years ago he had painted "The Happy Valley" after reading *Rasselas*. On that canvas, according to Whitman, he lavished color and intense light on grass, sky, and water until the exuberant final statement proved that nature is filled with "glowing blood." Since then Whitman had followed the career of this "least pushing" of artists and catalogued his progress from magazine engravings to hangings in the National Academy and the homes of Fifth Avenue patrons. By now their intimacy had grown to the stage where Talbot could confide his plans for a vast triptych. When he completed a group of scenic idylls his townsman ranked him with Allston and Cole, for in the best of these— "Indian Woods," "Rocky Scene on the Juniata," and "The Startled Deer" —he joined simplicity, boldness, and purity. Unable to buy one or an earlier Adirondack landscape, Whitman settled for the illustration of Bunyan's "Christian and the Cross" that had "exquisite touches of color and delicate outlines."

During the hours at the third-floor studio in Post's building, Whitman probed—after regaining his breath lost in the ascension—the reasons for his friend's success. Talbot, he concluded,

> has studied the great source of Art and Beauty, Nature herself, spending months in the mountains and woods, and by the borders of rivers and the sea—watching the sunset and the sunrise, and transferring to his canvas the play of light and shade, in its very reality. . . . We are sure that this is better than even "visiting Europe." Has Europe any better models in her galleries than Nature offers on American hill tops, and all over the broad spread of our fertile fields? Is the copy of a copy to be chosen, before the great Original itself? [11]

263

Some of the others in the Brooklyn circle were Thomson, known for marine subjects; Lester, the former consul at Venice, Free Soiler, art historian; and Walter Libbey, a young portrait painter. Flattered by Whitman's prophecy that his name would be heard in high places, Libbey asked him to pose. In these sessions Whitman heard at first hand the artists' aspirations and vexations; for if much had been done, more remained undone. Were Cooper's Effingham to return, he would find the little jewels of taste scattered rather than set in a national crown. The student too poor to travel to the Pitti Palace or the Louvre had to settle for casts at the National Academy. Officials of the New York Art Union, despite avowals that they rejected enough canvas to tent an army and budgeted no more than five per cent for overhead, stood accused of hanging mediocrity and squandering income on quarters rather than sponsoring needy genius; the few who received their subsidy never seemed to emerge. In rebuttal these officials argued that, unlike foreign galleries, nothing unchaste ever stained Art Union walls. As proof of devotion to original American subjects, they listed the winners of their annual distributions: Darley's scenes from Irving, Brown's "Aboriginal Hunter," Bingham's "Jolly Flat Boatmen."[12]

Whitman's friends feared the rise of a clique-dominated academy with power like that of fashionable Düsseldorf. There in a German town that lacked ancient abbeys or awesome nature, students spent years drawing for instructors who manacled them to laws that eliminated originality and poetry. The instructors stressed accuracy of outline and strong modeling rather than luminous color. Visitors to the hundreds of studios that lined the streets told of huge quantities of props, ranging from bishops' mitres to knights' spurs used for detailed rendering of religious and historic texts. One student, according to a tall tale, pursued realism so relentlessly that he led a horse near his easel, shot it, and then sketched the dying animal.

Whitman—in his role of little Ruskin—thought that this mode at its best produced works like the "Martyrdom of Huss" or "Old '76 and Young '48"; at its worst, paintings like the "Discovery of the Dead Body of Gustavus Adolphus," which had little to praise and nothing to remember. To defenders of the school's blatant technical bravura, he retorted that Americans bought Düsseldorf canvases for one reason: "We have no patience with the merely imaginative when we can get the real."[13]

The music lover who dared challenge the Lind claque now scolded the same errant taste in art. Rather than this very bad though popular mannerism of "sharp outlines and effects struggling to push themselves into notice," he preferred a natural style that pleased through its fusion of tone, softened edges, and a "delicious melting in" of every object. Talbot's harmony of color and form excited emotion, unlike Koehler's plodding "Germania." It was invariably fatal to any work of art, Whitman explained, "when the constructor endeavors to do too much. Nature laughs at such attempts." (This paraphrased the dictum in *Modern Painters* that "in art, every space or touch in which we can see everything, or in which we can see nothing, is false.")

For Whitman, imagination interpreted with simplicity and boldness was the greatest nerve "in the fingers of art." Why is it, he wondered, that some men labored for months to capture exact details and at last produced something fit only to be framed in a coffin pattern? Why did others take a dead coal, blow on it, and create a masterpiece? His answer would have pleased Ruskin:

> The principal aim of a work of art, to which all others are subordinate, is to embody the spiritual expression. Whatever the piece may be, landscape, historical composition, portrait, comic groups, or even still life, it is the spiritual part of it you want above all the rest. That is its soul, its animus, and makes art live. . . . The most exquisite draughting, the finest coloring, and the minutest truth, the mere forms of nature, are but the cold, dead corpses of art, if they have not the vivifying principle.

Fulton Street studio talk turned to ways of surviving financially in a time when it seemed to Whitman's friends that the public had thousands for Lind but not a farthing for native artists. As the unemployed journalist saw it, because they often lacked the shrewdness of the successful, they were fated to work in the dark, feeble and aimless, unless guided by a strong hand. (In the *Crescent* he had advertised for sale Gould's portrait of Schiller.) He suggested a Fourierist association similar to that sponsored by Greeley: "What a glorious result it would give, to form of those thousands a close phalanx, ardent, radical and progressive." But they chose to try a more feasible solution, a union of their own established in Fulton Street in 1850.

Nothing in *Modern Painters* had pleased Whitman more than the championship of Turner. Emulating Ruskin he publicized his own friends in newspaper columns that asked for critical precedence for them before they were, in his phrase, settled under six feet of heavy wet earth. When they in turn invited him to lecture at the Institute in March 1851 during the first distribution of prizes, he accepted gladly.

On a warm spring night after a walk under budding trees that brought to his memory Bryant's "Forest Hymn" with its celebration of enduring verdure by a spirit kindred to many artists, he stood on the same platform Emerson had used the year before.[14] His idiom, however, reflected not only the ode to beauty from *Nature* (recently reprinted) and the essay on "Art," but Ruskin and all others who preached the gospel of the sublime. In language more elegant that that of the paragraphs in which he had scolded materialists who valued only pigs in the pen and potatoes on the hill, the guest first honored his hosts for remaining aloof from the crass profiteers typical of a nation whose symbol was the steam engine. With brush and chisel each creator called to the feverish crowd "that in the life we live upon this beautiful earth, there may, after all, be something vaster and better than dress and the table, and business and politics." Each nourished the germ of "the truly great, the beautiful and the simple" and labored to disentangle all that obstructed the primal freshness of the earth. He hastened to correct the absurd separation of nature and art—Rousseau, "one of the noblest apostles of democracy," had indulged in this false dichotomy. All men possessed something of the artistic; the perfect man was the perfect artist.

In an era "distracted by frippery, cant, and vulgar selfishness" he found it refreshed the soul to contemplate an older civilization that gratified one's hunger for the intellectual and the ideal. Because Greek citizens were philosophers, poets, and musicians they provided model subjects for their artists who in turn sanctified the state. If creative emotion prevailed here in America as in antiquity, death itself would be shorn of its ghastly features. But what mockery to waste marble on the orthodox modern specimen! The tone of a Carlyle now dominated the Institute, as the lecturer excoriated every creature beyond the small room whose petty life showed

> contempt for all there is in the world, except money can be made of it; his entire vacuity of anything more important to him as a man than success in "business,"—his religion what is written down in books, or preached to him as he sits in his rich pew, by one whom he pays a round sum, and thinks it a bargain,—his only interest in affairs of state, getting offices or jobs for someone who pays him.[15]

Because he spoke to aspiring creators always in search of an ideal subject, Whitman turned from ridicule of fops and mercenaries to praise of great men. Washington and Kossuth became heroes because of their sensitivity to moral beauty: "Such men are not merely artists, they are artistic material"; therefore students were to end allegiance to false masters and abandon Düsseldorf imitation. Paris, Naples, and Rome provided the true academies; there lovers of beauty struggled and died for liberty, "a constituent part of all well developed artists." Out of these new graves ascended the august enthusiasm vital to art. As proof that ravaged Europe held material for canvas and marble—a lesson taught by Greenough who wanted stone pillars to be cemented with the blood of martyrs—Whitman read his "Resurgemus," timely now after reports of the brutality of soldiers. (Greenough had left Florence because he could not tolerate the sight of Austrians patrolling the streets.) The lecturer ended by assuring his audience of the rewards of freedom, for "under her umbrage Art must sooner or later tower to its loftiest and most perfect proportions."

His friendships with artists brought Whitman a degree of pain. Walter Libbey was dead the next year at twenty-six. The Brooklyn Art Union met little encouragement and dissolved. Soon commercial jealousy and pettiness began to destroy the prosperous Manhattan Union. There had always been regret at its use of a species of gambling to entice patronage, but no formal action resulted until the *Herald* charged that its officials were abolitionists who used funds earned by illegal means to help Henry Raymond establish the *Daily Times*. In its denial the *Times* described the Art Union president as a founder and leader of the major antiabolitionist group in the city, but could not silence Bennett. After trials and appeals the New York Supreme Court ruled that an illegal lottery indeed existed. The Union's holdings liquidated at auction, the fine building became a dance hall.[16]

It was time for the man who had offered financial advice to others to strengthen his own assets. Occasional columns and reprints of tales brought a few dollars, but hardly a living. A few extras came from bits of job printing and his retailing of *Love and Parentage* and other books wholesaled from Fowlers and Wells. His application for "any sort" of opening on the *New Yorker* failed, though baited with the lure that his ideas of salary were very moderate. After fruitless months he decided to rely on his own experience and the savings of years of regular work.

On 4 June 1851 "our amiable and talented friend" issued the first number of the weekly *Salesman and Traveller's Directory for Long Island.* The sheet was to appear every Wednesday; its price only fifty cents a year. Of all his many publishing ventures none had a humbler aim than the *Salesman.* "Admirably suited to the wants of the mercantile houses in the cities," it planned to advertise goods, inns, routes, and timetables of trains, boats, and stages throughout Queens and Suffolk. The erstwhile lecturer on the evils of commerce did not capitulate unconditionally to Mammon, for he promised to include original sketches and to avoid politics.[17]

The *Long Islander* found the first number interesting and well-printed, and quoted its account of the fisherman of Montauk. The *Advertiser* had little doubt of the success of the venture if initial standards and spirit were maintained. But Whitman suspended publication that same month—possibly because of competition from a paper started in Williamsburgh within days of the *Salesman.*

By the end of June he was in Greenport. If not so abundant as last summer, fish were available, the vegetables delicious, the milk purer than city swill, and the bay soothing. The local costumes were as bizarre as those worn by "supes"; the accent of an elderly Universalist with whom he discussed the tenets of that optimistic theology while digging clams was funnier than metropolitan comedy. All these "ministers to entertainment" eased the pain of another failure.[18]

18

EXFOLIATED

DONIZETTI'S *La Favorita* sung at Castle Garden after the vacationer returned from Greenport programed for him the entire human cycle: "the red fire of passion, the cavernous vacancy of despair, and the black pall of the grave." The tenor Bettini mourning misplaced love for the king's mistress typified man fated to endure a world that seemed magnificent but proved false—a moral the disillusioned politician believed universal as Shakespeare. By October 1851 courageous abolitionists in Syracuse led him to qualify this cynicism, when they rescued the fugitive slave Jerry from marshals and escorted him to Canada.

Other events these days touched long-time associations. That host and provider of comfort in time of drizzle and defeat, Dominick Colgan of the Eagle House, was arrested and fined for violating the Sunday liquor ordinance. Freed, he would serve again. At last the legislature authorized a park on the Heights, and citizens began to plan a memorial to the victims of the prison hulks. Frances Wright died, derided to the end by the orthodox but honored in lectures by Free Enquirers. All Brooklyn paused to mourn the patriarch General Jeremiah Johnson; reading his reminiscences had linked Whitman to the Dutch settlers and the Revolution. Then died Tom Hamblin, since 1830 synonymous with Manhattan theatre.[1]

An episode in Cuba reverberated here. When news from Havana confirmed the grim end of fifty Southerners captured in a filibustering raid, Captain Rynders and his Tammany ultras joined Mississippians in threatening reprisals against Spain. Whitman gave his sympathy, instead, to the living symbol of freedom, crushed by emperors and czars, when Kossuth came to America that December in search of means to reverse the calamity in Hungary. Accepting an invitation to visit Brooklyn, he was met by a troop of horse guards at Fulton ferry and escorted to the armory and Plymouth Church for orations at five dollars a ticket. No one in the audiences asked

269

the question posed by the *National Era*—his opinion of the bondage of three million Americans.

Excitement over the Noble Magyar gave way to the daily revelations in City Hall where the divorce trial of Forrest and his English wife combined the anglophobia of the Macready riots with sexual titillation. For Whitman the courtroom became the scene of conflicting loyalties. Forrest's lawyers were Theodore Sedgwick, the antimonopolist editor of Leggett's essays, and then John Van Buren. Charles O'Conor, a Hunker leader, defended Mrs. Forrest from the accusation of committing "indelicacies" with Willis and half a dozen other men. At the climax of his charge Van Buren entered what seemed to be conclusive evidence of guilt, the letter sent by a lover to "Consuelo"; to read its transcript published in the *Herald*—the courtroom seated only a hundred—was to find the illicit passion of a De Kock rather than the chaste restraint of Sand's heroine. The jury, however, swayed by O'Conor's skill in examining witnesses, returned a verdict against the actor for his morning "rehearsals" in Josephine Clifton's parlor and visits to an assignation house. Mrs. Forrest left City Hall richer by alimony of three thousand dollars a year and the gift of legal acclaim as an innocent woman.[2]

In this season when several banks collapsed, and businessmen called the money market tighter than a pair of new shoes, Emerson rode the ferry to Williamsburgh and lectured on wealth. In his easy, unaffected manner he suggested the cultivation of adhesiveness. Disappointed with this formula the local paper noted that most lectures in the transcendental idiom were humbug as patent medicine. However his series at Hope Chapel, which included "Egotism," led the *Tribune* to call him America's chief poet, philosopher, and seer.

Land reformers worried by the rise in rents and a veritable carnival of beggary by the unemployed increased their demands for free homesteads. With little to do Whitman trudged through thick mud to inspect what he found to be a wonderful example of Manhattan philanthropy, the new People's Wash and Bath House where wanderers could cleanse themselves and their clothing. His enthusiasm for a project that brought more credit to Americans than the building of a warship was reflected in a *Dispatch* article:

> In our time, we are moved to say, as occasion arises, hard words of that tyrant Capital, and its brood of pompous monopolists. But the sight of such an establishment as this Bath House, built by the

contributions of the richest men of the city, with an evident purpose of the profoundest philanthropy and no pecuniary gain at all, will go far to redeem a multitude of the sins of the overgrown and overgrasping nabobs of money.

Two cents bought a bath in the basement; five cents, a private room and bath on the first floor as fine as at the Astor House; ten cents, the ultimate in dressing facilities. The second floor rented stalls at five cents an hour for washing clothes sweet in hot Croton water and ironing them fresh.[3]

For the fourth time since coming of age, Whitman watched the approach of a presidential campaign, but unlike the other three when he had editorial control of a newspaper he endured enforced silence while Hunkers and Whigs convened in turn. The lobbying of delegates like Mike Walsh and Isaiah Rynders reminded a veteran of the race track with a dozen entries:

all the old nags to start, never having won a race, and all the young ones watched, and having neither blood nor appearance to recommend them. It is a clear case for black-leg management to come in for stakes. . . . The jobbers stationed at Washington have all opened their houses; wine and wassail is the order of the day.

After thirty-five ballots in Baltimore that winded both old and young nags—Cass, Marcy, Buchanan, Douglas—the crowded Democratic track had a late entry, Franklin Pierce of New Hampshire. "Who is General Pierce?" asked a Down East humorist. "It aint a fictious name, is it?" The *Times* identified him as "an average college student, an indifferent lawyer, a dull debater, an undistinguished public man, and an unsuccessful soldier." Abolitionists rated him no higher than a third-rate doughface politician. But on the forty-ninth ballot the race was his, along with a platform pledged to honor the Compromise.[4]

Two weeks later the Whigs also met in Baltimore and after fifty-three ballots chose General Scott, described by Greeley as an "immeasureably conceited, aristocratic ass." Friends of the senior warrior countered this charge of egotism by punning that it proved he had his *eyes* about him. The Cotton Whigs then further alienated northern voters by applauding the

Fugitive Slave Act. Following the crass maneuvers that typified both conventions, Whitman concluded that it would be retributive justice to make coffins of their platform planks.

Hawthorne, torn between loyalty to a Bowdoin classmate and knowledge that little time remained to fashion excellence, volunteered to write a campaign biography for Pierce. The *Times* called the apologia by the one-time Locofoco surveyor of Salem "Hawthorne's New Romance"; its author had descended to the depths of political pamphleteering and had become "an indiscriminate panegyrist and electioneering trickster," a party hack.[5] But the *Democratic Review*, which rated Pierce a great man, welcomed "N. Hawthorne, politician."

Addressing a petition to patriots of the entire land, the biographer expounded a concept of slavery as one of the evils "which divine Providence does not leave to be remedied by human contrivances, but which, in its own good time, by some means impossible to be anticipated, but of the simplest and easiest operation, when all of its uses shall have been fulfilled, it causes to vanish like a dream." He explained the constancy of Pierce's support of slavery as anchored in faith in the Constitutional rights pledged to the South; the firm advocate of Union never wavered at embracing the Compromise, though met by the obloquy that threatened a Northerner who "dared to love that great and sacred reality—his whole, united, native country—better than the mistiness of a philanthropic theory."

The creator of passionate Hester and Pearl could move Whitman, but not the doughface apologist who asked patience until a solution came from heaven—and ignored evidence that human contrivance in the Thirty-first Congress had strengthened slavery and that the trials of Jerry's rescuers proved slavery's iniquity. (Hawthorne would be buried in May 1864, the month of the battles of the Wilderness and Spotsylvania; Pierce stood with the family at the grave.) For the second time in four years the Free Soiler departed from the political Sodom—as he called the major parties. Unlike Lot's wife he never looked back.

To his dismay he saw that many Democrats who had bolted with him in 1848 now accepted Pierce. Among them Van Buren. In Jamaica Brenton printed campaign songs to the tune of "Old Dan Tucker":

> The Whigs they say it's all too fierce,
> To nominate that General Pierce,
> But the Democrats will learn them a thing,

By elevating both Frank Pierce and King.
So get out of the way for the People's got
A great dislike to General Scott.

At Masonic Hall in Pittsburgh on 11 August 1852 some two thousand people with another great dislike convened. The political origins of Joshua Giddings, Charles Francis Adams, Cassius M. Clay, G. W. Julian, Gerrit Smith, and other "Free Democrats," as they called themselves, were diverse; but huge banners heralded their unifying plan of "No compromise with slaveholders or doughfaces." In this Pennsylvanian Sheffield, stronghold of free white labor that worked the furnaces, forges, and rolling mills whose smoke blackened coaches until they looked like coal scuttles and turned visitors into chimney sweeps, the delegates denounced the two parties as hopelessly corrupt and unworthy of confidence since both had conspired at Baltimore to elevate cotton and debase conscience. Then, in the spirit of the invocation of Henry Wilson of Massachusetts, they vowed to hasten the day when every slave would stand and say, "I am a man, a brother, a freeman."

Whitman remained in Brooklyn but followed the detailed telegrams in the Manhattan press. Of the twenty-one resolutions presented by Giddings to the platform committee, none was cheered louder than the fifteenth which found the Fugitive Slave Act repugnant to the Constitution, the principles of the common law, the spirit of Christianity, and the sentiments of the civilized world: "We therefore deny its binding force upon the American people and demand its immediate and total repeal." A more impassioned indictment came from Smith, the philanthropist who had given land from his vast holdings to 3000 black farmers. A tall man with athletic figure and flowing beard, he delivered his minority report with sonorous voice and magniloquent manner; he called slavery piracy, and asked for the use of weapons against federal marshals, who were lower than sheep thieves: "The black man cannot esteem or respect us so long as we refuse to take the ground that resistance to the slavery of the black man is as imperative as resistance to the slavery of the whites."

As a scarred veteran of intrastate feuds, Whitman could accept the regional gloss of an Ohio man; Smith despairingly confessed little hope that a just God would spare a guilty nation from bloodshed: "He has lived among New York iniquity,—New York villainy,—New York sneaking, scheming and deception, and does not know the feeling of Western people on this subject." The Pittsburgh delegates further pleased the poet of "Re-

273

surgemus" when they extended sympathy to universal freedom for the brotherhood of man. And as an antimonopolist, Whitman approved their affirmation that public lands should be sold to the people, not granted to corporations.

The Free Democrats also turned to New Hampshire for their presidential nominee, Senator Hale, long proscribed by his state organization for defying instructions to vote for the annexation of Texas. Hunker accusations that he vagabonded through the country preaching abolition under the guise of lecturing had not silenced this jovial humanitarian. Known as the best joker in the Senate, he attributed his fame to the richness of material at hand and not to art. Chosen by the Liberty party and others at Buffalo but displaced by Van Buren—a grave error according to many there—Hale continued after that defeat to uphold free soil in the Senate and in the courts, where he defended fugitives with his considerable skill as a trial lawyer. Now, the slim chance of victory and his reluctance to endure a hard campaign away from home prompted his refusal; in fact he made his stand known before the delegates reached Pittsburgh.

Desperate for a leader, the Free Democrats ignored Hale's letter and on 12 August nominated him with Julian of Indiana, a former Whig, as vice-presidential candidate. When Whitman learned that Hale remained reluctant, he wrote to him on 14 August:

A word from a stranger, a young man, and a true Democrat I hope.

You must not only not decline the nomination of the Democracy at Pittsburgh, but you must accept it gracefully and cordially. It is well to know when to be firm against others' wishes; but it is better to know when to yield in a manly and amiable spirit.

Out of the Pittsburgh movement and "platform" it may be that a real live Democratic party is destined to come forth, which, from small beginnings, ridicule, and odium, (just like Jeffersonian democracy fifty years ago,) will gradually win the hearts of the people, and crowd those who stand before it into the sea. Then we should see an American Democracy with thews and sinews worthy this sublime age.

It is from the young men of our land—the ardent, and generous hearts—that these things are to come. Do you, then, yield to the decision at Pittsburgh, shape your acceptance to that idea of the future which supposes that we are at [present?] planting a renewed and vital party, fit to triumph over the effete and lethargic organizations now so powerful and so unworthy. Look to the young men—appeal specially to them. Enter into this condition of affairs, with spirit, too. Take two or three occasions within the coming month to make personal addresses directly to the people, giving condensed embodiments of the principal ideas which distinguish our liberal faith from the drag-parties and their platforms. Boldly promulge these, with that temper of rounded and good-natured moderation which is peculiar to you; but abate not one jot of your fullest radicalism. . . .

You are at Washington, and have for years moved among the great men. I have never been at Washington, and know none of the great men. But I know the people. I know well, (for I am practically in New York,) the real heart of this mighty city —the tens of thousands of young men, the mechanics, the writers, &c, &c. In all these, under and behind the bosh of the regular politicians, there burns, almost with fierceness, the divine fire which more or less, during all ages, has only waited a chance to leap forth and confound the calculations of tyrants, hunkers, and all their tribe. At this moment, New York is the most radical city in America. It would be the most anti-slavery city, if that cause hadn't been made ridiculous by the freaks of the local leaders here.

O, my dear sir, I only wish you could know the sentiments of respect and personal good will toward yourself, with which, upon seeing a telegraphic item in one of this morning's papers, that you would probably decline, I forthwith sat down, and have written my thoughts and advice. I shall make no apology; for if sentiments and opinions out of the great mass of the common people are of no use to the legislators, then our government is a sad blunder indeed.

How little you at Washington—you Senatorial and Executive dignitaries—know of us, after all. How little you realize that the souls of the people ever leap and swell to any thing like a great liberal thought or principle, uttered by any well-known personage—and how deeply they love the man that promulges such principles with candor and power. It is wonderful in your keen search and rivalry for popular favor, that hardly any one discovers this direct and palpable road there.[6]

Early in September Hale responded to the Free Democrats' mandate and stumped the North, but despite the fervor of audiences and the endorsement of his Brooklyn admirer he could not sway more than 156,000 voters. In local elections, Smith's district sent him to Congress, but Manhattan doughfaces elected the ex-pugilist and bartender, the Honorable William M. Tweed. Tammany celebrated with a "jollification." The inconsolable losers found the inaugural address of the fourteenth president, winner of all but four states, heavy with Fourth of July claptrap and eagerness for annexation of Cuba. Pierce pledged to enforce the Compromise.

During the next months as Whitman watched rivals within the victorious party contend for the loaves and fishes, he saw that the men who had returned to the fold had gained little. Before long these prodigal Soft Shells complained that unforgiving Hard Shells received favors beyond their ratio of votes. The continuation of this "great conchological controversy" ensured the barring from patronage of all who had truckled to Free Soil, but many blameless of heresy also found themselves "exfoliated." Despite his knowledge of the Pacific and the advice of powerful friends Melville failed to get assigned to the Sandwich Islands. According to *Putnam's* there were hundreds of other young men of letters, scientists, and artists to whom a secretaryship or consulate would come as a benefaction, but with the exception of Hawthorne they remained forgotten. Pierce deprived the nation of the harvest of their culture but sent to London Tammany Hard Shell Dan Sickles, an accused thief and pimp. While secretary to the legation Sickles would present a prostitute to Queen Victoria as "Miss Bennett of New York," thereby gaining revenge on the *Herald* for opposing his appointment.

As the bitterness in New York intensified until it was compared to a medieval *odium theologicum*, Whitman joined in condemning the rigid control of caucus and convention that made outcasts of the supporters of defeated candidates and nullified the wishes of the entire electorate. He sided with analysts who contended that given a direct choice no more than a few hundred people would have voted for Pierce. Now as he watched the execution of the "insolent" Fugitive Slave Act, Whitman promised defiance "by speech, by pen, and if need be, the bullet and sword."

Several years before, the *Morning News* had counseled American poets to abandon the practice of writing fugitive pieces and to court fame through publication of complete manuscripts. Whitman had seen the efficacy of this practice proved when Tupper was lionized during his visit to New York and when a new edition of Philip Bailey's *Festus*, inspired by "the hope of serving God as poet-priest," earned critical honor. (Along with its Universalist doctrine of the triumph of divine love over Lucifer, death, and hell, the twenty thousand lines of *Festus* contained deific, Uranus, an electric touch, the "soul of every atom," and a bard who "wakes and walks by night.") But the exfoliated politician, the editor deprived of a paper, the custodian of a stricken family had not been able thus far to emulate these writers. Recognizing his responsibilities, he sought ways to meet them amidst ominous signs of a troubled economy.

The journeymen carpenters of New York striking for seventeen shillings a day formed a procession five deep and a quarter of a mile long with banners complaining, "Everything is rising but carpenters' wages." Their average annual earnings, estimated the *Tribune*, did not exceed $400—not much more than rent for a decent dwelling. Room and board for a single man had jumped from $2.50 or $3.00 a week to $4.00 and $5.00. Joined by coach painters, cigar makers, masons, and men of other trades, the carpenters persisted in their demand for a ten to fifteen per cent increase, in the face of cries of "Socialism" and "Fourierism," and threats of replacement by immigrants or Negroes. Knowing that salvation for his family could not come from the hammer, an occasional piece in the papers, or inches of job printing, he pondered the solution through a cold winter which added temptation to the news from California that common laborers earned twenty dollars a day there.

That spring when the press reported that speculation in real estate had assumed the "bubble state" he made his headquarters in his father's shop at the corner of Cumberland and Atlantic and became a builder and seller of small houses. The venture seemed safe, for a shortage of housing had led landlords to raise rents; many Brooklynites moved to cheaper places in Williamsburgh. Increasing paralysis limited Walter Whitman's activity, but the son could draw on his years of experience in composing specifications for masonry casing, flooring, partitions, and roofing. By now two of his brothers, Andrew and George, also worked at the trade. And since 1830 Asher Benjamin's *The Practical House Carpenter* had guided many artisans.

Sale of the house on Myrtle Avenue in June 1852 for $3500 earned hundreds of dollars profit after three years of rent-free occupancy. That same month Whitman bought a lot on Cumberland Avenue—choicer sites from the General Johnson estate required brick structures—ordered materials, hired mechanics, and began to build two houses on it. By January he advertised one "genteel" dwelling for sale and moved his family into the second. Then he bought another lot. Continuing this lucrative cycle would enable him to present Louisa Whitman with an unencumbered deed to a dwelling on Ryerson Street.[7]

The connoisseur who bedecked his room with paintings and urged art lovers to patronize the Talbots and the Libbeys rather than the Düsseldorf technicians also guided the "good folks of Brooklyn, (who are well known to be eminently musical)," to halls filled with the sound of music he considered genuine. But those folks who remembered his ecstatic praise in the *Broadway Journal* and the *Eagle* for the "heart-singing" of the New England Cheneys or the Ethiopian Serenaders now met a reversal in his taste. "Ah," he exclaimed in a column in January 1852, "how can such an intellectual people as the Americans really are, countenance before them the nigger monstrosities and the sugar and water of the various 'families' who appear among us from time to time?"[8]

Ten years ago he had been one of many captivated when Dan Rice established a mode of entertainment. Cast against his will to play a Negro, Rice remembered a hostler who sang and danced,

> Turn about an' wheel about,
> An' do just so;
> An' eb'ry time I wheel about
> I jump Jim Crow!

Once he learned the songs and then adapted the steps to his bow legs, in a short month, reminisced the *Literary World*, "every urchin in the land was 'jumpin' Jim Crow, and every other urchin's sister tinkling the delightful aria upon her piano. In six, not a manager could fill his house or his pockets unless he infused a dash of darkness in the drama." Ensembles with banjo, tambourine, triangle, bone castanets, and fiddle toured America and England, delighting respectable citizens who arrived with wives and daughters

278

to applaud "Dandy Jim of the Caroline," jigs, hornpipes, double cuts, double shuffles. Their renown brought one group of minstrels an invitation to Buckingham Palace. Whitman's friends often heard him singing Ethiopian tunes in a voice marked by unique timbre; when the placard under the two great lamps at Mechanics Hall announced Christy's Minstrels he joined the throng. Proud to be known for "somewhat fastidious ideas about American music," he had assured his readers that something really great existed in Negro singing; here was entertainment that could form the base for native drama.

But by the turn of the decade despite the commercial success of Christy and other troupes, Whitman concurred with an anonymous coupleteer that the qualitative decline of African minstrelsy had been rapid and melancholy:

> This may be the music for the million, hurly burling,
> We will not hear it for a million sterling.

The easy humor of the first songs, the genuine mood of "Oh Hush" and "Dan Tucker" gave way to imitations in doggerel slang meant to please peanut chewers from rat-baiting pits at Five Points. Lyricists who had never seen an alligator or smelled magnolia blossoms wrote ditties filled with banana trees in Tennessee and sugar mills in Kentucky. Managers cast Ethiopians in "Lucy did lam a Moor" and other crude burlesques; some of the men dressed as females and danced with indecent gestures. The censors of this vulgarity were soon joined by antislavery leaders who exposed the paradox of Christians laughing at caricatures of human beings who deserved tears of sympathy. "God's alphabet"—their pious definition of music —should not spell debasement. Nor should adult entertainment consist of listening to pseudo-Negroes ejaculate "Yah! Yah! Yah!"

A few men intimately allied with the minstrels responded to the criticism. J. B. Fellows built a hall for a troupe and warned libertines that they were barred from his chaste shows. Stephen Foster blamed his would-be peers for using offensive language and declared to Christy his willingness to woo refined patrons. Safeguarding his reputation against widening prejudice the composer omitted his name from the title page of song sheets until, too late for his financial salvation, he knew that he had created a following. In 1852 his publishers sold 500 copies daily of "Old Folks at Home."

By then a succession of exposures to opera at Maretzek's Astor Place and the Castle Garden had proved to Whitman that this was the mode that sated his emotional hunger. What he called "human cravingness" led him to prefer the Italian baritone Badiali in the "Freedom" duet of *I Puritani* to the New Hampshire Hutchinsons in "The Maniac." Abby and her brothers had once made him weep. Now his tears came during Gennaro's deathbed *arioso*. Sable Harmoneons sighing for picayune butter at the plantation and the "warblers" of "The May Queen" no longer touched one who had heard Bettini in *Ernani*. Nor did it matter that the "beautiful, large, robust" tenor caroused nights away with faro and champagne. His clear, firm notes became a lark poised in heaven that trembled the soul.[9]

Like all Free Soilers he continued to applaud the Hutchinsons when they climaxed rallies with "Liberate the Bondsman" and "Get Off the Track to Make Way for the Car Emancipation." Their parody of calomel-dosing quacks always brought his laughter. But to hear a magnificent contralto was to discover a new planet soaring at ease through the universe. Exact correspondence for what he called the Creative Power no longer surfaced in country folk schooled by their parson, but in *bel canto* voices. After a night of *Lucrezia* he wrote:

> It is from such artists, and the hearing of such instrumentation, that the people of New York and Brooklyn, must habitually get the taste for genuine music, worthy of the name. For with all the commonplace of half-developed musical judgment about "fine old ballads," and "simple natural songs," it is to Italian music, from standard composers, that we must come at last, as to the ideal of what is most brilliant and effective in vocalism and with a properly appointed band. These, and the grand works of the old German composers, so exaltive and soothing. . . .[10]

In the past year he had bought a guitar and melodeon; now he spent $180 for a piano.

There were men who found fault with Marietta Alboni when she stood motionless on the stage of Metropolitan Hall dressed in a flounced white gown, holding a sheet of music and a fan. Only in her mid-twenties, her luxuriant proportions, complained *Harper's*, overpowered the limits of romantic beauty. "Art and the dress-maker can do much, but they are not omnipotent. They cannot . . . cheat the eye into the belief that a heroine of twelve stone is a sylph." A Falstaff in petticoats seemed the apt comparison. Others rated her acting as indolent and circulated the comment by Berlioz that six months of misery after marriage to him would rouse her sleeping fires. But from her debut in June 1852 to the farewell in May 1853, Whit-

280

man, who remembered that Consuelo had been called homely, exulted in the majesty of "this fully developed woman" and sided with all who saw noble beauty upon her brow and the poise of conscious power in her stage manner. In the phrase of the wit startled at the size of audiences in the Lenten season, he was among those for whom Alboni replaced all temptation.

Hearing the pure, round voice admirers called the beau ideal of a grand contralto, Whitman knew the sensation Sand had described when Consuelo sang the *Salve Regina* of Pergolesi that first revealed her genius. He exulted in the voluptuous richness of Alboni's tones guided by musicianship that never erred even in the finale of *La Sonnambula* and other touchstones of virtuosity. Whatever the demands of the score, she seemed natural and at ease. When Alboni moved from the concert hall to the operatic stage he sat in the upper tier of the Broadway and heard a series that continued to evoke his ecstasy. Surrounded by mechanics and roughs, he became entirely oblivious of all except the singer from the moment she came on stage until the final curtain. Her Norma sung half a note lower than in Bellini's score, became one of his "rare and blessed hours"; and almost forty years later he told friends of her overwhelming Lucia marked by genuine tears. When Alboni returned to Europe after "a most perfect" *Lucrezia*, he could second the testimonial in *Albion* that she had never "in intonation, phrasing, or execution sinned against perfect propriety, artistic rule or good taste."

When Henrietta Sontag arrived in New York, those boasting of the musical maturation of the "parvenu" metropolis asked if London or Paris ever presented the two ranking prima donnas at the same time. Though older than Lind or Alboni—"we are annoyed that Sontag, a staid matron of fifty is not all that we imagined she must have been at five and twenty," wrote an ungallant reviewer—the soprano retained flexibility and delicacy, showering roulades and arpeggios with the ethereal lightness that had astonished Goethe. Beginning in late September she offered Haydn's "With Verdure Clad," Italian arias, and "Home, Sweet Home." Then during the winter of that "meritorious season," she sang *Linda de Chamounix* and a brilliant Rosina in *The Barber of Seville*, for comic opera was her forte. (Strong gave away his ticket rather than hear Alboni, but exulted over Sontag's "girlish buoyancy and spirit.") Whitman called her magnificent and published in February 1853 his conviction that since she had unveiled the beauties of song to enthusiastic thousands at Niblo's, it was now "the theatre par excellence."[11] Sontag never returned to give further joy for within the year she was dead of cholera.

February also marked the debut at Niblo's of the pianist–composer, Louis Moreau Gottschalk. A friend of Berlioz and Chopin, the young musician from New Orleans was already famous for "La Bamboula" with its rhythms of the slave dances the *Crescent* editor had watched at Congo Square.

Entranced by the voice, Whitman also studied the face as revealed through old and new media. In the canvases of Charles Loring Elliot, whose hundreds of sitters included Bryant and Cooper, he saw the "tip-top performance" that by now his aesthetic creed equated with "simplicity, just the truth and no more, and some touches of a genius to understand what it means." (Consuelo's master, Porporo, taught his pupils that "simplicity is the essence of the great, the true, the beautiful in art.") At the Academy Whitman stood by the hour in front of the oils that led critics to consider Elliot a successor to Copley, Stuart, and Jarvis. Then in the street on the way home he noticed "how tame and doughy appeared all common faces, after the reflections of the human frontispiece, rich and electric with the glowing color of this remarkable painter." He confessed that some nights he dreamed of Elliot's men and women.[12]

He found few limners with comparable skill; furthermore, he believed that the genteel classes lacked paintable subjects. The inevitable results of such inept collaborations were myriads of bad portraits. Shoddy daguerreotypes, the work of untrained operators quick to exploit the popularity of a new medium, were also plentiful—except in Arkansas: "There ain't any doggertype man about here now," wrote Simon Suggs from Rackinsack. "There never was but won, and he tried his mershine on a lawyer here, and Lem was so mortal ugly it burst his mershine all to pieces trying to git him down." But in viewing a professional's work Whitman knew only fascination. Granted that black-and-white plates did not allow him to revel in color; but their faithful copying of living human features compensated by causing a welling of emotion.

Daguerreotyping was so profitable by 1851—the year of Daguerre's death—that a trade journal listed over 100 operators in Manhattan. As Whitman toured their establishments, his pride in the talent of these Holgraves grew until he asserted categorically that "in America alone, and mostly in New York, is daguerreotype taking really an *art*." Each of the "Priests of the Sun" displayed a choice assemblage of faces. On Brady's walls hung Victor Hugo and Eugène Sue. At Lawrence's with its thick carpets, splendid piano, lounges, and a huge skylight, Father Mathew on one side; across the room Henry Ward Beecher and his white-haired father. The Presbyterian Dr. Cox, the Congregationalist Dr. Patton, and the transcendentalist Dr. Spring formed an ecumenical group. A few feet away he "plumped" against the editor who remained a paradoxical "bundle of the best intentions, twisted here and there in the development"—Greeley with "Yankee cuteness in his eyes, but an all-embracing good will to men." At Gurney's, winner of a prize in the first national competition, Whitman came close to Alboni and noted features "chiseled in the nicety and truth of a Grecian sculpture"; the sorrows of Norma and Amina showed more clearly than from the high tier of the theatre. Here were actors, California gold diggers, cautious young men in need of tender Julia or Amelia Caroline, and a poet—"that is, he passes for such, while he lasts."

These encounters moved Whitman on 7 June 1853 to write in the *Star*:

> A thousand faces? They look at you from all parts of the large and sumptuously furnished saloon. Over your shoulders, back, behind you, staring square in front, how the eyes, almost glittering with the light of life, bend down upon one, and silently follow all his motions. . . . How many of these, whose faces look upon us, are now away in distant regions? How many are dead? What terrible changes have happened to them. . . .

It seemed inevitable that he would name Gabriel Harrison the most perfect of all the daguerreotypists. For years Whitman had known the bearded friend of Poe and Forrest (whose biographer he became), and president of the fourteenth ward Free Soil League. "Wild and unpruned as nature itself," according to his admirer, "but held in check by an organically correct eye for purity in form, color, and the symmetry of things," Harrison had worked as an engraver, and then as an actor. Coming to Brooklyn in 1848, he opened a theatre; when this failed he started a dramatic academy, then adapted Schiller's *Don Carlos*. But there was a richer living in daguerreotyping and in 1851, after a stint with Lawrence, he earned a prize at the London Crystal Palace. At the Fulton Street parlor whose facilities he advertised as the best in the country, he prepared portraits of a variety of subjects that would earn him a second medal at the New York Crystal Palace.[13]

Watching him polish oversize 14- by 18-inch silvered copper plates,

Whitman tried to isolate the source of Harrison's talent and concluded that it lay in spontaneous observation. One day Whitman posed for a portrait. Unlike the formal studies on an adjoining wall of gentlemen in full dress he wore clothing he found comfortable and healthy: a Spanish hat slanted back on his head, a flat-collared blouse open to show a red flannel shirt rather than a dickey, and mechanic's loose trousers and cowhide boots instead of snug gaiters and patent-leather shoes. Harrison's study revealed the fine head with its high brow, large shapely ears, full lips, powerful chest, but missed the color of the sunburned skin, the gray-blue eyes, the hair textured, as the poser said, like hay new-mown. It would soon serve, however, as the frontispiece to the book that contained a final version of a thousand faces.

Heralded as an event unique in American history the Crystal Palace, inspired by and named after Paxton's enchanting greenhouse in Hyde Park, opened in July 1853 with the lofty theme of making plain the laws of progress by displaying the changes in the world since the workshop had replaced the battlefield. In a huge shell erected in Reservoir Square for study and amusement, six thousand exhibitors seeking to extend the influence of pure and ornamental art and to awaken "a quicker sense of the grace and elegance of which familiar objects are capable," filled seventeen miles of naves and aisles—enough to stock a thousand country stores. The concept of honoring all who labored—mechanic, manufacturer, scientist—led ameliorists to believe that here at last was the symbol of the unity of mankind ever cherished by poets and philosophers.[14]

President Pierce and dignitaries from Great Britain (among them Charles Lyell and the future historian John Acton) attended the inaugural ceremonies and were drenched wet to the skin by rain that leaked through the unfinished roof and damaged some of the wares. The builder of small frame houses gladly paid a dollar for the entire week's admission and at last stood within what he called "an original, aesthetic, perfectly proportioned American edifice." The architects, Carstensen and Gildmeister, had shunned temples of Minerva and proved the utility of iron and glass for large structures. The British guests also admired the building and its encompassing ideals. Whitman would have responded to the geologist Lyell's observations noted at the site by Acton: "that if he were not so much occupied in thinking of what happened thousands of years ago, he would consider the contemplation of the political state of America most interesting and instructive. It is necessary to come here at intervals to see the wonderful progress that is being made."[15]

Marochetti's "Washington" held the station of honor under the 180-foot dome, but viewed from the ground level the metallic statue seemed as squat as Irving's Knickerbocker hogshead on skids. Among the other imported and domestic pieces were Thorwaldsen's "Christ and the Apostles," a group by Powers, and the largest collection of paintings ever assembled in an American gallery. From ten in the morning until ten in the evening, Whitman could examine English silver, Gobelin tapestries, Sèvres porcelain, Yankee clocks, sewing machines, presses, bindings, and instruments used in coastal surveys. Antislavery leaders thought it noteworthy that the World's Exhibition did not belie its name for the managers were more liberal than those of state and country fairs. They treated Negro spectators with courtesy and accepted the display case of the celebrated hair dyes and perfumes manufactured by John A. Jones of Baltimore—cited as proof of the capacity of his race when untrammeled by prejudice.

Every night under the light of thousands of gas lamps, Dodworth's Cornet Band and singers entertained. Beyond the perimeter, according to shocked clergy, groggeries thick as blackberries opened to serve the parched and the wearied; faro banks sprang up like mushrooms. To judge by Whitman's description some of his companions that summer and autumn were not lured to the Crystal Palace by the pure and ornamental: Bill Guess, a twenty-two-year-old driver, was "a thoughtless, strong generous animal nature, fond of direct pleasures, eating, drinking, fun." Peter, another driver, was a "large, strong-boned young fellow." If Thorwaldsen was not for them, the Crystal Palace also contained road scrapers, revolvers, ice creameries, five-legged calves, Lilliputians, and fat ladies. With their vocational expertness Bill and Peter may have voiced opinions in the debate over the statue of Andrew Jackson astride a charger rearing on its hind legs, for some visitors thought that Clark Mills had ensured the equestrian's stability by substituting the legs of a gigantic ox or elephant.

Whitman experienced proprietary pride when he came to the cases of daguerreotypes for those from New York and Brooklyn were superior to all others and none surpassed Gabriel Harrison's. The quality of the entire display, which included studies of the officers of Admiral Perry's expedition to Japan, led him to offer a dictum:

Indeed to do any work *good*, requires a vast deal more than people suppose; and we cheerfully welcome all good workmen in any thing. Nature alone is the perfect constructor and artist—never at fault for material or power of moulding it. Man experiments, blunders, tries again, despairs, gets a partial success, and is fain to shut his own eyes to the numerous shortcomings, and be satisfied if he can only make it pay.[16]

On 15 September 1855 the *Eagle* ran an unsigned review of the book by its former editor. The reviewer, under the impact of the encounter with an entire gallery of faces, may have intended more than metaphor in telling his readers that the poems formed a daguerreotype of the poet's inner being.[17]

19

AT HEART FREEDOM

AFTER THE FIRST FEW WEEKS the stiles of the Crystal Palace slowed as patrons with the exception of a few like Whitman sought newer sensations. Its financiers lacked profit, its virtues a poet. The London prototype had inspired Samuel Warren to commemorate that Temple of Wonder and Worship with a book about a poet-philosopher who mused there with his attendant spirit. Published in 1851 *The Lily and the Bee* earned its author both praise as the Milton of the exhibition and ridicule as a madman bereft of literary standards. For the 1854 edition reprinted by Harper, he added a gloss of the work: "Man, in his threefold relations to the Earth, to his fellowman and to God." In defense of the style he defined as rhythmical prose, he cited the choruses of *Samson Agonistes*. Breaking five thousand unrhymed lines into oddly stopped irregular stanzas, he often introduced his images with initial repetition:

> Here is a voluble smatterer: suddenly discomfited
> by the chance question of a curious child: and rather
> than own ignorance, will tell him falsely!
>
> . . . .
>
> Here is a philanthropist—thinking of blood-stained
> Slavery! [11]

For a while the huge diorama of Niagara continued to draw the curious to Hope Chapel. Smaller audiences heard Olmsted on astronomy and Youmans on the chemistry of vegetable growth. No Brooklyn lyceum accepted the suggestion, in an enthusiastic letter sent by "W." to the *Times*, that the chemist be invited there to repeat his lectures. In them he talked of ideas taken from the recently translated *Kosmos* of Baron von Humboldt. The pioneer popularizer of science had defined the scope of his title as "the assemblage of all things in heaven and earth," and in his volumes gave an

287

encyclopedic view of the universe, man, and language. Whitman soon addressed a note to himself to embrace and kiss "Kosmos words."[2]

The evershifting panorama of that wonderful street, as he called Broadway, now included the excitement of a museum holding forty tons of Egyptian antiquities. Dr. Henry Abbott, after twenty years as a physician in Cairo, hoped to earn a livelihood in New York by displaying relics of the Nile, but on some days Whitman found himself the only visitor to scan the hieroglyphics chiseled on slabs of limestone, the cases with pitch-blackened mummies, and the strips of papyrus that narrated life and death. From Dr. Abbott he learned aspects of the theology of Isis and Osiris before whom all human beings were equal. Their priests recognized immortality and the transmigration of souls, and celebrated the sanctity of every form of life by wearing gold dung beetles on their crests.[3]

Then George Aiken's six-act adaptation of *Uncle Tom's Cabin* came to the National after runs in Troy and Utica and, to the wonder of those including Mrs. Stowe who had abjured the theatre as Satan's synagogue, filled the house every night. The novelist on an extended visit to her brother in Brooklyn could corroborate the report in the *Daily Times* that Eva's love for the black child brought tears from people never beguiled into church— "the *proletaries* of a great city—wandering, marauding boy, the professional rowdy, the flash man, and even the outcast Pariah of our society—the prostitute." For three and a half hours these regulars sat with members of elite congregations and their pastors while Uncle Tom and Eva preached "the great ideas of Brotherhood, Equality, and religious responsibility." Some of the women in the third tier became unnerved by Cassy's confession; the few who tried to attend to their trade could not compete with a stage turned into an altar. Even the Bowery boys shouted "Hey, Hey!" in praise of Uncle Tom's exhortation to "taste ob de Lord's goodness."

Free Democrats, heartened by this powerful ally, rallied at the Tabernacle and heard Hale and Richard Henry Dana, Jr., by now a lawyer for fugitive slaves. (On the train Dana saw that four others in his car had copies of *Uncle Tom*.) In the judgment of these restive citizens the administration crawled like a toad to do the bidding of the South rather than flying like an eagle to unshackle humanity; their *National Era* scolded Young America for scolding British abolitionists. The Hard Shells of Tammany countered by entertaining Senator Foote of Mississippi and adopting the motto, "No Union with the enemies of the Union." In Whitman's candid prognosis these symptoms of chronic illness aggravated by the Compromise into gangrene would not be healed until the defeat of "poor lank" Pierce.

Manhattan celebrated New Year's Day of 1854 with noteworthy "semi-genteel rowdyism and dissipation." While editors, in their customary review of the old year, itemized an imbalance of disaster, news came of the sinking of the overloaded *San Francisco*. Sailing out of New York for the West Coast with civilians and troops for California garrisons, the ship had labored off Cape Hatteras through gales that washed two hundred passengers overboard. When the plight of the remaining five hundred became desperate, the captain of the *Antarctic* lay by four days and nights and kept the promise he chalked on a board, "Be of good Cheer, We will not desert you."

No samaritan rescued Europe from Napoleonic usurpation and war between Turkey and Russia; it seemed that tyranny, like the plague, had its epidemic season. At home there were depressed trade and a harvest damaged by drouth and the midge. Methodists and Baptists knew sectional cleavage over slavery, with those who remembered Bunyan alluding to their erstwhile brethren as By-ends following Religion for a pair of slippers; ultras vowed to meet at a new Philippi. Fortunately, Whitman had proof of the progress of other causes.

A physical culturist who studied Combe's *Principles of Physiology*, admired the rigid training routine of pugilists, bathed daily, swam, hiked, and resisted a tendency to alimentiveness (he loved raw oysters, steak, coffee, comb honey, blackberries), Whitman welcomed the diffusion of a philosophy of health. A devoted son and brother, he hailed Woman's Rights conventions—though drunken rowdies annoyed the delegates assembled in New York. The proclamation of women's equality by Owen, Saint-Simon, Fourier, and their disciples had fallen on sensitive ears; by now it seemed that Frances Wright had not lost all the campaigns in her thirty-year struggle to free her sex from bondage. At first calumny and ostracism had followed her public scrutiny of marriage and birth control, but now lecturers and publishers filled halls and shelves with expositions of what the wits called a fertile subject. Horace Mann on "Woman, the Inferior" was as frank as on the meager training of teachers. Lydia Bloomer shared platforms with Dr. Lydia Fowler, wife of Lorenzo Fowler, an early foe of corsetting and all tight lacings. Elizabeth Oakes Smith asked Brooklyn to change the role that cast men as the only responsible agents.

The man whose phrenological chart confirmed that he believed in "elevating and ameliorating the female character" tried to become—in the phrase of Mrs. Smith—an apostle of woman. After she had proposed a national costume, the bachelor agreed that a sensible garb would improve health and end the husband's expensive role as a silkworm. The "detestable stuff" they wore and the lack of fresh air and exercise produced a generation of "spleeny, sickly, feeble girls" sadly different from Louisa Van Velsor. But sceptics asked if the fashionable ten-pound quilted skirts were to serve as horse blankets and refused to join in singing to the tune of "O, Susannah":

> O the Bloomer! that's the dress for me!
> Soon may its beauty, freedom, health, appreciated be!

Railroad conductors would not honor tickets of girls in Bloomers; gentlemen called them hermaphrodites. When gangs of boys followed two wearers down Broadway and hooted until the police arrested the women rather than their tormentors, Whitman (to no avail) blamed the boys for conduct worse than that of redskins. Jeers of "hoop, hoop, hooray!" and mocking verse became common:

> And while retreating through the woods,
> And through the tangled fern,
> He tore his mustn't-mention-ems,
> And had to put on hern!

For ladies too shy to attend classes on female problems given free by Dr. Banning in language "strictly and deliberately chaste," or by Dr. Wieting, who uttered no word "that an angel might not hear or that any woman should fail to hear," the firm of Fowlers and Wells supplied texts to be studied in private. Secure in their faith that improvement was the leading characteristic of the century, and that they became public benefactors by executing the mandate of Gall and Spurzheim to investigate human origins and destiny with observation rather than theological dogmatism, the Fowlers and their brother-in-law, Samuel R. Wells, built their list from the "one idea-ism" of cranioscopy into a "literary and scientific museum."

With distribution assured through a national association formed in 1849, they went far beyond proselytizing converts to their system of twenty-six cortical localities and kept three presses busy printing the *Phrenological Journal*, pamphlets on the "business of life," astronomy, legal rights of wives, spiritualism, and the acquisition of charm, and Fuller's papers on *Literature and Art*. Bound in muslin or paper the pamphlets sold for fifty cents or less. Along with their swimming guides and *Water Cure Journal* (which described a method of treating the fatal dehydration of cholera), Whitman stocked copies of *Love and Parentage*, a 25-cent primer of eugenics that included "important directions and suggestions to Lovers and the Married, concerning the strongest ties and the most sacred and momentous relations of life."[4]

The Fowlers and their associates explored in print personal habits they considered pathological. Dr. Trall warned against "suicidal indulgence" in sexual appetite by those married couples who "provoke" the "sexual crisis almost every night." O. S. Fowler, who boasted that he had analyzed all human facilities except the one most important to human happiness, closed the last gap by circulating his *Amativeness, or Evils and Remedies of Excessive and Perverted Sexuality*—illustrated with candid case histories of the malfunction of the prime organ. (Whitman's amativeness scored six out of a possible seven—high.) Dr. Dixon, editor of *The Scalpel*, gained the praise of his Brooklyn neighbor by cautioning young onanists to end "self-pollution." The peculiarity of such men as Dixon, wrote Whitman, "is not that they think very differently from others, but that they say right out whatever they think." Dr. Draper urged wider knowledge of the human "ensemble." The Reverend Orville Dewey advanced the paradoxical thesis that the soul corrupts the body, and eulogized the sensory pleasures, particularly those arising from the faculty of touch and its extraordinary instrument, the hand.[5]

Legal prosecution often blocked the ameliorators, for the kin of those who tormented Frances Wright charged them with prurient aims. Higginson's *Woman and Her Wishes* was found to be "spicy"; Dr. Nichols, the first editor of the *Aurora*, was arraigned for teaching that the highest human law was gratification of passion without reference to the marriage tie; Brisbane was jailed for advocating free love. But the lectures and publications continued and Whitman learned their vocabulary and approved their program.

Early that January of 1854 the Washington telegraph sent news of an "insidious intent" by Senator Douglas, Chairman of the Committee on Territories. He had introduced a bill to organize the vast territory of Nebraska with or without slavery according to the constitutional wish of the residents. In two revisions later that month Douglas strengthened his bill to an explicit voiding of the Missouri Compromise—the statute had been in effect for thirty-four years and was held as sacred a contract as the Ordinance of 1787.

From the Senate, where the debate would last until 4 March, Sumner, Chase, and several allies published an "Appeal of the Independent Democrats in Congress to the People of the United States" denouncing the bill as a "criminal betrayal of precious rights," a plot to exclude American laborers and European immigrants from the Nebraska territory. In a speech that Lincoln liked, Seward detailed the threat of the imminent encroachment of slavery into these millions of acres, as well as in Cuba and Central America. Douglas furious that his motives were impugned, flayed the "pure, unadulterated representatives of Abolitionism, Free Soilism, Niggerism." (The retort credited to Seward: "Douglas, no man who spells Negro with two gs will ever be elected President of the United States.")[6]

Throughout the North the issue raged in press and pulpit while men convened either to defend Douglas or to hang him in effigy. Tammany— backed by Congressman Tweed—voted its approval of the bill, unmoved by pleas to avoid the brutal degradation of mechanics and laborers, white and black; but Emerson came to the Tabernacle to climax a series of hostile sessions. In Brooklyn after the largest demonstration in its history, three thousand citizens signed a denunciatory petition and sent it to Seward to bolster his stand.

By May 25 the "Leper Bill" had cleared the House and received final approval in the Senate. "Our vision of peaceful groups of free laborers," mourned *Putnam's*, "is changed into the contemplation of black gangs of slaves. A single act of legislation, like Satan, when he entered Paradise, has reversed the destinies of a world." "Two paltry pennies," wrote the *Daily Times* after the publication of the text, "will purchase the political death warrant of the Senator from Illinois." Seward's stock continued to rise in Brooklyn as well as in Springfield, for within the year a correspondent who identified himself as Walter Whitman, "a writer, for the press and other-

292

wise," asked to be placed on his mailing list. "I too have at heart Freedom, and the amelioration of the people."[7]

Douglas partisans fired cannon from Capitol Hill to celebrate their victory. Whitman and the many other foes vented emotion in the next few days by seizing a new opportunity to cry out against a hated law of what Gerrit Smith anathematized as "a bastard democracy, accommodated to the demands of slavery, and tolerating the traffic in human flesh."

In Boston on Wednesday evening, 24 May, a Negro about twenty-three years old, six feet tall, scarred on the cheek and marred on the right hand, closed the Brattle Street store of his employer, a deacon, and began to walk home. But before he reached it, seven white men surrounded him, identified themselves as officers, and took him to the courthouse where Colonel Suttle of Alexandria, Virginia, claimed him as Anthony Burns, his property, missing since 24 March. Serving the warrant issued by United States Commissioner Loring, the deputy marshal jailed Burns for the night. At nine the next morning Commissioner Loring began his examination. The prisoner seemed fearful that resistance would lead to the auction block at New Orleans, but after hearing his minister and Wendell Phillips he agreed to fight rendition. At this point Dana and C. M. Ellis, now acting as defense counsels, and Robert Morris, a Negro associate, asked and received postponement until Saturday.[8]

By Friday the first fragmentary accounts telegraphed from Boston had lengthened into columns of newsprint. When Commissioner Loring entered his classroom at Harvard Law School that morning, southern students cheered while Northerners hissed and groaned. In the evening Theodore Parker and Wendell Phillips heightened the excitement by addressing a crowd at Faneuil Hall; an assault on the courthouse followed in which one of the guards was killed and the Reverend Higginson wounded. In response to a report from the marshal, President Pierce wired, "Your conduct approved. The law must be executed." Marines came from Charleston and an artillery company from Fort Independence; Mayor Smith alerted the militia. When the trial resumed, federal soldiers with fixed bayonets patrolled the passage to the courtroom, which itself was filled by the marshal's guard, recruited from ex-convicts, blacklegs, and brothel keepers. Southerners, including Harvard law students, sat with Colonel Suttle. Unable to obtain the release of Burns through another court, the defense counsels on Saturday morning asked further time to prepare the case. Commissioner Loring at first refused, but after two hours of argument adjourned until Monday morning.

On Sunday—Ascension Sunday—when Parker rose to pray in the vast Music Hall, he read a statement sent from the Slave Pen by the prisoner asking the congregation to help restore the blessings of liberty "which, it is said, this government was ordained to secure." Delaying his prepared sermon on the war in Europe, Parker preached like an Old Testament prophet on "a man stolen in this city of our fathers" within sight of the graves of John Hancock and Samuel Adams. Later that day the rumor spread that Colonel Suttle had agreed to sell Burns for $1200, money raised by subscription, and a carriage readied for the liberated man. But when the sale failed to be announced on Monday some papers indicated that the owner feared the wrath of fellow Virginians if he returned without the slave. Suttle's counsel explained that the claimant, advised by many lovers of law and order, refused to negotiate.

Early in the week another detachment of marines came from the Portsmouth Navy Yard to support soldiers and militia. One captain of police resigned rather than perform a duty he declared odious, but it became obvious that all assaults would end in failure. Whittier wrote from Amesbury pleading for everyone who looked with horror upon the Fugitive Slave Act to abstain from violence: "Be calm, be patient—God rules, and oppression cannot endure forever."

The trial summation started on Wednesday. The defense argued that Burns had worked in Boston weeks before the date of the alleged escape, but the prosecution held the date immaterial in view of proven identity and ownership. Commissioner Loring then announced that he would render his decision on Friday. Hunkers and Cotton Whigs who had snubbed Dana in 1850 now stopped him in the streets and offered to pay the costs of the trial; some talked treason.

The Virginian's lawyer thanked the mayor for closing Faneuil Hall to inflammatory speeches and blasphemy, but three thousand delegates to a convention of Free Democrats at the Music Hall heard Hale and Giddings condemn the barbarism at the courthouse. One of the resolutions approved by the Free Democrats reflected a new strategy of political coalition that appealed to Whitman and others whose ballots had failed to pass the Wilmot Proviso or save the Missouri Compromise:

That in this crisis, when Liberty seems doomed to utter destruction, unless the whole North is rallied to her defence, the Free

Democracy are willing to relinquish all party considerations, and to forget all past hostilities—to disregard all minor differences; to sacrifice everything but their principles in order to secure an effectual union of true men against the mighty conspiracy of Slaveholders and Doughfaces, that now threatens to overthrow the peace, the honor, and the free institutions of the country.

At nine Friday morning in a courtroom cordoned with armed men Commissioner Loring read his verdict. Basing the decision on the established constitutionality of "the statute of 1850" and proof of the slave's identity, "the Court considers the claimant entitled to a certificate from him of a right to the fugitive." Troops then began to maneuver to clear a path to Central Wharf and the *John Taylor*. Mayor Smith called out his entire militia and in effect placed Boston under martial law. One hundred deputies formed a hollow square with Burns clad in black in the middle, and escorted by a thousand guards marched him to the ship. The procession as sinister to Whitman and others as that in Hawthorne's "My Kinsman, Major Molineux," passed under a coffin suspended by ropes; on its bottom plank someone had chiseled "Liberty." From other roofs fluttered cayenne pepper and cow itch. Women stared out of windows festooned with black cambric and cried "shame, shame"; sextons tolled bells. But with the exception of an old man cut by a lancer, the one casualty was a horse bayoneted when its teamster tried to break the line. After a delay caused by the lifting of a cannon on deck, the ship moved downstream to Fort Independence and transferred its cargo to the government cutter *Morris* which sailed at once for Norfolk.

On 13 June a Brooklyn poet sent to the *Tribune* the unsigned "Hail to the Stars and Stripes," a sardonic salute to the "flaunting lie"—the flag of the *Morris* waving over a pirate's deck that bore "a fellow-man/ To groan with fellow slaves." On 15 June the *Tribune* printed "The Freeman's Challenge," with an epigraph from Seward's militant speech on the passage of the Nebraska bill:

> Come from the Senate-hall and dull convention;
> Come from the pulpit and the crowded bar;
> We take the challenge for the long contention,
> And gird our armor for a ceaseless war!

The third poem written in Brooklyn—and the only one Whitman soon identified as his own—embodied his anger at those who rejoiced at the rendition of Burns, at the bullies who felled Dana with a slingshot, at Pierce who had wired the United States Attorney, "Incur any expense deemed necessary . . . to insure the execution of the law." An imaginary journey of nine hours on the railcars brought the balladeer to a Boston street corner, where he summoned phantoms of the Revolution from their hill graves down to the beleaguered city and alerted them to the onset of horror:

> If you blind your eyes with tears you will not see the
>   President's marshal,
> If you groan such groans you might balk the government cannon.

When an "hour with the living" proved "too dead" for the phantoms, he ordered them back to the hills; only King George belonged in this shamed place. He then directed the mayor to send a committee to England to exhume the royal coffin and return it on a Yankee clipper:

> Now call the President's marshal again, and bring out
>   the government cannon,
> And fetch home the roarers from Congress, and make
>   another procession and guard it with foot and dragoons.

Glued and crowned, the bones provided revenge, for "old buster" ruled again:

> Stick your hands in your pockets Jonathan . . . you
>   are a made man from this day,
> You are mighty cute . . . and here is one of your bargains.

In a letter to the Boston *Post* the attorney for the claimant thanked citizens for the firm and patriotic manner in which they had acted during the course of the trial and informed those who subscribed to the purchase fund that they could fulfill their benevolent wishes when Burns reached Virginia. Colonel Suttle honored his word but punctilio could not atone for gross damage. As Frederick Douglass saw it, after this newest display of slave power "there was no pause, no repose."[9]

That summer of 1854 Whitman watched violent men riot in the streets of Brooklyn incited by the same hostility that had bloodied the sixth ward during his *Aurora* editorship. At a time of continued massive Catholic immigration, Archbishop Hughes had paralleled the Carroll Hall contretemps of the earlier decade with a sermon in St. Patrick's on the decline of Protestantism; the printed text confirmed conditioned fear that his church sought world conversion. Nor had he hidden his hatred for Kossuth and other revolutionists. Early sentiment favorable to Pius IX hardened to scorn when the prelate reputedly poured maledictions on wounded Italian republicans and blessed French imperial hirelings who saved his throne. His nuncio Bedini roused hostile mobs during a visit to America to settle a dispute over church property, and finally fled New York on a tug. An ex-priest, Padre Gavazzi, "dealt thunderbolts at Popes, Cardinals, Jesuits, Priests, and Friars."[10]

One Sunday a sailor who called himself the Angel Gabriel crossed from Manhattan with an accordion player named Moses, and a bodyguard of nativist Know-Nothings wearing their white "wide-awake" hats. In a vacant lot he preached on "Purgatory for Popery and the Pope." Other street clerics exploited the theme many times in many cities as a wave of bigotry crested throughout the East. Attacked by Irish and German Catholics, Angel Gabriel retreated to the ferry and his home base.

The next Sunday he and a larger gang joined local Know-Nothings at the ferry. Their mission, according to rumor, was the burning of St. James' Church. Alerted Brooklyn Catholics who knew of the recent desecration of churches and convents met them on the route and exchanged insults. Then came volleys of stones, bricks, and pistol shots. Intervention by police and militia ended the physical violence but not the hatred.

As a builder Whitman had been meticulous and fortunate. His few houses, simple and sturdy, had not met the fate of many shoddy structures. (A nearby building collapsed in April 1854 and trapped a young fireman of Engine Company 20; freed after an hour of agony, the crushed victim of flimsy timber and poor mortar expired in the arms of brother firemen.)[11] The profit from sales bought milk, clothing, and other family necessities, and allowed indulgence in a bit of finery, the piano, a painting, and jaunts to Greenport, which he continued to prefer to Saratoga or Newport. Its white cottages, the garden vegetables, the Alhambra billiard saloon, the fishing and boating, the unfailing sea breeze at evening refreshed the city dweller. On his return he could afford a ticket to the new Academy of Music at Fourteenth Street to hear the latest recipient of superlatives—Grisi, whose Norma was called the finest show of dramatic genius ever seen on an American stage. Wealth, however, refused to extend its flush hand to a man with limited capital.

In the spring of 1854 the full force of depression struck the entire metropolitan area. Banks dissolved, private credit vanished, failures came daily to Wall Street, "to let" signs filled windows on Broadway and in Brooklyn. The stockholders of the Crystal Palace retained Barnum to salvage their investment, but even that egregious promoter could not lure customers with lifelike kicks—as he called the firemen quadrilles. Wages of artisans at the Navy Yard were cut from $2.50 a day to $2.25; longshoremen from $1.75 to $1.50; drivers to ten shillings. By December the *Tribune* reported that "the building of houses is rapidly coming to a close, and will be absolutely closed so soon as those now in course of construction are completed—for of them, there are few that could this day be sold except at a loss of twenty or thirty per cent, or perhaps much more." Idled carpenters and masons were joined by printers, whose shops had not endured a similar slackness in many years. The coldest days and nights in a quarter century added to the misery.

The idled builder observed the various ways of coping with the crisis. Some of the unemployed held meetings and counseled each other to seek work in the countryside or in distant towns; pleas for free flour also sounded. Citizens contributed funds and food; the Brooklyn Soup Association began to serve a boiler of soup at noon but before long the single file of supplicants emptied three boilers. Stewart opened a basement kitchen in his Manhattan emporium and gave away five hundred quarts of soup daily. Grisi and Mario volunteered their voices for a benefit concert. Since destitution was rising among seamstresses, Whitman suggested that they organize a collective farm on Long Island comparable to Spring's idyllic Eagleswood in New Jersey.

During this crisis the *Sunday Mercury* pleased him by reprinting "Revenge and Requital," for the parable of a samaritan braving alleys and cellars to nurse the victims of cholera had relevance; the community needed many "true sons and daughters of Christ." The Reverend Samuel Longfellow, Henry's brother, preached at the Second Unitarian Church of Brooklyn that hard times were retribution for years of extravagance and speculation; on the winter sabbath, as though to ward off despair, fresh flowers graced his pulpit. The projectors of the new *Crayon* defied commercial fact and offered their stricken countrymen the gospel of beauty as a cure for the hollowness of "money-pride"; rather than the statistics of Mammon, they chose to echo a text from the "Evangel of Art" in order to open eyes sealed to the perception of the outer world. The Philharmonic played Beethoven's *Eroica*. Benton in a well-attended lecture gave his pragmatic solution for easing the suffering of city dwellers—a transcontinental railroad to carry them to free land so spacious that twenty million families could homestead there.[12]

These measures and ideas did not end starvation. So many women solicited openly that the police began mass arrests, but they ignored the gangs of destitute young girls, filthy and obscene, who roamed the streets day and night. Touched by their suffering Whitman wrote "The New York Beggar," a poem printed on the same page of the *Mercury* with "Revenge and Requital." In forty-eight lines the poet prophesied the fate of a waif begging bareheaded and ragged in the snow:

> That child will be a woman—
>   Think you she will be chaste?
> Think you the language of her thought
>   With beauty can be graced?
> No—she will be a drunkard—
>   Drunk nightly in her den—
> A thief, a prostitute, and all
>   Before the age of ten.

W. admonished unsullied maidens who encountered this "loathesome thing" to show pity, for abandoned like her "You, too, had lived in sin."[13]

20

HOUSE OF HIMSELF

IN THE SAME HOUSE with a stricken father and deformed brother, on a homemade pine table in the room whose walls lighted by a single window held Talbot's "Christian" and old engravings of Bacchus and Silenus—a reviewer would soon charge that he stalked like a satyr amidst dainty dancers —Whitman began to build what he called in "Kosmos" a house of himself.[1] Jobless in his mid-thirties, knowing that resumption of editorship based on the political ascendancy of Free Soil lay at least two years in the future, he told himself that "Liberty is poorly served by men whose good intent is quelled from one failure or two failures or any number of failures." To firm his will not to stay idle and mute, he hung at eye level the motto, "Make the Work."

Some of his books and clippings also ordered a beginning. Consuelo in the passage that he read a score of times feared her debut until Master Porporo told her that only fools are timid: "Whoever is inspired with the love of art need fear nothing." Trismegistus in the epilogue to *La Comtesse de Rudolstadt* had composed a magnificent poem from the religions, politics, and art of all the ages. The *United States Review* had recently started a debate by wondering

> Say! will the Poet come?
> Or will this age be dumb,
> And die, its noblest thoughts
> By living lips unuttered?

A respondent affirmed that the poet would be found singing new carols at liberty's shrine, rather than dozing at the Irving House or puffing a cigar at a club or crawling in the dust for a pension.[2]

A Glasgow man, Alexander Smith, had recently published his evocative *A Life-Drama*. The appearance of this long dramatic poem in 1853 along with eleven shorter pieces had made the northern plebeian famous—or

300

notorious. Reared on the coast he used hundreds of oceanic images—"wonderful figures as ever I met in my life," said Emily Dickinson. (She also marked her copy of Tupper's *Proverbial Philosophy* as part of "a feast in the reading line.") Others complained of the poem's melodic and intellectual poverty, Ossianic mist, fancy run mad in tipsy disorder, and its scraps of Keats, Tennyson, and Bailey mixed with very bad whiskey. But Whitman heard "the true ring of the genuine metal" sound from *A Life-Drama* whose young hero Walter longs to write poetry. That autumn in his notice for the *Phrenological Journal*, as in a self-review two years later, he quoted an "electric passage" from *A Life-Drama* that announced a "mighty poet whom this age shall choose/ To be its spokesman to all coming times."[3]

Other imperatives there in his room and memory sanctioned substance and mode. Those who refused to honor new editions of *Nature* and the *Essays* and continued to call Emerson a treacherous marsh light had brought a lengthy protest to the front page of the *Daily Times* by a southern devotee, who isolated a singular trait in the transcendentalist's writings:

> The personal "I" is prominent. If not expressed, it is implied in the structure of every paragraph, in the utterance of every opinion, in the enforcement of every dogma. Emerson—the man—is one of the premises of the argument. All things are subjected to his individualism. It is not as independent matters for reflection, that he takes up history, science, art, but as parts of himself.

He had called new bards to cast away all conformity, and in his recent *Representative Men* had summoned hoarse singers of street ballads.[4]

From the introductory maxim that each created thing has its lover and poet, Emerson's volume offered solace and guidance to the exfoliated politician and aspirant author: Goethe's failures prepared his victories; Swedenborg's *Animal Kingdom* was "an anatomist's account of the human body, in the highest style of poetry," by a theologian who opened a foreground but lacked sympathy; the "warm, many-weathered world" was his "grammar of hieroglyphics." Montaigne, who sensed the undulation and flow of the masses of nature, knew the vast disproportion "between the sky of law and the pismire of performance under it." Napoleon wanted to "dazzle and astonish." Cheerfulness was one of Shakespeare's royal traits. Plato, "a great average man," saw contraries—death out of life, life out of death—and that it was "as easy to be great as to be small." Along with the chronicle of

301

these masters, Emerson assured a lesser mortal that the world still wanted its poet-priest.

The *Tribune* in August 1854 printed Thoreau's anathemas on the rendition of Anthony Burns, with his confession that since then he had lived within a hell called Massachusetts and plotted its murder. But the perfume of a white water lily, Thoreau said, brought confirmation that Nature remained virtuous. On the very first page of *Walden*, available in New York by autumn, Whitman found another precedent for the mode of his own manuscript:

> In most books, the *I* or first person, is omitted; in this it will be retained; that, in respect to egotism, is the main difference. We commonly do not remember that it is, after all, always the first person that is speaking.

Later pages of *Walden* carried the Concord ban on hollow ornamentation, both literary and architectural; beauty grew only "from within outward, out of the necessities and character of the individual, who is the only builder." And everywhere Thoreau in sustained meditation merged the waters of the Ganges with his pond. The lover of Vedantic philosophy, in search of the essence of its changeless reality, explained that nothing was too trivial for its holy teachers to include in their revelation of the identity of the soul. They taught eating, drinking, cohabiting, voiding excrement and urine, "elevating what is mean." Manhattan reviewers chided the "Yankee Diogenes" for talking of vast cosmic themes that he narrowed to mere self, but Whitman judged this singular pattern ideal. Thoreau would soon visit Brooklyn and spend a morning with the sweet-dispositioned man whom he praised as "the greatest democrat the world has seen."[5]

Poe would never again give gossips the chance to say they saw him measuring his length down Broadway as though on a surveying mission, but men of letters who prized his memory read "The Poetic Principle," printed posthumously in the *Union* magazine that had earlier carried a Whitman tale. The lecture that derided the epic mania, the didactic fallacy, and lauded the immortal instinct for beauty ended with a catalogue of a score of sources of true poetry.

Some of the authors shelved in Whitman's room provided quotations that he copied and used for end papers. From Whipple's remarks on Griswold's *Poets and Poetry of America* came affirmation that

America abounds in the materials of poetry. Its history, its scenery, the structure of its social life, the thoughts which provide its political forms, the meaning which underlies its hot contests, are all capable of being exhibited in a poetical aspect.

Ignoring Wordsworth's toryism, the democrat took from the laureate the paraphrasable law that every "original first-rate poet must make himself the taste through which he is to be fully understood and appreciated." Abolitionists called Carlyle's views on the Negro heartless, but the Smelfungus Redivivus who had abandoned criticism of worthless books justified a fresh attempt to create literature that would trace God's handwriting.[6]

The terminal illness of his father, urban noise, and old adversaries on Common Council interfered with Whitman's work in progress. Honoring the dying man's request, he took him somehow for a last visit to the Suffolk birthplace. One melancholy day he journeyed to Williamsburgh to buy a plot in the new Cemetery of the Evergreens, designed on elevated land by the landscape architect Alexander Jackson Downing. A single plot cost as little as $60, compared to $100 at Greenwood which was now crowded with 50,000 graves. Here Walter Whitman like an earlier member of the family, Salt Kossabone, could spend eternity on a hill watching the coming and going of ships.[7]

Another augury of domestic grief lay in the marriage of sister Hannah to Charles Heyde. Walt had introduced her to this landscape painter, musician, and poetaster, but before long he found his talented brother-in-law temperamentally odd and politically hostile—Heyde wrote verses honoring Tammany Hunkers. In time Walt called him the "bed-buggiest" man.

In need of quiet to sustain his self-cast role of aspirant psalmist who would dilate the living and drag the dead from their coffins, Whitman complained of carts, of vendors whose calls had once seemed musical, and of those chronic irritants, boys with firecrackers. The impromptu races through the streets would have been cheered at the Union track, but they did not please him; at night dozens of hogs ran loose through residential sections. Not since the Abdiel-like farewell to the *Freeman* had he been so eager to seek brief retreat, but officialdom blocked the way.

303

In the summer of 1854 railcars drawn by four horses had begun to serve Brooklyn; four cents on some routes, five on others, bought a ride to Williamsburgh, Bedford, or other neighborhoods. But to his annoyance Common Council banned the cars on Sunday. Petitioning like a Leggett for the happiness of communities he challenged this denial of a cheap, popular conveyance on the day of greatest need. Lest the issue be ignored as trivial, he amplified the protest into a definition of the role of a municipal officer as that of an agent who is not to meddle with the personal affairs and morals of his master. Prohibitive legislation connived by caucus emasculated the citizen and prevented him from becoming muscular; reliance on "restrictions of himself" rather than on hoggish laws formed a live man or woman. Fortunately those who wanted an athletic, spirited city had salvation in their own hands.

Common Council's denial of the request because of the fear that the cars would carry Angel Gabriel and other agitators seemed irrational, for a score of ferries ran on Sunday and no one dared stop them. In his manuscript Whitman restated his brief:

> Justice is not settled by legislators and laws . . . it is in the soul,
> It cannot be varied by statutes any more than love or pride or
> the attraction of gravity can . . .[8]

Whitman did not record whether the fall elections gave a choice of "strong-handed, big-brained" men or of more dry nurses. But at least two of its phases brought him back to the days of the *Aurora*. Exploiting the overt hatred of Catholicism, the Know-Nothings had moved from street corners to the ballot box. In addition to fellow bigots they recruited many voters angered by the proslavery politics of Hunkers and Whigs. Veteran Free Soilers resented their quick success, which threatened to fragment an emerging anti-Nebraska party, and cited their secret Union third-degree as an invitation to southern sympathy. Other citizens feared that the violent tactics of the Know-Nothings' many shoulder hitters presaged years of religious, ethnic war. When a brawl ended with the shooting of Bill Poole, a pugilist leader of the Manhattan Know-Nothings, over a hundred thousand escorted the coffin to Greenwood. On it they placed in silver letters, "I die a true American."

Temperance also became a key issue, but this time advocates of the Maine law took the place of Washingtonians in confronting the bottle demon. George Hall, who had been mayor of Brooklyn twenty years ago, ran again and won with his promise to end rum and rowdyism. Whitman did not write another *Franklin Evans* to further the revived crusade, though new material was at hand: a mechanic discharged from the Navy Yard because of drunkenness blew his brains out with a single-barreled revolver.

The winter brought further proof of depression when marching mechanics waved banners reading, "If work be not given we will help ourselves to bread." Soup kitchens served longer lines. Rows of houses with gaping windows stood unfinished, their owners bankrupt. Opera managers shortened the season. Fortunately, varied episodes provided distractions. Sceptics denied the validity of spirit rappings from the dead. A raid on a brothel ended in the shooting of a police officer and the disclosure that the pimp's free list included the name of another member of the force. To ensure Sunday abstinence Mayor Hall searched the *lager bier* saloons, though the keepers insisted that there was truer fire of friendship in one glass than in a wagon load of charcoal. Rum drinkers entrained for Jamaica where they sated themselves and then caroused. A judge of the circuit court awarded a Negress $225, half her claim against the Third Avenue railroad whose conductor had ejected her from the cars because of her color. George Curtis lectured in Brooklyn on "Success"; as an illustration he may have used *The Lamp-Lighter*—ten thousand copies sold in ten days. Dr. Raphael explained the sacred writing of the Hebrews.

When he returned to his manuscript Whitman assigned to it the Boston rendition ballad and the amplified lament over young men bloodied by European tyrants; so had Shelley mourned Castlereagh's victims in 1819. For his new poems he sought by the mode he called an "all-attracting egotism" to channel the local and temporary into the universal and eternal, the personal into the national. Autobiographer and historian, whatever he had once beheld or experienced, as Emerson said of Goethe, came to him as a model and sat for a portrait.

The scope of the work in no way awed him. He knew what to avoid: so-called fine writing based on the false premise of salon elegance; artificial writing that lacked precision, ease, and blood (the quality that animated

305

Talbot's landscapes); insincere writing born of cowardly submission to foreign standards or of the currying of favor with caste and sect, rather than of candid love and hate. Characterless performers had covered the land with weeds and chaff. He promised wheat and milk.

By now after studying Walker's *Dictionary*, that memento of New Orleans, as well as the new edition of Webster's and other lexicons, and Professor M. Schele de Vere's *Comparative Philology* with its chapter on American English, he prided himself on belonging to the small but majestic brotherhood of "language-searchers." Combining years of copy experience with the findings of that search deepened his admiration for colloquialisms engrafted on English stock.

Certain that thousands of idiomatic words ignored by impotent, dyspeptic dandies waited to be used by a poet with a passionate heart, he had begun to make "limber, lasting" lists that reached from aboriginal Paumanok through history, trades, shipyards, butcher stalls, and "bed houses." He chose tangible, textured words, names, and epithets that would give identity to his realities, whether of Christ walking the Judean hills, General Washington grief-stricken by the loss of troops, a "castrated" face, a "limpsey" fugitive slave, or a "wellhung" male consummating sexual mating. The touchstones were solidarity, strength, rudeness, and colloquial vibrancy that evoked the sound of the human voice he loved. Memories of sermons, lectures, books, and usages in his own earlier writings supplemented the lists. *Tuckahoe, kelson, omnific, snivel,* and *palpable* joined *Uranus, vivas, etui, embouchure,* and *hieroglyphic.*[9]

When the manuscript contained twelve poems he arranged the pages so that the last lines of the last poem affirmed the faith that could soothe his family:

> Great is death. . . . Sure as life holds all parts together,
>> death holds all parts together;
> Sure as the stars return again after they merge in the light,
>> death is great as life.

Then, as he acknowledged, he wrote a preface "with light and rapid touch," as though to add bulk.[10]

To create a title he joined printshop jargon to Old Testament incantation. Years ago holding a Harper catalogue, he had marveled at "leaves" that unwrapped a vast creation. Symbolic uses of grass were common, but the poet wanted to extend the prophecy of the preface, "Your very flesh shall be a poem." He found the apt sense in the oracular verses with which an earlier exile, Isaiah, had comforted his people:

> The voice said, Cry. And he said, What shall I cry? All flesh is grass . . . surely the people is grass.

(The Hutchinsons often sang a merry version:

> The horse bit his master;
> How came it to pass?
> He heard the good parson say
> All flesh is grass.)

It would have been fitting to add the *Leaves of Grass* to the Harper list, for the brothers were fellow Long Islanders. But instead of taking the manuscript to the great Cliff Street plant, Whitman carried it to Andrew and James Rome in the small, red brick building at Cranberry and Fulton and contented himself with this job shop that contained little more than an old press, a desk, and a backless chair. From the few battered fonts of the immigrant brothers who spoke with the accent of the descendants of Convenanters, he chose an imported Scotch face for the text and titling alphabets from the Bruce foundry in Williamsburgh. The Romes agreed to set the preface in ten-point type—or long primer leaded two spaces; the poetry in twelve-point cast on fourteen—thus approximating English—also leaded two spaces with the first word of each poem in capitals. Rather than the author's name in the traditional place under the 108-point "Grass," they would mount a stippled engraving by Samuel Hollyer of Harrison's daguerreotype on the verso of the preceding page of front matter. *Putnam's* called this manly correspondence "very proper in a book of transcendental poetry."[11]

With the customary allowance for overruns, the Romes would print an edition of approximately 800 in quarto format on what Whitman thought was rather poor paper. In daily visits the onetime journeyman often used stick and rule when composition of the 12 pages of preface and the 83 pages of poetry slowed because of unstopped sentences in the double-columned prose, sequences of ellipses, and irregular lines and stanzas. When the sheets came from the press he noticed uneven inking and typography less perfect than the kind he praised in his reviews of American publishers or of imports from the Chiswick craftsmen. But he delivered the sheets to a binder on Hudson Avenue, Charles Jenkins—not one of the exhibitors at the

Crystal Palace—and contracted to pay 32 cents a copy for books cased in the blind-blocked, green cloth popular in gift annuals. Triple rule gilt borders, and the title in a swirl of tendrils and roots on front, spine, and back would brighten the binding.[12]

All spring of 1855 Whitman waited for Jenkins to complete folding and pasting the sheets with caoutchouc into book format, to make covers and edges, and to apply the gold with heated blocks of brass. In April he heard that Anthony Burns was in Boston, a free man. He had been auctioned for $900 and then sold by a North Carolina trader to abolitionists for $1300. In May the *Star* ran "The Widow's Son," Whitman's early tale of a miraculous Christ. The twenty-fifth annual parade of pupils from local Sunday schools, including "those saved from dereliction," reminded the graduate of his childhood lessons at St. Ann's. The park on the Heights neared completion; the lawns were sodded, the serpentine paths graveled, and the trees and shrubs set. Patriots met again to plan to move the bones of the victims of the hulks on the day hallowed by the Battle of Long Island; the committee did not know that one of their neighbors had memorialized the battle in poetry. Reports of violence came from Kansas after the election there of a doughface ticket. Gerald Massey, another plebeian poet, published "Nebraska, or the Slavery Abolitionist to His Bride." Hale and "Incendiary" Seward returned to the Senate, dual signs of increasing hostility to the Pierce administration; they firmed Whitman's faith in the ultimate victory of a coalition formed, as he described in his preface, through "stern opposition" to slavery "which shall never cease till it ceases or the speaking of tongues and the moving of lips cease." Free Democrats, many Soft Shells, and Whigs adopted the name honored by Jefferson and banded together as Republicans. It was fitting that the New York members named a Wilmot man, Preston King, for the first slate.

The edition at last taking shape Whitman on 15 May 1855 visited George F. Betts, clerk of the United States court, Southern District of New York, and claiming the right as "Author and Proprietor" deposited the title of a book, *Leaves of Grass*. (In March Melville had come here with *Israel Potter*.) He then learned that Jenkins after completing 200 cases had subcontracted the remainder to Davies and Hand. The new binders charged 58 cents each for the first 138 copies, and then in a succession of economies over the next months omitted much of the gilding and all of the stamping of the title on the back; they also substituted boards for cloth, plain for

308

marbled end papers, and wrapped 150 sheets in pink, green, or blue paper. The bill for binding 804 copies totaled $201.32.[13]

That June the *Tribune* lauded the clipper ships out of Boston and Long Island yards with their sculptured hulls and 11,000 yards of canvas as a prime example of an indigenous art form; in another editorial it attacked the use of the hexameter in a translation of Goethe after both Southey and Longfellow had failed with the measure. The *Post* pegged the commercial value of a line of poetry at twenty-five cents by offering $25 for a "good poem" of a hundred lines inspired by Barnum's Baby Show. Puff critics named *Blanche Desmond* the best fiction of the season. *Putnam's* complained that national writing had degenerated into a vast stream of milk and water because citizens lacked the honesty or the intelligence to choose between good and bad.[14] (In its September issue the reviewer of the *Leaves of Grass* struggled through the "rough thicket" of "this gross yet elevated, this superficial yet profound, this preposterous yet fascinating book.") The brothers Duyckinck read proof of their *Cyclopaedia of American Literature*, unaware that it lacked a key entry.

Confined to the heat of the city Whitman missed cooling visits to Castle Garden, now a depot for immigrants rather than the most delightful of concert places. To sensitive nostrils the odor of ailanthus trees seemed worse than Peruvian guano or Argentine hides. The press reported that Lowell— also born in 1819 and now Longfellow's successor at Harvard—had sailed for Europe where he would land in time to hear that after months of bombardment Sevastopol had surrendered. For the man who remained at home there was baseball, with Hoboken beating the Eagles 21 to 19 in a seven-inning game; a kindly reporter praised the players and rejoiced that the teams multiplied. Scabby McClosky, who terrified Myrtle Avenue with rougher games, was at last jailed for six months, a change of residence that gratified the neighborhood. Coin counterfeiters also met their fate. Temperance advocates honored the sermons Lyman Beecher had given thirty years ago and warned mothers not to hire gin-sipping nurses who rationalized that "strong waters" improved the quality of breast milk. The Methodist church held a strawberry festival to raise money for the poor, but the talk may have been of a double suicide in a nearby brothel, the aftermath of a hopeless love shared by a patron and one of the staff; for days papers carried letters debating whether a prostitute deserved to be loved and mourned.

Celebrations of the Fourth of July started at sunrise Wednesday with

309

the customary salute fired from Fort Greene by survivors of 1812 and the ringing of church bells for half an hour. Buildings, coaches, and railcars showed bunting and spectators waved flags or handkerchiefs as cadets and veterans of the Fifth Brigade marched. Later many rode into the countryside or visited the Crystal Palace to see an enormous redwood tree erected under the dome. Fireworks in front of City Hall closed the festivities; the *chef d'oeuvre* of the pyrotechnicians represented an eagle resting on a shield capped by the word Liberty. According to every report patriotism was at a premium, unchecked by the new Maine-type prohibition law.

Unknown to all but a few patriots, Americans had another reason to rejoice on this seventy-ninth anniversary of independence—copies of *Leaves of Grass* could be bought the next day at Swayne's in Brooklyn and Thomas's in Manhattan. The *Tribune* advertised the price of the "thin quarto" as two dollars, but it was soon lowered to $1.25. Fowlers and Wells thought the edition format clumsy and uninviting but agreed to act as agents; however, out-of-town distribution remained haphazard. Irked by late receipt of the book, the *North American* complained that the winds of heaven were the publishers.

Who would think of fattening a race horse, Bryant asked in the belief that poverty and neglect did not curb creation. Disagreeing Whitman tried to ensure fulfillment of his prophecy in the preface that the nation would absorb its newest poet. He mailed a paper-bound *Leaves of Grass* to Emerson who in turn thanked him for "the wonderful gift." Then in the next few days he forwarded his own reviews to a local paper and two metropolitan periodicals, thereby earning the scorn of the *Times* for "an act that the most degraded helot of literature might blush to commit." In effect these reviews embodied extensions or postscripts to the preface, though *Albion* thought the longest one "a smart satire upon the present tendency of authors to run into rhapsody and transcendentalism." [15]

An inexorable visitation forced a halt to self-promotion. On 11 July, after long illness, Walter Whitman died at the age of 66. By then his son had made certain the resurrection of the family name. [16]

LETTERS FROM
A TRAVELLING BACHELOR

Number I

FISH, FISHERMEN, AND FISHING, ON THE
EAST END OF LONG ISLAND

Greenport, L.I., 9 Oct. [14 Oct. 1849][1]

At its easternmost part, Long Island opens like the upper and under jaws of some prodigious alligator; the upper and larger one terminating in Montauk Point. The bay that lies in here, and part of which forms the splendid harbor of Greenport, where the Long Island Railroad ends, is called Peconic Bay; and a beautiful and varied water is it, fertile in fish and feathered game. I, who am by no means a skilful fisherman, go down for an hour of a morning on one of the docks, or almost any where along shore, and catch a mess of black-fish, which you couldn't buy in New York for a dollar—large fat fellows, with meat on their bones that it takes a pretty long fork to stick through. They have a way here of splitting these fat black-fish and poggies, and broiling them on the coals, beef-steak-fashion, which I recommend your Broadway cooks to copy.[2]

Nobody knows, I think, what really good fish are, as you get them from your city markets. The firm fine-grained meat, white as snow, and of indescribable sweetness, of a good-sized blue-fish, black-fish, or poggy, taken from these waters, and cooked the same day for dinner or supper, is worth journeying a good way to taste. It hath the same relation to the city served fish as the pure breath of some whole-toothed country girl hath to the scent of almond-paste which the perfumer has furnished for the mouth of perhaps the most lovely metropolitan belle. I am convinced of one thing, (I must say my say out,) that even cleaning and salting fish for a few hours deprives

Letters from a Travelling Bachelor, previously uncollected, are reprinted from the New York Sunday *Dispatch*, 14 October 1849 through 6 January 1850. Number VIII is missing.

311

them of their best flavor—particularly the salting. Such weather as this, they will "keep" for thirty or forty hours at least; then let them be cleaned, and not salted till over the fire.

It is curious, and always instructive, to connect the physical peculiarities of certain localities, with the people's character there. Fish, now, and easy facilities for every body to catch them—what effects might you suppose? Effects really definite and weighty, do come from those causes, here, I am certain. Hundreds of poor men, with families, just rub on from year to year, never growing better off, and never worse; "the bay" stands between them and actual starvation, and they are never spurred on to any vigorous efforts after fortune. A kind of lazy pride is, from the same cause, begotten among many, who cannot afford it—the pride of poverty being the costliest in the world. Fish has its golden side, too. Besides what I have set forth in my praise of the food, when presented in its best form, the ease and promptness with which any one—child or woman, almost as well as man—can catch enough for a day's eating, serve many with a good meal, who could not otherwise get one. Fish, too, "moss-bunkers," innumerable, fertilize the grounds, and give body to the grain which constitutes perhaps the very bread you eat. As a cooling article of diet, a temperer of the blood, fish is proverbial. Imagine a community of straggle-limbed, yellow-faced, hard-fleshed sea-dogs—or a goodly infusion of such communities in the nation; do you suppose such a nation could ever degenerate and decay, as old Rome did with her Sybarites? No, indeed. And though my compound adjectives above do not describe the ideal of masculine good looks, there is something surpassingly welcome in the sight of these sinewy and huge-pawed fellows.

I went down to Montauk Point a day ago, (whereof you shall have an account one of these times,) and we came among a band of such amphibious men,—great unshaved, gigantic-chested beings, with eyes as clear as coals, and flesh whose freedom from the gross humors of artificial life told its tale in the dark and unpimpled brown of their faces and necks. One feels not a little ashamed, after mixing with such tough knots of humanity, to be so particular against sleeping in a lately scrubbed room, or a draught of wind from some chink in the window. These men—hundreds of 'em in the regions hereabout—make their beds and sleep soundly on the salt hay, or in the sails of a boat, or on the ground—go half stripped for days and days up to their waists in water—eat raw salt pork, seasoned with a little vinegar, (or perhaps bad rum,)—and, thus continuing for many seasons, live to a good old age, and die of Time more than of Sickness. Would they turn out so, were they to study our dietetic oracles, and be lanceted and calomeled occasionally?[3]

If you understand any thing of what I try to describe, you must get the idea of a race of men, even individual specimens of whom you never see in New York, where you see almost every thing. I have mentioned the eyes of these old fishermen; they are the eyes of hawks, piercing and sharp. I never saw such eyes in other old men, or young men either.

A little to the east of here, but in sight when you sail down to Montauk Light-House, are a whole island full of these peculiar personages, the Block Islanders. They have the foregoing characteristics, in double intensity. Their very hair is a sort of seaweed, and the Block Island babe makes for the shore with its first creep. Shelter Island and Gardiner's, Fisher's, and Plum Islands, also partake of the briny cast; but as you don't positively have to hold the hair on your head by main force, when the sea gale blows over them, Block Island, which is quite out in the ocean, and used to the exhibition of wind and water power on the most sublime scale, goes ahead.

When I was down, for the moment, among those Montauk chaps—I forgot to say before that they were preparing to catch the sea-bass—I took some little pains to return the considerable courtesy they showed me, by first, finding out what politeness I might do them in response. Of the specimens I tried, all they wanted to fill up the measure of their perfect content, was, some plug tobacco and the latest election news! The tobacco I had not, but made them happy by the gift of two stray numbers of the *Tribune*, which were in my pocket. There they would stay, on what was equal to the sea-shore, twenty miles from any human habitation, except that of the Light-House keeper; there they would stay for many a week, entirely cut off from communication with "the public." I suspect those two *Tribunes* were completely got by rote. It was a pity I didn't happen to have anything better.

One of the men had the most magnificent Newfoundland dog, young but full-grown, that I ever saw—probably a finer no one ever saw. He was black as tar. He would dash off in the water, and out—and in and out again. All of a sudden, while his master was talking with me, and his brilliant (I really cannot find the right word,) vitreous eyes were vibrating from mine to the surface of the sea, he broke off from his talk, and in a loud quick tone called the dog to our side, just as he was splashing in to try another of his equatic excursions.

"Do you see that?" said the fisherman to me, pointing to something like a small black chip, slowly moving edgeways on the surface of the water. "That's a shirk. I've no idea of losing my dog by a darned shirk!"

An hour before I had been thinking of a little swim along there, although the day was cool. It was altogether too cool, after that. On the same occasion there was the prettiest of marine exhibitions—prettier, to my eyes, than any New York yacht race that ever tapered off with the "prize," or a dinner in that yellow edifice which used to puzzle us so at Hoboken. Two hundred men, in a hundred skiffs, catching bluefish by trailing! Imagine the skiffs, real beauties, too, darting like swallows, and managed by five-score bold and expert water-dogs, each ambitious of doing some dare-devil maneuver that would eclipse his fellows—the sails bulging like the puffed cheeks of an alderman, and anon dipping in the water, or making the boat turn sharper corners than I ever saw boat turn before—a hundred men ceaselessly employed in hauling in the lines, taking off the fish, and casting out again—and then such a casting out! Such a length as they made the bones fly! such a twirl of the rope! no twisting, although the coils be many! such superb attitudes, equal to any thing in Greek statues! such ready expedients to avoid any obstacle to the incessant hauling in, and throwing out of those lines, and the rapid depositing of fish in the boats, which seemed, to my eyes, to rival the celerity with which a "fast compositor" deposits type in his stick! the flashing of the white bones in the sunlight, and the ornamental flourishes which the "fancy ones" among the young fishermen would cut with their lines in the air—and all this done under the swiftest motion of their vessels in a stiff breeze over the dark sparkling waters! All silent, too, was the spectacle, except the slapping of the waves on the shore of the promontory, and the occasional screech of a sea-bird. Here they intertwined among each other, to and fro, in and out and around—much like the sparkles of moonlight that you can see sometimes of a summer night dancing in the East River—or any other river, I suppose, when the water is smooth, and the moon bright.[4]

But perhaps I should have told you that the blue-fish is a very voracious creature; so voracious that, instead of a bait, we fasten a piece of bone, or even a white rag, to the usual place on the line, and so let it trail from the stern of the boat. The greedy fish snaps it down at a gulp. Two or three lines, fixed off in this way, are often appended to one boat; and then, if the fish be plenty, one man must work himself. Sometimes two men "throw out" from one boat, and so on. Very often, too, the sharp teeth of the blue-fish ease the boat of hooks, bones and all.

314

My friends on sea-bass intent (they were waiting for a particular wind, or something to complete their nets, I think,) looked with a sort of superciliousness, I discovered, on the blue-fish business. I found one buying a basket of the fish, from a boat which just came in loaded; and when I was curious enough to ask him why, while they were waiting, he and his mates didn't go out and catch for themselves, he gave me to understand that sea-bassers never demeaned themselves in that way.

Item, a consolation for wearers of beards; a full-whiskered grizzled old chap—young and old, however, were thorough sons of Esau—informed me how experience had proved to all sea-bassers and other fishermen, that an application, while out there, of the razor or shears was equal to aches, chills and neuralgic twinges forthwith, and that their sovereign'st defence against the same and all kindred attacks, was to let their beards and hair grow.

PAUMANOK

Number II

OLD GRAVE YARDS ON EAST LONG ISLAND—ONE OF THE PREACHERS—WHALING VESSELS

Greenport, L.I., 17 Oct. [21 Oct. 1849]

Some tatters of the mantle of Old Mortality have surely descended to me, for I find a real enjoyment in exploring the ancient burial places of East Long Island. The other day, while returning from a long walk to Oyster-ponds Point—the north mate of Montauk Point—I turned off the road, to ascend some bleak and stony hills. They were close upon the Sound, and had an unusually bare and dismal and lonesome appearance. Between a couple of the largest, what should I come upon, but an old grave yard, and a very large one, too. Not a single inscription upon the stones, could be made out with ease; and only a few could be made out at all. It was a weird looking place; the wind piped its thousand trebles over the hill-tops on each side, and a sullen base came from the shore near by, yet down there not a breath of the wind could be felt. There were hundreds of graves, all of generations *long* before our own; but from some reason or other, no new burial appeared to have taken place there for many many years. Several of

315

the tomb-stones were large flat ones, even with the ground, and quite covered with moss and stone-rust. Some were crumbled away, some just poked out a few inches of their tops, above the surface. 'Twould have been curious to decipher the inscriptions upon them; but one needed to make a day's work, perhaps several days, for any satisfactory result that way.

At Southold, (90 miles from New York, by the L.I. Railroad,) there is another very old grave yard. Perhaps the two are the oldest in the United States. That at Southold is in good preservation, and is still used. It contains the graves of many of the "oldest inhabitants," some of whom were buried as early as 1620 and 30. And the neighbors have a commendable way of resetting the monuments when they get to crumbling from age, and of re-cutting the inscriptions, which I was very much pleased at. One of the old stones has this upon it:

> "Here lyeth interred the body of Colonel
> "John Youngs, Esquire, late one of
> "His Majesty's Council of the Province
> "of New York, who departed this
> "life the 12 day of April, Anno
> "Domini 1698, aged 75 years."

As it is a pretty rare thing to find in fresh preservation in our republic, such tangible and avowed presence of "one of His Majesty's Council," the story seemed to me worth printing. Then here is another:

> "To the blessed memory of Mrs. Mary
> "Hobart. Born in Boston, who after
> "she had served in her own age,
> "By the will of God fell on sleep
> "in this on the
> 19 of April 1698.
> "Aged 55 years, 11 months and 17 dayes."
> "Desir'd she Liv'd
> Lamented she did
> Dye   yet still she
> Lives in precious memory."
> "My soul ascends
> Above the Stars."

Many of the inscriptions must be really interesting if one could only make them out. But it needs more than an idle hour's time; and an hour or so was all I had to spare.

Large and venerable grave yards are very numerous all over Long Island, particularly at this end of it. Many of them are placed upon hills, and are without trees or shrubbery. As you travel along the roads you see the white tomb-stones, group after group, some far, and some near. I suppose you know that Long Island is quite equal to any part of North America in the antiquity of its settlement, and in the desire of its sons and daughters to be buried among their kindred.

It is a great pity that some of that feeling which has, of late years, led to the setting apart of beautiful and wooded grounds for burial, had not prevailed of old, when it could have been done so much more easily and cheaply. The feeling, however, does not seem to take start in country places, even yet. I notice that they put their dead in singularly dreary and dismal spots, bad of view and bad of everything, connected with locality. Some sandy stony hill, hopeless for the growth of any crop, is generally selected. Must we say the choice is from that sort of "thrift, thrift," which served up certain meats at the wedding-table of Hamlet's step-father? [1]

I have noticed, too, that a funeral in the country is indescribably chilly and depressing. Let me start somebody to thinking why—for I am sure, whoever has attended such a funeral will recall to mind the same fact, and will find a great difference between its scenes and the like solemnity in a city.

Talking of funerals allows me to slide off in some remarks upon the performances at one of the "meetings" in this village, last Sunday night. The regular preacher was absent, and his place was supplied by certainly one of the oddest of human specimens. (I saw him the next morning cheapening a gun in a neighboring shop). If he was a wag, he succeeded to perfection in burlesquing the sermon: if serious, it was a seriousness as funny as Mitchell's or Placide's in their dreadful travesties. [2] You may imagine something of the gentleman's style when you know that he earnestly demanded of the audience, "Do you imagine Christ was such *hypocricat* as that?" Shade of Mrs. Malaprop! *"Hypocricat"*! About every third or fourth attempt at rolling off a sentence would stick him in the mud; whereupon he would extricate himself by an unintelligible jabber, containing no distinct words— a decidedly "unknown tongue." One of the contingencies he put before the audience was the being "as rich as *Zeros*"! And as to moods and tenses, and

317

the good old rule of "a verb must agree with its nominative," &c, the work was a slaughter beyond precedent. My poor handkerchief, when I pulled it from my pocket the next morning, was what the wolverines might call "tetotaciously chawed up." I had done it in the agonies between my laughter and attempted decorum.

On Saturday last, we all gathered on the dock, to see the departure of a whaler. Formerly there was quite a flourishing business carried on from here, in fitting out such ships, and receiving them back again. But lately it has declined. They have mostly returned weary enough, but not heavy laden. I am told that the raw hands who go out in these whalers make a poor business of it. Some of them barely get enough to repay their outfit. The captain gets his sixteenth or twentieth "lay," and one or two others share equally well; but the hands generally leave the ship as poor as they entered it, except in experience. I am told that whales have been scarce of late years; and that very few vessels from any quarter, get full cargoes. The ship that left here last Saturday has been on two whaling voyages from this port—neither of them very successful. Her owners are persevering fellows. I almost wonder they didn't start her off to California.[3]

PAUMANOK

Number III

SOME POETICAL COMPARISONS BETWEEN COUNTRY AND CITY.—THE OLD COUPLE ON SHELTER ISLAND.— A BIT OF ARGUMENT—OR AN ATTEMPT ANY HOW

Southold, L.I., 24 Oct. [28 Oct. 1849]

Quiet, homely and passionless, is the life of these East Long Islanders, compared with existence in a great city like New York. Now that old Dutch Dr. Zimmermann, who wrote so profoundly and acted so foolishly, commends "solitude" as the greatest developer and establisher of virtuous conduct, and intellectual and scientific improvement.[1] Also, it is a common way among writers to speak in the same strain—to make much of "the soothing pleasures of retirement," and the "calm delights of obscurity." We hear these gentlemen talk about life in the country as surely productive of a fine unsophisticated character in man or woman.

I know from the frequent bent of my own feelings, that yearning for the freshness and quiet of the country—that love of freedom from the ligatures and ceremonies of a life in town. But to be born and "brought up" in an out of the way country place, and so continue there through all the stages of middle life—and eat and drink there only, and "dress up" of a Sunday and go to church there—and at last die and be buried there—is that an enviable lot in life? No, it is not. The burying part may be well enough, but the living is much such living as a tree in the farmer's door-yard.

Undoubtedly as a general thing we United Statesers have enough of the restless in us, never to settle anywhere, longer than a few seasons. But Long Island is an exception. The people are tenacious of the place, and the places, from the brown sand of Napeague Beach, far east, to the white sand of Coney Island Point, far west. Here about the eastern parts, in particular, I find whole villages, or rather scattered hamlets, whose residents were born, and will live and die here, many of them having been only once or twice away from home over night, and very many who never visit the city of New York, during their whole lives! A very large majority never entered a theatre or read a play, or saw a piano or any thing worthy to be called sculpture or painting. Only a fraction of them take newspapers—and the books I frequently find to be nothing later than the "Children of the Abbey," "Rinaldo Rinaldini," "Alonzo and Melissa," or those interesting horrors of Calvinism by Masters Fox and Baxter.[2] I am aware that these people might be very intelligent, and very manly and womanly, without ever having seen a play or a piano—and therefore I only mention that as a specimen of their primitiveness. But the vegetating forever in one little spot of this wide and beautiful world—the absence of books—the getting *set* in the narrow notions of the locality where they live—serve to dwarf and distort much of the goodly elements of their own nature; and increase the same rude effects to the third and fourth generation.

Yes, Messrs. of the city: I have found no precept more strongly taught, by my rambles among this often hospitable and quite invariably honest and sturdy race, then that of, *Let everyone mix for at least some part of his earlier life with the bustling world of the great towns.* Such towns have, for many an age, borne the accusations of moralists, and been warned against by timid fathers and affectionate mothers. Yet were we a coarse and unhewn structure of humanity without them. Living in the country, in an insulated way, never wears off the husk upon one's manners, never sharpens conversational powers, rarely develops the intellect or the morals to the perfection they are capable of—and generally leaves a man in that condition of unbakedness, appropriately called "raw." Advantages there are, truly; but they are preserved on the same principle as the father's who, fearing his son *may* be drowned, lets him never go in the water to learn to swim.

Isolated country life, I perceive, encourages avarice and a singular sort of egotism. Penuriousness is almost universal among the farmers here, and their families; and "living by one's self" is carried to a remarkable extreme.

The other afternoon, tired and sweaty, after a long scramble over the hills and among the woods of Shelter Island, (a fertile "collection of land surrounded by water," in extent some ten miles by three,) I came down to the shore, opposite Greenport, and found myself just too late for the little ferry boat, which crosses only at long intervals. Nigh the shore ran up a beautiful creek, the water whereof was as clear as plate glass; and the mouth of this creek and the shore helped form a fine knoll whose sides were adorned with thrifty oaks and so forth, altogether a very goodly and wholesome spot. Through a gate, some five or six rods, was a large two-story double house, and the barns and outbuildings gave token to the fatness of the land. The whole air of the spot was so inviting, that I dispatched a ragged little urchin who came down to view me, back again to the house, asking if I could get a bowl of bread and milk. They had no bread, was the answer sent me, but I could have some milk and hominy. I presently found myself at the table of this well-stored dwelling, spooning up some skimmed milk and coarse burnt hominy. An old woman, the mistress of the place, bustled about, and regaled my repast with many words: her husband had gone over to Greenport after "things": she had no servants, and never wanted any: she had had nine children, all of whom were living, but none lived home: they, that is her husband and herself, had settled there thirty-eight years ago. Wasn't she sometimes lonesome? No, she never wanted company—her husband and she found they "got along" best as they were. I noticed large numbers of cows in the neighboring fields: were they hers? Yes: the cheese and butter were sent to market. Those thrifty orchards? Yes, they produced well; the apples were sold. Divers fatting hogs, in the pens; they also were designed for market. Those flocks of poultry, and the daily products of eggs. O, they were not for "poor folks" to consume—they, too, increased the weight of the money bags.

Shortly the farmer himself came home. He had been across the bay, to "the store," for various purchases. I was amazed to notice that they were just such articles as a workingman's family in New York might get, butter, bread, candles, lard, salt fish, and so on—all by the small quantity! And I discovered, by-and-by, that this man had a good farm of nearly three hundred acres, and money out at interest, and two or three other farms for sale! His farms he put out on shares: all his part of the product was sold over to the stores, and he purchased, by the peck and pound, just enough to live on, from season to season.

Notwithstanding all the old woman's apologies, and protestations, I saw plainly enough that they always lived in this half starving manner. I really could not eat the thin milk and coarse burnt corn; but, as I rose, I put down a shilling on the table. The fierce clutching look of the woman's eyes, as she sidled toward the money, made me sick. It told more than I could write on pages of paper; and it told a degrading story of avarice and wretchedness.

Thirty-eight years agone, that couple, then probably just married and young, had settled down there; and from that time forward they had made money and raised children—the latter, probably, because they found it more economical than hiring people to work on the farm. I cannot describe to you their remarkable queernesses of look and manner. The old woman was fat, but her face, the color of copper, had none of the jolly or motherly expression of most fat old women. Her restless black eyes shifted constantly to and fro, and she seemed to be under the influence of an unsatisfied demon of motion, for she waddled and trotted without a single moment's cessation. Neither a physiognomist nor a phrenologist would have been pleased with her face and head—or the man's either.

The old man had piercing gray eyes, that fixed upon you firmly, and looked you through, with an intense look. His manner and the still-expression (you know what I mean?) of his features didn't trouble one like the woman's; for one don't notice such things so strikingly in a man. But that expression corresponded perfectly with the facts aforesaid—that not one of their nine children lived home—that they had no servants—that they were rich—and that they seized ravenously on my shilling! I almost forgot to say that the wife's mother, a superannuated relic of mortality, aged ninety-two, still lived with them.

I have been somewhat particular in drawing this little "family picture" for you, because, with fewer or greater modifications, it stands good for a sadly large number of Long Island and New England country people, with probably one exception. There are few of the farmers, or farmers' wives about east Long Island who will take shillings for a cup of milk and a slice of bread to the wayfarer. Doubtless the same exception holds good in New England.

321

You would be amazed, in peregrinating around these quarters, at finding out the number of people who *live alone*. The other day, I turned off the road to call at the hut of a venerable hermitess, that used to remind me of some of the old women in Scott's novels, with her short blanket-cloak, her horn-rimmed spectacles, and her long hickory staff. I made the acquaintance of the dame of a Sunday, some years since, on which occasion she gave me a specimen of her vocal powers, evidently then in full vigor. A small gift purchased her good will, and our acquaintance has been preserved by annual instalments. Poor, half-deranged, old creature! She lived all alone, in a miserable cottage, some distance from the road—all alone, for many years, though those who were related to her, and who were rich, would have taken her to stay with them, but she would not. Strange and ridiculous, and—but sacred be the poor old crone's weak traits, for she is under the sod. I found the old cottage unoccupied. The paper blinds were up at the windows, and a wild black cat scampered under the house; and a neighbor told me that the old woman had died some six months ago.

To the north of the village, again, in a small two-roomed dwelling, lives a man by himself—an old fellow, who for years has done his own cooking and washing—and made his own shirts, for what I know. He is a fat, stolid looking old man. Benevolence and philoprogenitiveness have made themselves scarce on his skull-cap.

Truly, I might go on, and jot down a long string of these solitary people, who betake themselves aside from their kind, and seem to resist companionship the more they need it by growing old. Sometimes, in the middle of wide "plains," or on the edge of extensive woods, or otherwheres at a great distance from any neighbor, I find families living, who see no one but their own members for days in succession. They hear no news, till it is old—sometimes not the most startling and important occurrences, till months after they are printed in the city papers. And all this within a hundred miles of New York!

From the people themselves I have learned that, generally, at first, it was irksome to them, and they felt solitary enough; but in a very few seasons they liked it better, and by and by it was inexpressibly annoying to be long in a thick town, or surrounded closely by neighbors. They came to *love* their far-removed habitations, and, if their children went away, the old people would stick with double tenacity; and if one of the old people died, the other would still remain in the same place, and would not move away!

Such were the ones, who, when newly married, had bought lands very cheap in those remote spots, and gone to make a living there. But there were others, who from childhood had grown up on similar farms by themselves, surrounded by deserts of plain, or pine, or scruboak; and this class, too—so individuals of them told me—felt happier in their solitude than they could bring themselves to feel where the dwellings were less sparse.

Does some one suggest that from the scattered nature of a country population, vice is scarcer? It appears so, but it is not probably so in reality. *In proportion*, there is as much wickedness in country as in towns. What I mean is this: Suffolk county, L.I., has about 40,000 inhabitants, New York city has eight or ten times that number—does any one suppose that any fair average eighth part of the city generates more vice, or contains more, than Suffolk county? And I believe that the county I mention has as sternly honest a race of inhabitants as any in the Republic.

There is also a great amount of error as to the physical advantages of country life. The *air* is wholesomer, of course; but that advantage is generally counterbalanced by evils in other points. The country child is put to hard work at an early age; he soon loses the elasticity of youth, and becomes round-shouldered and clumsy. He learns to smoke, chew, and drink, about as soon as his town prototype. The diet of country people is generally abominable; pork and grease, doughy bread, and other equally indigestible dishes, form a large portion of their food. They work very much too hard, and put too heavy labors upon the youthful ones. The excessive fatigue of a hurried harvest, in the hottest season of the year, thoroughly breaks the constitution of many a boy and young man.

So much have I informally written, because what I *have* written is by no means the popular view, although the truth. Does any one infer that I would advise country-boys to betake themselves to the city right off? God forgive me, if it should tend that way: no! The city hath its perils, too, and very likely the novice would find them great ones. Yet would I have no child reared up in the barbarous ignorance of so many quite well-off country families. And I say that, no matter what moralists and metaphysicians may teach, *out of cities the human race does not expand and improvise so well morally, intellectually, or physically.* Nor do I yield the point when some one goes farther than our own land, to London, or Paris, or manufacturing Glasgow or Manchester.

PAUMANOK

323

Number IV

LONG ISLAND PLACES—BROOKLYN—BEDFORD—EAST NEW YORK—JAMAICA—UNHEALTHINESS OF TOO MUCH SHRUBBERY—HEMPSTEAD—"THE PLAINS," AN ILLUS-TRATION OF THE BEAUTIES OF LAND MONOPOLY—SETTLEMENTS ALONG THE LINE OF THE LONG ISLAND RAILROAD—FARMINGDALE—"THE BRUSH"—A HINT TO CARPET DESIGNERS

[4 Nov. 1849][1]

We left the roofed and roomy Depot—one might almost call it *grounds*—of the Long Island Railroad, at the South Ferry, just five minutes after the "half past nine" which is advertised as the starting time; an allowance of grace which I recommend to all other lines, for it is very customary and very provoking, as the last monents approach, to be under the necessity either of losing your wind or losing your journey. For my own part, I have more than once chosen the latter alternative. Besides, what is more ridiculous than a man, red-faced and sweaty, running after the steamboat or the cars? How such an unfortunate wishes he could sink into the earth, when he has shrieked out for the engineer or the pilot to "hold on!" and they heed him no more than the dead—and the passengers all look back and smile!

It is a noticeable fact, now, on the Long Island Railroad, that hardly anybody will sit in the car that immediately follows the locomotive; it never becomes occupied till all the other places are taken. That a collision occurred some ten or twelve months ago, in which the forward car and its inhabitants suffered most, is the reason why. How careful we are of our precious lives!

The bell rings, and winds off with that sort of a twirl or gulp, (if you can imagine a bell gulping) which expresses the last call, and no more afterwards: then off we go. Every person attached to the road jumps on from the ground or some of the various platforms, after the train starts—which, (so imitative an animal is man) sets a fine example for greenhorns or careless people at some future time to fix themselves off with broken legs or perhaps mangled bodies. The orange women, the newsboys, and the limping young man with long-lived cakes, look in at the windows with an expression that says very plainly, "We'll run alongside, and risk all the danger, while you find the change." The smoke with a greasy smell comes drifting along, and you whisk into the tunnel.

The tunnel: dark as the grave, cold, damp, and silent. How beautiful look Earth and Heaven again, as we emerge from the gloom! It might not be unprofitable, now and then, to send us mortals—the dissatisfied ones, at least, and that's a large proportion—into some tunnel of several days' journey. We'd perhaps grumble less, afterward, at God's handiwork.[2]

Even rattling along after the steam-engine, people get a consciousness of the unrivalled beauties of Brooklyn's situation. We see the line of the new Fifth Avenue, and the hills of Greenwood, and swelling slopes that rise up from the shore, Gowanus-ward. Also the little cove that makes in by Freeks's mill, and the meadows to the south of Penny Bridge, and the green knolls and the sedgy places below the aforesaid Fifth Avenue, and toward Bergen Hill.

Brooklyn! Brooklyn! thou art indeed a Dame Beautiful. But thou canst never have a fresh face, and clean stockings, till those Water Commissioners are appointed, and have done their duty.

Bedford is the first stopping-place. Rich and moist land, here, gives a deep hue to the plentiful vegetation, but unfortunately puts a taint of fever and ague in the air, at the same time. With such a state of things it is by no means the wisest idea in the world to nearly smother one's dwelling in trees and shrubbery, as is the practice with divers of the Bedfordians. To the north of the railroad several new streets and avenues have lately been opened, and modicums of ground facing thereon are in the market. I noticed a group of gentlemen up there, most of whom had the prying appearance of examiners and purchasers, and one of whom showed speculation in his eyes as sure as ever an auctioneer bawled in Wall street.

East New York, spread out as flat as a pancake—Cypress Hills Cemetery, with its white-painted tower, (looking like some solitary bachelor,)—and then Union Race Course. An unusually long halt here, and the getting out of divers people—among others some gents possessing the unmistakeable look, with fancy-colored broadcloth and plenitude of jewelry, that help one to identify the blackleg. For there was to be a race there that day, and another train, two hours later, was to bring the mass of the company.

As far as we had come, and onward to Jamaica, the ground on both sides of the road presented a pleasing appearance. Partly-reaped cornfields, buckwheat, cabbages, turnips, and potatoes—apple orchards with the yellow fruit—farms and farm-yards, and farm operations, and cattle—were to be *enjoyed*; for it was really enjoyment to look at them. I never knew the crops on Long Island to yield better or show better, take them in the lump, than this fall and the past summer.

Jamaica is embowered in the same deep dead green, indicating the sort of rich loam, aforementioned, favorable to the disease which makes quinine a drug that is no drug. Trees and shrubbery add to the prettiness of any house, and, indeed, are indispensable; but sunshine is indispensable too. A reasonable amount of trees, ye people with country cottages! but let no window in your houses, nor square foot of ground around them be without the wholesome rays of the sun at some period of the day.

Jamaica is composed mostly of one long street, which is nothing else but the turnpike. It is lined closely by trees, which again have an inner lining of the same, sprinkled with shrubbery. As you enter the village you pass a pretty place some years since owned and occupied by Hackett the actor; more lately by Mr. Judd, a retired New Yorker. Then there is John A. King's residence, unseeable from the road, through the impervious trees. I saw Mr. K. just return from an agricultural fair, somewhere east. He holds his years well. He is in Congress, you know, for the two winters to come.[3]

Old Dominie Schoonmaker still flourishes in Jamaica. He used to preach oftener in Dutch than English—and was halved between two congregations; but that was long ago. Of late years his flock have built a large handsome church, and otherwise given in to the vanities of the world; but I guess the Dominie still lives in his old parsonage, and can talk Dutch and toss off a joke, or a glass of wine, as well as forty years ago.[4]

As you walk through *the street* of Jamaica, every house seems either a store or a tavern. There are two newspapers, one by Mr. Brenton, otherwise "Dr. Franklin," a good soul; and the *Long Island Farmer*, by Mr. Willis. Charley Watrous, I see, has retired from the dignities of the printing office, having probably made an "independent fortune," as that is so common a sequence of publishing a newspaper. Jamaica has a large old established Academy for Boys, "Union Hall," and a more lately commenced Academy for Girls; the former is in charge, these many years, of Henry Onderdonk, an accomplished man of letters, whose interesting work on the Revolutionary Incidents of Long Island will hold a standard place in all our complete libraries.[5] The infinitude of Jamaica stores and public houses allows an inference, which is the truth, viz: that farmers, travellers, marketmen, and other passengers on the turnpike through the village, give it all its trade and retail business. It has no manufactories, and has not been what is called a "growing place" for many years, and probably will not be.

After leaving Jamaica, and Brushville which is three miles east, we stretch out pretty soon upon "the Plains," that prairie-like and comparatively profitless expanse of land. The character of the country now becomes flat, and bare of trees; the houses are far from each other, and there is an uncomfortably naked and shrubless look about them. As the locomotive whisks us along, we see to a great distance on both sides, north and south—and see, mostly, large square fields, a great portion of which is devoted to pasturage.

The "Branch," or turning off place for Hempstead, is about eighteen miles from Brooklyn. A cluster of houses has been built up here, in the midst of the wide expanse, and a tolerable degree of traffic is carried on; of course all derives its life-blood from the Railroad. Hempstead, otherwise "Clamtown," otherwise "Old Blue," is some two miles to the south; which two miles you pass over on a railway, in cars drawn by horses that the crows, as they fly overhead, must feel astonished at not having got, some time before. The village is rather a pleasant one, of perhaps 1400 inhabitants. It hath a Presbyterian tinge, of the deepest cerulean; and in one of its graveyards is buried Henry Eckford, the naval architect, who once held the office of chief constructor at the Brooklyn Navy Yard, and built that noble piece of seacraft the ship of the line Ohio. Branching out from Hempstead, in a southeasterly direction is the fine south turnpike, that leads along through (among other places,) Merrick, Babylon, Patchogue, Speonk, Good-Ground, away east to the Hamptons.

For some miles east of the Branch, there is little but a mighty stretch of these uncultivated Plains. True, there are some patches enclosed alongside of the railroad, here and there.—Around Hicksville, there is quite a group of these small settlings. Hicksville! that place of vanished greatness! O, what a cutting up of lots, and selling them off at high prices, there was here, in "the time of the great speculations," years ago! An immense city *was sure* to be that same Hicksville: *now* its sovereign sway enfolds a large unoccupied tavern, a few pig-pens, a very few scattered houses, and aforesaid little enclosures. But joking not, I shouldn't wonder to see Hicksville gradually pick up, and be a tidy, little hamlet, in the course of five or six years.[6]

The great obstacle of improvement, all about here, is the monopoly of most of this immense tract of plains, by the town of Hempstead, the people whereof will not sell, nor divide it among themselves even, as was proposed a few years ago. If they *would* consent to sell, the town treasury would be

327

prodigiously the gainer; and, cut up in strips, the land would be cultivated, adding to the looks of that region, to productiveness and human comfort, to the wealth of the town of Hempstead, and consequently decreasing the rate of its taxes. Some portions of the Plains, belonging to the town of Oysterbay, have been sold; and are taken up and settled on immediately.

Land Monopoly shows one of its beauties, most pointedly, in this matter. I don't know, indeed, where one could go for a more glaring and unanswerable argument of its evils. Here is good land, capable of ministering to the existence and happiness of thousands upon thousands of human beings, all lying unproductive, *within thirty miles of New York city*, because it is monopolised by one principal owner! I know the people have the right of pasturing their cattle, horses, and sheep, on the plains—but that privilege, however widely used, does not develope one twentieth of the natural resources of the land. Thousands of acres of it are covered with nothing but "kill-calf," and other thousands, where nothing grows, could be redeemed by two or three seasons' cultivation and manuring.

At Farmingdale, anciently known under the appellation of "Hardscrabble," you begin to come among the more peculiar specimens of humanity which good old Long Island produces. (Though I ought not to have overlooked the goodly village of Jericho, two miles north of Hicksville—a Quaker place, with stiff old farmers, and the native spot of Elias Hicks.) Farmingdale rears its towers in the midst of "the brush," and is one of the numerous offspring of the Railroad, deriving no inconsiderable portion of its importance from the fact that the train stops here for the passengers to get pie, coffee, and sandwiches.

We are now in the midst of the aforementioned "brush," a growth of pine and scruboak, mostly, though interspersed with birch, sumach, and other modest-sized trees. But at this time it is beautiful exceedingly! I can sit and gaze admiringly for miles and miles, at those colors that the chemistry of the autumn has profusely dyed every leaf withal. Deep and pale red, the green of the pines, the bright yellow of the hickory, are the prevailing hues, in numberless lovely combinations. I have often thought that those who make designs for carpets could get most excellent hints from these autumn garnishings. How pleasing and graceful would be a carpet pattern, richly covered with figures and colors, closely imitated from what one sees here —how much better than the tasteless, meaningless, and every way unartistical diagrams that we walk over, now, in the most fashionably carpeted parlors.[7]

328

In my next letter, I shall take the reader 'way to the jumping off place of the island.

PAUMANOK

Number V

REGION OF "THE BRUSH"—DEER PARK—BABYLON—AN OLD MINISTER AT OYSTER BAY—NORTH AND SOUTH SIDES—RAILROAD STOPPING-PLACES—SETTLING IN THE BRUSH—RIVERHEAD—TRAINING DAY—SOUTH-EAST L.I. —MONTAUK PENINSULA—NORTH PRONG—GEOLOGY— SOUTH BAY—INSCRIPTION IN OLD GRAVE YARD—SHELL HEAPS

[11 Nov. 1849]

For more than 40 miles, east of Farmingdale, (which is some 30 miles from New York,) the L.I. Railroad passes through a region of monotonous "brush," or pine barrens, much of the latter covered with burned trunks, black and gloomy enough.[1] Not many years since, the deer had their haunts here, and an occasional hunting party would succeed in shooting one or two; the sport is now rare, however. I saw one handsome doe, coming down on the cars—the trophy of a gent who was more used to John Does than any other sort. He was mighty proud of his luck, and has doubtless astonished hundreds of fellow lawyers, around Nassau street, and the City Hall, with narratives of his chase, by this time.

Deer Park, (we Americans seem to christen new localities according to contraries, like the way dreams go,) is the next hamlet east of Farmingdale. It is a little cluster of houses in the midst of the woods, as indeed are nearly all the succeeding places of stoppage, for many miles. Off against here, on the south side of the island, and distant five miles, is Babylon, a town which, in conjunction with Islip, certainly produces the largest musketos and the most tiplers, of any known community of its size. Many old sportsmen, who used to put up at Captain Dodd's, there, will feel surprised to see the familiar fat face of "Madame Dodd" behind the bar of the shabby accommodation house, at Deer Park. For you must know that Madame Dodd is a character of these regions; she wears a prodigious turban upon her head, and dis-

329

penses gin or ginger-bread with the smiling grace of a French woman. On the north side, off against this same quarter, is Huntington, one of the prettiest villages of the island. The township of Huntington is a Democratic "banner town;" giving from five to eight hundred majority. Nigh at hand are the pleasant villages of Cold Spring and Oyster Bay. The latter place has still resident within its limits one of the oldest pastors, probably in America, Rev. Marmaduke Earle, who has preached regularly, and taught school, for fifty consecutive years, in the same place! Mr. E. is an example of what prudence, temperance, and obedience to physical propriety, will do for a fellow. Though of quite delicate constitution, he has attained fullness of age seldom vouchsafed to man, has experienced very little illness, and his faculties, old as he is, are quite as clear as in people not half his age. In Oyster Bay, too, they show you the mossy rock on which stood Fox when he preached in the woods, causing a great hubbub among the people, and turning many in the way of getting "born again."

The north side of Long Island, adjacent to the Sound, and for a couple of miles inward, has a more varied and hilly character; while the south side is almost invariably level. This difference prevails, the whole length of the island.

Suffolk station, Thompson, and Medford, are stopping places, like the previous ones, completely embosomed in dwarf oak and pines. They are the depots of folks and chattels for or from, Islip, Sayville, Patchogue, Bellport, Fireplace, etc., on the south side, and Comac, Smithtown, Stony Brook, Letauket, Ronkonkoma Pond, and so forth on the north side. Wampmissic and Yaphank, are ditto ditto,—and so is St. George's Manor. This region used to be a great place for putting obstructions on the track of the railroad. The people openly defended and stood by each other in that scoundrelly crime, and it is wonderful that some horrible accident didn't happen there. It was the dread of the whole road. Since the administration of the present President of the road, Mr. Weeks, and the popular Superintendent, Mr. Ives, the obstructions and quarrels have quite ceased. For there were also, in those days, perpetual quarrels and lawsuits between the people there, and the Railroad Company.

The 40 miles of "brush," aforementioned, is by no means an inspiriting spectacle to see, as you may imagine. Here and there, through the wilderness, tracts have been purchased at a very low price, and people have put up places to live in, and cleared and cultivated portions of the surrounding wilderness. I have kept the run of three or four of these hardy and persevering

330

settlers, and have watched their progress from year to year, with much interest. They are gradually "progressive," and in a few years will have fertile and valuable farms, the almost exclusive results of their own exertions. Many large owners of land here will give away alternate portions in it, on condition that the recipient will settle on it, and build and "improve." (What do you say when I tell you that the same thing was done with lots in Main street, Brooklyn, less than forty years ago?—Owners gave away alternate lots, to be built on, so that the remaining ones would fetch more.)

Really, the work to be done here in this desert of half grown trees, is not harder than in many new settlements out west. But there the hardships and tough times are universal. Here, within a short distance, are so many well off families, that it makes a most annoying contrast. It is a perplexing paradox that where all are poor nobody is poor.

Riverhead, the central town of Suffolk county, is 75 miles from New York. It is a sober, quiet, old place. I stopped there a few days, and visited the lions. An old wooden jail and court house is the most venerable thing of the sort, I presume, on Long Island. An expert adept in city crime, however, would easily show it a clean pair of heels. "General training day," I had an opportunity of here noticing, has dwindled away altogether from its old pomp and circumstance. Formerly, Riverhead, on its annual occurrence, presented the appearance of some great camp, or beleaguered city, or an excited mess of warriors bustling around and getting ready for the fray. Eatables, drinkables, and frolic, were the accompaniments; the girls came from far and near, and many nigger fiddlers, and there was dancing and making merry, and no going to bed. All the young fellows of the county had to be there present, "armed and equipped as the law directs," and they *were* there. But O what a falling off this last training presented! Some forlorn looking youths, and poor middle-aged men, with rusty guns—and the officers, almost as numerous as the men! It was a very melancholy sight, the way those disconsolate ones were marched around, and occasionally stopped and put through the motions. I was told that the demon of "commutation" had even penetrated the rural districts of Suffolk county, and people paid their three quarters, and staid at home.

A suit was in progress, at Riverhead, in which a brother of an engineer who was killed by a collision on the rail road, over a year ago, was plaintiff. I believe he recovered a thousand dollars damages of the company. To the widow of another man who was killed, the company paid nearly five thousand dollars. Such items must "eat into the profits."

331

East and south of Riverhead, for some distance, the soil is hideously barren and sandy. Still farther south, however, it becomes a bit better. There is quite a watering place, on the shore, called by the euphonious name of Quogue. Here, (or somewhere not far off,) is the termination of the only magnetic telegraph I know of on Long Island. It extends to Brooklyn, and is used to give information of the approach cityward of vessels; said information being used by speculators in a manner they best know how.

Onward east from Quogue, the road leads through Southampton and Bridgehampton, to the ancient and primitive village of Easthampton, which, if you except Amagansett, a trifle farther, is as far as the civilization of the Empire State extendeth in the direction of the rising sun. For the peninsula of Montauk has only some huts for the sheep, horse, and cow herds, who tend the immense droves put to graze there. Yet this strip contains much very excellent land, uncultivated as it is for more than twenty miles. I know of no prettier garden spot, or a finer field of corn, than I saw adjacent to the very lighthouse on Montauk point, whence if you go any farther you go into the sea.

From Riverhead, following the railroad, which keeps to the north prong, you behold the town of Jamesport, which lies on the shores of Peconic bay —then the Hermitage, and the vast thoroughfares of Mattituck and Cutchogue. Afterward come the farms and thrifty looking houses of Southold, a comfortable place I think, and so on to Greenport. Sag Harbor, one of the most populous of the Long Island towns next to Williamsburgh, lies in a sheltered part of the other shore. From Greenport it is some six or seven miles to Oyster Pond point, which is the jumping off place of the before-mentioned north prong. A first-rate jumper, though, could almost jump to Plum Island, a small spot that lies a little beyond.

The geological formation and traits of Long Island are full of interest, to the man of science. If I were not afraid of running on a snag, or in other words showing my ignorance, I would like to expatiate a little on these points. On the very summits of the range of hills that goes through the middle of the island are sometimes rocks of large size, and at the tops of other gush forth springs of the sweetest water. The south bay, 70 miles in length, from Hempstead to Brookhaven, is another feature: it is navigable, and full of fish, and has only two or three outlets through the great beach which hems it along the south. By-the-bye, there is a Canal Company, so-called, which will soon remove the obstructions between an uninterrupted communication through the long strip of water, so that vessels of moderate

332

draught can go from Peconic bay to New York. This will be a most desirable guard against dangers from the coast navigation, which is very much jeopardised by east and south flows.

In my former notes on the grave yards of east Long Island, I find I omitted the following inscription, found in the old place of burial at Southold. The latter village, as I narrated in one of the former letters, is as old as any settlement on Long Island, and that old grave yard is bigger and more crowded than many similar places in large towns.

> Here Lyeth Buried te Body of
> Mr. Barnabas Horton
> Born at Housley in Lester-shire,
> in Old England, & Dyed at
> South-hold, te 13 day of July
> 1680, aged 80 years
> Here sleeps te Body tombed in its Dust
> Till Christ shall Come & raise it with the Just
> My Soul ascended to te Trone of God
> Where with sweet Jesus now I make Aboad
> Then hasten after Me my dearest Wife
> To be Pertaker of this Blessed Life
> Hear & obey His public sacred Word
> And in your Houses call upon His name
> For oft I have advis'd you to te Same
> Ten God will bless You with your Children all
> And to this Blessed Place He will you call
> Hebrews, H. &ye 4.—He being dead yet speaketh.
> Also, at his feet
> Lie the remains of his youngest son
> JONATHAN HORTON
> The first captain of Cavalry
> in the county of Suffolk
> He died Feb. 23, A.D. 1707, Æ 60

The names cut on most of the tombstones at Southold, old and new, were Horton, Youngs, and Conkling, the names of the first settlers—an instance of the tenacity with which Long Islanders adhere to their native soil.

One of the singular features I have noticed along the shores of Southold, and sometimes at quite a distance from the shores, is the frequency of immense shell-heaps, some of them the size of small hills, although accumulated there hundreds of years ago. They are pointed to as the sites of long decayed Indian villages.

PAUMANOK

Number VI

AN ADVENTURE ON HEMPSTEAD PLAINS, YEARS AGO

[18 Nov. 1849]

One of my old friends for the last fifteen years has made it his annual custom to go down on Long Island, for purposes of recreation, sporting, and to get sniffs of the sea air that sweeps over every part of that amphibious sort of territory. It was on one of these occasions, some ten years since, that he met with a little adventure wherewith he has, in my hearing at least four times regaled a suppertable; and I consider it worth putting in print. All the additional preface necessary is the motto of the knights of the garter, *"honi soit qui mal y pense."*

Frequent mention has been made in these veracious letters of the Plains, and the reader is probably aware what a wild and wide stretch of desert they are; but ten years ago they were still more so. Only here and there at intervals of many miles over their immense surface, a hut or hovel was situated, in whose door or window the chance passer-by, of a summer day, would behold a startled bare-footed woman, and divers children, looking upon him as if they had not seen a stranger for months before, which very likely they had not.

My friend aforesaid had gone out to shoot on the Plains (stopping awhile on his way farther east) one fine but not sunshiny morning, and had met with tolerably good luck, when, toward the middle of the day, a drizzling sort of rain-shower came up, which was succeeded by a light fog. Thoughtless of whither he was going—for a New Yorker never thinks of such a thing as *he* losing his way anywhere—he kept tramping on until after the lapse of two hours he suddenly came at right angles upon some tracks made in a loamy spot, and saw at once that they were his own, and that he had, as frequently happens in such cases, been marching round-about, and at last returned to the same ground he had travelled over before.

334

The narrative of the efforts my old crony made that afternoon, (the fog deepening meanwhile) to get on the right road for home, would be tiresome to the reader—unless he could hear it from the unfortunate man himself, when it is funny enough.

We jump at once to night-fall, or a bit afterward, when, tired and drenched through, the hapless sportsman fortunately espied a light, which proved to come from a rude yet by no means comfortless cottage, consisting of exactly one room, and "nothing else." He knocked at the door, told his story, and was consoled with the comfortable assurance that there was no other house within five miles—and that there was only one bed in the cottage, the occupants whereof were the couple then and there present, having been married some six or eight months.

"Na'theless," said the young farmer, who was half undressed, his wife being already in bed, and listening, "Na'theless, we can 'commodate ye, if ye'll sleep with us. Sukey is not much of a body, and the bed is big and strong, and I dare say you are tired out like. Come in; come in."

My friend was indeed tired, and thankfully accepted the honest fellow's offer. The intruder proposed that he himself should lie on the floor; but there was a scarcity of covering, and neither the wife nor husband would consent to such a thing, protesting that they would do so themselves first. The wanderer of course demurred to that; and the final conclusion was that the primitive offer of the host was accepted as at first made, he of course lying down in the middle, and the new comer, after a moderate supper, found room enough on one side of him.

That our hero had a most excellent sleep, and was disturbed by no dreams, is as true as that it would be well for many of our city youth to purchase slumber by similar vigorous exercise. He slept indeed so well, that he was only partially awakened by the sound of a voice speaking loudly and suddenly early in the morning:

"Massy sakes!" it exclaimed, "O, Derrick! Derrick!" (which was the farmer's name) "the cow has got in the buckwheat lot! I declare she's broke down the fence, and may be been there all night!"

The wife was leaning up on her elbow in bed, and looking out of the uncurtained window, which gave a good view of three or four little fields, containing probably most of the farmer's produce. Derrick sprung up at once! Hauling on his trowsers, and rubbing his eyes, he sallied forth to eject the rebellious cow, and save his grain. The wife gazed after him a moment, then giving a stray glance at the stranger as he lay apparently sound asleep, she relapsed back into her own slumber with perfect composure.

My friend, be it known, is the most modest of men—and now what the deuce to do, was the question. His perplexities were cut short by the loud clear voice of the young man outside:

"Suke! Suke! for God's sake come here. I can't get the darned cow out, except you help me."

Sukey answered the summons like an obedient wife, and the skies looked bright again. No sooner was the woman, (who, far less fastidious than my friend, made no bones of jumping out and deliberately putting on her gown, before his eyes, although he shut them, as in decency bound,) out of doors, than the relieved child of modesty was out of bed, and ensconced in his well dried clothes, the outer and heavier portions of which had been hung the previous evening in front of the fire place.

After breakfast neither the young man or his wife could be prevailed on to accept more than a couple of shilling pieces. They were perhaps the reader imagines, excessively primitive in their notions; undoubtedly, but my sporting friend describes them as more than ordinarily intelligent, and evincing every sign of uprightness and kindness. He has since visited them more than once. Their simplicity, unsuspiciousness, and goodness, have not degenerated, although they live in a thicker neighborhood; and their farm is now quite fertile and valuable, and they have a large family of children.

PAUMANOK

Number VII

ABOUT SOME MATTERS NEARER HOME—THE CROTON
RESERVOIR—WHAT OF IT A HUNDRED YEARS HENCE
—THE GROUNDS AND HOUSES BELOW MURRAY'S HILL
—UNION SQUARE AND ITS ARISTOCRACY—GRACE
CHURCH—AN HOUR AMONG THE PICTURES OF THE
INTERNATIONAL ART UNION

[25 Nov. 1849]

I have just been up paying one of my monthly visits to the lower Croton Reservoir, on 40th street. Of the latter part of an afternoon, it makes a

336

delightful little jaunt to go out, (if on foot, so much the better,) and see the sunset, from the broad walk on the top of this reservoir. A hundred years hence, I often imagine, what an appearance that walk will present, on a fine summer afternoon! You and I, reader, and quite all the people who are now alive, won't be much thought of then; but the world will be just as jolly, and the sun will shine as bright, and the rivers off there—the Hudson on one side and the East on the other—will slap along their green waves, precisely as now; and other eyes will look upon them about the same as we do.[1]

The walks on the battlements of the Croton Reservoir, a hundred years hence! *Then* these immense stretches of vacant ground below, will be covered with houses; the paved streets will clatter with innumerable carts and resound to deafening cries; and the promenaders here will look down upon them, perhaps, and away "up town," toward the quieter and more fashionable quarters, and see great changes—but off to the rivers and shores their eyes will go oftenest, and see not much difference from what we see now. *Then* New York will be more populous than London or Paris, and, it is to be hoped, as *great* a city as either of them—great in treasures of art and science, I mean, and in educational and charitable establishments. Even now, however, as one sweeps his glance from the top of the Reservoir, he can see some seven or eight splendid charities, wholly or partially under the umbrage of the State. Let them prosper and increase, say I. If the moneys of the people only go plentifully for the great purposes of Benevolence and Education, no matter how heavy the taxes or how large the loans. They will be like bread cast upon the waters, and we shall indeed find it again after many days.

Ages after ages, these Croton works will last, for they are more substantial than the old Roman aqueducts, which were mostly built on the surface of the ground. And crowds of busy feet will patter over this flagging, years hence, and here will be melancholy musings, and popping the question, and perhaps bargains and sales, long long after we of the present time are under the sod.

Coming down the hollow-echoing stone stairway, one stops a minute to read the large marble tablet, on which are inscribed the names of the Croton functionaries and contractors and master operatives. You learn that,

"The Aqueduct commences at the Croton river, five miles from the Hudson river, in Westchester county. The dam is 250 feet long, 70 feet wide at bottom, 7 at top, and 40 feet high, and built of stone and cement.

It creates a pond five miles long, covering an extent of 400 acres, and contains 500,000,000 gallons of water. From the dam the Aqueduct proceeds, sometimes tunnelling through solid rocks, crossing valleys by embankments and brooks by culverts, until it reaches Harlem river, a distance of thirty-three miles. It is built of stone, brick and cement, arched over and under, 6 feet 9 inches wide at bottom, 7 feet 8 inches at top of the side walls, and 8 feet 5 inches high; it has a descent of 13½ inches per mile, and will discharge 60,000,000 of gallons every twenty-four hours. It crosses the Harlem river on a magnificent bridge of stone, 1,450 feet in length, with 14 piers, 7 of them bearing arches of 80 feet span, and 7 others of 50 feet span, 114 feet above tide water at the top. The receiving reservoir at Eighty-sixth street, 38 miles from the Croton dam, covers 35 acres, and holds 150,000,-000 of gallons. The distributing reservoir on Murray's Hill, in Fortieth street, covers 4 acres, and is constructed of stone and cement, 45 feet high above the street, and holds 20,000,000 of gallons. Thence the water is distributed over the city in iron pipes, laid sufficiently deep under ground to protect them from frost. The whole cost of the work has been about $13,000,000. The water is of the purest kind of river water. There are laid below the distributing reservoir in Fortieth street more than 170 miles of pipe, from 6 to 36 inches in diameter."[2]

The elevated and stony grounds about here will cost their owners dearly to get them graded and paved in the monotonous style required by most of our American cities. I always think it a pity that greater favor is not given to the natural hills and slopes of the ground on the upper part of Manhattan Island. Our perpetual dead flat, and streets cutting each other at right angles, are certainly the last things in the world consistent with beauty of situation.

From "Murray's Hill," on which the reservoir is built, you descend into the city, by any of these great wide avenues, or the Bloomingdale road. There are some very elegant houses out here; one Gothic affair, in particular, belonging I believe to Capt. Marshall, formerly of the Liverpool liners.

We get presently into the aristocratic neighborhood of Union Square. The fountain is playing, and so let us stroll about here a few minutes. Those tall and stately edifices, with their high marble stoops and iron balconies; the rich and glowing drapery inside the plate glass windows; here and there a private carriage waiting at the doors: these are the domiciles of what are called the "upper ten." Perhaps you fancy that this elevatedness of wealth and furniture, is significant of a like elevatedness of intellect, purpose, and heart, in the people. By no means. Here and there, among them, you find beautiful and sweet-souled women, and learned and chivalrous men; so you do among common people. But the great body of "fashionables" are vulgar, flippant and overweeningly selfish. Nine-tenths of the families residing in these noble dwellings, have "sprung from nothing," as the phrase is—by which is intended that their parents were hucksters, laborers, waiters, and so on; which made the said parents not a whit the worse, but, on the contrary, they were perhaps more sensible and respectable than the children who would burn with shame if their daddies or granddaddies were to start up before them, like Hamlet's, in their habits as they lived.

Whoever "keeps" Union Park, deserves a good word in the papers. For a cleaner, more trimly swept place, with better arranged shrubbery and flowers, we know not of in any city. The fountain here plays more frequently than any of the other fountains—at least it is always playing when I visit the Park.

Coming out of the lower gate of Union Square, (these oval or triangular spaces are always called *squares*) the eye is attracted by several palace-like residences, one on the corner of Broadway; and by the Church of the Holy Innocents on University Place.

Grace Church, somehow, fails to impress the mind at once with a character of beauty, or any quality synonymous with its name. The tall white spire, the prolific tracery and ornament, and fret-work, make one wonder and ask how much it all cost, and so on; but the subtle sense of the beautiful is not satisfied. You are painfully impressed with the notion of a rich, showy and tasteless congregation, who "tried to do something, and couldn't." The mellowing and sanctifying influence of time, *may* perhaps do something for this church. We hope so, for there is yet a disagreeably garish and flaunting air about it.[3]

Coming down Broadway, one must not overlook the exhibitions of pictures, in the rooms of the American and International Art Unions. The former is "noticed" in so many prints, that we give what little space we have remaining for this letter to a few lines about the International. Never before has any art exhibition in America contained pieces or work of such high order as this. Long, long half hours have I passed looking at "The Dead Christ," by Ary Scheffer.[4] It has grown into my very soul. The face and breast of the Saviour are exhibited, with the grave clothes raised from them, and the prostrate head of his mother resting on his breast. There are

339

three other female figures, whose faces exhibit different developments of grief. The countenance of the Sacred Corpse is beyond all description; he or she who can look upon it without the deepest emotion must be insensible to the great achievements of art. Yet the painting is entirely free from any strained effect, any daring attempt at wonderful things: it is after the severest forms of simplicity and spirituality. The serene grief, too great for words, of the female at the left is beautifully expressed—and the bitter wailing of the aged woman more in the background almost touches the ear—but the face of the mother is too intense for depicting, and it is bowed and hidden on the cold bosom of Christ. No tricks of ambitious color, or "warm light," or any thing of that sort, mar this great picture.

"The Christian Maiden converting her Betrothed," is a large and rich painting by Gendron, and was presented to the International by the French Republic. A young man, seated, is instructed in religious matters by a beautiful female who stands behind him, and pointing over his shoulder, to the open book in front, rests her neck confidingly against his head. The picture is highly finished, and its adjuncts are all complete, and well delineated.

"The Republic," also a donation from France, is a large sized painting— a female figure, emblematical of a Free Government. There is nothing particularly new or striking about it. The attitude of the female, and the expression in her face, are serene and majestical; her ample form is clothed in classically flowing drapery, and her head is surrounded by laurel.[5]

Perhaps the most attractive and popular pictures, however, are "Children leaving School," "The Convalescence," and "The Grandfather's Festival," by Waldmuller. The first named is certainly one of the most remarkable paintings ever produced. Its variety of scene and expression, all comprised in a small compass, and without violent contrasts, is beyond that of any picture I ever saw. A score and more of children are just tumbling out of school, and there they are with all the vivacity and gleesomeness of their age. One has received a medal, a little girl is laughing in her pleasure at examining it; another is reaching her hand out over the crowd, for her grandfather, who has come after her; one little fellow appears to have the toothache; one is going to strike a young foe, but is restrained by the sister— and so on. It is incomparable! The expression of the old man, in "The Convalescence," is a solemnly beautiful gratitude; he has recovered from illness, and as the spring warms the cherry blossoms, he is helped through the door of the cottage into the open air.

"The Fish market," by Duval le Carmus, "Head of our Saviour," by

Paul Delaroche, a female head by Court, "Rigolette and her Family," by the same, and one or two others are the remaining choice pieces of the exhibition.

We think highly of the effect of works of art on the minds and characters of the people, and warmly hope that both Art Unions, and more associations of the same kind which may come in future, will flourish well, and continue to send out among the masses of the people, the seeds of a love for beauty as it is embodied in Art. The unavoidable progress of such institutions is toward a better and higher standard of excellence every year. But the International seems to leap at once, like Minerva, into mature fulness, as respects the standard of excellence in its pictures. We doubt whether any exhibition of similar size in any city of Europe, has contained a better average of merit than this. There are, it is true, plenty of other pictures, of as extraordinary worth—but a dozen pictures of the very first class have never yet been collected at the same place in America before.

PAUMANOK

Number IX[1]

SITUATION OF MONTAUK POINT—LIGHTHOUSE—FER-
TILITY—AN INVALID FISHERMAN—OPIUM EATING—
STRANGE DOINGS AT MONTAUK—SICKENING TURN OF
AFFAIRS—A DINNER AT LAST SECURED—THE PROCES-
SION—THE DINNER—THE START FOR HOME—NIGHT—
A DASH OF SENTIMENT—SUNRISE—BREAKFAST—MORE
EXCITEMENT—ARRIVAL HOME

[16 Dec. 1849]

Montauk Point! how few Americans there are who have not heard of thee —although there are equally few who have seen thee with their bodily eyes, or trodden on thy green-sward. Most people possess an idea, (if they think at all about the matter,) that Montauk Point is a low stretch of land, poking its barren nose out toward the east, and hailing the sea-wearied mariner, as he approacheth our republican shores, with a sort of dry and sterile countenance. Not so is the fact. To its very extremest verge, Montauk is fertile

341

and verdant. The soil is rich, the grass is green and plentiful; and the best patches of Indian corn and garden vegetables I saw last autumn, were within gun shot of the salt waves of the Atlantic, being just five deg. east longitude from Washington, and the very extremest terra firma of the good state of New York.

Nor is the land low in situation. It binds the shore generally in bluffs and elevations. The point where the lighthouse stands—and it is the extreme point—is quite a high hill; it was called by the Indians *Wamponomon*—by modern folks Turtle-hill. The lighthouse here is a very substantial one of an old-fashioned sort, built in 1795; the lights are two hundred feet above the level of the sea. Sheltered in a little vale, near by, is the dwelling of the keeper and his family, the only comfortable residence for many miles. It is a tolerably roomy cottage—a sort of public house; and some inveterate sportsmen and lovers of nature in her wild aspects, come here during the summer and fall, and board awhile, and have fun.

I went out to the very edge of the cliff, and threw myself down on the grass, and tossed aside my slouchy wool hat, and looked to the eastward. The sea was in one of its calmest phases. A hoarse low roar, only, gave some token of its fiercer vitality—a sort of *living* roar, it seemed to me, for it made me think of great storms, and wrecks; and the despairing and dying who had groaned erewhile upon those waters. In a former letter I have described the appearance of the catchers of blue-fish, darting about in their swallow-like boats and trailing their lines. It was upon these men and their maneuvers that I was now gazing.

An invalid-looking man came slowly up the hill while my eyes were out upon the sea there. He seemed to be about nothing in the way of employment, and as he looked curiously and half-bashfully toward me, I called to him. He was a fisherman he told me, by occupation, and had come there to work with the rest.

"But I couldn't stand it," he continued, coughing in a bad hacking way, "went out in the water, and got pretty cold, I had a dead pain all over here," placing his broad hands over the regions of his stomach, lungs and heart.

We got directly into conversation—which, by-and-by merged into an account of his life, fortunes, and sickness. He further confessed to me that he had for years been in the habit of eating large quantities of opium. He had also lost his appetite.

"Have you had no medical advice?" I asked.

342

"No"; he felt no faith in doctors; besides it was expensive and trouble-some. Notwithstanding his ailments, however, he still continued his opium eating.

The man, at my request, showed me one of the globules which he was in the habit of taking daily. It was frightfully large! He was also becoming troubled frequently with a pain and swelling in one of his legs, which would ache and then remain torpid awhile, so that he could not walk, and then swell up to double its natural proportion. He was a large robust-sized man, of good original development, but very much emaciated in the face, and with bad stuff in his eye balls. He told me that he worked whenever he could, and liked well to come a-fishing, from which sport he was only deterred by the imperious suddenness of the before-mentioned pain in all the important vital organs, that followed his getting wet and chilled. He was better dressed than the ordinary fishermen and—probably gratified at the interest of a city stranger, and liking to talk over his troubles and be condoled—he told me that he had parents who lived toward the middle of the island, who were well off, and wished him to come home to them. He had married, years ago, and moved near Sag Harbor; though his wife was dead, and he had no family.

From the man's statement, it needed not much physiological knowledge, to tell that there was a general abstraction of the vital stimulus of the great organs,—the "dead pain" as he well-expressed it,—a lethargic slowness of the functions of the heart, stomach and liver. Besides he must have had some pulmonary affection; the cough signified a sorry state of things that way. Opium was a poison to him—and had undoubtedly brought him to the pass I saw, and was vitiating his blood, as instanced in the swelled and painful leg.

I advised him by all means to stop his fishing employments—for he ex-pressed a design to stay until the party he was with went home, and mean-while to go out with them whenever he felt well enough. I was at a loss to enjoin the cessation of the opium or not; but, laying before the poor fright-ened fellow the plain condition and probabilities, I told him by all means to get himself home to his old mother's nursing care, to lay by for a while, and to get the advice of a trusty physician, after stating all the symptoms and habits he had just related. And his accidental talk with me was the first rational colloquy the man had had with any living being on the subject.

We talk a great deal about "the intelligence of the age," and so on; but truly there is ignorance enough yet among the masses to grow up in moun-tains of sickness, destitution and vice.

343

By the by, this opium eating, may be more prevalent in county districts than one would think. At Southold not many days before, I had come across a man, who, from the same practice, achieved himself into a helpless state, and a painful swelling of the limbs. For many years, he had supported himself and family, by fishing, gunning, and light jobs; but out of his narrow income he must invariably get the little monthly box of opium! The day I saw him at Southold, he was going to the alms house, and there the poor helpless fellow is at this moment.[2]

As every man was master of his time between our arrival, and the period of dinner, I took a good long ramble for several miles to and fro. To a mineralogist, I fancy Montauk Point must be a perpetual feast. Even to my unscientific eyes there were innumerable wonders and beauties all along the shore, and the edges of the cliffs. There were earths of all colors, and stones of every conceivable shape, hue, and density, with shells, large boulders of a pure white substance, and layers of those smooth round pebbles called "milk-stones" by the country children. There were some of them tinged with pale green, blue, or yellow—some streaked with various colors —and so on.

We rambled up the hills to the top of the highest—we ran races down— we scampered along the shore, jumping from rock to rock—we declaimed all the violent appeals and defiances we could remember, commencing with "Celestial states, immortal powers, give ear!" away on the ending which announced that Richard had almost lost his wind by dint of calling Richmond to arms. I doubt whether those astonished echos ever before vibrated with such terrible ado. Then we pranced forth again, like mad kine—we threw our hats in the air—aimed stones at the shrieking sea-gulls, mocked the wind, and imitated the cries of various animals in a style that beat nature all out! We challenged each other to the most deadly combats—we tore various passions into tatters—made love to the girls, in the divine words of Shakespeare and other poets, whereat the said girls had the rudeness to laugh till the tears ran down their cheeks in great torrents. We indulged in some impromptu quadrilles, of which the "chasez" took each participant couple so far away from the other that they were like never to get back. We hopped like crows; we pivoted like Indian dervishes; we went through the trial dance of *La Bayadère* with wonderful vigor; and some one of our party came nigh dislocating his neck through volunteering to turn somersets like a circus fellow. Every body caught the contagion, and there was not a sensible behaved creature among us, to rebuke our mad antics by comparison.[3]

Most appalling news met us on returning from this nice exercise! *Our master of the revels had utterly failed to negotiate a dinner for us at the cottage!* Three several parties had been in advance of ours, that day, and had eaten up the last crumb in the house! Wasn't this enough to make Rome howl?

But it was no time to howl any more—we had already sharpened our appetites quite enough by that sort of sport. Something must be done, and quickly. A very fat, tender, plump-looking young woman, was already trying to hide herself from the ravenous looks of two or three of the most alimentively developed of our party—when we luckily spied a flock of well grown chickens feeding near the cottage door. We had still lots of bread and butter aboard the sloop. Moreover, were there not the freshest and finest fish to be bought within stone-throw? And couldn't we get potatoes from that garden, and onions likewise? And what was better than *chowder?*

Our almost collapsed hearts now bounded up again like young colts. We proceeded in solid phalanx to the landlady,—the Mrs. Lighthouse-Keeper— and with an air which showed we were not going to stand on trifles, gave voice to our ultimatum. The landlady attempted to demur, but the major domo loudly proposed that if all else failed, we should eat the landlady herself; and this motion being passed by acclamation, the good woman gave in.

Six fat pullets had their heads off in as many minutes—and shortly afterwards we made a solemn procession down to the water, each man carrying a part of the provender, in its raw state. For we determined to cook our meal on board the sloop, and owe no thanks to those inhospitable shores. Our faithful major at the head, carried a large sea-bass; next followed the young sailor with the six headless chickens, whose necks (like Pompey's statue,) all the while ran blood; next the fat girl with a splendid head of cabbage— behind whom marched the continuation of us, each furnished with something to make up the feast. Toward the rear came I, possessed of a stew-pan, purchased at a great price, and borne by me, I hope, with appropriate dignity.

All worked to a charm. Amid laughter, glee, and much good sport, (though I and the fat girl cried bitterly, peeling onions,) we cooked that dinner. And O ye Heavens, and O thou sun, that looked'st upon that dinner with a glow just as thou wast dipping thy red face below the western horizon—didn't we enjoy it? The very waters were as quiet as a stone floor, and we made a table by placing three boards on some barrels, and seats by other boards, on half barrels. But the strongest part of all is that when we got through there were fragments enough to rival the miraculous remains of the feast of the five loaves and two fishes. I shall remember that dinner to my dying day.

We pulled up stakes, and put for home. But we had overstaid our time, and the tide too.—Night came on. It was calm, clear and beautiful. The stars sparkled, and the delicate figure of the new moon moved down the west like a timid bride. I spread a huge bear-skin on the deck, and lay flat on it, and spoke not a word, but looked at the sky and listened to the talk around me. They told love stories, and ghost stories, and sang country ditties; but the night and the scene mellowed all, and it came to my ears through a sort of moral distillation; for I fear, under any circumstances, 'twould have appeared stale and flippant to me. But it did not then; indeed quite the contrary.

I made my bed in the furled sail, watching the stars as they twinkled, and falling asleep so. A stately and solemn night, that, to me—for I was awake much and saw the countless armies of heaven marching stilly in the space up there—marching stilly and slowly on, and others coming up out of the east to take their places. Not a sound, not an insect, interrupted the exquisite silence,—nothing but the ripple of the water against the sides of the vessel. An indescribable serenity pervaded my mind—a delicious abnegation of the ties of the body. I fancied myself leaping forward into the extent of the space, springing as it were from star to star. Thoughts of the boundless Creation must have expanded my mind, for it certainly played the most unconscionable pranks from its tabernacle lying there in those fields of hempen duck.

Sunrise found us alive and stirring. We he-creatures departed for an island near by, on whose sedgy creeks there was the look of wild birds. Over the sand, here, we issued a second edition of the proceedings on the hills and shores of Montauk. But, owing to the absence of the terraqueous girls, we didn't have as good a time. After all, what a place this wretched earth would be without the petticoats!

A plentiful breakfast was ready when we returned: the Lord only knows whence came all the viands, for they appeared to rise, like Venus, from the froth of the sea. However, I asked no questions, but ate thankfully.

Up sails, then, and away!—a clear sky still overhead, and a dry, mild wind to carry us before it. I was astonished at the amount of vitality that resides in man, and woman too. One would have thought the exertions and outpourings we had performed within the last twenty hours, should have

346

left us cooled down a little. Angels bless you, sir! 'twas no such thing. Fast and loud rose the voices again, the clear upper notes of the girls, and laughter and singing. We knew we should soon be home—down amid the clouds and commonplaces—and we determined to make the most of it. And we *did*.

Ah, my dear friend, I despair of putting upon paper any true description of that condensed Babel. Our shouts transpierced the wounded air. Even the dullest of us seemed filled with mental quicksilver which rose higher and higher, until there seemed some chance of not enough being left in our heels to anchor us fast upon earth. Truly those were wonderful hours!

We hove in sight of the steeples and white-paint of home, and soon after, the spirits we had served deserted us. (There was no brandy aboard, mind, and hadn't been.) We landed at the dock, and went up to the village, and felt the tameness of respectable society setting around us again. Doubtless it was all right; but as for me, I fancied I felt the mercury dwindling down, down, down into the very calves of my legs.

PAUMANOK

Number X

AN INTERESTING JOURNEY DOWN FULTON STREET AND ACROSS FULTON FERRY—OBJECTION TO STRAIGHT STREETS—ARCHITECTURE OF THE LANDING—HOLT'S HOTEL, AND THE BUILDER—THE CLERKS—THE BOAT— VIEW FROM THE RIVER—CROSSING IN THE DEPTH OF WINTER, AND IN A DENSE FOG—SCENES—ACCIDENTS— THE BRIDGE PROPOSITION

[23 Dec. 1849]

Many books have been written, to describe journeys between the Old and New World, and what was done or seen therein, and afterward. But we know of no work—at least we feel sure none has yet been issued by the Harpers, Appletons, or any of our great publishers—describing a voyage accross the Fulton Ferry. This is the more remarkable, as that is a jaunt taken every day by myriads of people. Besides, we have ourself seen authors, editors, reporters and all departments of the "press-gang" go aboard the boats of the Fulton Ferry Company, (after depositing two cents with the gentleman at the gate,) and cross over—sometimes even coming back again on the same boat. (This latter, doubtless, to get the pure air, at the economical price of a penny a trip.)[1]

Fulton street—we are going down the one on the New York side—is not what may be called the prettiest one in town. Neither is it after the straightest sect of streets. On the contrary, it is rather ugly, and very much crooked. It is an old street. It probably came in with the Knickerbockers. We are free to assume that it once had some Dutch name, before it was christened after the great applier of steam to boat moving. We suggest an inquiry that way to some antiquarian, and solemnly believe that if he were to burrow out the facts which bear on this interesting subject, he would get something more than his labor for his pains.

While upon the subject, let us in confidence reader, just whisper to you that we are no friend to thoroughfares that are rigid and right-angular. The checker-board principle applied to laying out a town is our abomination. What romance is there about it? Such exactness reduces one to despair! What is left for you to see, after you have traversed *one* of such avenues? Nothing. When you "go" one, you have gone the whole. Much more do we prefer the winding and curvicular arrangement. We like to come upon new shows—to turn a bend, and behold something fresh. Uniformity! Why it's the taste of the vulgar. Nature hath nought of it. The skies, the earth, the waters, and the woods laugh in your face, at such rectangular tediousness. But we are digressing.

Architecturally there is nothing great in Fulton street—unless it be the United States Hotel, down near the Ferry. When it was built, that was the greatest specimen of a Hotel in New York. Mr. Holt, the putter-up, had made a hundred thousand dollars out of cheap eating houses under the Fulton market. He commenced with less than ten dollars; he and his wife did the work, and waited on the customers. The ambition of the man's heart was to build a *great Hotel*. Accordingly, in "dear times," he put out contracts for the tall-storied concern we have mentioned. He spent his hundred thousand dollars, and went on giving notes and mortgages for some twice as much more. He finished it. Proudly and contentedly he entered it as lord and master. But alas, alas! how transitory is human pride! The "days of the speculation" passed like a dream, after having lighted many fools the way to dusky death. Mr. Holt was unable to satisfy his mortgages, which, somehow, *had* to be satisfied. Consequently the great Hotel was sold, for just short of the amount of the aforesaid mortgages, and poor Mr. Holt was left without a dollar of his hundred thousand![2]

But here we are at the Ferry entrance, after having passed, without personal outrage, the stream of carts, omnibusses, and all sorts of wheeled horrors, that surround, (like things Milton describes,[3]) the entrance to the great space beyond. The piece of architecture before us is of wood, well painted. It is of the simplest order of the genus roof. Under its shadow are many small edifices—besides a large plank floor.

It has been a wonder to us that the Ferry Company do not put up, there, substantial and useful buildings, of stone and iron, with fine large entrances. They are rich enough to do it, and the investment would be better than any stocks in Wall street. Put this hint in your memory, gentlemen.

Pause a moment under this pine canopy, and you will find food for observation, and thought too. There is the special room where "No gentlemen are admitted unless accompanying ladies." There are two other rooms for the masculine gender. Outside there is always a crowd waiting, stamping its feet with impatience for the boats—as if Time didn't fly fast enough without wanting to hurry it. The most impatient gentlemen here are the young clerks. It is perfect agony for them to be just half a second too late for the boat. On such occasions you may see what a struggle it costs them to restrain their legs from leaping into the river. The time until the arrival of the next boat, (which extends from a second to three quarters of a minute,) these excited youths pass in a state of mind which must be felt before it can be realized. Then to see them wait at the very edge of the wharf, and spring on the incoming boat, to the manifest danger of fat personages standing placidly in front! Afterward, the rush for the farther end—the sharp glance around, to see whether there are any fashionable coats aboard—the intense earnestness with which our youthful friends watch for the premonitory symptoms of the boat's starting! Ah, these city clerks are a peculiar race; on all occasions, you can tell them with as much certainty as you can tell a New England voice.

Then we put off—for the bell has tapped twice. Perhaps we have come on the "Manhattan," the newest of these steamers. Behold the roomy and high-ceiling'd ladies' cabin, its clear, open, airy sweep, and the colored glass windows, giving a glow to the light. The seats are cushioned most comfortably, and all around run pipes containing "hot stuff" to warm the air these cold winter times. The ladies, too, *they* form not the least part of the pleasantness. When the cabin is full, and they are seated in close rows all along from one end of the cabin to the other, it takes a fellow of some nerve to run the gauntlet through that cabin. For our part, we always feel our heart beat quicker when we attempt it—and are fain to pop down in a seat before we get half way. But then every body knows we have an unusual amount of modesty.

Who has crossed the East River and not looked with admiration on the beautiful view afforded from the middle of the stream? The forests of the New York shipping, lining the shores as far as one can see them—the tall spire of Trinity looming far up over all the other objects—various other spires—the tops of the trees on the Battery and in the Parks—these we have left behind us. In front stands Brooklyn—Brooklyn the beautiful! The Heights stretch along in front, lined now with dwellings for nearly the whole extent; but with space still left for a Public Promenade, if it be applied to that purpose *soon*. To the left of the Heights, the open mouth of Fulton street, the great entrance to the city—up whose vista you can see many of the principal Brooklyn buildings, particularly the square squatty tower of St. Ann's Church. Away to the left lies the Navy Yard, and the great Dry Dock, now nearly finished. Then Williamsburgh, another place of beauty. She too, has her high banks, and they show admirably from the river.

On the other side our eyes behold a still more varied scene. Governor's Island, in shape like a well proportioned wart, looks green even at this season of the year; and those straight, regularly planted poplars are in perfect accordance with the military character of the place. Far to the distance is Staten Island, and the Jersey shore. The Battery Point is hidden by the masts of the shipping.

A moving panorama is upon all parts of the waters. Sail craft and steamboats are in every direction. Observe, too, the dexterity with which our pilot plies between the crowd that cross his way. He can shave by, to the verge of a hair. He makes all allowances for the strength of the tide, and "brings her in" at the appointed time, as a fine rider manages a well-trained horse.

Nor should we omit to mention a good point connected with the management of these boats. Each one has a respectable person, elderly and staid, who keeps things strait, and acts, when there may be need, as chevalier to the ladies. My old friends, Mr. Doxsey and Mr. Van Duyne are in this department.

Soon, now, will come the time for big cakes of ice in the river. We have a fondness for crossing then,—particularly when we have to go "all the way round Robin Hood's barn." Why, bless your soul! in our day, we have

350

taken a forced trip, and a merry one, round Governor's Island, between starting from Brooklyn and arriving at New York; filling up time enough, in clear sailing, to go from New York to Poughkeepsie. It is now several winters since the ice has been so "fixed," as to permit crossing the East River on foot. We remember such things, however, and have, on our own legs, done that feat of courage. We came marvellously near taking a trip down the day, however, for the ice got dislodged again and was moving maliciously off—leaving us just time, by hard "scrouging," to hop on the end of a certain pier, with the determination never again to trust our flesh on a mass of congealed water.

There is another favorite time we have for crossing at the Fulton Ferry. It is when a heavy fog spreads itself. We like to start out, and listen to the muffled tolling of the bell in the distance, and go prowling slowly along, with divers men on the look-out for breakers. We are not sure but we enjoy a bit—just a *little bit*, of danger—nothing, of course, that would give us the chance of taking to the cold water, but just a spice of excitement. After some time, we come out, perhaps, near the Catherine Ferry. Then the nervousness of those who are in a great hurry—merchants wanting to get to their business, clerks, and people who have engagements that they fear will have to be broken.

There is "a great deal of human nature," to be seen in crossing the Fulton Ferry. All imaginable sorts and styles of rational and irrational life, besides a variety of manufactured matter, transmits itself there, from one shore to the other. We like too, to cross at night, when there is a clear sky; always feeling sorry that the jaunt isn't ten times as long. Yes, yes; for some of the nicest of the "happy ten minutes" that glitter in one's experience, have we been indebted to the Fulton Ferry.

Fortunately for our nerves, we have never yet seen a serious accident on this great passage line. It is sickening, though, what things do sometimes happen here! A fellow in his haste, jumps *at* the landing, from the incoming boat—misses his footing!—slips!—O, horrible!—falls between the steam-moved mass, and the solid timbers of the wharf! Stout faces, then, grow ashy, and the bravest are appalled! But the hands attached to the boat, spring to the rescue. What they do, depends upon the circumstances of the case; but they always act promptly, effectively, and for the best.

We notice there is much talk, just at present, of *a Bridge* to Brooklyn. Nonsense. There is no need of a bridge, while there are incessantly plying such boats as the Manhattan, the Wyandance, and the Montauk. If there be

351

any spare energy, let it be applied to improving the indifferent accommodations at Catherine ferry, and the wretchedness of that at Jackson street. Also, to completing the proposed lines from the bottoms of Montague street and Bridge street.

PAUMANOK

Number XI

SOME DIMINUENDOS (ORIGINAL,) PICKED UP DURING INTERMISSIONS OF TRAVEL, OR WHILE "WAITING FOR THE BOAT"

[6 Jan. 1850]

TESTS OF TRAVELLERS.—You may know an Englishman of whom there is always a good proportion in our public conveyances—by his brusque and vacant air—sovereignly indifferent to the fact of any one's existence, near by, except his own. The German is generally unaffected, and, though never officious, is always good-humored, and responds to any call on his civility. Frenchmen are more gratuitously polite. The highly bred Irishman, and the educated American seem to me the pinks of travellers. Women invariably have a better travelling behavior than men.

A WELL-KNOWN FACT EXPLAINED.—It is acknowledged that in the United States people get rich faster than in any other country. It is calculated by some statistician that there are eleven millions of Advertisements published annually in the American newspapers. Isn't the second fact a satisfactory explanation of the first?

THE LAW'S DELAY.—Over two hundred cases are on the docket of the Supreme Court of the United States, at Washington. The Court decides about thirty cases, annually, on an average; while from fifty to seventy new ones ask audience of it every year.

PARIS NEWSPAPERS.—We make the following extract from the letter of a friend—a practical "type," now in the French capital:
"Cheap newspapers are now common in Paris. There are thirty dailies. Unfortunately the publishing business is very insecure; if you say anything

the government dislikes, your forms are knocked into pi, and your press pitched in the street."

SOMETHING OF A CUSTOMER.—England, during the last twenty-seven years, has paid the United States over Fifteen Hundred Millions of Dollars, for the single article of Cotton.

COUSINLY SPITE.—A well-known attack upon America in the *Foreign Quarterly Review*, supposed to be from Charles Dickens, asserts that—

"The ruling maxim of the life of Mr. Sampson Brass's father, *Suspect Every Body*, is now the dominant fashion of the Republic. On the side of the People, it sprang from their too close proximity to the election of their chief magistrate: from that of the President, it received in some sort justification and means of growth, by that too immediate contact with popular breath which dims the most stainless reputation: but it is the newspapers that, through every smallest function of the State, have made it what it is."[1]

The first charge was never made against the American people before—and will not be replied on by any body, except a very ignorant and bigoted man. Our national folly, indeed, is *too much confidence*. The prime cause of the business disarrangements which in times past have operated, and now operate to a degree over the land, is, that men have placed *a blind faith in one another*, and in institutions that, results prove, were not worthy that faith. How warmly do we receive all the eminent men who come to us from the Old World! What a long list of ridiculous capers are annually enacted in compliment to every foreign nation? We do *not* suspect;—we receive the stranger with open arms—and smile as he seats himself under the protection of our banner, and prepares to enjoy the blessings of our wide land and free government, on equal grounds with ourselves. We have thrown the doors far open, and with a generosity which no European nation parallels, we take those who come to us by the hand, not merely to bestow a *few* of our good gifts, but *all*—a voice in our elections—free chance with us for wealth and honor, and, in many cases, exemption from burdens that rest on our own shoulders.

The "close proximity," spoken of by the English writer, is one of the finest and most admirable traits of the American Government. The Englishman, we have little doubt, cannot see its beauty.

NEW AMERICAN AUTHORESS.—Mrs. Emma D. M. Southworth, (whose novel of "Retribution" was published a few months ago by the Harpers,) is a new American authoress, of unusual native grace and vigor. With a very little more practice, and the exercise of—what is perhaps hard to a female writer—*condensation*, she will take rank among the best literary women of the land.[2]

INSANITY.—It is a curious fact in reference to the insane, that each of that unfortunate class appears to be sane upon some points. Is it not equally a fact, with reference to those we call sane, that each appears to be *insane* upon some point?

CANADA.—A writer in a Washington print argues that if Canada should be annexed to the United States, the runaway slaves from the South would be hunted up and returned, according to "the compromises of the constitution." The idea is consistent with law, perhaps; and yet we wouldn't give a dime for all the wool and ivory that comes back from the north in the way mentioned.

LOCALITIES OF THE SENSE OF TASTE.—Writers upon such subjects say that the perception, to the taste, of *sweet*, lies at the edges of the tongue—of *bitter*, at its root—and of *sour*, or acids, at the tip. This may be all true enough, but it is a curious theory; any one, however, can test it for himself.

NEW THEORY OF DREAMS.—The old theory of Dreams is, that the faculty or tendency most active during waking hours, continues to operate on the subject after he falls asleep and dreams. A modern physiologist, however, argues that the dreamer is generally under the control of organs that have not been exercised enough in the day, and which seize an opportunity to make it up when the Lord of the Palace of the Mind nods upon his throne.[3]

YOUTH OF LIFE, ON THE YOUTH OF THE DAY AND THE YEAR.—"How glorious," (so ran the thoughts in the heart of an intellectual boy,) "How glorious appears the earth, of a fine spring morning! I am but in the beginning of life, and my heart has not lost its sympathy with the cheerful and bright in nature. Then there is—for there *must be*—so much to make a man happy on earth; there is love, there is enjoyment. One should pluck only the pleasant branches; what need of taking the ill-favored thorns?"

How many thousands of boys have had such trains of imaginings—as they stood, eager, cheerful, and confident, on the portals of manhood! How many thousands of men have looked back on such thoughts—some with smiles, some with sorrow, some with anger. But all have looked back with that compassion one feels for one's own unreasonable vagaries.[4]

NOTES

CHAPTER 1

1. The daily press of Manhattan joined Long Island weeklies in covering Webster's tour. The Whigs had used "Locofoco" as a derisive epithet since 1835.

2. The ballad stanza is from J. O. Terry, *Poems* (New York, 1850), p. 95. Terry claimed that his songs and satires illustrated "the manners and customs of the ancient and present inhabitants of Long Island."

3. The obituary notice of Major Cornelius Van Velsor appeared in the *Democrat*, 7 August 1839: "Died at Cold Spring, on the 3rd inst. . . . aged about 80 years." This is two years later than the date given in genealogies. The Trent Collection at Duke University contains the "democratic and heretical" tag. It is reprinted in Clarence Gohdes and Rollo G. Silver, *Faint Clews & Indirections* (Durham, N.C.: Duke University Press, 1949), p. 46.

4. *Democrat*, 29 September 1840.

5. *Huntington Town Records*, ed. Charles R. Street (Huntington, N.Y., 1887); *Records of the First Church in Huntington* (Huntington, N.Y., 1899); Katherine Molinoff, *Some Notes on Whitman's Family* (Brooklyn, 1941).

6. Robert C. Murray, *Fish-Shape Paumanok* (Philadelphia: American Philosophical Society, 1964).

7. Whitman kept at hand Benjamin F. Thompson's account in *The History of Long Island* (New York, 1843), 1: 214–26. In the Brooklyn *Times*, 3 July 1857, Whitman concluded that the battle had "more momentous results" than any other fought upon the American continent. In the extended editorial campaign to build a monument to the men who had been imprisoned in the hulks anchored a few rods offshore, he often itemized British transgressions. At the Broadway in February 1849, one of his friends, C. Edwards Lester, staged *Kate Woodhull*, a play which followed the popular interpretation of Woodhull's death. A recent historian, W. H. Sabine, suggests that Woodhull defected and that his fatal wound was self-inflicted.

8. Timothy Dwight, *Travels in New England and New York* (New Haven, 1822), 2: 314.

9. Along with his father's attitude toward deism, the son recorded his own praise of Paine's "most precious service" to the "embryo Union" in *Specimen Days*. See *Prose Works, 1892*, ed. Floyd Stovall (New York: New York University Press, 1963), 1: 140–42.

10. The Van Velsor name appears in Huntington records by 1745. Whitman took pride in the fact that the heritage of the famous publishers, the Harper brothers, paralleled his own. Joseph Harper, a Long Island farmer and carpenter, had also married a Dutch girl.

11. William Cobbett, *A Year's Residence in the United States of America* (New York, 1818), p. 228.

12. See Shelley's "Sonnet: England in 1819" and "The Mask of Anarchy." In New Hampshire the father of Horace Greeley lost the family farm; in Manhattan the Society of Tammany issued an *Address* that condemned bankers and called the nation an "overgrown and pampered youth . . . vaulting and bounding to ruin."

CHAPTER 2

1. With their editorial penchant for reminiscence, the Long Island (later Brooklyn) *Star* and the Brooklyn *Eagle* provide descriptions that supplement Ralph H. Weld, *Brooklyn Village, 1816–1834* (New York: Columbia University Press, 1938). Among the village leaders was Adrian Van Sinderen. In time his family would bequeath a Whitman collection to Yale University.

2. *Eagle*, 4 June 1846.

3. Two survivors, Freneau in "The British Prison Ship" and Thomas Dring in *Recollections of the Jersey Prison Ship* (Providence, R.I., 1829), reported the horrors of the hulks. Whitman, who read Dring, later memorialized "The Wallabout Martyrs" as "The stepping stones to thee . . . America."

4. *Star*, 7 July 1825; Walt Whitman, *Lafayette in Brooklyn* (New York, 1905). Two lists of books placed in the library survive: *Catalogue of Books Belonging to the Brooklyn Apprentices Library Association*, 1828 and 1842. The lines are from Joseph Rodman Drake's "To a Friend," New York *Mirror*, 3 March 1832.

5. Frances Wright, *Views of Society and Manners in America*, ed. Paul R. Baker (Cambridge, Mass.: Harvard University Press, 1963). Moving from praise of the American government, statesmen, and the "lord of the wilderness," Daniel Boone, the *Views* ended harshly: "The sight of slavery is revolting everywhere, but to inhale the impure breath of its pestilence in the free winds of America is odious beyond all that the imagination can conceive."

6. Lancaster had received an enthusiastic welcome during his visit to New York in 1820. The description of Whitman's elementary school appeared in the *Star*, 30 March 1831, and is reprinted in Florence B. Freedman, *Walt Whitman Looks at the Schools* (New York: King's Crown Press, 1950).

7. *Walt Whitman's Diary in Canada*, ed. William S. Kennedy (Boston, 1904). Whitman also attended Sunday school at the Dutch Reformed church.

8. Whitman in his essay on Hicks in *November Boughs* used *The Journal of the Life and the Religious Labours of Elias Hicks* (New York, 1832). See *Prose Works, 1892*, ed. Floyd Stovall (New York: New York University Press, 1963), 2: 626–53. See also *Letters of Elias Hicks* (Philadelphia, 1861); Bliss Forbush, *Elias Hicks, Quaker Liberal* (New York: Columbia University Press, 1956). Moncure Conway believed that Paine rose again in Hicks; the press often linked the two in eulogies or assaults. Though the presence of the Friend and his doctrines remained with Whitman, we shall see that in maturity he moved in one phase far beyond Hicks' position by frequent avowals of love for Christ.

9. Not often given to enthusiasm, Mrs. Trollope in *Domestic Manners of the Americans* (New York, 1832), p. 73, described Frances Wright on the lecture platform: "It is impossible to imagine anything more striking than her appearance. Her tall and majestic figure, the deep and almost solemn expression of her eyes, the simple contour of her finely formed head, unadorned, excepting by its own natural ringlets; her garment of plain white muslin, which hung around her in folds that recalled the drapery of a Grecian statue, all contributed to produce an effect unlike anything I have ever seen before, or ever expect to see again." Revealing letters sent by Frances Wright to newspapers in self-defense (for example, to *The Workingman's Advocate*, 30 June 1830) span all her visits to America; they remain uncollected.

10. In the *Free Enquirer* he found tributes to Paine and Hicks. The title reflects Godwin's influential *Enquiry Concerning Political Justice*.

11. Constantin Volney, who visited America on a colonizing mission, had earned his reputation as a historian with a two-volume study of Egypt and Syria. He then became secretary of the National Assembly and a senator under Napoleon. First published in France in 1791, *Les Ruines, ou Méditation des Empires* excited Jefferson into beginning a translation, but Joel Barlow, an intimate friend of Volney, completed that task. A New York edition became available to the Whitmans in 1828. Shelley admired *Les Ruines* (so did Lincoln), but in Timothy Dwight's judgment reading it made a man "an absolute profligate."

The *Free Enquirer* library sold Godwin, Paine, and Mary Wollstonecraft's *Rights of Woman*.

12. Walter Hugins, *Jacksonian Democracy and the Working Class: A Study of the New York Workingmen's Movement, 1829–1837* (Stanford, Calif.: Stanford University Press, 1960).

13. *Eagle*, 11 October 1847. Coleridge thought that his mind became "habituated to the Vast" through his reading of the *Arabian Nights*.

CHAPTER 3

1. Whitman included the Hartshorne reminiscence in the 28 May installment of a series that he wrote for the Brooklyn *Advertiser* in 1850. Murphy was admitted to the Bar in 1833 and became a partner in John A. Lott's firm. By 1848 both men, political powers in city and state, led the Hunker opposition to Whitman, now the Free Soil editor of the Brooklyn *Eagle*. Accounts of apprentice experiences appear in Horace Greeley, *Recollections of a Busy Life* (New York, 1868); M. W. Hamilton, *The Country Printer, New York State, 1785–1830* (New York: Columbia University Press, 1936).

2. The Sands Street ministry returned to Whitman's memory years later with the aftermath of notoriety that followed charges of immorality caused by Maffitt's second marriage.

3. "The panic became great," observed Finney, "and many Christian people fled into the country." Charles G. Finney, *Memoirs* (New York, 1878), p. 321. One of the characters in Harold Frederic's *The Damnation of Theron Ware* observed that the cholera epidemic created Methodists "hand over fist."

4. The American response to the death of Scott was tantamount to a period of national mourning. New Yorkers met at the Stock Exchange and pledged funds for a monument.

5. James F. Beard, the editor of Cooper's *Letters and Journals* (Cambridge, Mass.: Harvard University Press, 1960), notes that the press often insulted Cooper through animal images: a tomcat, bulldog, tiger, a salamander at home in the fire of controversy, a trout rising to newspaper flies. See also *Memoirs of James Gordon Bennett, By a Journalist* (New York, 1855).

6. The humorist, Major Jack Downing, boasted of the "capital fun" on the tour as Jackson received thanks for "presarvin the Union." In New York Van Buren and Governor William Marcy rode with Jackson. This symbolic alliance of national hero and Albany Regency seemed to proclaim the invincibility of the Democratic party.

7. Spooner's *Star*, an autobiographical essay in the Long Island Historical Society, and the other Brooklyn papers, including Whitman's Brooklyn *Eagle*, contain biographical material.

8. *Eagle*, 27 November 1847. *The Last Days of Pompeii* was one of several melodramas written for Hamblin by Louisa Medina.

9. Whitman's "The Old Bowery" in *November Boughs* is but one of his frequent accounts of Manhattan theatricals. William Leggett, the editor and drama reviewer for *The Critic*, was a friend of Forrest. See also Richard Moody, *Edwin Forrest* (New York: Knopf, 1960); Floyd Stovall, "Whitman and the Dramatic Stage," *Studies in Philology* (July 1953), pp. 513–39. Whatever Forrest's limitations, he sponsored playwriting contests and acted in the prize winners. None of them was a masterpiece. To untangle the plot of *Metamora*, a critic said, became as difficult as discovering perpetual motion, but in it an American writer used indigenous material and evoked sympathy for an exploited race. As a result of exacting study and careful production Forrest did more than any other native actor to honor Shakespeare's texts and spread vital interpretation throughout the land.

10. J. K. Paulding, in a letter to T. W. White of the *Southern Literary Messenger* in July 1834, wrote, "I want to see something wholesome, natural, and national. The best thing a young American writer can do, is to forget that any body ever wrote before him; and above all things, that there are such caterpillars as critics in this world." Ralph M. Aderman, ed., *The Letters of James Kirke Paulding* (Madison: University of Wisconsin Press, 1962), p. 149.

11. Jay Leyda, *The Melville Log* (New York: Harcourt Brace, 1951), 1: 72. Melville's uncle gave him J. Orville Taylor's *The District School* (New York, 1834), to help him manage thirty charges. Whitman may also have found this guide useful.

12. The minutes of the debates are reprinted in Katherine Molinoff, *An Unpublished Whitman Manuscript: The Record of the Smithtown Debating Society, 1837–38* (Brooklyn, 1941).

NOTES

1. Freneau's stanza is from "Occasioned by a Legislation Bill Proposing a Taxation upon Newspapers." The *Mirror* on 9 June 1838 described the common editorial formula that filled American newspapers: horrid accident; outrage; look to your doors; new works; steamboat explosion; attack on rival editors.

2. *Specimen Days*, in *Prose Works, 1892*, ed. Floyd Stovall (New York: New York University Press, 1963), 1: 287. The *Knickerbocker* magazine for July 1850, pp. 108–09, gave a rhapsodic description of Huntington with its white houses, flowers, wood laurel, tree-lined roads, its 170–year-old church, and its cemetery with stones broken by cannon balls fired during the Revolution. John Burroughs in *Whitman* (Boston, 1901), p. 28, quotes two Huntington men who remembered the young editor "brimful of life, reveling in strength, careless of time and the world, of money and of toil; a lover of books and jokes."

3. *Long Islander*, 12 July 1839; *Farmer*, 17 July 1839.

4. *The Critic* ran from 1 November 1828 to 2 May 1829. Leggett sought to follow the epigraph he chose from Johnson: "All truth is valuable; and criticism may be considered as useful when it rectifies error, and improves judgment; he who refines the public taste is a public benefactor." America, Leggett insisted, would continue to have "nondescript polylogues" rather than a powerful national drama as long as it abided by the judgment of English critics.

5. William F. Byrdsall, the secretary, published *The History of the Locofoco or Equal Rights Party* (New York, 1842).

6. The essays in *The Plaindealer*, 1836–1837, as individual in their tone as those in *The Critic*, provide the essence of Leggett's political philosophy. "There can be no surer test of the purity of our conduct," he told maligners, "than the offence it gives to the class of persons who have expressed their censure."

7. Theodore Sedgwick, Jr., ed., *A Collection of the Political Writings of William Leggett* (New York, 1840). Bryant and Whittier joined Sedgwick in writing biographical sketches of Leggett. Among more recent studies is Richard Hofstadter's "William Leggett, Spokesman of Jacksonian Democracy," *Political Science Quarterly* (December 1943), pp. 581–94.

8. *Democrat*, 18 September 1839.

9. *Democrat*, 4 September 1839. On 16 October Whitman continued his definition of "true democracy" by calling it a system which sought "the advancement of our great cause, and not of individuals. . . . The people's benefit—the progress of popular rights —and a politick and prudent administration of our government—make our bond of union and the base of our strength."

10. *Democrat*, 6 November 1839.

11. Maurice Bucke believed in addition that Whitman attended the Jamaica Academy "when a big lad." *Walt Whitman* (Philadelphia, 1883), p. 22.

12. Nine of the "Sun-Down" pieces have been recovered. See Emory Holloway, ed., *Uncollected Poetry and Prose* (New York, 1921), 1: 32–51; Herbert Bergman and

William White, "Walt Whitman's Lost 'Sun-Down Papers,' Nos. 1–3," *American Book Collector* (January 1970), pp. 17–20.

13. Brenton prefaced Whitman's "Card" with the statement that "we cannot but think the public will be glad to be convinced, in so spirited a manner, that threats and bravado are not to be allowed to stop freedom of speech."

14. *Plebeian*, 14 October 1842.

CHAPTER 5

1. Lydia M. Child, *Letters from New York* (New York, 1843), p. 13.

2. Orestes Brownson, "American Literature," *Boston Quarterly Review* (January 1839), pp. 1–21. His remarks came in response to Emerson's lecture on "Literary Ethics" and were designed to refute the assertion that the creation of literature depended "entirely" on the individual will. In Brownson's view, literature was "the expression and embodiment of the national life. Its character is not determined by this man or that, but by the national spirit." He also contributed to the *Free Enquirer* and the *Democratic Review*.

3. Gulian Verplanck's copyright bill, enacted in 1831, merely secured American literary property for twenty-eight years, with a renewal privilege for the same period. Reciprocal international protection would not become law until after the Berne Convention of 1887. Emerson in *English Traits* quoted an Englishman: "As long as you do not grant us copyright, we shall have the teaching of you." See also John W. Ostrom, ed., *The Letters of Edgar Allan Poe* (Cambridge, Mass.: Harvard University Press, 1948), 1: 164; Sidney P. Moss, *Poe's Literary Battles* (Durham, N.C.: Duke University Press, 1963); Eugene Exman, *The Brothers Harper* (New York: Harper and Row, 1965).

4. See Merle M. Hoover, *Park Benjamin* (New York: Columbia University Press, 1948).

5. Brooklyn *Eagle*, 6 April 1847. The *Herald* on 30 July carried the fullest report of the speech. In the crowd that day was Samuel E. Johnson of Brooklyn; some years later he helped Whitman start *The Freeman*.

6. O'Sullivan's leadership of the crusade to end capital punishment is described more fully in a later chapter. He was of course not the only Democratic leader who held aloof from attacking slavery. Benjamin F. Butler in the campaign of 1840 even boasted of the opposition of the party to abolitionism and insisted that Harrison's favoring of abolitionism had led him to the Whig nomination.

7. As early as November 1839 "The Great Nation of Futurity" in the *Review* expressed faith in "our high destiny." Later, in the 1840s, the phrase became "manifest destiny." The very first paper in the magazine, in October 1837, spoke of the need to apply the democratic principle to both politics and literature. Later numbers aligned the literature of American democracy against that of English feudalism, and by August 1842 had added a theological tenet: "The sincerest Christian should be the firmest democrat."

8. O'Sullivan helped to start the New York *Morning News* in 1844. In effect he then competed with Whitman, editor of the New York *Democrat*.

9. *Brother Jonathan*, 9 September 1843. Mathews' *The Career of Puffer Hopkins* was published in 1842. The *Brother Jonathan* also carried poetry by Ferdinand Freiligrath. Thirty years later he translated Whitman into German.

10. John Neal, *American Writers*, ed. Fred L. Pattee (Durham, N.C.: Duke University Press, 1937), pp. 89–90; John Neal, *Wandering Recollections of a Somewhat Busy Life* (Boston, 1869). His "What Is Poetry?" appeared in the *Union*, January 1849.

11. When the *Brother Jonathan* printed "My Departure" on 11 March 1843, this editorial note prefaced the poem: "The following wants but a half-hour's polish to make of it an effusion of very uncommon beauty."

James Nack's "The Lonely Heart," circulated by Leggett, illustrates the ultimate scope of popular maudlinity:

> I had a father—he is dead!
> A mother—she no more is mine!
> A sister—on her grave I tread!
> And brothers—they in death recline!
> I had a friend—he rent the tie!
> I had a loved one—ruthless fate!
> What is she now? And what am I?
> Oh God! this heart is desolate!

12. *Brother Jonathan*, 26 February 1842, pp. 243–44. The weekly retained a witty equilibrium during the frenzy that surrounded the tour: "Will he write a book?" an editorial asked. "We hope so. . . . We have been trolloped—let us be bozzed."

13. New York *Aurora*, 2 April 1842. Neal called Bennett "the worst and most dangerous man who has ever had charge of a newspaper in this or any other country. We impute to his villainous course much of the crime that has disgraced this city."

14. Dickens in *Martin Chuzzlewit* showed his contempt for the Bennett style through his characterizations of Colonel Diver, editor of the *Rowdy Journal*, and Jefferson Brick, his war correspondent. The novelist titled the other Manhattan papers the *Sewer*, the *Stabber*, the *Family Spy*, the *Peeper*, the *Plunderer*, and the *Keyhole Reporter*.

CHAPTER 6

1. Charles Lyell, *Travels in North America, in the Years 1841–42* (New York, 1845). Joseph Jay Rubin and Charles H. Brown, in *Walt Whitman of the New York Aurora* (State College, Pa.: Bald Eagle Press, 1950), reprinted editorials and news paragraphs from the rare file of surviving material. By 1842 some thirty daily and weekly newspapers were being published in Manhattan.

2. Thomas L. Nichols, *Forty Years of American Life* (New York, 1874). *The Con-*

servator in July 1901 carried William Cauldwell's reminiscences of his time as a young journeyman in the *Aurora* shop. *Hamlet* was misquoted: "And crook the pregnant hinges of the knee/ Where thrift may follow fawning." In the years since the Whitman family had moved from Suffolk, the alien population of metropolitan New York had jumped from eleven per cent to thirty-five per cent.

3. *Aurora*, 9 April 1842; Brooklyn *Eagle*, 30 March 1842.

4. Dickens found that Americans pursued lectures as avidly as though they were concerts and balls.

5. Emerson's series of lectures on "The Times" included "Introductory," 3 March; "The Poet," 5 March; "The Conservative," 7 March; "The Transcendentalist," 9 March; "Manners," 12 March; and "Prospects," 14 March. Greeley and Bryant also reported each lecture in depth, but Bennett held aloof: "Emerson is a young man of very respectable talent. . . . He has not yet found out the nature and source of all of the evils of which he complains."

6. Clarke had come to Manhattan from his birthplace in Bath, Maine; he ended his impoverished existence on 5 March 1842. Nichols, in the belief that all "the Archangel of the Almighty" needed to be immortalized was a sympathetic audience, had published twelve of Clarke's poems in the *Aurora*, though he found them "difficult to unravel as a skein of tangled gold." Whitman, like his predecessor, knew Clarke and recoiled at the callousness of the final prank played upon him—the unfulfilled promise of a rendezvous with a beautiful woman.

7. William O. Bourne, *History of the Public School Society of the City of New York* (New York, 1891); John R. Hassard, *Life of the Most Reverend John Hughes, D.D.* (New York, 1866); Louis D. Scisco, *Political Nativism in New York State* (New York: Columbia University Press, 1901); E. M. Connors, *Church–State Relationships in Education in the State of New York* (Washington, D.C.: Catholic University Press, 1951).

8. The press reported every phase of the controversy in Manhattan and Albany. The diaries of Mayor Philip Horne and George Templeton Strong and the journals of Charles Lyell also reflected the bitter mood. On 15 November 1841, Lyell noted that "In New York the Roman Catholic priests have recently agitated with no small success for a separate allotment of their share of the education fund. They have allied themselves, as in the Belgian revolution, with the extreme democracy to carry their point, and may materially retard the general progress of education."

Governor Seward, in commiserating with Bishop Hughes, said that "philanthropic conceptions for the improvement of society come in conflict with existing interests founded in existing prejudices." According to a witness at the Chicago convention in 1860, Seward's sympathy for the education of Catholic children may have cost him the Republican presidential nomination, for the issue was revived there "afresh as a danger signal." Alexander K. McClurg, *Recollections of Half a Century* (Salem, Mass., 1902), pp. 212–19.

9. Virtually every issue of the *Aurora* in March and April contained editorial opinion on the proposed law.

10. The Sunday *News* and the Sunday *Mercury* accused Whitman of Nativism. On 18 April he denied having this bias. In the *Aurora*, as later in the *Eagle*, he quoted

Jefferson on "the absolute and lasting severance of the church from the state," but some of his press contemporaries refused to accept this as his philosophical source and insisted that he was intolerant. So far as I have been able to discover, Bishop Hughes blamed Bennett rather than Whitman for serving as the "fountain of all the vituperation, calumny, and slander." But on 29 March 1842, the *Herald* insisted that though it was not a friend of Bishop Hughes, it could not approve "the gross, beastly, shocking attacks" in "certain newly established" papers. These "are unjustifiable, barbarous." Later the *Herald* identified Whitman as the attacker. Meanwhile *The Journal of Commerce* was also hurling epithets on behalf of the Protestants.

11. *Aurora*, 3 May, 16 May 1842. Whitman cited the transfer of Herrick's allegiance to Tyler as the main cause of his departure from the *Aurora*; a month earlier Whitman had called Bennett a pimp for accepting Tyler's patronage. In the *Star*, on 6 January 1845, he lamented the fatal hour when the *Aurora* withdrew from the "bright circle" of fashionable society, "of which it was the cynosure, and became lost in the storm and darkness of Tylerism."

12. *Aurora*, 29 August 1842.

13. *Atlas*, 1 July 1860.

CHAPTER 7

1. The *Atlas*, 26 June 1853, described the operation of the *Tatler*. Copy from the daily paper was transferred to the Sunday *Times* until the publishers sold their shop to Major Noah, who joined his *Messenger* to the *Times*. "It then began to improve in character and circulation." See also Thomas O. Mabbott, "Walt Whitman Edits the Sunday *Times*: July, 1842–June, 1843," *American Literature* (March 1967), pp. 99–102.

2. "A Legend of Life and Love" had the widest popularity, with reprinting in the *Brother Jonathan*, the *Tribune*, the *Sun*, and the *Democrat*, as late as 7 August 1849. "Death in the School–Room" was reprinted in papers as varied as the *Brother Jonathan* and the *Farmer*. The one tale that received qualified praise was "The Angel of Tears." The *Tribune* thought it "betrays a good, healthy tone of thought and feeling, but is decidedly inferior in point of grace and taste to previous papers by the same author" (3 September 1842).

3. Sophia Hawthorne told friends that her husband could not afford to send O'Sullivan anything except short stories. Poe was dismayed when he learned that contributors to the *Review* earned two dollars a page, a dollar under the average, but as he knew too well, many publishers paid nothing.

4. The *Herald* gave no reason for its failure to print the sketches and engravings.

5. Noah joined Whitman in praising Slamm for mild temper, gentle manners, and pure intentions. Indeed the *Plebeian*, during the time of Whitman's association with it, reflected the idealism of the editorial motto: "As long as any of the race are miserable, none can be truly happy."

6. Godwin was Bryant's son-in-law, and had worked as one of the editors of the

Evening Post. His fine essay on Shelley in the *Democratic Review*, December 1843, pointed out the poet's meliorative concept of poetic function, while the prospectus of his *Pathfinder*, started that year to help find both cause and cure of social misery, explained that its editor intended to espouse simple principles: "They may be expressed in the words Freedom and Progress." Richard Henry Dana, Jr., on a visit to Manhattan in February 1844, dined with Godwin and found him "a man of strong mind, but a hopeless radical in all his notions." Robert F. Lucid, ed., *The Journal of Richard Henry Dana, Jr.* (Cambridge, Mass.: Harvard University Press, 1968), 1: 234.

7. There is much stark evidence of the vast quantity of "souls in soak" in the nineteenth century. J. B. Durand, in *The Life and Times of A. B. Durand* (New York, 1894), reported "drunken lawyers, drunken doctors, drunken ministers, drunkards of all stages" (p. 11). Lawyers seemed especially derelict, as indicated by the witticism of "practitioners at more than one bar." Gerrit Smith testified that in his village of Peterboro, New York, the proportion of drunkards was higher than one man in two. The traveller H. B. Fearon, in *Sketches of America* (London, 1819), found that the quantity of malt liquor and spirits drunk by New Yorkers "much exceeds the amount consumed by the same extent of English population" (pp. 27–29). As early as 1815 a Brooklyn group attempted to suppress drunkenness on the Sabbath. By 1829 the village had its temperance society; the Reverend McIlvaine of St. Ann's was aided that year by a former associate of Beecher at Litchfield, Daniel Carroll.

8. Mason Weems in *The Drunkard's Looking Glass*, circulated by tract societies, listed "Golden Receipts Against Drunkenness": "Drink no longer water, but use a *little* wine for their stomach's sake. Also, cyder, ale, beer, etc." Weems recognized social and business pressures: "Never marry but for love. Hate is repellent; and the husband saunters to the tavern. . . . Debts and duns have filled the world with sots." The quantity of tracts increased each year; in 1833 two million copies of a sermon by the Reverend Eli Merill circulated.

9. *Brother Jonathan*, 11 June 1842. For views of the Washingtonians see John B. Gough, *Platform Echoes* (Hartford, Conn., 1884); W. H. Hawkins, *The Life of John Hawkins* (Boston, 1862); John Marsh, *Temperance Recollections* (New York, 1866). This was the Washingtonian pledge: "We whose names are annexed, desirous of forming a society for our mutual benefit, and to guard against a pernicious practice which is injurious to our health, standing and families, do pledge ourselves as gentlemen, that we will not drink any spiritous or malt liquors, wine or cider."

10. The fault may have been Whitman's since the twentieth chapter is a reverie of wandering "through the cities of a mighty and populous empire," and seems to belong after the next chapter. Thomas L. Brasher has provided an accurate text of *Franklin Evans* in his edition of *The Early Poems and the Fiction* (New York: New York University Press, 1963).

11. *Aurora*, 21 March 1842.

12. All these reviews appeared during the last week of November and proved to be profitable. Years later Whitman told Horace Traubel that the book sold so well that "they sent me fifty dollars more in two or three weeks."

13. *Herald*, 27 November 1842.

NOTES

14. Emory Holloway, "More Temperance Tales by Whitman," *American Literature* (January 1956), pp. 577–78.
15. *Herald*, 4 July 1843.
16. Whitman reprinted *Franklin Evans* in the Brooklyn *Eagle* under the title of *Fortunes of a Country-Boy; Incidents in Town—and his Advetures at the South.*

CHAPTER 8

1. Kennedy's *Quodlibet*, published in 1840, is a witty attack by a prominent, literate Whig upon the conduct of Jacksonians during the 1830s. The novel examines the withdrawal of the deposits, the war on Biddle, the depression, and the Independent Treasury.
2. *Aurora*, 11 March 1842.
3. *Aurora*, 24 March 1842. As editor of the Brooklyn *Eagle* during the quickening furor over free soil, Whitman began to resent Calhoun's "ardent advocacy" of southern interests "above all else."
4. *Aurora*, 12 March 1843.
5. Whitman wrote about Fellows in his essay "In Memory of Thomas Paine," in *Specimen Days*. See *Prose Works, 1892*, ed. Floyd Stovall (New York: New York University Press, 1963), 1: 140–41. Moncure Conway, in *Life of Thomas Paine* (New York, 1892), 2: 422–23, reports more of Whitman's comments on Fellows. While working with Vale on the Paine biography that was published in 1841, Fellows also wrote the preface to an edition of Paine's works.
6. In 1843 the Spartan Association compiled *Sketches of the Speeches and Writings of Michael Walsh: Including his Poems and Correspondence*. In one of his letters "the champion of the shirtless" also named himself "the greatest and purest reformer of the age." Walsh vowed hostility toward "every species of Usurpation, Tyranny, Oppression, and, especially, Monopoly." Whitman some fifteen years later wrote his obituary. Losing power and office, Walsh became a drunkard, fell one night, and died of a broken neck (Brooklyn *Times*, 18 March 1859).
7. Elliot B. Gross, " 'Lesson of the Two Symbols,' An Undiscovered Whitman Poem," *Walt Whitman Review* (December 1966), pp. 77–80.
8. *Sun*, 7 September 1843. Other papers reported that Saunders spent time in the Tombs reading books on banking and currency!
9. The *Herald* refused to side with the *Tribune* and the *Post*, joining Senator Walker and other annexationists. On 1 May Bennett wrote, "It is our firm conviction—that sooner or later, not only Mexico, but Canada, Oregon, and all, will be absorbed in the mighty bosom of the North American Republic. It is destiny." But Channing called Tyler a Guy Fawkes: "To think that a President of this Republic should have gone haggling and begging to those ungrateful robbers, who stole a Mexican province, that he might induce them to share with this country their booty."

10. *Evening Post*, 18 July 1844; *Plebeian*, 17 October 1844. The biographers of Silas Wright seem to have been unaware of the extent of Whitman's involvement in this gubernatorial campaign.

11. *Tribune*, 19 July 1844.

12. On 3 April 1847, the Brooklyn *Advertiser* dared anyone to deny "that the editor of the *Eagle* was a Whig some few seasons before he was hired to write locofoco editorials for the *Eagle*." On 5 April the paper demanded to know his allegiance in the summer of 1841 and whether he did not later bitterly oppose the nomination of Silas Wright to be governor. The next day Whitman refuted each of the charges. First he quoted from the published accounts of his speech at the mass meeting on 29 July 1841 to censure the Whigs. "As to our ever having opposed the nomination of Silas Wright," he told Brooklynites, "we were one of the instruments in the latter part of July '44, of first making his nomination, through a Democratic daily, published in New York City. . . . Silas Wright's name was kept flying at the head of a paper we edited."

As with the *Statesman*, no file of the *Democrat* survives. It is possible, however, to trace some of its history through scattered accounts by contemporaries.

13. Washington *Globe*, 6 and 10 September 1844. Whitman's editorial position here paralleled that of Slamm, whose *Plebeian* insisted that Texas should become an integral part of the republic.

14. *Niles Register*, 12 October 1844, p. 83.

15. The *Morning News* spoke of "The Lost and Found Letter" on 30 September and 7 October; the *Tribune* returned to it on 29 November.

16. *Plebeian*, 4 December 1843. These unsigned opinions match others Whitman soon published.

17. *Tribune*, 21 December 1843 and 18 January 1844. Emerson had recently given five lectures in Manhattan.

18. *Herald*, 6 and 15 August 1844; *Foreign Quarterly Review* (January 1844), pp. 291–324. Griswold's anthology, as well as volumes by Bryant, Longfellow, George Colton, and others motivated the author of the *Review* article, who began with a slur: " 'American poetry' always reminds us of the advertisements in the newspapers, headed 'The best substitute for Silver.'—if it not be the genuine thing, it 'looks just as handsome, and is miles out of sight cheaper.' " Then followed the charge that America was a refuge for convicts, derelicts, and "Pariahs of the wide earth." How could poetry "spring out of an amalgam so monstrous and revolting?" After venting wrath on most of Griswold's entries, the author extended qualified praise to Halleck, Bryant, Longfellow, Poe, and Alfred B. Street.

CHAPTER 9

1. In 1836 Rantoul gave his impressive brief to the legislature. Like Whitman, he was an ardent Democrat. See Luther Hamilton, ed., *Memoirs, Speeches and Writings of Robert Rantoul, Jr.* (Boston, 1854).

2. Leon Radzinowicz, *A History of British Criminal Law and Its Administration from*

1750 (London: Stevens, 1948–1968); David B. Davis, "The Movement to Abolish Capital Punishment in America, 1787–1861," *American Historical Review* (October 1957), pp. 23–46. American reformers often quoted Lafayette: "The punishment of death has always impressed me with sentiments of horror, since the execrable use made of it in the Revolution."

3. The hatchet murder of Helen Jewett in a brothel and the failure of the jury to return a verdict of guilty against the accused led to cynical public conclusions about the venality of the judicial system.

4. While one trial was underway Lydia Maria Child wrote to a friend, "For a fortnight past, the whole city has been kept in a state of corroding excitement, either of hope or fear." *Letters from New York* (New York, 1843), p. 223. See also Edward Livingston, *Remarks on the Expediency of Abolishing the Penalty of Death* (Philadelphia, 1831).

5. For his *Report* O'Sullivan drew upon the work of the Massachusetts reformer mentioned above, Robert Rantoul, Jr.

6. Tilden, Godwin, Augustus Graham, and many other prominent men praised O'Sullivan's *Report*, but the Reverend George B. Cheever became a vociferous opponent. This clergyman was a leader in temperance reform, but in sermons from his Allen Street pulpit and in the pamphlet *Punishment by Death: Its Authority and Expedience* (New York, 1842) insisted upon the sentence pronounced in Exodus and Leviticus.

7. "Revenge and Requital" appeared in July–August 1845; the *Morning News* reprinted it on 11–12 August. "A Dialogue" appeared in November 1845; the *Star* prefaced its reprinting on 29 November with the suggestion that "perhaps the reader may receive some new notions in the perusing of it."

8. Thomas O. Mabbott, ed., *The Half-Breed and Other Stories by Walt Whitman* (New York: Columbia University Press, 1927). The *Democratic Review* for July 1842, which carried Whitman's "A Legend of Life and Love," contained a description of Catlin's work.

9. *Broadway Journal*, 3 May 1845.

10. *Sunday Times*, 10 October 1847. Noah regretted the suspension of the *Aristidean*: "It was worthy of a better fate, some of its matter being equal to any we have read." Leggett had also turned to Luke for a poem, "The Widow's Son Raised from the Dead."

11. *Advertiser*, 5 April 1847. The first volume of the *American Review* included "The Raven," essays on Emersonian transcendentalism, and an appeal for the writing of American literature. See T. R. Rajasekharaiah, *The Roots of Whitman's Grass* (Rutherford, N.J.: Farleigh Dickinson Press, 1970) for the possible impact on Whitman of Hindu material published in the *American Review* by J. D. Whelpley.

12. *Morning News*, 31 January 1845. The *Advertiser*, 3 December 1846, claimed that Whitman had described his own earnings when he wrote the day before of "a very fair American writer who receives only five dollars a month for contributing to a certain magazine." The *Advertiser* added, "The publisher and readers of the magazine containing such 'fair' compositions are the only parties really entitled to sympathy and commiseration."

13. *New York in Slices by an Experienced Carver* (New York, 1849), p. 54. The *Herald*, in the same article referred to below, denouncing Whitman's editorship of the

Aurora, added this comment about Manhattan journalists: "There is a set of men in New York perpetually revolving about in the current of political events, like chips in an eddy of the Mississippi."

14. "Literary Life of Thingum Bob, Esq."

CHAPTER 10

1. Americans who sought to end the use of cesspools, fouled drinking water, un-regulated slaughter houses, and polluted dairies had the monumental example of two British reformers: Edwin Chadwick, who published *The Sanitary Conditions of the Labouring Population* in 1842, and John Simon, health officer of the city of London.

2. *Star*, 2 April and 10 May 1845. On 22 February 1845 the *Star* printed Harriet Beecher Stowe's "Generous Slaveholder."

3. Horace Mann, *Lectures and Annual Reports on Education* (Cambridge, Mass., 1867). His *Seventh Report*, published in 1844, became notorious when Boston teachers countered his charges with a defense of corporal punishment. For a valuable collection of Whitman's columns on education, see Florence B. Freedman, *Walt Whitman Looks at the Schools* (New York: King's Crown Press, 1950).

4. The *Hints* are also miniature reminders of the pamphlets issued by the American Tract Society to redeem sinners, such as "My Young Friend and His Cigar."

5. *Star*, 27 October 1845. Though the *Star*—as well as the influential Hamilton Literary Society—boycotted the theatre, its columns remained open to accounts of lectures on Shakespeare and to the program of the American actor Murdoch. Whitman suggested that capital could be invested in a building for the production of "musical pieces, dramatic readings, varied concerts, clever comic pieces (not regular comedies or plays), tasty pantomimes, and all kinds of vocal and instrumental harmony."

6. *Mirror*, 8 March 1845.

7. The *Star* questioned the motives of "Young America" on 30 April 1845. On 4 July Charles Sumner, in a speech at Tremont Temple, also answered those who sought a militant solution to the Oregon question: "In our age there can be no peace that is not honorable; there can be no war that is not dishonorable."

8. *Star*, 17 December 1845. The article that had angered Whitman was "English Politico-Commercial Companies."

9. There is evidence that Whitman had access to the *Eagle* before his formal inheritance of the editorship, for on 22 January the paper had reprinted his "Shirval."

CHAPTER 11

1. The files of the *Eagle*, indispensable to a study of Whitman's career, are extant. For a recent investigation see Thomas L. Brasher, *Whitman as Editor of the Brooklyn*

NOTES

Daily Eagle (Detroit: Wayne State University Press, 1970). Cleveland Rodgers and John Black published two volumes of *Eagle* editorials in *The Gathering of the Forces* (New York, 1920). For the Polk administration see Milo M. Quaife, ed., *The Diary of James K. Polk during His Presidency* (Chicago, 1910); Charles Sellers, *James K. Polk, Continentalist, 1843–1846* (Princeton, N.J.: Princeton University Press, 1966); Glenn W. Price, *Origins of the War with Mexico* (Austin: University of Texas Press, 1967).

2. The *Morning News* began to attack the political policies of the *Eagle* in October 1845 and intensified its charges until Marsh's death.

3. H. D. Donovan, *The Barnburners* (New York, 1925); Dixon R. Fox, *The Decline of the Aristocracy in the Politics of New York* (New York, 1919); and Ivor D. Spencer's biography of William L. Marcy, *The Victor and the Spoils* (Providence, R.I.: Brown University Press, 1959), trace the conflict within the Democratic party.

4. James P. Shenton, *Robert John Walker* (New York: Columbia University Press, 1961). Unlike some of the Manhattan editors Whitman persisted in praising the legislation and its chief advocate. "The Democratic Party," he wrote on 12 December 1846 despite his reservations, "owe Mr. Walker a debt of honor and gratitude for his untiring and dauntless advocacy." In some of his earlier editorials—"Shaving and Shinplasters," "The Last Kick of the Tariff Men"—he had spoken for mechanics and laborers against speculators and manufacturers. As the debate over a revived Independent Treasury intensified, he considered its passage of prime importance and on 6 November 1846 cited the determination of true Democrats to divorce state from bank. "With that measure, we stand or fall. Up or down, we will never desert it."

5. *Star*, 21 April 1846. The *Star* resented Whitman's "furious democracy" and his strenuous opposition to the Whig program of internal improvements financed by the state treasury.

6. "Gowanus," the Brooklyn correspondent for George Evans' *Young America*, filled his paragraphs with caustic inventories of the city's liabilities: "We have our Hunkers, Cliques, Clubs, and Coteries. . . . And also many of the blessed institutions of other renowned cities, such as poor houses, prisons with their paupers." He refused to support any measure to increase Brooklyn's debt, which he said would be paid "by the toil and sweat of homeless, landless labor."

7. Spencer, *The Victor and the Spoils*, p. 177; John A. Garraty, *Silas Wright* (New York: Columbia University Press, 1949). On 29 July Whitman, worried by internal strife, stressed that the *Eagle* "is committed to neither of the 'factions' which raised such a row last winter at Albany. We have a prodigious fancy for keeping the *Eagle* aloof and clear from all clique and personal influence." But by 1 September he had begun to expose Governor Wright's enemies.

8. *Eagle*, 7 November 1846. After he examined election statistics he recognized the plight of the party: Wright had received 50,000 fewer votes than in 1844.

9. Frederick von Raumer, *America and American People* (New York, 1846). Von Raumer was Professor of History at the University of Berlin. His preface established the tone of his survey: "Many at home had prophesied to me, that when I returned from the United States, I should be cured of all *favorable* prejudices, and bring with me an *unfavorable* opinion of the country and the people. How differently it turned

369

out! All the trifling disagreeableness of the journey have utterly lost their importance; while the truly great and wonderful phenomena and facts still remain like the sun-lighted peaks of the Alps, in full splendor before my eyes."

10. In the first weeks of his editorship, in "Illy Paid Labor in Brooklyn," 26 March 1846, he wrote, "There is hardly anything on earth, of its sort, that arouses our sympathies more readily than the cause of a laborer, or a band of laborers, struggling for a . . . mere pittance and standing out against the exactions of grinding 'bosses' and speculation."

11. He would soon join Gould in New Orleans. In addition to attempting to earn a living as a painter, Gould wrote verse for the *Eagle* and for Manhattan papers. In 1848 his *A Bouquet of Poesy* appeared "Published by the Author and for sale at the Principal Bookstores." Whitman surely remembered, later in his own career, this self-publication of a volume of poetry.

12. "Gowanus" remained hostile throughout the discussion. "The landless rent payers of Brooklyn," he told readers of *Young America*, "have already entailed upon them a heavy debt, and it is about to be enlarged. So hurrah for high rents, low wages, specu-lation, humbug, and monopolies, a splendid City Hall, a poverty-stricken people, crime, misery, and degradation."

CHAPTER 12

1. By now a veteran printer, Whitman also recognized the technical scope of the *Pictorial Bible*.

2. *Eagle*, 12 March 1846. Later that month he "confidently recommended" Brady's daguerreotype parlour at Fulton and Broadway "to those of our Brooklyn friends who desire a correct and artistical likeness"; in July he gave two columns to Plumbe's Gallery.

3. Poe's reviews of *Fashion* appeared in the *Broadway Journal*, 29 March and 5 April 1845. Poe—like Whitman—searching for verisimilitude, asked for "natural art . . . based in the natural laws of man's heart and understanding." Mrs. Mowatt's acting impressed Whitman as much as her playwriting; he thought her performance in *Fazio* more powerful than Fanny Kemble's.

4. *Morning News*, 13 January 1845. In an earlier notice of the same tour, a critic insisted than Kean tore passion to pieces and "stormed enough to satisfy the wildest admirer of the violent."

5. *Advertiser*, 2 September 1846. On 1 September Whitman began to answer those who objected to his comments on the Keans, and he continued his "Honest Opinions" throughout his stay on the *Eagle*. On 12 February 1847, in one of his strongest state-ments, he repeated his formula for "resuscitating" the American stage through the discarding of newspaper puffery.

6. The English actor Vandenhoff supported Whitman's ranking of American per-formers, and called Susan Cushman "the best walking-lady" on the American stage,

Placide "the best actor in his varied line." Whitman itemized, on 30 September 1846, the mannerisms he found a common curse: "the hysterical jerking of the voice, at the end of sentences—the inane smile . . . the stale professional tricks that are as common place in theatricals as certain . . . phrases are in newspaper reporting."

7. *Mirror*, 3 September 1846. "Woodman, Spare That Tree" had become a popular song when Henry Russell set the lines to music.

8. Before the performance, however, he had written, on 16 November 1846: "That sanguinary and remorseless gentleman, Mr. Charles Kean, is to murder King John (pitiable Shakespeare!) tonight, and Sunday."

9. *Advertiser*, 28 September 1846. All in all, Whitman would notice or review over 400 books in the *Eagle*.

10. The Tupper review appeared in the *Eagle* on 20 February 1847 under the fanciful heading, "Twigs from the Press-tree." See M. F. Tupper, *My Life as an Author* (London, 1886), pp. 148–50.

11. Frederica Bremer's visit to America brought favorable publicity to her fiction. Whitman also had access to *The Home, Strife and Peace*, and *The H—— Family*.

12. *Eagle*, 31 May and 27 September 1847. For the impact of Sand see Esther Shephard, *Walt Whitman's Pose* (New York: Harcourt Brace, 1938). On 1 February 1847 Whitman wrote with enthusiasm of Douglas Jerrold's *St. Giles and St. James*: "No morbid sentimentality is encouraged by it—no covert licentiousness, or gilded aristocratic vice. . . . All readers will derive from it none of the evil of the sickly school of romance writing."

13. Ralph M. Aderman, ed., *The Letters of James Kirke Paulding* (Madison: University of Wisconsin Press, 1962), pp. 454–55. "From the time of Byron and Moore," complained Paulding, "poetry has principally consisted in cursing and kissing. It has either all gall or honey. Now, however, it either deals in outrageous complaints about nothing, or transcendental extacies inveloped in such an impenetrable fog of mysticism, that the Reader . . . knocks his head against it in the dark."

14. "Home Literature," in the *Eagle*, 10 July 1846, is an editorial on national literature. Whitman had appealed on 9 July 1846 for the government purchase of Catlin's "Memorials of the Red Man"; on 22 July he brooded over the loss of paintings and memorials "so emphatically American, and of such decided importance to Art and to our national History." Catlin, in turn, gave his advocate a print of the Seminole chief, Osceola.

15. *Eagle*, 26 April 1846.

16. Though Whitman did not know Mathews as a friend, he knew his work; *Puffer Hopkins* and *Franklin Evans* shared a review.

17. In one way the choice of title for the address caused, I believe, confusion among Whitman students. Literary "Young America" and political "Young America" were quite different. Mathews, like Whitman, wanted in essence a quickened version of "our own" national spirit in literature, drama, art, music, and architecture, "elevating and enlivening our daily life." Political "Young America" found its motivation in territorial aggrandizement. There is no evidence that Mathews or Duyckinck or any other member of so-called literary "Young America" accepted Whitman as an ally—or contributor. Later chapters of this book prove Whitman's hostility to political "Young

America." See John Stafford, *The Literary Criticism of "Young America"* (Berkeley: University of California Press, 1952).

18. *Eagle*, 12 January 1847. Whitman amplified his definition of "monkeyism" as "a few gentlemen . . . getting together, and 'adoring' and 'doting' on Byron, Scott, and 'sentiment.' "

19. *Eagle*, 10 February 1847.

20. In "Slavers and the Slave Trade," 18 March 1846, Whitman printed an account of the horrors of slave ships. On 29 May he called himself a reformer "in our humble way—disposed to go the length of the string, for improvements of all kinds, political first, and others afterward." Later editorials on "New States: Shall They Be Slave or Free?" and "American Workingmen, versus Slavery," 22 April and 1 September 1847, reflect his free-soil commitment.

21. *Atlas*, 23 January 1848. On 21 January the New York *Globe* reported that "Mr. Whitman, late editor of the Brooklyn *Eagle*, has drawn upon him the opposition of the Conservatives, who have controlled the party hitherto in Brooklyn." The next day the *Globe* added, "We know Mr. Whitman, the discharged editor, to be strong in favor of free territory, and free white labor in such territory as we may acquire from Mexico, and have been informed that this was the principal cause of the dismissal."

22. *Eagle*, 14 February 1847. Some of the other lines of the valentine are graphic:

> One of the great men of the day—your *friends* will tell you so,
> And you are bound to trust their words, believing all you know.
> A goose quill (what an emblem apt!) oft-sette behind your ear,
> A collar broad and clothes to match do constitute your gear;
> And then what bursts of eloquence your ready hand can trace,
> To fill upon your dusky sheet the most conspicuous place.

CHAPTER 13

1. *Tribune*, 18 January 1849; *Advertiser*, 19 January 1849.

2. In addition to Gould, other men known to Whitman had written of New Orleans. Among them were Nichols, the first editor of the *Aurora*, and L. F. Tasistro, a *Herald* reporter and actor.

3. *Crescent*, 5 March 1848. On 23 March the *Crescent* again defined its position: "We will keep clear from the maelstrom of party politics." The extant files of the *Crescent* and the *Picayune* are indispensable. Whitman also described limited phases of his New Orleans experience in *Specimen Days*, in *November Boughs*, and in a manuscript reprinted in Emory Holloway, ed., *Uncollected Poetry and Prose* (New York, 1921), 2: 77–79.

4. The *Crescent* on 5, 6, and 10 March 1848 printed his description of the journey, "Excerpts from a Traveller's Note Book." The schedule and itinerary are given in *Appleton's Railroad and Steamboat Companion* for 1848.

5. *Sunday Times*, 2 April 1848. This letter, written 21 March, and a second, written 12 May and printed 21 May, have remained unnoticed in the files of the weekly published by the man Whitman called "our esteemed friend Major Noah." The *Sunday Times* in the summer of 1849 printed three unsigned items based on New Orleans subjects that may also have been written by Whitman.

6. The *Picayune* on 26 February 1848 listed the cargo manifest of the *St. Cloud*. The lines of poetry are from the last stanza of the 24-line poem, "The Mississippi at Midnight," published in the *Crescent* on 6 March 1848.

7. There has been some confusion about the Whitman residence in New Orleans, caused by the similarity in the names of Lafayette Square and Lafayette suburb. The latter would have been some three miles from the *Crescent* office.

8. The charges by General Scott against Generals Worth and Duncan were dropped by the court of inquiry. The court then agreed that General Pillow had claimed "a larger degree of participation" at Contreras than facts justified, but refused to censure him for the alleged writing of the boastful letter signed by Leonidas. The *Crescent* ridiculed the affair as "the Pillow-case." The *Picayune* printed on 22 April General Taylor's terse statement of political faith: "I am a Whig but not ultra Whig."

9. The *Crescent* headed its anti-treaty editorial of 9 March 1848, "A Sorry Business." Other hostile editorials followed: for example, 11 March, "A Peace Between This Country and Mexico is Impossible"; 3 May, "Mexico Must Be Subdued." The fact that a British naval squadron had reached Nicaragua on 1 January 1848 added to the expansionist zeal of anti-treaty Americans.

10. In *The War in Nicaragua* (Mobile, Ala., 1860), Walker revealed the depth of the motives that drove him to eventual death. He had utter contempt for the "mad rhapsodies" of Rousseau and the "ravings about equality and fraternity" that had inflamed the fathers of the American Constitution. Insisting that force alone could bring stable relations between the "pure white American race" of the United States and the "mixed Hispanic-Indian race" of Mexico and Central America, he used that method to repeal the decrees that had ended slavery in Nicaragua, and scoffed at the "false humanity" of France and England in Jamaica and Santo Domingo. As to the economic future of North America, he found it difficult to conceive that capital could be saved from the attacks of the majority in a pure democracy, "unless with the aid of a force that gets its strength from slave labor."

11. *Crescent*, 6 March 1848.

12. Jeff's letter, one of the four sent home to the family, was dated 14 March 1848 and is contained in Edwin Haviland Miller, ed., *The Correspondence of Walt Whitman*, Vol. I: *1842–1867* (New York: New York University Press, 1961), pp. 27–36.

13. The *Literary World* on 28 October 1848 had begun A. Oakley Hall's series, "A Manhattaner in New Orleans." The section on the press covered the *Picayune* and the *Delta* but not the *Crescent*.

14. Whitman thought her Juliet was "gentle, yet impassioned," and mentioned her performance in a least three different issues. In his *Crescent* sketch, 2 May, Samuel Sensitive is in love with a beautiful woman named Julia. For a period history see John S. Kendall, *The Golden Age of the New Orleans Theatre* (Baton Rouge, La.: Louisiana State University Press, 1952).

15. Whitman attended Gliddon's lecture on Egyptian archeology and told *Crescent* readers on 17 March that "we were astonished."
16. The author of these lines whose poetry appeared often in the *Crescent* was Whitman's friend, Gould. On 10 May the paper carried "The Beggar Girl" by Rambler, possibly Whitman's own pseudonym, for as we shall see he used the same subject in 1854.
17. *Crescent*, 7 April 1848. R. T. Clark, "The German Liberals in New Orleans, 1840–1860," *Louisiana Historical Quarterly* (January 1927), pp. 137–38, describes the city as the gathering place of refugees from Metternich and other despots. Clark quotes a revolutionist who found sanctuary there: "All class of the population, the wealthy as well as the laborers . . . the press in all languages, vie with each other in activity for the salvation of Europe."
18. *Crescent*, 16 May 1848. Several editorials expressed sympathy for the Chartist demands for universal suffrage, but doubted the national readiness for revolution.
19. *Eagle*, 19 July and 24 September 1849. Irked by his conduct of the *Freeman*, the *Eagle* insulted Whitman often that year.
20. *Sunday Times*, 21 May 1848.
21. Whitman's own reminiscences are contradictory, for he wrote both of the quarrel and of satisfaction with his position.
22. The letter was signed by P. W. W.—Peter W. Wilson.
23. "The Beggar Girl" (see note 16) had been subtitled "Lights and Shadows of the Heart."

CHAPTER 14

1. *Advertiser*, 23 June 1848; *Tribune*, 3 July 1848.
2. Whitman returned home just after the Barnburners had demonstrated at City Hall to reject the official delegates to the Baltimore convention. Later in June, he joined the crowd that cheered the delegates to the Utica convention. The protests gained momentum during July, while the Senate debated the bill of the Clayton committee to establish territorial governments for Oregon, California, and New Mexico.
3. Van Anden's anger seems to have been exacerbated by Lees, who printed these lines in the *Advertiser*:

> Six months since or so
> Not longer, we know—
> The Eagle was a rabid barnburner;
> But No. 3 said
> "Van, heels over head,"
> And Van grew a somerset turner.

The speakers at Washington Hall, in the opinion of the *Eagle*, had "abandoned even the color of Democracy—and assumed the sable mantle worthy of their black intentions."
4. A famous shorthand reporter, Oliver Dyer, transcribed the major speeches: *Phono-*

graphic Report of the Proceedings of the National Free Soil Convention (Buffalo, 1848).

5. Richard H. Sewall, *John P. Hale and the Politics of Abolition* (Cambridge, Mass.: Harvard University Press, 1965), pp. 95–104.

6. The manuscript list of subscribers for the proposed *Banner of Freedom* is in the Feinberg collection. Seth B. Hunt, one of the Brooklyn family that published the *Merchant's Magazine* and a delegate to Buffalo, had evidently compiled it.

7. *Freeman*, 9 September 1848. This single extant issue is in the Duke University Library.

8. *Advertiser*, 13 September 1848; *Star*, 1 November 1848; J. F. Kernan, *Reminiscences of the Old Fire Laddies* (New York, 1885), pp. 107–09.

9. This essay in the *Massachusetts Quarterly Review* offered more useful exposition than the survey of "Indian Poetry" in the *Westminster Review* for October 1848, which Whitman underscored and saved. Along with Colebrooke, the British periodical quoted Emerson: "Language is an edifice, to which every forcible individual contributes a stone." In January 1849 the *Westminster* summarized the study of Indian and Egyptian theology in *Lectures upon Ancient History* by the German scholar Whitman admired, von Raumer.

Sermons heard in Brooklyn churches provided a frequent though less exotic source of ontological theory. On 31 January 1847 Whitman was stirred by the Reverend Dr. Mason, a guest preacher from New York. The object of the discourse, the editor noted the next day, was "to make palpable the nature of the soul" and to illustrate its immortality. His friend and familiar contributor to the *Eagle*, the Reverend Mr. Thayer, was known as a fluent metaphysician.

10. Quoted in the *Advertiser*, 1 November 1848. In this editorial Whitman indicted some of his former associates:

It follows quite naturally, that the regular Democratic organ here, the *Eagle*, should be Hunker . . . which it is, up to the hub. It is surrounded by Hunkers, and the oldest friends of the owner are Hunkers; which makes the result natural enough. Those old fellows who have reigned supreme, and cut and carved "public opinion" on the nominations so long—and many of whom have grown rich from office—are not going to yield, either, without a long struggle.

11. Melville to Evert Duyckinck, 24 February 1849. Jay Leyda, *The Melville Log* (New York: Harcourt Brace, 1951), 1:288.

12. Quoted in the Williamsburgh *Daily Times*, 30 April 1849. With the *Freeman*, Brooklyn now had four daily papers. The *Advertiser* on 25 April quoted Whitman again on his opponents:

Old Hunkerism we detest in all its forms and developments. With it and its leaders we never had any sympathy; there was no love lost between us. . . . We despised the tactics they pursued and they returned the compliment right heartily. Without any real talent, or even a tolerable share of the popular love, these men have "managed" themselves into office, and into the control of the Democratic party here.

13. The *Advertiser*, 14 June, and the *Daily Times*, 15 June 1849, described the visit to the asylum by thirty "distinguished citizens" of the county.

14. Whitman's "violent hostility" to the measures of Dr. Goodrich, the local health officer, reflected his memory of the epidemic of 1832. But in 1849 medical science had not yet isolated the *vibrio cholerae* (first identified by Robert Koch in 1883) or blocked its transfer from water contaminated by human fecal waste. It was this epidemic of 1849 which provided Dr. John Snow of London with proof that the source of the disease was water-borne.

15. The phrenological profile is reprinted in Clarence Gohdes and Rollo G. Silver, *Faint Clews & Indirections* (Durham, N.C.: Duke University Press, 1949), pp. 232–36. See also Edward Hungerford, "Walt Whitman and His Chart of Bumps," *American Literature* (January 1931), pp. 350–84; John D. Davies, *Phrenology: Fad and Science: A 19th-Century American Crusade* (New Haven: Yale University Press, 1955). Whitman's visit established a degree of rapport, for the *American Phrenological Journal* in October 1849 reprinted a *Freeman* editorial in praise of the *Tribune*: "Although we differ from the print in several very important matters of political economy, we are none the less willing to acknowledge its unequalled merit as an American press; generally dignified, always talented, and ever marked by a heart-felt desire for the true elevation of the people."

16. *Advertiser*, 1 June 1849.

17. Quoted in the *Advertiser*, 5 June 1849. Irritated by this paper's frequent mention of Whitman, the *Eagle* charged Lees with using the *Freeman* to drive a wedge between the factions of the Democratic party for the sake of gaining an easy Whig victory at the polls.

18. *Daily Times*, 2 and 7 August 1849.

19. *Star*, 19 September 1849. The next day the *Advertiser* noted, "The organ of Free Soil has changed its tune and gives none of its free music as formerly." A week later, back from a visit to England, Lees found changes here: "If death has been busy, Hyman has not been idle—for our friend, the old Mr. Hunker, has taken into his fond embrace, Miss Barnburner. . . . So Mr. Whitman took the Barnburner flag, principles and party away with him." The *Eagle* in response called Whitman "a very crying child. . . . Like Oliver Twist, he was always asking for 'more.'"

CHAPTER 15

1. *Democrat*, 18 September 1849. Brenton had followed Whitman's activities with friendly concern. As recently as 8 May he had noted the use in the *Freeman* of Beecher's "Lectures to Young Men on Idleness"; on 7 August he had reprinted "A Legend of Life and Love."

2. *Advertiser*, 22 September and 4 October 1849.

3. Whitman showed especial tenderness for this sister. From New Orleans he had sent word of the longing to have "Mary and her children come to pay us long visits" on the "quiet little farm" he hoped to own.

4. In September 1847 the *Eagle* had run three letters, titled "East Long Island Correspondence," which he wrote after a Suffolk tour. See Emory Holloway, ed., *Uncollected Poetry and Prose* (New York, 1921), 1: 174–81. Now, over the signature Paumanok, he amplified the earlier descriptions. The first letter appeared in the Sunday *Dispatch* of 14 October 1849; six additional ones followed weekly. On 2 December the paper printed "Pickings-up about Brooklyn." The issue for 9 December, containing the eighth letter, is missing. On 16 December came the ninth, followed the next week by the tenth. On 6 January 1850 the *Dispatch* printed the eleventh and last letter.

Published by Williamson and Burns at 61 Ann Street, the *Dispatch* sold for three cents. A "fearless advocate" of free land to settlers, the paper examined the merits of a railroad to the Pacific, favored Étienne Cabet's Icarian communism, and honored the memory of Leggett by reprinting his writings. Among its poets were Gould and Charles S. Heyde, who soon married Hannah Whitman.

5. *Dispatch*, 4 November 1849. The letters did not appear in chronological sequence. In numbers 36–39 of the historical sketches in the Brooklyn *Standard* in 1861–1862, he used material taken, often verbatim, from the *Dispatch*. See Holloway, ed., *Uncollected Poetry and Prose*, 2: 306–12; Emory Holloway and Vernolian Schwarz, eds., *I Sit and Look Out* (New York: Columbia University Press, 1932), pp. 165–68; and Henry M. Christman, ed., *Walt Whitman's New York* (New York: Macmillan, 1963), pp. 171–88.

6. Whitman later told the readers of the *Standard* that he sailed to Montauk "last autumn." In reality he had made the trip thirteen years earlier.

7. This poignant episode appeared in the *Dispatch* on 16 December 1849.

8. I believe that this letter first appeared in the missing *Dispatch* of 9 December, and that Whitman used his own copy for the *Standard* series.

9. *Dispatch*, 21 October 1849.

10. *Dispatch*, 25 November 1849.

11. The Manhattan press revealed that Ary Sheffer had been paid $4,000 for "The Dead Christ." Whitman returned often to see the painting; as we see in the next chapter, his interest in art was growing.

12. *Dispatch*, 23 December 1849.

CHAPTER 16

1. Brenton placed "A Card" in the *Democrat*, 24 April 1849, announcing *The Printer's Book* and inviting contributors. When he published the collection on 20 November 1849, it had a new title, *Voices from the Press*.

2. I found descriptions of the *News* in the New York *Pathfinder* of 17, 24, and 31 December, and in the *Star*, of 20 December. On 21 December the Williamsburgh *Times* noted that "Our talented friend Walter Whitman, Esq., late of the Brooklyn *Freeman*, is connected with the *News*."

3. The suspension of the *News* marked the end of Whitman's editorial career in Manhattan.

4. Citation of the *News'* comments on these subjects can be found in the *Democrat*, 5 February 1850, and the *Star*, 28 February 1850. On 4 March the *Pathfinder* had a brief obituary of the *News*: "Peace to its ashes."

5. The *Eagle* seemed to delight all during the summer of 1850 in tracking Whitman's comings and goings. The "Postscript" of 29 May is typical: "We stop the press to announce the re-appearance in our midst, of the 'man in the luxuriant shirt collar.' He came over this afternoon in the Fulton street ferry—left hand side. Starch dealers will do well to hold on in anticipation of advanced prices."

6. Whittier's lines are from "To Pius IX."

7. On 28 August the *Dispatch* reprinted the poem.

8. The tone and language both of "Resurgemus" and of the ballad Whitman later wrote to protest the rendition of Anthony Burns resemble that of the invocation to the Giles lecture he quoted in the *Eagle*, 10 December 1847:

> Let *them* come who have fallen on the field of battle. Call back the sunken-hearted, and the weary-souled, in this cause. Call back a million martyrs from their graves. Call the witnesses from the stake, and men and women from the bloody scaffold. . . . Make the tombs of the earth, the caverns of the mountains, and the depths of the sea, give up their dead, who championed this great right of man, and fell for it.

9. Brownson wrote at length on prosody in his essay, "Longfellow's Evangeline and Kavanagh," *Brownson's Magazine* (January 1850), pp. 56–86.

CHAPTER 17

1. Howe published his *Report Made to the Legislature of Massachusetts upon Idiocy* in 1848. Earlier he had organized a school for retarded youths and issued a noble challenge: "Shall we, who can transmute granite and ice into gold and silver . . . shrink from the higher task of transforming brutish men back into human shape?" Harold Schwartz, *Samuel Gridley Howe* (Cambridge, Mass.: Harvard University Press, 1956).

2. The *Advertiser* printed forty-four "Paragraph Sketches" between 18 May and 6 June 1850. In a prefatory note Whitman explained: "Our readers will see that we do not aim at making these brief biographies anything at all like complete. They are more of 'passing mention,' than aught else; claiming but an humble place as compositions, and depending entirely upon their interest to Brooklyn people, who are supposed to know most of the personages mentioned. They are, indeed, as our title says, nothing in the world more than 'Paragraph Sketches.' "

3. *National Era*, 31 October 1850. See Rollo G. Silver, "Whitman in 1850: Three Uncollected Articles," *American Literature* (January 1948), pp. 301–17. Dr. Bailey also published in his weekly Whittier's moving eulogy of Leggett and a brief dissection of Whitman's doughface nemesis: "This country can scarcely produce more

than one Daniel R. Dickinson." Dr. Bailey attempted, however, to disclaim "the honor of being the organ of the abolitionists" and named as his subscribers Free Soilers, anti-slavery Whigs, and antislavery Democrats. "We aim at the establishment of a principle, not of a party."

4. The letters concerning Jenny Lind appeared in the *National Era* on 31 October and 21 November 1850.

5. Longmans had published a three-volume translation of *King Eric and the Outlaws* in London in 1843.

6. William White, "Whitman's First 'Literary' Letter," *American Literature* (March 1963), pp. 84–85.

7. Whitman defended the "Greek Slave" in the *Crescent*. The other items in this paragraph are a small sampling of the press coverage given to art news during these years. The list could be expanded to include lectures like those by Henry James, Sr., in 1851.

8. John Effingham's judgments are in *Home as Found*, 1838. Privately Cooper displayed less optimism. In letters to Greenough he insisted: "As for any feeling with either the arts or literature," the American public "has none. There is a pretending swagger on the subject, and doubtless an individual, here and there is an exception, but. . . . There is nothing; but a greedy rapacity for money. . . ." As late as 1843 he told the sculptor, "This is no country for the arts or letters."

9. Whitman saved Deland's article, which had appeared in a continuation of the *Union Magazine* that ran "The Shadow and the Light of a Young Man's Soul" in 1848. Greenough collected his papers in *Aesthetics in Washington* (1851) and *The Travels, Observations and Experiences of a Yankee Stonecutter* (1852). Whitman had the opportunity then to read again "American Architecture," first published in 1843. See Harold Small, ed., *Horatio Greenough, Form and Function: Remarks on Art* (Berkeley: University of California Press, 1947).

10. Both volumes of *Modern Painters* were available by 1846; *The Seven Lamps of Architecture* by 1849. See Roger B. Stein, *John Ruskin and Aesthetic Thought in America, 1840–1900* (Cambridge, Mass.: Harvard University Press, 1967). "Little Ruskins of Art" appeared in the New York *Daily Times*, 16 December 1854. Other British critics also had an impact upon Americans. Lowell memorized passages of Benjamin Robert Haydon's lectures on *Printing and Design*, 1844–1846.

11. Whitman devoted an entire column to Talbot in the *Dispatch*, 19 May 1850. He also wrote about the painter in the *Advertiser*, 4 April 1850; *Star*, 30 April 1850; *Phrenological Journal*, February 1853. James T. Callow, *Kindred Spirits: Knickerbocker Writers and American Artists, 1807–1855* (Chapel Hill: University of North Carolina Press, 1967), p. 249, lists both praise and censure for Talbot in New York magazines of the 1840s.

Observations on the correspondence between art and nature came often during these years. Thoreau filled "Thursday" of *A Week on the Concord and Merrimac Rivers* with his concept; the invocation at the American Art Union on 30 September 1851 had for its text, "Art, the Interpreter of Nature; Nature, the Interpreter of God." Others used Coleridge's definition of art as "the mediatress and reconciler of nature and man."

12. The frequent carping at the taste of the directors led to witticisms:

"The Art Union is certainly doing a great deal for our art," observed a young Rapin.

"How so?" asked his friend, "have they bought one of your pictures?"

"Oh, no; nothing of that sort. But they are determined that there shall be no poor paintings in the next Exhibition of the Academy; they have bought them all up to distribute to their subscribers."

13. *Advertiser*, 21 December 1850. In addition to the Talbot essay in the *Dispatch*, Whitman in the space of a year placed four others on art in the local press: *Advertiser*, 4 April and 21 December 1850; *Star*, 30 April 1850; *Post*, 1 February 1851.

14. Emerson had come to New York and Brooklyn through the agency of Marcus Spring, the Free Soiler Whitman knew well.

15. The *Advertiser* on 3 April 1851 reprinted the lecture. Ruskin, in the "Lamp of Life," wrote that "money will not buy life," while Carlyle, in "The Hero as Man of Letters," deplored the omnipotence of cash: "I will say rather that, for a genuine man, it is no evil to be poor; that there ought to be Literary Men poor—to show whether they are genuine or not!"

16. Libbey, when he died, had just begun to receive recognition for "The Message" and "The Match Boy." Another ironic note: Whitman's association with artists led him to introduce Charles Heyde to his sister Hannah; their marriage proved catastophic.

The *Daily Times* and other friends continued their efforts to save the Art Union until the terminal court decree in June 1852. "Had it not been for the Art Union," wrote the *Literary World*, "what masses of its admirers would have limited their artistic experience to the windows of print shops and the mezzotints of the monthly magazines."

17. Friends on the *Democrat* and the Williamsburgh *Times* noticed the advent of the *Salesman*, but none recorded its suspension.

18. If the stanzas "To Julia" in the *Advertiser*, 30 June 1851, initialed "W.," are Whitman's, success in romance also held aloof:

> Were I the happy man; so blest
> With Julia's pure and holy flame,
> I'd seek her out, and never rest
> Till Julia changed her *other* name.

CHAPTER 18

1. Among the deaths that of Lees of the *Advertiser* in October 1851 should be noted again. The Free Enquirer who lectured in Brooklyn in 1852 was Gilbert Vale, an old friend. Vale, now a resident of Williamsburgh, led ceremonies honoring Paine and moved that the deist's name be engraved on a block of marble and sent to the National Monument in Washington to counter a gift from the Vatican.

2. The *Herald* rushed into print the entire testimony. In its way the trial reflected a

continuation of nationalistic rivalry, with Forrest venting anger over the hostile reception given him in England.

3. The Williamsburgh *Times* on 4 May 1852, under the title "Visit to the People's Bath and Wash House—A New Era," identified the article as "from the pen, we judge, of our friend Walter Whitman, and, will be read with avidity by every one who takes an interest in 'progress.' The People's Bath and Wash House is a little specimen of what can be done by a unity of effort—in other words—it is another step toward the new Social Era."

4. Francis Blair, Jr., made the race-track comparison; Major Jack Downing ridiculed the nomination in one of his popular letters. Richard Henry Dana, Jr., supported the judgment of both Whitman and Raymond: Pierce was a "doughfaced Militia Colonel, a kind of third rate—or, at most, state politician." Robert F. Lucid, ed., *The Journal of Richard Henry Dana, Jr.* (Cambridge, Mass.: Harvard University Press, 1968), 2: 516.

5. The New York *Daily Times* attacked Hawthorne's campaign role on 28 August and 25 September 1852.

6. Richard H. Sewall discovered this letter during his research on the Hale papers. It is printed in Edwin Haviland Miller, ed., *The Correspondence of Walt Whitman*, Vol. I: *1842–1867* (New York: New York University Press, 1961), pp. 39–40.

7. Documents in the Feinberg collection reveal the sequence of Whitman's dealings as builder and realtor. See Charles E. Feinberg, "A Whitman Collector Destroys a Whitman Myth," *Papers of the Bibliographical Society of America* (Second Quarter, 1958), pp. 73–92.

8. *Star*, 23 January 1852. The *Star* also printed his column of praise for the music at Niblo's Garden. See also Max Maretzek, *Crotchets and Quavers; or, Revelations of an Opera Manager in America* (New York, 1855); Hans Nathan, *Dan Emmett and the Rise of Early Negro Minstrelsy* (Norman: University of Oklahoma Press, 1962).

9. Badiali made his American debut on 22 April 1849; Bettini, on 5 December 1850. After hearing Bettini several times, Whitman called him the best tenor in America; his Gennaro in *Lucrezia Borgia*, sung in January 1852 at Niblo's "with sweetness and subdued melancholy," confirmed this judgment.

10. *Star*, 23 January 1852. Manhattan indeed heard "grand works," for the Philharmonic gave the *Eroica* and Theodore Eisfeld directed Haydn and Beethoven quartets at the Apollo. But Whitman did not write in detail about these programs.

11. *Star*, 10 February 1853. Other critics who joined in praising "the magnificent Sontag" justified Whitman's earlier comments on Lind. The *Herald* found that Sontag "uses no claptrap means of astonishing her auditory, does not resort to any of those musical ventriloquisms adopted by Jenny Lind . . . but relies on her purely legitimate artistic merits."

12. "An Hour among the Portraits," *Star*, 7 June 1853.

13. Whitman wrote about Harrison several times: *Star*, 24 May 1852 and 7 June 1853; *Eagle*, 27 August 1853. See also Harrison's *The Progress of the Drama, Opera, Music and Art in Brooklyn* (Brooklyn, 1884).

14. The catalogue of the Crystal Palace is in B. Silliman and C. R. Goodrich, eds., *The World of Art and Industry Illustrated* (New York, 1853).

15. "Lord Acton's American Diaries," *The Fortnightly Review* (November–December 1921), p. 917.

16. *Eagle*, 27 August 1853. He did not show comparable enthusiasm for the paintings hung at the Crystal Palace; too many of them were in the Düsseldorf mode. Nor did he mention King's bust of Webster.

17. The new *Crayon* magazine in January 1855 also turned to photography to explain that in Whitman's aesthetics "the great poet is he who performs the office of the camera to the world, merely reflecting what he sees—art is mere reproduction" (pp. 30–32).

CHAPTER 19

1. Warren's technique is illustrated here—as was Tupper's earlier—to show the existence of certain prosodic variations in the years before the first *Leaves of Grass*. If it is unsound to say that these guided Whitman, it is equally unsound to ignore their existence and reception.

2. New York *Daily Times*, 23 February 1853; Horace Traubel, ed., *An American Primer by Walt Whitman* (Boston, 1904), p. 12. Poe dedicated *Eureka* to von Humboldt. By 1852 Harper had published a translated edition of the bulk of von Humboldt's writings.

3. Whitman's visits to Dr. Abbott's collection became the basis for "The Egyptian Museum," an article in *Life Illustrated*, December 1855; reprinted in Emory Holloway and Ralph Adimiri, eds., *New York Dissected by Walt Whitman* (New York: R. R. Wilson, 1936), pp. 27–40.

4. The *National Era*, 5 July 1849, described the scope of the Fowlers–Wells establishment in "Phrenology and the Fowler Publications." See John D. Davies, *Phrenology: Fad and Science: A 19th-Century American Crusade* (New Haven: Yale University Press, 1955); Robert M. Young, *Mind, Brain and Adaptation in the Nineteenth Century* (Oxford: Oxford University Press, 1970).

5. The phrenologists also ranged beyond the physical: The April 1852 issue of the *Phrenological Journal* devoted a column to tracing the etymology of "loafer" to a Manhattan baker whose large loaves attracted the lazy, who were soon therefore known as "loafers." The February 1853 issue noted that "Christian and the Cross," another "warm and glowing work" by Talbot, was "in the possession of Walter Whitman, of Brooklyn." Both the information and the language suggest that Whitman contributed to the *Journal* at this time as well as two years later.

6. He reprinted the Seward anecdote in the Brooklyn *Times*, 14 May 1859.

7. Edwin Haviland Miller, ed., *The Correspondence of Walt Whitman*, Vol. I: *1842–1867* (New York: New York University Press, 1961), pp. 41–42. He asked for Seward's speeches "and any government, congressional or other publications of general interest, especially statistics, census facts" and reports of the Smithsonian Institution. The petition to Seward has not survived but surely Whitman signed it.

8. The sequence of events described here follows the reports wired to New York newspapers.

9. *Life and Times of Frederick Douglass, Written by Himself*, with an introduction by Rayford W. Logan (New York: Collier, 1962), p. 293.

10. Williamsburgh *Times*, 9 May 1853. Gavazzi lectured in Brooklyn that month and his "scathing sarcasm" precipitated a near riot; the next month he aroused another audience to violence.

11. Whitman soon gave his poetic version of the death of the fireman.

12. *Sunday Mercury*, 16 April 1854.

13. "The New York Beggar" treats in abbreviated form the sensational material in Solon Robinson's *Hot Corn*, published that year by one of the editors of the *Tribune*. Robinson traced in detail the path followed by girls from beggary to prostitution.

CHAPTER 20

1. "Kosmos" appeared in the 1860 edition of *Leaves of Grass*. In its review of the first edition in September 1855, *Putnam's* wondered, "Precisely what a kosmos is, we trust Mr. Whitman will take an early occasion to inform the patient public."

2. "The Poet" appeared in the *Review* of January 1853, pp. 61–63; its answer, "To the Author of 'The Poet,'" in March, pp. 206–07. Maurice Bucke printed Richard Watson Gilder's expression of the same theme, "When the True Poet Comes," in *Walt Whitman* (Philadelphia, 1883), p. 134.

3. *Phrenological Journal*, September 1853; October 1855. The American edition sold 20,000 copies in a year. *A Life-Drama* has passages Whitman may have found evocative:

> 'Twas at the close of a long summer day,
> As we were sitting on yon grassy slope
>
> . . . .
>
> As ghost-like, from the dim and tumbling sea
> Starts the completed moon.

His admiration for Smith continued. In the Brooklyn *Times*, 5 September 1857, he wrote, "The lovers of poetry in these degenerate . . . days will rejoice with us that the author of 'A Life-Drama' is about to issue a volume of 'City Poems,' which will doubtless be worthy of his fame."

4. New York *Daily Times*, 17 February and 1 March 1853. Emerson had lectured in Manhattan the year before.

5. Thoreau gave this judgment in a letter to H. G. Blake, 19 November 1856, and amplified it in a second letter to Blake on 7 December 1856. Walter Harding and Carl Bode, eds., *Correspondence of Henry David Thoreau* (New York: New York University Press, 1958), pp. 441–45.

6. Whipple's statement first appeared in the *North American Review*, January 1844,

and then in the 1850 edition of *Essays and Reviews*. Carlyle's comments were in the "Corn-Law Rhymes" in the 1845 Carey and Hart edition of the *Essays*.

7. The Cemetery of the Evergreens began to be developed in 1851. The president of the corporation was Whitman's friend, Samuel E. Johnson.

8. The lines appeared in the twelfth and last poem of *Leaves of Grass*. The *Eagle* on 7 July noticed with approval his memorial to the Common Council but claimed it did not have space to print it. The *Star* answered that the author's "sentiments are by no means ... the vox populi."

9. *Comparative Philology* (New York, 1853) by de Vere, a member of the University of Virginia faculty, is one manifestation of an increasing interest in language in America. See "America's Mightiest Inheritance," the article Whitman wrote for *Life Illustrated* (6 April 1856), reprinted in Emory Holloway and Ralph Adimiri, eds., *New York Dissected by Walt Whitman* (New York: R. R. Wilson, 1936), pp. 52–53; Horace Traubel, ed., *An American Primer by Walt Whitman* (Boston, 1904); C. Carroll Hollis, "Names in *Leaves of Grass*," *Names* (September 1947), pp. 129–56; "Whitman and the American Idiom," *Quarterly Journal of Speech* (December 1957), pp. 408–20.

10. In a letter to Thomas Dixon of Sunderland, England, on 30 June 1870, he admitted that the Preface "was written hastily while the first edition was being printed in 1855—I do not consider it of permanent value." Edwin Haviland Miller, ed., *The Correspondence of Walt Whitman*, Vol. II: *1868–1875* (New York: New York University Press, 1961), pp. 99–100.

11. J. Johnston and J. W. Wallace, in *Visits to Walt Whitman in 1890–1891* (London, 1917), p. 138, repeat a conversation in which Whitman disputed the Romes' description of the type used, "saying he believed it was entirely 'English,' while Rome thought it was only 'an English face.'" The contradiction may have come as a result of the use of "English" as a name for both fourteen-point type and the place and style of casting.

The Bruce titling alphabets used for *Leaves of Grass* are, in turn, 72 point No. 16 for *Leaves*; 22 point No. 13 for *of*; 108 point No. 116 for *Grass*. Place and date on the title page are unidentified "fat face" type. The heading over the poetry text is 28 point "Style 1" cast at the Bruce foundry.

12. For descriptions of the binding see these Whitman catalogues: *The Oscar Lion Collection* (New York Public Library, 1953); Lewis M. Stark and John D. Gordon, *A Centenary Exhibition from the Lion Whitman Collection and the Berg Collection of the New York Public Library* (New York Public Library, 1955); *First Books by American Authors* (New York: Seven Gables Bookshop, 1955).

13. Gay Wilson Allen, "Regarding the Publication of the First *Leaves of Grass*," *American Literature* (January 1956), pp. 78–79; William White, "The First (1855) *Leaves of Grass*: How Many Copies?" *Papers of the Bibliographical Society of America* (Third Quarter, 1963), pp. 22–24.

14. *Putnam's* in January 1855 despaired, after many anxious years, of "the advent of the coming poet who is to take away from America the sin and the shame of never having produced an epic, or a lyric, commensurate with Niagara and the Rocky Mountains." The viable alternative seemed to be Negro minstrelsy: "There is no turn-

ing aside for flowery metaphors, or forcible expression—no straining for effect—no lugubrious whining over the hero's downfall—no moralizing his unhappy fate. Even the jingle of rhyme is wanting" (pp. 73–74).

15. Emerson sent his letter on 21 July 1855. *Albion* on 8 September 1855 reprinted part of "Walt Whitman and His Poems," a self-review that the poet had placed in the *United States Review* that month. *Albion* added, "its main fault in a literary point of view—that it suggests the notion of a man reviewing his own work—is not of much importance."

16. Obituaries in the press told of Walter Whitman's "long and prostrating illness"; the *Star* specified paralysis as the cause of death.

LETTERS FROM A TRAVELLING BACHELOR

I

1. With the exception of the removal of errors by *Dispatch* pressmen and the addition in brackets of the publication date of each of the *Letters*, the text remains unchanged.

2. The trip to Greenport on the railroad that had been completed in 1844 took a minimum of three and a half hours. Once there, Whitman could lodge with Mary and Ansel Van Nostrand, his sister and brother-in-law.

3. J. Hector St. John (Michel Guillaume Jean de Crèvecoeur) in *Letters from an American Farmer* (London, 1782) had similarly noticed differences between forest dwellers and plainsmen.

4. Whitman would use the images of the black chip and the bluefishermen in the 1855 *Leaves of Grass*.

II

1. As an example of "the setting apart of beautiful and wooded grounds" Whitman had in mind the construction site of the new Cemetery of the Evergreens.

2. Both men were dominant on the Manhattan stage. Billy Mitchell became famous with burlesque roles and that of Vincent Crummles in *Nicholas Nickleby*. The acting of Henry Placide, whom Forrest called the best comedian of the era, ranged from Sir Peter Teazle to Grandfather Whitehead and dialect farce.

3. Though the venerable whaling industry of Long Island never equaled that of New Bedford and Nantucket, three towns in the 1840s outfitted a combined fleet of more than fifty ships yearly. Ishmael could have embarked from Sag Harbor (where Cooper bought part ownership in a whaler), Cold Spring Harbor, or Greenport. By 1849 the need to sail to the far Pacific had diminished profits, and California gold soon lured the most "persevering" owners.

III

1. Dr. John Zimmerman, born in Bern in 1728, climaxed an eccentric, antidemocratic career with the four-volume *Solitude*, 1784–1786.

2. *Children of the Abbey* (1796) by Regina Maria Roche; *Rinaldo Rinaldini* (1798) by Christian August Vulpius; and *Alonzo and Melissa* (1804/1811) by Isaac Mitchell/Daniel Jackson are variations on the popular Radcliffe theme. Whitman agreed that all three deserved the criticism given the first: "Extremely sentimental, mysterious, and improbable." *Alonzo and Melissa* offered local readers a moated Gothic castle built on Long Island.

The "interesting horrors of Calvinism" are John Foxe's *Book of Martyrs* (1563) and Richard Baxter's *The Saints Everlasting Rest* (1649–1650).

IV

1. Whitman did not include the place or date for this *Letter* and the next ones.

2. Many Brooklynites resented the tunnel and the passage of the trains along Atlantic Avenue. While editor of the Brooklyn *Times*, Whitman cited the public fear of fire and of injury to pedestrians and horses.

3. James H. Hackett was the original Nimrod Wildfire of Paulding's *The Lion of the West* (1833). Whitman enjoyed quoting one of his robust brags: "My father can whip the best man in old Kaintuck, and I can whip my father."

John Alsop King, sixty-one at the time of the bachelor's visit, was an antislavery Whig whose congressional record would appeal to a Free Soiler. King later voted against the Compromise of 1850 and the Kansas–Nebraska legislation of 1854, and led other New York Whigs into the Republican party. Ten years before, he and his family, ardent defenders of issues paramount then—the Bank, high tariff, international improvements—had antagonized the young Locofoco reporter of the Jamaica *Democrat*. Now, mutual opposition to the expansion of slavery made them allies.

4. Long Island papers recorded the death of "Old Dominie" in April 1852 at the age of 75.

5. On the *Eagle* Whitman often referred to Henry Onderdonk's *Documents and Letters Intended to Illustrate the Revolutionary Incidents of Queens County* (New York, 1846). Watrous bought the *Farmer* in February 1840 and competed with Brenton's *Democrat*. As Whitman knew after years in shops, fortune was not a common sequence of publishing a newspaper.

6. Hicksville—named after a railroad executive and not Elias Hicks—resumed its growth as the country recovered from financial crisis.

7. In the second poem of the *Leaves of Grass*, he included "The designs for . . . carpets."

V

1. Their major objective being swift connection to Boston—via ferry from the north fork rail terminal to Stonington—engineers had plotted the main line through the flat central barrens and had avoided towns.

VII

1. This paragraph and Letter X foreshadow "Crossing Brooklyn Ferry."
2. While working in Manhattan in 1842, Whitman joined in celebrating the completion of the project. The city now had water for drinking and, as George Templeton Strong noted, will "at last stand a chance of being cleaned—if water *can* clean it."
3. From its consecration in 1846, Whitman had never responded to James Renwick's Grace Church with the enthusiasm he gave to the Croton aqueduct the young engineer had helped to build. The Gothic spire and transepts, the velvet-cushioned pews, the rich congregation all failed, he insisted, to evoke a sense of religion or beauty—except in an upholsterer.
4. Goupil, Vibert of Paris announced in December 1849 the establishment of an International Art Union in New York "for the promotion of the taste for the Fine Arts, in the United States of America, by introducing through the means of a perpetual Free Gallery, the *chefs d'oeuvres* of the European School of Art." The firm also began publication in February 1849 of the *International Art Union Journal* and a series of lithographs that included Mount's "The Power of Music" and Kollner's "Views" of American scenery. Sheffer, known as "the poet of the painters and the painter for the poets," had preceded "The Dead Christ" with "Christus Consolator."
5. Whitman did not name the painter of "The Republic" because he remained anonymous. See Albert Boime, "The Second Republic's Contest for the Figure of the Republic," *Art Bulletin* (March 1971), pp. 68–83.

IX

1. The titles of this *Letter* and the next two are shortened in the *Dispatch* to "From a Travelling Bachelor."
2. Crèvecoeur had noted that the women of Nantucket ingested a dose of opium every morning; Brooklyn chemists sold unlimited quantities of the drug. In the first poem of the *Leaves of Grass* Whitman remembered the addict: "The opium eater reclines with rigid head and just-opened lips."
3. The first "violent appeal" remains unidentified; the second is from *Richard III*, Act V. During her American tour Fanny Elssler included the dance from *Le Dieu et la Bayadère*, the ballet opera produced in 1830 with music by Auber and libretto by Scribe. The bachelor did not record who danced the amorous courtesan to his God.

X

1. Whitman's recognition in 1849 of the literary value of the journey and the remarks here in the *Dispatch* are preliminaries to "Crossing Brooklyn Ferry."
2. Stephen B. Holt opened his six-story, 250-room hotel in January 1833. From then on Whitman could see it while he stood on the deck of a ferry or walked Brooklyn Heights. Mrs. Holt's share in the venture led to the *Macbeth* allusion; she spent years sewing the hotel linens.

3. Whitman had recently finished reading the new illustrated edition by Harper of the works of the man he called "the great poet of heaven and hell."

XI

1. Mr. Sampson Brass is the unscrupulous attorney in *The Old Curiosity Shop.* "The Newspaper Literature of America" (October 1842), pp. 197–222, was the "well-known attack" whose anonymous author flayed the "infamous . . . degrading and disgusting" press dominated by the *Herald.*

2. E. D. E. N. Southworth's career did not quite fulfill the prophecy. Hardly the best of literary women, she became the most prolific, and after *Retribution,* first serialized in the *National Era* in 1847, wrote sixty novels that replaced *Rinaldo Rinaldini* on the tables of Long Islanders.

3. Fowlers and Wells, to whose list and *Phrenological Journal* Whitman had access, published several physiology texts and articles on dream phenomena; the hypotheses of Drs. Robert McNish, John Abercrombie, and Karl Friedrich Burdach had reached America from Scotland and Germany. By 1855 Whitman would write:

> I dream in my dreams all the dreams of the other dreamers,
> And I become the other dreamers.

4. The last two "Diminuendos" are omitted, for they are mere fillers. This *Letter* lacks a signature—as though Whitman admitted its hasty composition. By now his editorial work on the *Daily News* was demanding priority.

INDEX

c4